Money,
Banking, and
Macroeconomics

ECONOMICS INFORMATION GUIDE SERIES

Series Editor: Robert W. Haseltine, Associate Professor of Economics, State University College of Arts and Science at Geneseo, Geneseo, New York

Also in this series:

AMERICAN ECONOMIC HISTORY—*Edited by William K. Hutchinson**

ECONOMIC DEVELOPMENT—*Edited by Thomas A. Bieler**

ECONOMIC EDUCATION—*Edited by Catherine Hughes*

ECONOMIC HISTORY OF ASIA—*Edited by Molly K.S.C. Lee**

ECONOMIC HISTORY OF CANADA—*Edited by Trevor J.O. Dick*

ECONOMICS OF EDUCATION—*Edited by William Ganley**

ECONOMICS OF MINORITIES—*Edited by Kenneth L. Gagala*

HEALTH AND MEDICAL ECONOMICS—*Edited by Ted J. Ackroyd*

HISTORY OF ECONOMIC ANALYSIS—*Edited by William K. Hutchinson*

INTERNATIONAL TRADE—*Edited by Ahmed M. El-Dersh**

LABOR ECONOMICS—*Edited by Ross E. Azevedo*

MATHEMATICAL AND ECONOMIC STATISTICS—*Edited by Joseph Zaremba**

MATHEMATICAL ECONOMICS AND OPERATIONS RESEARCH—*Edited by Joseph Zaremba*

PUBLIC POLICY—*Edited by Michael Joshua**

REGIONAL ECONOMICS—*Edited by Jean Shackleford**

RUSSIAN ECONOMIC HISTORY—*Edited by Daniel Kazmer and Vera Kazmer*

SOVIET-TYPE ECONOMIC SYSTEMS—*Edited by Z. Edward O'Relley*

TRANSPORTATION ECONOMICS—*Edited by James P. Rakowski*

URBAN ECONOMICS—*Edited by Jean Shackleford**

*in preparation

The above series is part of the
GALE INFORMATION GUIDE LIBRARY

The Library consists of a number of separate series of guides covering major areas in the social sciences, humanities, and current affairs.

General Editor: Paul Wasserman, Professor and former Dean, School of Library and Information Services, University of Maryland

Managing Editor: Denise Allard Adzigian, Gale Research Company

Money, Banking, and Macroeconomics

A GUIDE TO INFORMATION SOURCES

Volume 11 in the Economics Information Guide Series

James M. Rock

Associate Professor of Economics
University of Utah

Foreword by Axel Leijonhufvud

Professor of Economics
University of California, Los Angeles

Gale Research Company
Book Tower, Detroit, Michigan 48226

Library of Congress Cataloging in Publication Data

Rock, James M
    Money, banking, and macroeconomics.

    (Economics information guide series ; v. 11)
(Gale information guide library)
    Includes indexes.
    1. Money--Bibliography. 2. Monetary policy--
Bibliography. 3. Banks and banking--Bibliography.
I. Title.
Z7164.F5R63   [HG221]   016.332   73-17585
ISBN 0-8103-1300-6

To

Lillian Leverenz Rock

and

Carroll George Rock

VITA

James M. Rock is currently associate professor of economics at the University of Utah. He received a B.S. in geography and an M.S. in rural sociology and agricultural economics from the University of Wisconsin--Madison and a Ph.D. in economics from Northwestern University. Rock has been a statistician and an economist for the federal government and has taught at the University of Wisconsin--Oshkosh.

Rock has published articles in the areas of macro and monetary economics, industrial organization, economic education, feedback control economics, economic history, and the economics of crime and punishment. In 1969 he founded and remains adviser to INTERMOUNTAIN ECONOMIC REVIEW, the first student-edited journal in economics. He is also an associate economics editor for INTELLECT.

If he must dabble in science, keep him on economics and sociology; don't let him get away from that invaluable "real life."

C. S. Lewis, THE SCREWTAPE LETTERS

CONTENTS

Foreword   xiii
Preface   xv
List of Selected Books of Readings   xvii

Chapter 1 – Overview of Money, Banking, and Macroeconomics   1
  Introduction to Macro–Monetary Economics   1
    Economic Organization   1
      Microfoundations vs. No Microfoundations:
        The Aggregation Problem   5
      Equilibrium vs. Disequilibrium   6
      Perfect Competition vs. Imperfect Competition   7
      Static vs. Dynamic, Certainty vs. Uncertainty,
        and Real vs. Monetary   8
      Policy Prescriptions and Conclusion   10
  General Sources   10
    Surveys   10
      Essays   10
      Conferences and Symposiums   13
    Collected Readings   19
      Single Author   19
      Multi–authored: Festschriften   24
      Multi–authored: General   26
    Textbooks   34
      Money and Banking and Monetary Economics   34
      Macroeconomics and Growth   38
  Library Sources   45
    Guides to Sources   45
    Guides to Articles: Current   45
    Guides to Articles: Historic   46
    Guides to Books and Monographs: Current   48
    Guides to Books and Monographs: Historic   49
    Encyclopedias   50
    Guide to Citations   50
    Guide to U.S. Government Documents   51
  Macro–Monetary Basic Library   51

Contents

Over Time and Through the Literature 51
  Before Keynes 52
  Keynes 54
  After Keynes 55
    From the GENERAL THEORY to 1950 56
    1950 to 1960 59
    1960 to the Present 63
  References 69

Chapter 2 – Financial Intermediation and Commercial Banking 75
  Introduction 75
  Sources 75
  History 75
  Theory 77
    Portfolio Theory 77
    Inside-Outside Money 82
    Optimal Quantity of Money 84
  Practice 86

Chapter 3 – Macro-Monetary Theory 95
  Introduction 95
  Sources 95
  Early Theory 95
    Quantity Theory of Money: Classical 95
    Quantity Theory of Money: Friedmanite 96
    Contra-Quantity Theory of Money 98
  Later Thought: Theoretical and Applied 99
    Contemporaries of Keynes: Rivals and Friends 99
    Contemporaries of Keynes: Underground 101
    Business Cycles: Theory, Econometric Models, and
      Forecasting 102
    National Income and Flow of Funds Accounts: Theory
      and Application 112
  Keynes 114
    His Works and Works about Him 114
    Interpretations of the GENERAL THEORY before 1956 116
  Post-Keynes Analysis 123
    Equilibrium Theory: Orthodox Consensus and Neoclassical
      Synthesis 123
    Disequilibrium Theory 133
  Post-Keynes Aggregation 140
    Income, Consumption, and Saving 140
    Investment and Inventory Theory 147
    Real and Monetary Multipliers and the Accelerator
      Relation 156
    Labor Market 160
    Output Relations 161
    Money Demand: Definition and Value 164
    Money Supply 178
    Interest Rate: Theory 182

Contents

Interest Rate: Term Structure 187
Growth, Accumulation, and Distribution 191

Chapter 4 - Central Banking 207
Introduction 207
Sources 207
History 207
Theory 210
Practice 213

Chapter 5 - Stabilization Policy 217
Introduction 217
Sources 217
Problems 217
Unemployment and Growth 217
Inflation and Deflation 219
Relation between Employment and Prices 224
Tools 227
Fiscal Policy 227
Monetary Policy 230
Comparisons and Monetary Aspects of Fiscal Policy 238
Incomes and Human Resources Policies 243
Policy Controversies 245
Monetary Commissions 248

Author Index 251
Title Index 263
Subject Index 275

FOREWORD

Students of macro and monetary economics at all levels will be grateful to Dr. Rock for this volume. The field is one in which it is particularly difficult to gain a reasonably organized overview of the literature. There are several reasons for this.

First, and most obviously, the flow of new publications in this field rose mightily in the 1960s and is still running high. Most general economics journals came to allot increased space to monetary economics. In addition, many new journals were established, and among them some specializing in monetary economics. The swelling flood of publications is a problem for workers in all areas of economics but those in the monetary field have been disproportionally inundated in the last ten or fifteen years.

So the obvious problem is that of the sheer volume of new work. If established professionals sometimes find it discouragingly hard to keep up with the flow, students entering the field have all the more reason to be daunted by the accumulated stock. Fashions in economic research change. Perhaps the tide will again recede. But the 1960s revival of professional interest in monetary economics drew new entrants into the field in large numbers. The division of labor increased with the extent of the market. The number of relatively distinct specialized subfields in money, banking, finance, and macroeconomics has grown. This second development has also made the field more difficult to survey--and it is not a development at all likely to be reversed.

Third, and most important, the student of monetary economics will today have to recognize the lack of a firmly established orthodoxy. A generally accepted doctrine is a boon to the aspiring professional; it structures the subject, determines certain propositions to be true and others to be false, judges some approaches to be promising and others uninteresting, assigns great and general importance to some contributions and marginal or specialized significance to others. But, while a settled orthodoxy makes things easier, its very capacity to dictate answers to the most interesting questions may also rob research in the field of intellectual excitement.

Foreword

Monetary economics today promises the student a good deal of excitement. By the same token, it cannot offer him structured coherence. For more than a decade conflicting theoretical images of what the world is like have contended incessantly for attention and allegiance in the journals with no assured settlement in sight. But it is not just the conflicts between theoretical hypotheses that make the literature hard to master. The unsettled state of the field is marked also by the large variety of approaches that theoretical model-builders and empirical investigators alike are trying to bring to bear on the recalcitrant issues.

For all these reasons a source book such as this one should be most welcome. Students, instructors, and research-workers will all have occasions to find that the work that Dr. Rock has undertaken offers the rest of us considerable savings in time and trouble. To accurately characterize the content or contribution of a book or technical article in a sentence or two is of course impossible, and Dr. Rock wisely refrains from attempting such thumbnail abstracts. But users of this book will find, I think, that his brief comments provide just enough clues to filter out the literature they need to consult for a particular research purpose without letting major contributions slip by unnoticed.

Axel Leijonhufvud
Professor of Economics
University of California
Los Angeles, California

PREFACE

MONEY, BANKING, AND MACROECONOMICS is a source book for undergraduates, graduates, librarians, and interested laypersons. This area of economics consists of historical, institutional, and theoretical aspects of the national economy.

The first chapter is devoted to an introductory overview of macro-monetary economics, as this area has come to be called. The difficulties of arriving at
definitive answers in macro-monetary economics are previewed in the essay on
economic organization. The number of variables that may need to be considered
when speculating about the national economy grows over time as do the possible
combinations and permutations.

To simplify the acquisition of general macro-monetary knowledge, textbooks,
surveys, conferences, and collected essays and articles were assembled and eval-
uated. Twenty books of readings were selected as an informal guide to the
best articles written--in terms of originality and/or pedagogy. The articles ap-
pearing in these books of readings are designated by the number of the reading
book or books in which they are reprinted. The books of readings are numbered
by alphabetical order in the List of Selected Books of Readings and in chapter
1. In addition, slightly over one hundred of the best books and articles are
cited in the basic library essay--Over Time and Through the Literature--which
summarizes macro-monetary economics historically and doctrinally.

The first chapter also explains how areas of interest to economists and others
may be kept current through the use of selected library sources. The library
sources listed were chosen with the assistance of Frieda McCoy and Eloise
McQuown of the University of Utah library.

The four remaining chapters cover the main interests of macro-monetary economists:
"Financial Intermediaries," "Macro-Monetary Theory," "Central Banking," and
"Stabilization Policy." The books and articles that have been annotated were
selected from this fast growing and large area of economic literature. To obtain a
representative selection, reading lists (covering graduate and undergraduate courses
in money and banking and macroeconomics) were solicited from over twenty of
the leading universities in the United States and the bibliographies for both

Preface

Oxford and Cambridge universities were also included. In addition, the AMERICAN ECONOMIST (vol. 18, Fall 1974) carried the macroeconomic reading lists of more colleges and universities, and they too were annexed. To this massive number of possible entrants were added the selective reading lists that appear in MACROECONOMICS AND MONETARY THEORY (by Harry G. Johnson) and MONETARY THEORY (edited by Robert W. Clower) and, of course, those selections I have collected. All books and articles that appeared in two or more reading lists were automatically included in this book. Over one-half of the selections were chosen in this way. Of the unreplicated books and articles, approximately two-thirds were included. The fact that so many of the articles and books were duplicates is a strong sign, on the one hand, that there is general agreement among macro-monetary economists on what constitutes the core literature in this field. On the other hand, the almost equally large number of unduplicated selections means that there is still much disagreement as to where the emphasis should be in this field. My choices are biased somewhat by my professors at Northwestern University: Meyer Burstein, Bob Clower, Bob Crouch, Bob Eisner, and Franco Modigliani.

A great deal of thanks also goes to Dave Ashby, Lynn E. Jensen, Don Roper, Allen Sievers, and Mike Shields who have added their expertise to the final selection process. Jean Arment and Kevin Johnson have both breathed life into the professorial fantasy of undergraduates who enjoy intellectual curiosity without getting paid for it. The editing was expertly done by Virginia Pett, Dedria Bryfonski, and Denise Allard Adzigian of Gale Research Co. Financial support was received from the University of Utah Research Fund. My deepest gratitude is reserved for my wife Bonnie, and Jenny, Peter, Jimmy, and Sara who have provided me with enough interruptions over the past three years to delay the completion of this book for a year--and thus allow it to be more "up-to-date."

Ephraim, Wisconsin 1977

LIST OF SELECTED BOOKS OF READINGS

[1]   Carson, Deane, ed. MONEY AND FINANCE: READINGS IN
THEORY, POLICY, AND INSTITUTIONS. 2d ed. New York:
John Wiley & Sons, 1972. 507 p.

[2]   Clower, Robert W., ed. MONETARY THEORY. Baltimore: Penguin
Books, 1970. 360 p.

[3]   Fellner, William, and Haley, Bernard F., eds. READINGS IN THE
THEORY OF INCOME DISTRIBUTION. Homewood, Ill.: Richard
D. Irwin, 1946. 734 p.

[4]   Gibson, William E., and Kaufman, George G., eds. MONETARY
ECONOMICS: READINGS ON CURRENT ISSUES. New York:
McGraw-Hill Book Co., 1971. 523 p.

[5]   Gordon, Robert A., and Klein, Lawrence R., eds. READINGS IN
BUSINESS CYCLES. Homewood, Ill.: Richard D. Irwin, 1965.
731 p.

[6]   Haberler, Gottfried, ed. READINGS IN BUSINESS CYCLE THEORY.
Homewood, Ill.: Richard D. Irwin, 1944. 510 p.

[7]   Harris, Seymour E. THE NEW ECONOMICS: KEYNES' INFLUENCE
ON THEORY AND PUBLIC POLICY. New York: Augustus M. Kelley,
1947. 717 p.

[8]   Johnson, Walter L., and Kamerschen, David R., eds. MACRO-
ECONOMICS: SELECTED READINGS. New York: Houghton
Mifflin, 1970. 415 p.

[9]   Lekachman, Robert, ed. KEYNES' GENERAL THEORY: REPORTS
OF THREE DECADES. New York: St. Martin's Press, 1964. 359 p.

Selected Books of Readings

[10] Lindauer, John, ed. MACROECONOMIC READINGS. New York: Free Press, 1968. 424 p.

[11] Lutz, Friedrich A., and Mints, Lloyd W., eds. READINGS IN MONETARY THEORY. Homewood, Ill.: Richard D. Irwin, 1951. 514 p.

[12] Mitchell, William E., et al., eds. READINGS IN MACROECONOMICS: CURRENT POLICY ISSUES. New York: McGraw-Hill Book Co., 1974. 514 p.

[13] Mittra, S., ed. DIMENSIONS OF MACROECONOMICS: A BOOK OF READINGS. New York: Random House, 1971. 572 p.

[14] _____. MONEY AND BANKING: THEORY, ANALYSIS, AND POLICY. New York: Random House, 1970. 643 p.

[15] Mueller, M.G., ed. READINGS IN MACROECONOMICS. 2d ed. New York: Holt, Rinehart and Winston, 1971. 490 p.

[16] Shapiro, Edward, ed. MACROECONOMICS: SELECTED READINGS. New York: Harcourt, Brace and World, 1970. 485 p.

[17] Smith, W[arren]., and Teigen, R.L., eds. READINGS IN MONEY, NATIONAL INCOME, AND STABILIZATION POLICY. 3d ed. Homewood, Ill.: Richard D. Irwin, 1974. 556 p.

[18] Smithies, Arthur, and Butters, J. Keith, eds. READINGS IN FISCAL POLICY. Homewood, Ill.: Richard D. Irwin, 1955. 606 p.

[19] Thorn, Richard S., ed. MONETARY THEORY AND POLICY. New York: Random House, 1966. 683 p.

[20] Williams, Harold R., and Huffnagle, John D. MACROECONOMIC THEORY: SELECTED READINGS. New York: Prentice-Hall, 1969. 537 p.

Chapter 1

OVERVIEW OF MONEY, BANKING, AND MACROECONOMICS

INTRODUCTION TO MACRO-MONETARY ECONOMICS

If national policy makers had a better understanding of the determinants of the performance of economies, reasonable national economic goals might be obtainable. Economists have been entrusted to ferret out the causal chains. As James Tobin has said, "The strategy is to build models that lay bare the essentials of the phenomena under study; the art is to find those simplifying abstractions that clarify and do not distort."[1] However, words such as "clarify" and "distort" subjectively reflect only what we wish to discern. So we cannot be sure that our models really describe the phenomena. In the meantime, the phenomena are continually evolving.

This essay reflects on the many problems with which economists are concerned in trying to understand the causal chains. There are more questions than answers. Research is currently being undertaken at all levels of the contour map presented below. The contour map used here illustrates levels of abstraction rather than different elevations.

Economic Organization

Our world is weird.[2] It may appear to be simple to comprehend (and, consequently, to abstract) or it may appear to be difficult to comprehend. Perception is in the eye of the beholder.

---

[1] James Tobin, "Macroeconomics," in ECONOMICS, ed. N.D. Ruggles (Englewood Cliffs, N.J.: Prentice-Hall, 1970), p. 44.

[2] Don Juan says, "For you the world is weird because if you're not bored with it you're at odds with it. For me the world is weird because it is stupendous, awesome, mysterious, unfathomable. . . ." Carlos Castaneda, JOURNEY TO IXTLAN: THE LESSONS OF DON JUAN (New York: Simon & Schuster, 1972), p. 92. Our world is also funny and slightly irreverent; see Donald Barthelme, "The Teachings of Don B.: A Yankee Way of Knowledge," in GUILTY PLEASURES (New York: Farrar, Straus and Giroux, 1974), pp. 53-62.

What we perceive may be illusion, hallucination, or reality; the distressing aspect is how often the same image may change from one to the other.[3] We hope to divine the future by understanding the past, but the past is a subjectively created ideology that grows day by day.[4] Although constantly improving means of communication allows information to be transmitted more rapidly, this in no sense should be construed always to mean better information. That is, information may change our image of the world, but is it illusion, hallucination, or reality?

Albert Einstein conceived of the universe as a four-dimensional manifold made up of three dimensions of space and one of time. Thus, we have learned from the theory of relativity that time influences space as well as space influencing time. The same is true in human relationships, with one major addition.[5] Time is not a mere dimension in the "human affair"; the distinction among past, present, and future time is meaningful.[6]

Saint Augustine, in less scientific but more poetic language, perceived time itself to be a three-dimensional manifold of memory, present experience, and expectations.

> What now is clear and plain is that neither things to come nor past
> are. Nor is it properly said, "There be three times: past, present,

---

[3]"In an illusion the error stems from the interpretation. In an hallucination it is the sensation itself which is garbled." Andre Maurois, ILLUSIONS (New York: Columbia University Press, 1968), p. 25. Image is what one believes is true--subjective knowledge. See Kenneth E. Boulding, THE IMAGE: KNOWLEDGE IN LIFE AND SOCIETY (Ann Arbor, Mich.: University of Michigan Press, 1956).

[4]"The past is always a created ideology with a purpose, designed to control individuals, or motivate societies, or inspire classes." J. H. Plumb, THE DEATH OF THE PAST (Boston: Houghton Mifflin Co., 1970), p. 17.

[5]"The logical basis of the theory of relativity is the discovery that many statements, which were regarded as capable of demonstrable truth or falsity, are mere definitions." Hans Reichenbach, "The Philosophical Significance of the Theory of Relativity," in ALBERT EINSTEIN: PHILOSOPHER-SCIENTIST, ed. Paul Arthur Schilpp (New York: Cambridge University Press, 1949), 1:293. But, remember well this caveat of his: "The parallelism between the relativity of ethics and that of space and time is nothing more than a superficial analogy, which blurs the essential logical differences between the fields of volition and cognition." Ibid., p. 289.

[6]The seminal work relating time, irrationality, and economic knowledge is: G.L.S. Shackle, EPISTEMICS AND ECONOMICS: A CRITIQUE OF ECONOMIC DOCTRINES (New York: Cambridge University Press, 1972). T.S. Eliot is especially insightful in "Burnt Norton" from FOUR QUARTETS. Another book that looks at time is Kurt Vonnegut, Jr., SLAUGHTERHOUSE-FIVE (New York: Dell, 1969).

and to come"; yet perchance it might be properly said: "There be three times: a present of things past, a present of things present, and a present of things future." For these three do exist in some sort, in the soul, but otherwise do I not see them: present of things past, memory; present of things present, sight; present of things future, expectation.[7]

Consequently, memory and sight are used to formulate one's expectations of the future. However, each person's expectations will be modified by his position in space-time;[8] his space-time relationship will be further modified by his objectives and his constraints; and his objectives and constraints will, no doubt, be influenced by his heritage, wealth, mental and physical characteristics, and so forth. As Kenneth Boulding has said, "There are no such things as 'facts.' There are only messages filtered through a changeable value system."[9]

Because past, present, and future messages are filtered differently by each individual, the image of the world that is projected is different for everyone. Often one's image of a particular problem is distorted because not all messages received are essential to that problem. This is where the strategy and art of model building are necessary.

What messages each person perceives to be nonessential are selected out. For if one did not, a person would be engulfed by the tide of images.[10] Only "essential" messages should be allowed to influence the actual decision. Decision making by macro-monetary economists is carried out in much the same way. Of course each economist, as with each noneconomist, has his own set of filters.[11]

---

[7]Saint Augustine, THE CONFESSIONS, translated by Edward Bouverie Pusey, in GREAT BOOKS OF THE WESTERN WORLD, vol. 18, (Chicago: Encyclopaedia Britannica, 1952), book xI, par. 26, p. 95 a,b.

[8]Again, in the words of Don Juan, "To believe that the world is only as you think it is, is stupid. . . . The world is a mysterious place." Castaneda, p. 73. For a coherent discussion of ideology, visions, and value judgments see Maurice Dobb, THEORIES OF VALUE AND DISTRIBUTION SINCE ADAM SMITH (New York: Cambridge University Press, 1973), pp. 1-37.

[9]Boulding, p. 14.

[10]Aldous Huxley believed that "The function of the brain and of the nervous system is to eliminate, not to produce [images]." Maurois, p. 26.

[11]Albert Einstein commented in a speech in honor of Max Planck, "Man tries to make for himself in the fashion that suits him best a simplified and intelligible picture of the world: he then tries to some extent to substitute this cosmos of his for the world of experience, and thus to overcome it." Banesh Hoffmann, ALBERT EINSTEIN: CREATOR AND REBEL (New York: Viking Press, 1972), pp. 221-22. It is impossible to know all that influences the consciousness of man. See Robert E. Ornstein, THE PSYCHOLOGY OF CONSCIOUSNESS (San Francisco: W. H. Freeman, 1972).

This is the reason why there is presently a plethora of static or dynamic, equilibrium or disequilibrium macro-monetary models of the economy, each competing to become the dominant orthodoxy. In addition, any model may generate contradictory results by employing different sets of assumptions.

This short introduction to model building is meant to reveal only the most obvious pitfalls to the unwary. No one has ever built (or will ever build) the perfect theoretic model of the economy. The reason is not difficult to understand. The world seen by Don Juan or the world seen by Castaneda is also the world of the economist. The object of inspection changes as it is inspected.

> The world which the economic theoretician must study is protean in
> the profoundest sense. . . . In order to achieve demonstrative
> proof, the economic theoretician must reject time. In order to
> reflect the human predicament, he must consider time as the fact
> above all facts. . . .[12]

The economic theoretician has no choice but, in Shackle's words, to "doublethink." Economic models cannot be comprehensive; they must exclude each other if their purpose is either to achieve demonstrative proof or to reflect the human predicament. There is complementarity, not substitutability.

Methodology is an additional problem area in economic theory. Is a theory an instrument for prediction of observable reality or is it a description of observable experience?[13] As growth of knowledge theories are applied, rightly or wrongly, to the history of economics, alternative propositions somewhere between these two polar positions have gained additional adherents.[14] Kuhnian "revolutions" and Lakatosian "research programs" are competitive ways of explaining the evolution of knowledge.[15] Whether or not changes in economic theory can be accounted for by either of these two methods is not the issue here. The issue is: What is the goal of a theory? Intellectually certain knowledge is its goal. Theories, however, are often too complex to be readily useful; modeling is necessary.

Modeling an economic theory is, itself, a sampling process. Certain assumptions are made and weighted. The model builder implicity makes an all-important

---

[12]Shackle, pp. 254-55.

[13]The methodologies of Paul Samuelson and Milton Friedman have recently been critiqued by Stanley Wong: "The 'F-Twist' and the Methodology of Paul Samuelson," AMERICAN ECONOMIC REVIEW 63 (June 1973): 312-25. An excellent list of references is included.

[14]For an introduction to this movement see: Spiro J. Latsis, "Situational Determinism in Economics," BRITISH JOURNAL FOR THE PHILOSOPHY OF SCIENCE 23 (August 1972): 207-45.

[15]The approaches of Thomas S. Kuhn and Imre Lakatos are examined critically in: Imre Lakatos and Alan Musgrave, eds., CRITICISM AND THE GROWTH OF KNOWLEDGE. New York: Cambridge University Press, 1970.

reservation. He assumes that the assumptions "which have been enumerated, specified and presented for the assignment of weights are the only relevant ones."[16] Because there are numerous choices to be made, it is important that a road map, or better yet a contour map, be provided to illustrate the various levels of choices facing a macro-monetary model builder. The essay will cover, in large scale, these five levels: I. Microfoundations vs. no microfoundations; II. Equilibrium vs. disequilibrium states; III. Perfect vs. imperfect competition; IV. Static vs. dynamic, certainty vs. uncertainty, and real vs. monetary; V. Policy prescriptions and conclusions.

MICROFOUNDATIONS VS. NO MICROFOUNDATIONS:
THE AGGREGATION PROBLEM

We commence with three questions. First, is it possible to encapsulate macro-monetary economics in a single model? As already indicated, it is impossible to achieve demonstrative proof and to reflect changing time in a single model.

A second question deals with whether or not there should be or needs to be a relationship between macro-monetary economics and microeconomics. Currently economists are divided on whether or not macroeconomics needs an explicit microeconomic foundation. The degree to which the actions of individual households and firms influence the national economy is still in question.

Before John Maynard Keynes's THE GENERAL THEORY OF EMPLOYMENT, INTEREST AND MONEY (1936), economic theory as taught in England was composed of two branches: principles and money. Principles (microeconomics) was, in essence, a study of market behavior under the influence of supply and demand, i.e., the determination of relative prices of goods and factors. There existed no "macro" economics as such. Money dealt with the real world problems of absolute price levels and trade cycles. The change in emphasis from Keynes's A TREATISE ON MONEY (1930) to the GENERAL THEORY was his determination to "deal thoroughly with the effects of changes in the level of output." His method of analysis, however, depended on explicit and revised microfoundations. The revision was necessary because the orthodox supply schedule for labor used in the TREATISE is consistent with voluntary unemployment but completely disregards involuntary unemployment. Thus, a tentative affirmative answer is given to the question of whether macro-monetary economics should have an explicit microeconomic foundation. An emphatic yes is given to the need for a revision of pre-Keynes microeconomics as they are applied to macroeconomics.

The third question that needs answering is: If macro-monetary economics has a microeconomic base, what kind of microeconomics is it? The two main microeconomic theories in use have been Marshallian and Walrasian. The usual price-quantity correspondence for Walras is $q = f(p)$; for Marshall it is $p = g(q)$. In a

---

[16]Shackle, p. 15, emphasis in the original.

competitive equilibrium context, it is an algebraic triviality to invert from one to the other. But a disequilibrium context is a different matter, even assuming algebraic equivalence. The philosophical and axiomatic foundations of these two microtheories are different; hence, inversion does not always give the same answer.[17]

If we follow Keynes's approach, as do most macro-monetary economists, the next problem is that of aggregation. "Aggregation is a process whereby a part of the information available for the solution of a problem is sacrificed for the purpose of making the problem more easily manageable."[18] (Macroeconomic theory, consequently, is doubly abstracted from reality.) Even though the "index problem" (aggregation of nonhomogeneous items, e.g., apples and pears) is insolvable, worthwhile index numbers may be constructed. Part of the art of macroeconomic theorizing is to determine the "correct" split between the cost of handling and the cost of sacrificing additional information for the purpose at hand.

EQUILIBRIUM VS. DISEQUILIBRIUM

What state, equilibrium or disequilibrium, best describes our economy? Does the economy always have a tendency to move toward or away from a stable condition? Is stability or instability the "natural" state? There is no doubt that our economy is historic (i.e., changeable) rather than static. However, most macro-monetary models now in use are static equilibrium ones. There is support for the statement that static models are easier to understand and to work with. Nevertheless, a restriction of their unbridled use is necessary for they may promote false policy prescriptions (e.g., the famous British "Treasury View" that investment, both public and private, must equate with an unchanging amount of saving, even though excess stocks of factors were available). Joan Robinson has said it best:

> Once we admit that an economy exists in time, that history goes one way, from the irrevocable past into the unknown future, the conception of equilibrium based on the mechanical analogy of a pendulum swinging to and fro in space becomes untenable. The whole of traditional economics needs to be thought out afresh.[19]

---

[17]Axel Leijonhufvud, "The Varieties of Price Theory: What Microfoundations for Macrotheory?" Department of Economics, UCLA, Discussion Paper Number 44 (Los Angeles, 1974).

[18]H. A. John Green, AGGREGATION IN ECONOMIC ANALYSIS (Princeton, N.J.: Princeton University Press, 1964), p. 3.

[19]Joan Robinson, "What Has Become of the Keynesian Revolution," CHALLENGE: THE MAGAZINE OF ECONOMIC AFFAIRS 16 (January/February 1974): 8. The equilibrium vs. disequilibrium controversy is highlighted by Nicholas Kaldor, "The Irrelevance of Equilibrium Economics," ECONOMIC JOURNAL 82 (December 1972): 1237-55 and F. H. Hahn, ON THE NOTION OF EQUILIBRIUM IN ECONOMICS (New York: Cambridge University Press, 1973).

PERFECT COMPETITION VS. IMPERFECT COMPETITION

For the same reasons that timeless models are "preferred" by textbook writers to dynamic disequilibrium ones, so too are perfectly competitive macro-monetary models preferred as an additional simplification. Keynes's model was perfectly competitive; Roy Harrod and Joan Robinson could not convince him of the importance of marginal revenue deviating from average revenue. Consequently, it was necessary for Keynes to find reasons why a "competitive" economy did not equilibrate (e.g., lack of effective demand, user cost, fixed money wages, liquidity trap).

Subsequently, the relaxation of one or more of the restrictions assuring perfect competition has opened new macro-monetary theoretic avenues. The assumptions of free and perfect information, homogeneous products and factors of production, and complete flexibility of all prices are most often relaxed in current macro-monetary theory. We will dispose of the information restriction first. If information is not costless, it may cost either time and/or money. If information is imperfect, it may be due to either illusion, hallucination, or because some informational signals were lost. In each case, disequilibrium may be caused or continued within an economy. For example, independent demanders and suppliers may not agree on an equilibrium price when they do not know if excess demands or excess supplies will occur, or if the normal stability conditions will be reversed. Information flows are of vital interest when history is actually being made, but perfectly competitive models ignore this point.

The restriction on flexibility and homogeneity could refer to prices or quantities. Most economic models do allow quantities to be completely flexible, just like putty, and, consequently, only one "homogeneous" commodity price and one "homogeneous" factor price is necessary because both commodities and factors are homogeneous "globs."[20] On the other hand, prices in most Keynesian models are less than completely flexible; they are, however, completely homogeneous by Jevons's law of indifference (i.e., prices for identical items are identical over time and space). Over the years the theoretical discussion has moved from price rigidities to the speed of relative price movements. Controversy has centered around the respective adjustment speeds of prices and quantities--that is, prices and quantities of both products and factors (primarily labor). An additional dispute has to do with whether or not adjustment speeds vary depending on the stage of the cycle the economy finds itself in.

As macro-monetary models move away from timeless competitive models to a more dynamic setting, the restrictions on information, as well as the adjustment speeds

---

[20]Because all goods are assumed to be physical consumption goods, all the problems inherent in dealing with services and capital goods are avoided.

and heterogeneity of price and quantity, are of importance. Models from which policy prescriptions are written should no longer be couched solely in timeless (vs. dynamic), certainty (vs. uncertainty), and real (vs. monetary) terms.

STATIC VS. DYNAMIC, CERTAINTY VS. UNCERTAINTY, AND REAL VS. MONETARY

The macro-monetary theoretic problems concerning time, uncertainty and the real versus monetary mix of variables cannot be discussed independently very well because of their interrelationships. Consequently, the reader is asked to keep the following figure in mind (p. 9). In what follows the interrelationships expressed by the box diagram are of utmost importance.

Once the idea of a static world has been abandoned, it becomes relevant to discuss different views of the future. These views can be either short run or long run. Most macro-monetary models use Marshall's nomenclature: "short run" means labor is variable but capital is fixed (changing capital utilization occurs); "long run" means both capital and labor are variable.

If time is allowed to be continuous, the distinction between stocks (time reference only) and flows (time dimension as well as time reference) becomes meaningful. Investment in one period does add to capital stock in the next; saving becomes wealth (savings) in the same way. Also, not to be forgotten are the reverse processes, depreciation and spending out of savings (dissaving). A dynamic analysis should be in terms of processes not states; adjustment speeds are relevant and so are their rates of change. Acceleration and deceleration give some sense of reality to growth and capital theory.

The increased uncertainty brought about by a more distant future has already been broached. A current subject of controversy is whether expectational investment decisions, the most unstable of macroeconomic aggregates, can be classified as risky (measured by probabilities), or as uncertain. G.L.S. Shackle has called uncertainty the "kaleidic factor." He feels Keynes's investment function is as ephemeral as the mosaic of a kaleidoscope--not risky.[21] Investment decisions have a number of mutually exclusive answers. If one decision is right, the other, necessarily, must be wrong. There are no probabilistic truths, everything changes with every turn; there is only uncertainty. Risk (probability) is never right; it is a simple means of averaging error.

In a static, certain world there is no need for money. Interest-bearing assets would always be preferred to cash as a store of value, if there were no doubt as to their future value. If receipts and expenditures can be synchronized, there also is no need for money as a medium of exchange. But in a dynamic world abounding with uncertainty, money is a necessity. Liquidity provides the

---

[21]G.L.S. Shackle, A SCHEME OF ECONOMIC THEORY (New York: Cambridge University Press, 1965), p. 48.

Box Diagram of Theoretic Interrelationships

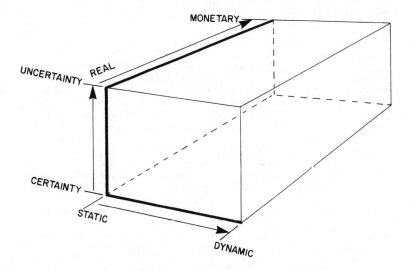

additional luxury of delaying decisions, but this advantage must be pitted against the cost of lost opportunity.

Over time macro-monetary analysis has placed more or less emphasis on the differences among the six variables (static, dynamic, certainty, uncertainty, real, and monetary) that have been analyzed in this section. Theoretical writing has begun to move away from the static-certainty-real corner of the box diagram.

POLICY PRESCRIPTIONS AND CONCLUSION

We live in a dynamic world; the messages may remain the same but the filters are constantly changing. For example, during the Great Depression it became clear that aggregate demand was not independent of aggregate supply; laborers must be employed to create products, as well as to create effective demand. More recently, the Marshallian market-day supply schedule (completely inelastic) has become for many raw resources the long-run supply schedule (except, of course, for labor). Thus, both economic problems and their solutions have changed drastically over time.

In the 1930s Keynes diagnosed the ills of the economy to be those of depressed prices and a lack of effective demand. In the 1970s the ills are inflation along with a shortage of aggregate supply, brought on by a pessimistic view of raw resources--excepting labor. The problems and perhaps the solutions appear to be reversed but the two main culprits, money and labor, have not changed. Money and labor have more in common than is generally realized. There is a critical minimum amount of both human capital and liquid financial capital necessary before the production and exchange process will work equitably and efficiently. However, if labor and money are in excess they can cause an economy to cease to function. Labor is a resource only so long as it is fed, educated, etc., or else it becomes a detriment. Likewise, money is only worthwhile as long as there is faith in its value; once the faith is shattered the economy will revert to a less efficient barter economy or economic anarchy. The transition from a monetary economy may not be smooth. There is a need for continued theoretic research into the mysteries of the macro-monetary economy. Policy prescriptions will always be value judgments. Only if the economy is modeled to reflect the "essential" messages do we have any hope that our policy prescriptions will be relevant. The economist is in charge of the filtering.

GENERAL SOURCES

Surveys

ESSAYS

Brunner, Karl. "A Survey of Selected Issues in Monetary Theory." SCHWEIT-ZERISCHE ZEITSCHRIFT FUER VOLKSWIRTSCHAFT UND STATISTIK 107 (March 1971): 1-146.

Brunner's survey is divided into eight sections: (1) "The Nature of Our Problem," (2) "The Micro-Analysis of Money," (3) "The Transmission Mechanism," (4) "Issues Associated with Alternative Views on the Transmission Mechanism," (5) "Impulse Forces and Dynamics of Economic Fluctuations," (6) "An Elaboration of the Monetarist Hypothesis," (7) "The Supply and Control of Money," and (8) "The Analysis of Monetary Policy."

Dernberg, Thomas. "Income and Employment Theory." In INTERNATIONAL ENCYCLOPEDIA OF THE SOCIAL SCIENCES, edited by D. L. Sills, vol. 7, pp. 122-31. New York: Macmillan, 1968.

Dernberg gives a quite elementary exposition of this subject--not much different than the textbook he coauthored. (See Textbooks: Macroeconomics and Growth.)

Fellner, William [J.]. "Employment Theory and Business Cycles." In A SURVEY OF CONTEMPORARY ECONOMICS, edited by Howard S. Ellis, vol. 1, pp. 49-98. Homewood, Ill.: Richard D. Irwin, 1948.

Notwithstanding the advance of ideas, aggregate processes are treated as given, although, in reality, they fluctuate during the cycle. Since this book was published, employment theory has become less integrated with value theory. The areas covered are: (1) "The Analytical Framework: The Quantity Theory vs. Variants of the Saving-Investment Approach," (2) "Trends and Cycles," (3) "Rigidities and the Problem of Uncertainty," and (4) "Policies."

Friedman, Milton. "Post-War Trends in Monetary Theory and Policy." NATIONAL BANKING REVIEW 2 (September 1964): 1-9. Reprinted in [10].

The world changes. There is now a feeling that money matters.

Haley, Bernard F. "Value and Distribution." In A SURVEY OF CONTEMPORARY ECONOMICS, edited by Howard S. Ellis, vol. 1, pp. 1-48. Homewood, Ill.: Richard D. Irwin, 1948.

Especially because of the writings of John R. Hicks and Paul A. Samuelson, value theory was becoming totally Walrasian--breaking away from the Marshallian value theory in Keynes's GENERAL THEORY. Distribution theory, on the other hand, was more firmly wedded to the ideas growing out of the GENERAL THEORY, especially the theories of wages and interest.

Hicks, John R. "Monetary Theory and History: An Attempt at Perspective." In his CRITICAL ESSAYS IN MONETARY THEORY, pp. 155-73. New York: Oxford University Press, 1967. Reprinted in [2].

Hicks looks back in history to compare Keynes and those whom he called classics. It is his view that the type of monetary theory which becomes current is determined by history. The greater the challenge the better the theory.

Johnson, Harry G. "Major Issues in Monetary Economics." OXFORD ECO-
NOMIC PAPERS 26 (July 1974): 212-25.

He lists three "most fruitful lines of future . . . research": (1) "The
Foundations of Monetary Theory and the Integration of Monetary
and Value Theory," (2) "The Optimum Quantity of Money and Related Issues," and (3) "The International Monetary System."

_____. "Monetary Theory and Policy." AMERICAN ECONOMIC REVIEW 52
(June 1962): 335-84. Reprinted in [19].

This is one of a series of survey articles sponsored by the Rockefeller
Foundation. Four broad topics are covered: (1) dichotomy and
neutrality of money, (2) theory of the demand for money, (3) theory
of the supply of money, monetary control and monetary dynamics,
and (4) monetary policy. Excellent bibliography, although dated.

_____. "Recent Developments in Monetary Theory." INDIAN ECONOMIC
REVIEW 3 (February and August 1963): 29-69 and 1-28.

In this essay Johnson surveyed recent developments in monetary
theory with respect to six major questions originating in Keynes's
GENERAL THEORY: (1) "The Role of Money in the Economy,"
(2) "The Propensity to Consume," (3) "The Propensity to Invest,"
(4) "The Demand for Money," (5) "The Supply of Money," and
(6) "Monetary Policy."

_____. "Recent Developments in Monetary Theory--A Commentary." In MONEY
IN BRITAIN: 1959-1969, edited by D.R. Croome and H.G. Johnson, pp.
83-114. New York: Oxford University Press, 1970.

The essay surveys developments in monetary theory since the Radcliffe Report. Johnson's emphasis is less on unifying strands of
thought and rather more on current controversy. The themes discussed are: (1) the revival of monetarism, (2) the rehabilitation
of Keynes, (3) fundamentals of monetary theory, (4) problems associated with financial intermediation, (5) money in growth models,
and (6) theory of inflation and economic policy.

Smith, Warren L. "On Some Current Issues in Monetary Economics: An Interpretation." JOURNAL OF ECONOMIC LITERATURE 8 (September 1970): 767-
82.

The issue of interest to Smith is the integration of portfolio theory
with the theory of income generation. In a rambling format the
models of Pesek and Saving and the monetarists are discussed and
criticized.

Tobin, James. "Macroeconomics." In ECONOMICS, edited by Nancy D. Ruggles, pp. 44-54. Englewood Cliffs, N.J.: Prentice-Hall, 1970.

> The survey is at the informed laymen level. This is the Yale School approach.

Villard, Henry H. "Monetary Theory." In A SURVEY OF CONTEMPORARY ECONOMICS, edited by Howard S. Ellis, vol. 1, pp. 314-51. Homewood, Ill.: Richard D. Irwin, 1948.

> Monetary theory after the Second World War was in a sad state. Monetary policy was broadly ineffective during the Great Depression. Keynesian theory shifted interest from the quantity of money to the level of output and employment. Villard divided his survey into five areas of interest: (1) "The Changing Monetary Environment and the Decline of the Quantity Equation," (2) "Monetary Equilibrium, Period Analysis, and the GENERAL THEORY," (3) "Liquidity Preference and Interest," (4) "War Finance," and (5) "The Postwar Heritage."

Weintraub, Sidney. "Theoretical Economics." ANNALS OF THE AMERICAN ACADEMY OF POLITICAL AND SOCIAL SCIENCE 376 (March 1968): 145-62. Reprinted in [13].

> A survey of the best studies in theoretical economics. Over 200 works are cited. Also see his earlier survey in the same journal with the same title (352 [March 1964]: 152-64).

CONFERENCES AND SYMPOSIUMS

Bach, G.L., et al. "The State of Monetary Economics." REVIEW OF ECONOMICS AND STATISTICS 45, supplement (February 1963): 3-155.

> This supplement is in two parts: "Monetary Economics" and the "Report and Staff Papers of the Commission on Money and Credit." The outstanding contribution is by Franco Modigliani, "The Monetary Mechanism and Its Interaction with Real Phenomena," pp. 79-110. This is a mid-1950s updating of his classic "Liquidity Preference and the Theory of Interest and Money." ECONOMETRICA 12 (1944): 45-88.

Brunner, Karl, ed. "The Federal Reserve Discount Policy: A Symposium." JOURNAL OF MONEY, CREDIT AND BANKING 2 (May 1970): 1-34.

> Papers by Robert C. Holland, Thomas R. Atkinson, Donald D. Hester, and Deane Carson discuss the problems inherent in an independent central bank. The issues remain unsettled.

_____. "1969 Conference of University Professors." JOURNAL OF MONEY, CREDIT AND BANKING 3, supplement (May 1971): 321-603.

Five sessions were held: (1) "The Comparative Merits of Fixed versus Flexible Exchange Rates," (2) "A New Look at Monetary Policy Instruments," (3) "Survey of Econometric Models of the Financial Sector," (4) "Criteria for Determining the Efficiency of Monetary and Fiscal Policy," and (5) "The Evolution of Financial Institutions."

_____. "A Symposium: The President's Commission on Financial Structure and Regulation." JOURNAL OF MONEY, CREDIT AND BANKING 3 (February 1971): 1-34.

Five economists were asked to discuss the role and function of the president's commission. What are the social costs and benefits of the existing regulations and constraints?

_____. TARGETS AND INDICATORS OF MONETARY POLICY. San Francisco: Chandler Publishing Co., 1969. 348 p.

These are papers read at a 1966 conference by the same name. Additional chapters, to obtain a more representative view, were contributed by J. Tobin, Gramley and Chase, Hendershott, R. Weintraub, Meltzer and Brunner. The conclusion is that interpretation and determination of monetary policy is a difficult problem to resolve.

_____. "Two Major Issues in Recent Monetary Policy: A Symposium." JOURNAL OF MONEY, CREDIT AND BANKING 2 (February 1970): 1-55.

The issues were: (1) the control of interest rates payable on bank deposits and (2) the variability of monetary policy. Papers were given by James Tobin, Milton Friedman, Paul Samuelson, and Allan H. Meltzer. A classic liberal-conservative confrontation.

Clayton, George, et al., eds. MONETARY THEORY AND MONETARY POLICY IN THE 1970'S. New York: Oxford University Press, 1971. 272 p. Also paperbound.

One of a series of conferences of the Money Study Group, which together contain most of the important recent macro-monetary work done in Britain.

Conference on Research in Income and Wealth. STUDIES IN INCOME AND WEALTH. New York: National Bureau of Economic Research (distributed partially by Princeton University Press), 1937- . Various years.

The National Bureau has published in these volumes the original research of numerous economists. Volumes 15, 16, 18, 19, 22, 25, 27-29 are especially useful.

Croome, David R., and Johnson, Harry G., eds. MONEY IN BRITAIN: 1959-1969. New York: Oxford University Press, 1969. 314 p. Also paperbound.

A summary of monetary theory in Britain since the report of the
Radcliffe Committee--1959 to 1969. H.G. Johnson's survey of
the literature for those ten years is especially worthwhile.

Eckstein, Otto, ed. THE ECONOMETRICS OF PRICE DETERMINATION. Washington, D.C.: Board of Governors of the Federal Reserve System and Social
Science Research Council, 1972. 397 p. Also paperbound.

The purpose of this conference was to study four equations (price
adjustment, wage adjustment, price expectations, and normal utilization) which form a subsystem of a complete model. The introductory comments by J. Tobin, pp. 5-15, are the place to begin.

Federal Reserve Bank of Boston. MONETARY CONFERENCE SERIES, no. 1.
Boston: 1969- . Paperbound.

From June 1969 to September 1973, eleven conferences were held.
All are available from the Federal Reserve Bank of Boston. The
proceedings of most interest are: No. 1, CONTROLLING MONE-
TARY AGGREGATES, June 1969, 174 p.; No. 5, CONSUMER
SPENDING AND MONETARY POLICY: THE LINKAGES, June
1971, 315 p.; No. 8, POLICIES FOR A MORE COMPETITIVE
FINANCIAL SYSTEM, June 1972, 221 p.; No. 9, CONTROLLING
MONETARY AGGREGATES II: THE IMPLEMENTATION, September
1972, 184 p.; No. 10, ISSUES IN FEDERAL DEBT MANAGEMENT,
June 1973, 257 p.

Haberler, Gottfried, ed. "Paradoxes in Capital Theory: A Symposium."
QUARTERLY JOURNAL OF ECONOMICS 80 (November 1966): 503-83.

The symposium contains contributions by Luigi L. Pasinetti; Paul A.
Samuelson and David Levhari; Michio Morishima; Michael Bruno,
Edwin Burmeister, and Eytan Sheshinski; P. Garegnani; and a summary by Samuelson. Levhari and Samuelson confirm that the non-
switching theorem is false.

Hahn, Frank H., and Brechling, F.P.R., eds. THE THEORY OF INTEREST
RATES. New York: St. Martin's Press, 1966. 381 p.

The proceedings of this International Economic Association conference
are divided into three groups: (1) "Theories of Asset Preference,"
(2) "Money, Interest Rates, and Equilibrium Models," and (3) "Interest, Growth, and Inter-Temporal Allocation." Another I.E.A.
conference of interest is: Lutz, F.A., and Hague, D.C., eds.
THE THEORY OF CAPITAL. New York: St. Martin's Press, 1961.
428 p.

Harris, Seymour E., ed. "Budgetary Concepts: Symposium." REVIEW OF ECO-
NOMICS AND STATISTICS 45 (May 1963): 11-47.

This is an analysis of U.S. budgetary account and policies.

Fifteen well-known economists expressed their views.

_____. "Controversial Issues in Recent Monetary Policy: A Symposium."
REVIEW OF ECONOMICS AND STATISTICS 42 (August 1960): 245-82.

The debt management and monetary policies of the Eisenhower Ad-
ministration were carefully analyzed by S.E. Harris, J.W. Angell,
W. Fellner, A.H. Hansen, A.G. Hart, H. Neisser, R.V. Roosa,
P.A. Samuelson, W.L. Smith, W. Thomas, J. Tobin, and S.
Weintraub.

_____. "The Controversy over Monetary Policy." REVIEW OF ECONOMICS
AND STATISTICS 33 (August 1951): 179-200.

The monetarists are Lester V. Chandler and Milton Friedman. The
fiscalists are A.H. Hansen, Abba Lerner, and James Tobin. Time
changes but opinions don't--often.

Horwich, George, ed. MONETARY PROCESS AND POLICY: A SYMPOSIUM.
Homewood, Ill.: Richard D. Irwin, 1967. 400 p.

The symposium was held during the "happy times" immediately after
the 1964 tax cut--happy times for the fiscalists. The papers are
gathered under four headings: (1) "High Employment and Price
Stability," (2) "Possible Instability of the Financial Structure,"
(3) "Effects of Monetary Policy" (split into three subheadings),
and (4) "International Constraints."

Johnson, Harry G., ed. "Conference of University Professors." JOURNAL OF
MONEY, CREDIT AND BANKING 1 (August 1969): 303-681.

The introduction by Harry G. Johnson and the poems composed by
Kenneth Boulding makes this issue informative and entertaining.
The issues were all monetary in nature: theory, institutions, and
policy.

Johnson, Harry G., and Nobay, A.R., eds. THE CURRENT INFLATION.
New York: St. Martin's Press, 1971. 215 p.

The third in a continuing series of conference papers by the best
British economists. All twelve papers are devoted to the problems
of inflation, with special emphasis on the Phillips curve and incomes
policy.

_____. ISSUES IN MONETARY ECONOMICS: PROCEEDINGS OF THE 1972
MONEY STUDY GROUP CONFERENCE. Vol. 4. New York: Oxford University Press, 1974. 608 p.

This is a collection of the papers presented at the fourth Money
Study Group Conference. The papers are centered on four issues:
(1) "Money in the International Economy," (2) "Recent Developments in Monetary Theory," (3) "Money and Economic Activity,"

and (4) "Recent Developments in British Monetary Policy."

Lakatos, Imre, and Musgrave, Alan, eds. CRITICISM AND THE GROWTH OF KNOWLEDGE. New York: Cambridge University Press, 1970. 282 p. Also paperbound.

These papers were originally given at the 1965 International Colloquium in the Philosophy of Science held at Bedford College. The positions of T.S. Kuhn, I. Lakatos, and Karl Popper are critically discussed.

Lipsey, Richard G., ed. "Symposium on Production Functions and Economic Growth." REVIEW OF ECONOMIC STUDIES 29 (June 1962): 155-266.

The articles are by Kenneth J. Arrow, Nicholas Kaldor and James A. Mirrlees, Paul A. Samuelson, Robert M. Solow, Joan Robinson, J.E. Meade, D.G. Champernowne, J. Black, and Richard Stone and J.A.C. Brown. Although the M.I.T. versus Cambridge, England battle appears to be evenly fought, logic is with England.

Malinvaud, E., and Bacharach, M.O.L., eds. ACTIVITY ANALYSIS IN THE THEORY OF GROWTH AND PLANNING. New York: St. Martin's Press, 1967. 349 p.

This book is the proceedings of a 1963 conference held by the International Economic Association. The seminal article by Tjalling C. Koopmans, "Economic Growth at a Maximal Rate," QUARTERLY JOURNAL OF ECONOMICS 78 (August 1964): 355-94, also appears here (pp. 3-42).

Mints, Lloyd W., et al. "A Symposium on Fiscal and Monetary Policy." REVIEW OF ECONOMICS AND STATISTICS 28 (May 1946): 60-84.

Lloyd Mints's contribution "Monetary Policy" pp. 60-69 is reprinted in [18]. Mints, a member of the Chicago school, emphasizes the importance of free markets, price flexibility, and monetary (versus fiscal) policy in maintaining general economic equilibrium with a high level of employment. A.H. Hansen, H.S. Ellis, A. Lerner, and M. Kalecki were part of the symposium.

Mirrlees, James A., and Stern, N.H., eds. MODELS OF ECONOMIC GROWTH. Proceedings of a conference held by the International Economic Association at Jerusalem, 1970. New York: John Wiley & Sons, 1973. 394 p.

The volume contains fifteen previously unpublished papers in the areas of: (1) growth experience, (2) growth and the short run, (3) technological growth, (4) capital growth, (5) optimal growth, and (6) growth in developing countries. The introduction by Mirrlees, which attempts to convince the reader that growth models are useful and that their uses can be criticized, is first rate. An index is included.

Niehans, Jurg, ed. "The Universities-National Bureau Conference on Secular Inflation." JOURNAL OF MONEY, CREDIT AND BANKING 5, supplement (February 1973): 237-593.

> Jurg Niehans's introduction, pp. 237-41, gives a good summary of the articles and comments. Niehans makes an interesting point that because an unstable unit of account may impose costs, the unit of account may join the medium of exchange in the center of future monetary theorizing.

Parkin, Michael, ed. ESSAYS IN MODERN ECONOMICS. THE PROCEED-INGS OF THE ASSOCIATION OF UNIVERSITY TEACHERS OF ECONOMICS: ABERYSTWYTH 1972. With A.R. Nobay. New York: Barnes & Noble Books, 1973. 411 p.

> Out of a total of nineteen articles, one is on Keynes and seven on macro-monetary economics. Elizabeth Johnson's article, "The Collected Writings of John Maynard Keynes: Some Visceral Reactions," gives one a clearer picture of how Keynes, the great man, worked and wrote. Frank Hahn's article, "On the Foundations of Monetary Theory," re-echoes the concern that all other economic theory, besides monetary, treats money as unessential. An index is included.

Rousseas, Stephen W., ed. INFLATION: ITS CAUSES, CONSEQUENCES AND CONTROL. Wilton, Conn.: Calvin K. Kazanyian Economics Foundation, 1968. 59 p. Paperbound.

> The two main papers given at the symposium were: Robert M. Solow, "Recent Controversy on the Theory of Inflation: An Eclectic View," and Phillip Cagan, "Theories of Mild, Continuing Inflation: A Critique and Extension." The discussants were Albert G. Hart and James Tobin.

Stein, Herbert, et al. POLICIES TO COMBAT DEPRESSION. National Bureau of Economic Research. Princeton, N.J.: Princeton University Press, 1956. 427 p.

> This is the proceedings of two conferences held in Princeton, N.J. --the first on October 30-31, 1953, and the second on May 14-15, 1954. There was a feeling at that time that the United States was increasingly vulnerable to an economic decline.

Uzawa, Hirofumi, ed. "Symposium on the Theory of Economic Growth." JOURNAL OF POLITICAL ECONOMY 77, supplement (July/August 1969): 573-719.

> This symposium was held at the University of Chicago in November 1967. The paper by Miguel Sidrauski, "Rational Choice and Patterns of Growth," pp. 575-85, has generated the most continuing interest. This collection of papers was dedicated to the memory of Miguel Sidrauski.

Collected Readings

SINGLE AUTHOR

Domar, Evsey [D.]. ESSAYS IN THE THEORY OF ECONOMIC GROWTH. New York: Oxford University Press, 1957. 272 p.

> The best essays written by the other half of the Harrod-Domar growth theory duo. Domar has written a very informative foreword which puts his essays in perspective.

Friedman, Milton. DOLLARS AND DEFICITS. Englewood Cliffs, N.J.: Prentice-Hall, 1968. 279 p. Also paperbound.

> A collection of Friedman's more popular writings from the past two decades. The first essay "Why Economists Disagree" is very insightful, especially about Friedman.

_____. THE OPTIMUM QUANTITY OF MONEY. Chicago: Aldine Publishing Co., 1969. 296 p.

> A collection of the most recent articles by the leader of not only the Chicago school, but of all monetarists. The title essay is original with this volume.

Harrod, Roy F. ECONOMIC ESSAYS. New York: St. Martin's Press, 1952. 314 p.

> The fifteen pieces in this varied collection range in time from the pre-Joan Robinson-Edward Chamberlin "Notes on Supply" and "The Law of Decreasing Cost" to the current (and rather counterrevolutionary) "Theory of Imperfect Competition Revised" and "Supplement on Dynamic Theory."

Hayek, Friedrich A. PROFITS, INTEREST AND INVESTMENT. New York: Augustus M. Kelley, 1939. 266 p.

> This collection of essays, by a Nobel Laureate, retain their importance because of the emphasis on investment and, especially, the role of expectations on investment. "The 'Paradox' of Saving," pp. 199-263, first published in 1929, is of current importance.

Hicks, John R. CRITICAL ESSAYS IN MONETARY THEORY. New York: Oxford University Press, 1968. 231 p.

> Twelve essays are included of which only two and part of a third had been published previously. The first three essays have a common title, "The Two Triads." The triads are the functions and the motives for holding money. The ninth essay, "Monetary Theory and History--An Attempt at Perspective," is an excellent narrative comparing Keynes and the classics. The last three essays are in

the history of doctrine. Thornton, Keynes's TREATISE ON MONEY, and Hayek are discussed. All the essays have something new to say.

Johnson, Harry G. ESSAYS IN MONETARY ECONOMICS. Cambridge, Mass.: Harvard University Press, 1967. 332 p.

This is a collection of ten previously published articles. The most significant are: "Monetary Theory and Policy." AMERICAN ECONOMIC REVIEW 52 (June 1962): 335-84; "Recent Developments in Monetary Theory." INDIAN ECONOMIC REVIEW 6 (February and August 1963): 29-69 and 1-28; "A Survey of Theories of Inflation." INDIAN ECONOMIC REVIEW 6 (August 1963): 29-66; and "Money in a Neo-Classical One Sector Growth Model." Reprinted in [2] [16]. This last reference is an elaborated and corrected version of "The Neo-Classical One Sector Growth Model: A Monetary Economy." ECONOMICA 33 (August 1966): 265-87. These articles are all from part 1: "Monetary Theory." Part 2 is "Monetary and Fiscal Policy Issues in North America," and part 3 is "Monetary and Fiscal Problems of Developing Countries."

_____. FURTHER ESSAYS IN MONETARY ECONOMICS. Cambridge, Mass.: Harvard University Press, 1973. 366 p.

Fifteen previously published essays on domestic and international monetary issues are reissued. It is intended as a sequel and complement to his ESSAYS IN MONETARY ECONOMICS (1967). All five articles in part 1, "General Monetary Theory," are annotated in this book. (None of the articles from part 2, "International Monetary Theory," or part 3, "The International Monetary Crisis," have been annotated.) The annotated articles are: (1) "Recent Developments in Monetary Theory--A Commentary." In MONEY IN BRITAIN, 1959-1969, edited by David R. Croome and Harry G. Johnson, pp. 83-114. New York: Oxford University Press, 1970; (2) "The Keynesian Revolution and the Monetarist Counter-Revolution." AMERICAN ECONOMIC REVIEW 61 (May 1971): 1-14; (3) "Problems of Efficiency in Monetary Management." JOURNAL OF POLITICAL ECONOMY 76 (September/October 1968): 971-90; (4) "Inside Money, Outside Money, Income, Wealth and Welfare in Monetary Theory." JOURNAL OF MONEY, CREDIT AND BANKING 1 (February 1969): 30-45; and (5) "Is There an Optimal Money Supply?" JOURNAL OF FINANCE 15 (May 1970): 435-42.

_____. MONEY, TRADE, AND ECONOMIC GROWTH. Cambridge, Mass.: Harvard University Press, 1962. 199 p. Also paperbound.

The two essays of most importance are: "Monetary Theory and Keynesian Economics." PAKISTAN ECONOMIC JOURNAL 8 (June 1958): 56-70; and "The GENERAL THEORY After Twenty-Five Years." AMERICAN ECONOMIC REVIEW 51 (May 1961): 1-17.

These articles are both from part 2: "Money." Parts 1 and 3 are entitled "Trade and Growth," and "Economic Growth," respectively.

Kahn, Richard [F.]. SELECTED ESSAYS IN EMPLOYMENT AND GROWTH. New York: Cambridge University Press, 1972. 239 p.

Lord Kahn's paper on the multiplier, which is now such a familiar tool in economics, is included. With regard to it, Kahn has written ". . . often cited but apparently little read." All of the essays, except the last, were reprinted in their original form.

Kaldor, Nicholas. ESSAYS ON ECONOMIC POLICY. 2 vols. London: Gerald Duckworth, 1964. 315 p. and 342 p.

The policies which were advocated by Keynes are defended herein.

———. ESSAYS ON ECONOMIC STABILITY AND GROWTH. Glencoe, Ill.: Free Press, 1960. 302 p.

Every essay in this collection was influenced by the work of J.M. Keynes. The essays are divided into these areas: (1) "Speculation, Liquidity Preference and the Theory of Employment," (2) "The Theory of Economic Fluctuations," and (3) "The Theory of Economic Growth." The introduction gives a chronology of thought.

———. ESSAYS ON VALUE AND DISTRIBUTION. Glencoe, Ill.: Free Press, 1960. 238 p.

This collection of Kaldor's articles deals with the problems of equilibrium, imperfect competition, welfare economics, capital and distribution. Many were published in the thirties. The introduction is most interesting reading.

Kalecki, Michal. SELECTED ESSAYS ON THE DYNAMICS OF THE CAPITAL-IST ECONOMY, 1933-1970. New York: Cambridge University Press, 1971. 198 p.

Three papers are included which were published in Polish before the GENERAL THEORY appeared and include many of its essentials. The economics taught at Cambridge University is, in many ways, closer to the writings of Kalecki than to those of Keynes.

Koopmans, Tjalling C. THREE ESSAYS ON THE STATE OF ECONOMIC SCI-ENCE. New York: McGraw-Hill Book Co., 1957. 243 p.

The three essays are entitled: "Allocation of Resources and the Price System," "The Construction of Economic Knowledge," and "The Interaction of Tools and Problems in Economics." The utilization of mathematical tools to better understand economic theory is the purpose of this book. It was for his work in mathematical economics that he was honored with a Nobel Prize.

Lerner, Abba P. ESSAYS IN ECONOMIC ANALYSIS. London: Macmillan and Co., 1953. 394 p.

Part 4 of this collection of essays is devoted to "Employment and Interest." Abba Lerner's out-pouring of significant articles during the 1930s and 1940s is simply amazing.

Marshall, Alfred. OFFICIAL PAPERS. Edited by John Maynard Keynes. London: Macmillan and Co., 1926. 428 p.

This volume contains all of Marshall's contributions to official inquiries on economic questions except for his work on the Labour Committee, of which he was a member.

Metzler, Lloyd A. COLLECTED PAPERS. Cambridge, Mass.: Harvard University Press, 1973. 611 p.

A collection of twenty-four essays and articles, four of them previously unpublished. Metzler was a leader of early post-World War II macroeconomics. Almost everything he wrote has become a classic.

Mundell, R[obert]. A. MONETARY THEORY. Pacific Palisades, Calif.: Goodyear Publishing Co., 1971. 201 p.

A collection of his reprinted articles and new material. The book is divided into two sections: (1) "New Ideas in Monetary Theory," and (2) "The World Economy."

Pasinetti, Luigi L. GROWTH AND INCOME DISTRIBUTION: ESSAYS IN ECONOMIC THEORY. New York: Cambridge University Press, 1974. 161 p.

There are six essays collected in this volume; five are dated (1958-62), but three have not previously been published (one was written in 1971-72). The rate of profit is exogenously determined in long-run equilibrium by the natural rate of growth divided by the capitalist's propensity to save. The theme is: In the long run, capital is independent of the rate of profit.

Patinkin, Don. STUDIES IN MONETARY ECONOMICS. New York: Harper & Row Publishers, 1972. 262 p.

Most of the papers included, except the first four, were published since the second edition of his MONEY, INTEREST, AND PRICES (1965). The article on the neo-quantity theory, "The Chicago Tradition, the Quantity Theory, and Friedman," pp. 92-117, is of special interest.

Robertson, Dennis [H.]. ESSAYS IN MONEY AND INTEREST. New York: William Collins, 1966. 256 p. Paperbound.

The essays have been collected from three volumes published during

Sir Dennis's lifetime: ESSAYS IN MONETARY THEORY (1940), UTILITY AND ALL THAT (1952), and ECONOMIC COMMEN-TARIES (1956). Sir John Hicks made the selection and contributed a memoir.

Robinson, Joan. COLLECTED ECONOMIC PAPERS. 4 vols. Atlantic Highlands, N.J.: Humanities Press, 1951, 1964, 1965, 1973. 248 p., 284 p., 315 p., 268 p.

The compleat Joan Robinson.

_____. ESSAYS IN THE THEORY OF ECONOMIC GROWTH. New York: St. Martin's Press, 1964. 148 p.

The four essays are in part reprinted and in part original. They constitute an introduction to her THE ACCUMULATION OF CAPI-TAL (Homewood, Ill.: Richard D. Irwin, 1956. 440 p.).

_____. THE RATE OF INTEREST AND OTHER ESSAYS. New York: St. Martin's Press, 1952. 170 p.

The tone of the essays is dynamic. The following essays are included: "The Rate of Interest," "Notes on the Economics of Technical Progress," "The Generalization of the GENERAL THEORY," and "Acknowledgments and Disclaimers." The penultimate essay expands the GENERAL THEORY into a dynamic model. In the last essay, she discusses the writers who have influenced her most.

Tobin, James. ESSAYS IN ECONOMICS. Vol. 1: MACROECONOMICS. Chicago: Markham Publishing Co., 1971. 542 p. Vol. 2: CONSUMPTION AND ECONOMETRICS. New York: American Elsevier Publishing Co., 1975. 492 p.

The first volume, MACROECONOMICS, is divided into three parts: (1) "Macroeconomic Theory," (2) "Economic Growth," and (3) "Money and Finance." The second volume, CONSUMPTION AND ECONOMETRICS, consists of four parts: (4) "Inflation and Unemployment," which continues the macroeconomic theme of volume one; (5) "The Consumption Function," (6) "Rationing," and (7) "Econometrics," all of which are concerned with consumer behavior. These are the articles the head of the Yale school feels are his best.

Warburton, Clark. DEPRESSION, INFLATION, AND MONETARY POLICY. Baltimore: Johns Hopkins Press, 1966. 440 p.

These are nineteen of his articles selected from the 1945-53 period. Warburton was the first post-World War II economist to emphasize the role of money supply in economic growth.

MULTI-AUTHORED: FESTSCHRIFTEN

Baran, Paul A., et al. PROBLEMS OF ECONOMICS AND PLANNING: ESSAYS IN HONOUR OF MICHAL KALECKI. Oxford: Pergamon Press, 1966. 494 p.

> This volume contains thirty-two original essays. The article by Joan Robinson, "Kalecki and Keynes," pp. 335-41, is a fine critique of the origins of employment theory. There was no attempt made to categorize the essays.

Bentzel, Ragnar, et al. ECONOMIC ESSAYS IN HONOUR OF ERIK LINDAHL. Stockholm: Economist Tidskrift, 1956. 412 p.

> The essays by Sir John Hicks, "Methods of Dynamic Analysis," pp. 139-51, and Johan Akerman, "The Cumulative Process," pp. 393-412, are still of current interest.

David, Paul A., and Reder, Melvin W., eds. NATIONS AND HOUSEHOLDS IN ECONOMIC GROWTH. ESSAYS IN HONOR OF MOSES ABRAMOVITZ. New York: Academic Press, 1974. 414 p.

> Fifteen original papers by the well-known and not so well-known. The second section on "Macroeconomic Performance: Growth and Stability" is of special interest.

Eltis, W.A., et al. INDUCTION, GROWTH AND TRADE: ESSAYS IN HONOUR OF SIR ROY HARROD. New York: Oxford University Press, 1970. 386 p.

> This collection of twenty-four original papers is divided into four parts: (1) "Philosophy," (2) "Growth and Development," (3) "International Trade," and (4) "The Firm." The first nineteen pages are a personal memoir of Sir Roy Harrod by Robert Blake.

Gayer, A.D., ed. THE LESSONS OF MONETARY EXPERIENCE: ESSAYS IN HONOR OF IRVING FISHER PRESENTED TO HIM ON THE OCCASION OF HIS SEVENTIETH BIRTHDAY. New York: Farrar & Rinehart, 1937. 462 p.

> The essays are from fourteen different countries. The articles by Marriner S. Eccles and Alvin H. Hansen bear re-reading.

Horwich, George, and Samuelson, Paul A., eds. TRADE, STABILITY, AND MACROECONOMICS: ESSAYS IN HONOR OF LLOYD A. METZLER. New York: Academic Press, 1974. 576 p. Also paperbound.

> Parts 3, 4, and 5 on inventory fluctuations, macro-monetary theory, and growth are of interest. All are original articles by outstanding economists.

Kurihara, Kenneth K., ed. POST KEYNESIAN ECONOMICS. New Brunswick, N.J.: Rutgers University Press, 1954. 460 p.

A collection of original articles dedicated to the memory of John
Maynard Keynes, each taking the GENERAL THEORY as a frame
of reference. The articles are divided into three groups: (1) "Monetary Theory and Policy," (2) "Economic Fluctuations and Growth,"
and (3) "Aggregative Economics and Testing." Articles by Martin
Bronfenbrenner, Don Patinkin, L.R. Klein, and Franco Modigliani,
among others, are of enduring value.

Metzler, Lloyd A., et al. INCOME, EMPLOYMENT, AND PUBLIC POLICY:
ESSAYS IN HONOR OF ALVIN H. HANSEN. New York: W. W. Norton,
1948. 379 p. Also paperbound.

This is a great collection of original articles by leading economists.
The articles are arranged in three groups: (1) "Determinants of
Income," (2) "Social Setting," and (3) "Economic Policy."

Strumpel, Burkhard, et al. HUMAN BEHAVIOR IN ECONOMIC AFFAIRS.
San Francisco: Jossey-Bass, 1972. 590 p.

The twenty-five essays in honor of George Katona are divided into
six sections: (1) "Introduction," (2) "Economic Psychology and Behavioral Science," (3) "Understanding and Comparing Consumer Behavior," (4) "Predicting Consumer Behavior," (5) "The Consumer in
a Changing Environment," and (6) "Poverty and Social Welfare."
Katona's concluding essay is a good introduction to the psychology
of economics.

Whittlesey, C.R., and Wilson, J.S.G., eds. ESSAYS IN MONEY AND
BANKING IN HONOUR OF R.S. SAYERS. New York: Oxford University
Press, 1968. 327 p.

Commercial banking, central banking, and international finance are
the subjects of most all the essays. The authors are both English
and American.

Wolfe, J.N., ed. VALUE, CAPITAL, AND GROWTH. PAPERS IN HONOUR
OF SIR JOHN HICKS. Edinburgh: Edinburgh University Press, 1968. 564 p.

This is a collection of twenty-two original essays by well-known
economists. All of the papers are derived from Hicks's thought.
An introduction by the editor gives an insight on Nobel Laureate
Hicks.

Wright, David McCord, et al. MONEY, TRADE, AND ECONOMIC GROWTH:
IN HONOR OF JOHN HENRY WILLIAMS. New York: Macmillan, 1951.
343 p.

The seventeen original essays are separated into the three areas of
Williams's interest: (1) "International Organization and Trade,"
(2) "Macroeconomic Theory and Policy," and (3) "Monetary Theory
and Central Banking." Essays by Tobin, Samuelson, Robertson, and

Roosa are especially noteworthy.

MULTI-AUTHORED: GENERAL

Note: As an indication of what articles are of sufficient worth to be reprinted, twenty of the best general books of readings were selected as a sample. The books are numbered from one to twenty, according to their author alphabetical listing. The number (or numbers) of the readings book in which an article has been reprinted is listed in brackets after the bibliographic material for that article.

Boorman, John T., and Havrilesky, Thomas M. MONEY SUPPLY, MONEY DEMAND, AND MACROECONOMIC MODELS. Northbrook, Ill.: AHM Publishing, 1972. 526 p. Paperbound.

This readings book may be used as a textbook. The authors give an overview of the problems discussed in the articles. Additional bibliography and questions are listed at the end of each chapter.

Carson, Deane, ed. BANKING AND MONETARY STUDIES. Homewood, Ill.: Richard D. Irwin, 1963. 441 p.

This volume was a project of the Office of the Comptroller of the Currency, published in commemoration of the centennial of the national banking system. The essays give slight historical treatment of monetary problems, with the thrust of the book in the direction of the institutions of today and their related problems.

[1] _____ . MONEY AND FINANCE: READINGS IN THEORY, POLICY, AND INSTITUTIONS. 2d ed. New York: John Wiley & Sons, 1972. 507 p. Paperbound.

Over 90 percent of the articles in the second edition are new, reflecting the rapid developments in money and finance. Carson's introductions to the chapters are most helpful. The book is divided into six parts: (1) "The Supply of Money," (2) "Commercial Banking," (3) "The Federal Reserve System: Structure, Goals, Indicators, and Instruments," (4) "Monetary Theory," (5) "Monetary Policy," and (6) "International Monetary Arrangements and Problems."

Cass, David, and McKenzie, Lionel W., eds. SELECTED READINGS IN MACROECONOMICS AND CAPITAL THEORY FROM ECONOMETRICA. Cambridge, Mass.: M.I.T. Press, 1974. 520 p.

The topics selected range in date from 1935 to 1966. All of the articles are highly mathematical in their arguments.

Clark, John J., and Cohen, Morris, eds. BUSINESS FLUCTUATIONS, GROWTH, AND ECONOMIC STABILIZATION. New York: Random House, 1963.

The majority of the articles included in this reader are from the

1940s and 1950s. The essays are organized in the following classification: (1) "Varieties of Business Fluctuations," (2) "Empirical Analysis of Business Cycle Theory," and (3) "Economic Stabilization." An extensive bibliography is included.

[2] Clower, Robert W., ed. MONETARY THEORY. Baltimore: Penguin Books, 1970. 360 p. Paperbound.

This is a superb collection of recent articles in monetary theory. Clower added commentaries and a bibliography which are most helpful. The areas covered are: (1) "Money and the Mechanism of Exchange," (2) "Traditional Doctrine: The Quantity Theory of Money," (3) "Contemporary Theory: Neo-Walrasian Equilibrium Analysis," (4) "Monetary Theory and Keynesian Economics," and (5) "Money and Economic Growth."

Entine, Alan D., ed. MONETARY ECONOMICS: READINGS. Belmont, Calif.: Wadsworth Publishing Co., 1968. 510 p. Paperbound.

Sections: (1) "Commercial Banking: Problem of Competition and Control," (2) "Financial Intermediaries and Commercial Banks," (3) "Monetary Instruments," (4) "Monetary Indicators," (5) "Monetary Theory and Policy in a Closed Economy," (6) "Monetary Theory and Policy in an Open Economy," (7) "Monetary Policy: Evaluation and Alternatives."

[3] Fellner, William [J.], and Haley, Bernard F., eds. READINGS IN THE THEORY OF INCOME DISTRIBUTION. Homewood, Ill.: Richard D. Irwin, 1946. 734 p.

The best articles on income distribution published before 1946 as selected by a committee of the American Economic Association. A bibliography of the literature on national income and distribution is included. The contents include articles in the areas of: (1) "Concept of Income and Distribution," (2) "Production Function and Marginal Productivity," (3) "Wages," (4) "Interest," (5) "Profit," and (6) "Rent."

[4] Gibson, William E., and Kaufman, George G., eds. MONETARY ECONOMICS: READINGS ON CURRENT ISSUES. New York: McGraw-Hill Book Co., 1971. 523 p. Paperbound.

This collection is divided into six major parts: (1) "Money, Monetary Policy, and Economic Activity," (2) "The Definitions of Money," (3) "Federal Reserve Control of the Money Stock," (4) "Money, Price Expectations, and Interest Rates," (5) "Indicators of Monetary Policy," and (6) "The Incidence of Monetary Policy."

Gies, Thomas G., and Apilado, Vincent P., eds. BANKING MARKETS AND FINANCIAL INSTITUTIONS. Homewood, Ill.: Richard D. Irwin, 1971. 416 p. Paperbound.

The thirty-eight essays are divided into three general sections: (1) "Structure and Competition in Banking," (2) "New Directions in Asset, Liability, and Capital Management," and (3) "Regulation and Allocative Efficiency."

[5] Gordon, Robert A[aron]., and Klein, Lawrence R., eds. READINGS IN BUSI-NESS CYCLES. Homewood, Ill.: Richard D. Irwin, 1965. 731 p.

This is the second volume to appear in the American Economic Association's series of republished business cycle articles. This volume has more mathematical and econometrical articles. Eight areas of interest are covered: (1) "Theory," (2) "Methodology," (3) "Econometric Models," (4) "Studies of Particular Variables," (5) "Long Cycles," (6) "International Aspects," (7) "Forecasting," and (8) "Policy."

[6] Haberler, Gottfried, ed. READINGS IN BUSINESS CYCLE THEORY. Homewood, Ill.: Richard D. Irwin, 1944. 510 p.

The best articles in business cycle theory published before 1944 as selected by a committee of the American Economic Association. The articles were divided into six parts: (1) "Over-all Picture of the Business Cycle and Method of Analysis," (2) "Saving, Invest-ment and National Income," (3) "The Multiplier, Acceleration Principle and Government Spending," (4) "Monetary Theory of the Business Cycle," (5) "Underconsumption Theory and Secular Stagna-tion Thesis," and (6) "Special Commodity Cycles." An extensive bibliography is included.

Hahn, Frank H., ed. READINGS IN THE THEORY OF GROWTH. New York: St. Martin's Press, 1971. 290 p.

The best articles on economic growth theory from the REVIEW OF ECONOMIC STUDIES as selected by Frank Hahn.

Hansen, Alvin H., and Clemence, Richard V., eds. READINGS IN BUSINESS CYCLES AND NATIONAL INCOME. Enl. ed. New York: W.W. Norton, 1964. 588 p.

The thirty-seven selections are arranged in seven groups: (1) "His-torical Episodes," (2) "Business Cycle Theories," (3) "Economic Dynamics," (4) "Econometrics," (5) "International and Interregional Aspects," (6) "Long Cycles," and (7) "Cycle Policy." This book is complementary to the American Economic Association's READINGS IN BUSINESS CYCLE THEORY, edited by Gottfried Haberler. Referenced by [6].

Harcourt, G.C., and Laing, N.F., eds. CAPITAL AND GROWTH. Balti-more: Penguin Books, 1971. 383 p. Paperbound.

Capital theory, because of ideology or difficulty, generates more

confusion than substance. Both sides of the controversies over
capital and growth are included.

[7] Harris, Seymour E., ed. THE NEW ECONOMICS: KEYNES' INFLUENCE
ON THEORY AND PUBLIC POLICY. New York: Augustus M. Kelley, 1947.
717 p.

> A superb collection of pre-1950 articles analyzing the economics
> of Keynes. Almost all of the well-known economists are repre-
> sented. Seymour E. Harris has done a masterful job of editing
> and introducing the various chapters. Some of his introductions
> to the writings of others have become classics in their own right.

Hester, Donald D., and Tobin, James, eds. FINANCIAL MARKETS AND
ECONOMIC ACTIVITY. New York: John Wiley & Sons, 1967. 266 p.

> A collection of the Yale school's 'portfolio-balance' approach to
> monetary analysis. The first essay is most famous, James Tobin's
> "Commercial Banks as Creators of 'Money'." This is one of three
> volumes by the same editors; this one stresses macroeconomics.

Hunt, E.K., and Schwartz, Jesse G., eds. A CRITIQUE OF ECONOMIC
THEORY. Baltimore: Penguin Books, 1972. 476 p. Paperbound.

> This readings book tries to explain why man may not get what he
> is worth--both positively and negatively one presumes. Part 3 on
> the capital controversy and income distribution is of special inter-
> est. Selections by Robinson, Dobb, Nuti, and Garegnani are in-
> cluded; there are none from M.I.T.

Johnson, Harry G., et al., eds. READINGS IN BRITISH MONETARY ECO-
NOMICS. Oxford: Clarendon Press, 1972. 620 p. Also paperbound.

> Put together by the British Monetary Study Group. British insti-
> tutional arrangements are emphasized. The areas covered are:
> (1) "Money and Economic Activity," (2) "The Demand for Money,"
> (3) "The Supply of Money," (4) "Efficiency," (5) "Financial Inter-
> mediaries," (6) "Debt Management," and (7) "Monetary Policy."

[8] Johnson, Walter L., and Kamerschen, David R., eds. MACROECONOMICS:
SELECTED READINGS. New York: Houghton Mifflin Co., 1970. 415 p.
Paperbound.

> The areas of interest covered are: (1) "The Macroeconomy," (2)
> "Consumption and Investment," (3) "The Money Sector," (4) "Wages,
> Prices, and Employment," (5) "Growth," and (6) "Macroeconomic
> Policy."

Keiser, Norman F., ed. READINGS IN MACROECONOMICS: THEORY,
EVIDENCE AND POLICY. Englewood Cliffs, N.J.: Prentice-Hall, 1970.
596 p. Paperbound.

This readings book is divided into five main topical sections: (1) "Income Theory, Consumption and Investment," (2) "Monetary Theory and Policy," (3) "Fiscal Policy," (4) "Economic Growth Determinants and Policy," and (5) "Policy Goals: Techniques and Constraints." Many of the articles have been abstracted.

[9] Lekachman, Robert, ed. KEYNES' GENERAL THEORY: REPORTS OF THREE DECADES. New York: St. Martin's Press, 1964. 359 p. Also paperbound.

Nine distinguished economists have each written two essays about John M. Keynes and his GENERAL THEORY: E.A.G. Robinson, W.B. Reddaway, R.F. Harrod, D.G. Champernowne, Abba P. Lerner, Jacob Viner, Gottfried Haberler, Paul M. Sweezy, and Paul A. Samuelson. Six wrote their first essay within one or two years of the GENERAL THEORY's publication; three wrote ten years later at Keynes's death; and they all wrote again during 1962-63 for this volume.

[10] Lindauer, John, ed. MACROECONOMIC READINGS. New York: Free Press, 1968. 424 p. Paperbound.

General economic policies are given most emphasis. The nine parts are entitled: (1) "Consumption," (2) "Investment and Capital," (3) "Money and Interest," (4) "Income and Employment," (5) "Income Fluctuations and Growth," (6) "Inflation," (7) "General Policy Considerations," (8) "Monetary Policy," and (9) "Fiscal Policy."

[11] Lutz, Friedrich A., and Mints, Lloyd W., eds. READINGS IN MONETARY THEORY. Homewood, Ill.: Richard D. Irwin, 1951. 514 p.

A selection of the best articles in monetary theory made by a committee of the American Economic Association. An extensive classified bibliography is included. The major topics covered are: (1) "Integration of the Theory of Money and the Theory of Price," (2) "The Demand for and the Supply of Money--the Value of Money," (3) "Money, Rate of Interest and Employment," and (4) "Monetary Policy."

[12] Mitchell, William E., et al., eds. READINGS IN MACROECONOMICS: CURRENT POLICY ISSUES. New York: McGraw-Hill Book Co., 1974. 514 p. Paperbound.

The book is divided into ten chapters. Each chapter begins with an editor's introduction. The chapter titles are: (1) "Measurement of National Income, Wealth, and Money Flows," (2) "Resource Allocation and National Priorities," (3) "Macroeconomic Forecasting," (4) "The Tradeoff between Full Employment and Price Level Stability," (5) "Fiscal and Monetary Policy: Impact and Indicators," (6) "Economic Stabilization: The Role of Fiscal and Monetary Policy," (7) "The Monetarist Approach to Economic Stabilization,"

(8) "Wage-Price Controls," (9) "The International Economy," and (10) "Economic Growth." The articles in this readings book are less technical than most.

[13] Mittra, S., ed. DIMENSIONS OF MACROECONOMICS: A BOOK OF READINGS. New York: Random House, 1971. 572 p. Paperbound.

This book of readings has some articles reprinted in full, some are summarized by the editor, and some are cited only. The readings are divided into fourteen categories: (1) "Macro Methodology," (2) "Models," (3) "General Equilibrium of Income and Employment," (4) "Post-Keynesian Economics," (5) "Consumption and Investment," (6) "Macro Distribution and Expectation," (7) "Money, Interest, and Monetary Theory," (8) "Prices, Inflation, and Monetary Policy," (9) "Fiscal Theory and Policy," (10) "Monetary and Fiscal Policy," (11) "Income Fluctuations," (12) "International Trade, Finance, and Order," (13) "Planning, Development, and Growth," and (14) "Economic Policy."

[14] _____. MONEY AND BANKING: THEORY, ANALYSIS, AND POLICY. New York: Random House, 1970. 643 p. Paperbound.

This readings book was developed as a "multiauthored" textbook. The areas covered are: (1) "The What, Why, and for Whom of Money," (2) "Banks, Nonbanks and the Market," (3) "Central Banking System," (4) "Instruments of Monetary Control," (5) "Varieties of Monetary Theory," and (6) "Monetary and Fiscal Policy." Most emphasis is placed on area 6. Many of the articles have been condensed by the editor.

[15] Mueller, M.G., ed. READINGS IN MACROECONOMICS. 2d ed. New York: Holt, Rinehart and Winston, 1971. 490 p. Paperbound.

A good collection of classic articles. The subjects covered are: (1) "Determinants of the Level of Aggregate Income," (2) "Consumption," (3) "Investment," (4) "Money, Interest, and Income," (5) "Wage Rates, the Price Level, and Employment," (6) "Fluctuations and Growth," (7) "Policy Issues," and (8) "Income Stabilization and Forecasting."

Parker, R.H., and Harcourt, G.C., eds. READINGS IN THE CONCEPT AND MEASUREMENT OF INCOME. New York: Cambridge University Press, 1969. 410 p. Also paperbound.

This readings book has collected the most important literature in accounting and economics on the concept and measurement of income.

Pontecorvo, Givcio, et al., eds. ISSUES IN BANKING AND MONETARY ANALYSIS. New York: Holt, Rinehart and Winston, 1967. 245 p.

This book mainly deals with monetary phenomenon in a banking sense. Chapters are written by noted experts with a commentary on the issue at hand by another well-known authority. Chapters 1 and 2 are basically demonstrative chapters with respect to the banking system today. Chapters 3, 4, and 5 discuss policy ramifications in the monetary field, while chapters 6, 7, and 8 provide insight into new ideas in the field.

Prager, Jonas, ed. MONETARY ECONOMICS: CONTROVERSIES IN THEORY AND POLICY. New York: Random House, 1971. 448 p. Paperbound.

A number of the articles included have been edited. The contents are divided into ten parts: (1) "The Controversy Over the Definition of Money," (2) "Issues in Commercial Banking," (3) "The Structure of the Federal Reserve System," (4) "The Money Market and the Federal Reserve," (5) "Keynes Versus the Quantity Theory," (6) "The Tools of Monetary Policy," (7) "Problems of Monetary Policy," (8) "Rules Versus Discretion," (9) "Inflation: The Phillips Curve Controversy," and (10) "International Monetary Economics."

Ritter, Lawrence S., ed. MONEY AND ECONOMIC ACTIVITY: READINGS IN MONEY AND BANKING. Boston: Houghton Mifflin Co., 1967. 464 p. Paperbound.

Sections include: (1) "Introduction to a Monetary Economy," (2) "Commercial Banking," (3) "Instruments of Central Banking," (4) "The Theory and Practice of Monetary Policy," (5) "Fiscal Policy and Debt Management," and (6) "World Economy."

Sen, Amartya, ed. GROWTH ECONOMICS. Baltimore: Penguin Books, 1970. 549 p. Paperbound.

This is an excellent selection of previously published articles. There are twenty-one readings in eleven parts: (1) "The Harrod-Domar Model," (2) "Neo-Keynesian Distribution Theory and Growth," (3) "Ingredients and Types of Equilibrium Growth," (4) "Factor Substitution and Neo-Classical Growth," (5) "Critiques of Basic Growth Models," (6) "Money and Growth," (7) "Two-Sector Growth Models," (8) "The von Neumann Model," (9) "Technology and Growth," (10) "Measuring Contributions to Growth," and (11) "Public Policy and Growth." The thirty-one page introduction by Sen is well worth the price of the book; he cites approximately one hundred and fifty references.

[16] Shapiro, Edward, ed. MACROECONOMICS: SELECTED READINGS. New York: Harcourt, Brace and World, 1970. 485 p. Paperbound.

The readings are aimed mainly at the economics graduate student. The articles are divided into eight parts: (1) "Income and Consumption," (2) "Investment," (3) "The Public Sector and Income Determination," (4) "Money and Interest," (5) "Money, Interest,

and Income Determination," (6) "Growth," (7) "Inflation," and
(8) "Macroeconomic Policy."

Shell, Karl, ed. ESSAYS ON THE THEORY OF OPTIMAL ECONOMIC GROWTH.
Cambridge, Mass.: M.I.T. Press, 1967. 316 p. Paperbound.

These essays were given at a 1965-66 seminar at M.I.T. They all
contribute either to the "Ramsey Problem" or "golden rules." An
excellent selected bibliography was prepared by the editor and E.
Sheshinski.

[17] Smith, W[arren]. L., and Teigen, R[onald]. L., eds. READINGS IN
MONEY, NATIONAL INCOME, AND STABILIZATION POLICY. 3d ed.
Homewood, Ill.: Richard D. Irwin, 1974. 556 p. Paperbound.

Relatively few pages are devoted to the historical and institutional
details of the money and capital markets. The seven chapter headings are: (1) "The Theory of Income Determination," (2) "Commercial Banking and Financial Intermediaries," (3) "The Federal Reserve System," (4) "Fiscal Policy," (5) "Monetary Policy," (6) "International Finance," and (7) "Coordination of Economic Policy."

[18] Smithies, Arthur, and Butters, J. Keith, eds. READINGS IN FISCAL
POLICY. Homewood, Ill.: Richard D. Irwin, 1955. 606 p.

The best articles in fiscal policy published before 1955, as selected
by a committee of the American Economic Association. The section
headings are: (1) "Introduction," (2) "Fiscal Policy in Recovery,"
(3) "Fiscal Policy and Inflation," (4) "Fiscal Policy and the National Debt (Monetary Policy)," (5) "Fiscal Policy and Stability,"
(6) "Burdens of the Budget and Debt," and (7) "Fiscal Policy and
Economic Growth."

Stiglitz, Joseph E., and Uzawa, Hirofumi, eds. READINGS IN THE MODERN
THEORY OF ECONOMIC GROWTH. Cambridge, Mass.: M.I.T. Press, 1969.
576 p. Also paperbound.

A good selection of articles on early mathematical growth theory.
The growth models of Harrod, Domar, Tobin, Solow, and Swan are
reprinted along with commentaries.

[19] Thorn, Richard S., ed. MONETARY THEORY AND POLICY. New York:
Random House, 1966. 683 p.

The best selection of macro-monetary papers published during the
fifties and early sixties. The articles are separated into six parts:
(1) "Introduction," (2) "The Demand for Money," (3) "The Integration of Monetary and Value Theory," (4) "The Supply of Money,"
(5) "The Rate of Interest," and (6) "Monetary Policy."

Ward, Richard C., ed. MONETARY THEORY AND POLICY. Scranton, Pa.:

International Textbook, 1966. 570 p. Paperbound.

> The ten basic chapters, which include several articles by noted experts, include: (1) "Nature of Money," (2) "Central Banking," (3) "Investments in Monetary Policy," (4) "Money and National Debt," (5) "Money in the Economy," (6) "Interest Rates," (7) "Money in the Business Cycle," (8) "Money and Liquidity," (9) "International Monetary Relations," (10) "Commodity Standards." The broad chapter divisions and number of authors contained result in readings that illuminate specific points rather than giving a general overview.

[20] Williams, Harold R., and Huffnagle, John D. MACROECONOMIC THEORY: SELECTED READINGS. New York: Prentice-Hall, 1969. 537 p. Paperbound.

> A very good collection of theoretical articles in three general areas: (1) "Classical Economics and Keynes," (2) "Keynesian Economics: the Classics and the Keynesians," and (3) "Theory of Economic Growth." The second area is subdivided into: "Theory of Consumption"; "Theory of Investment"; "Theory of Money, Interest, and Employment"; and "Theory of Price Level, Money Wage Rates, and Employment."

Wolf, Harold A., and Doenges, R. Conrad. READINGS IN MONEY AND BANKING. New York: Appleton-Century-Crofts, 1968. 488 p. Paperbound.

> Sections: (1) "The Structure and Operations of Commercial Banks," (2) "The Federal Reserve System," (3) "Monetary Theory and Monetary Policy," (4) "Non-Bank Financial Institutions," (5) "Fiscal Policy and Debt Management," (6) "Inflation, Stability, and Growth."

Textbooks

Textbooks are textbooks are textbooks. Only those with some unique quality have been annotated. All have been published since 1968 or, if not, they have unusual merit.

MONEY AND BANKING AND MONETARY ECONOMICS

Barger, Harold. MONEY, BANKING AND PUBLIC POLICY. 2d ed. Chicago: Rand McNally & Co., 1968. 730 p.

Barro, Robert J. and Grossman, Herschel I. MONEY, EMPLOYMENT AND INFLATION. New York: Cambridge University Press, 1975. 324 p.

> A graduate text that reformulates the underlying theory of microeconomic functions to look at macroeconomic problems from a different perspective.

Besen, Stanley M. INTRODUCTION TO MONETARY ECONOMICS. New York: Harper & Row Publishers, 1975. 224 p.

Boughton, James M., and Wicker, Elmus R. THE PRINCIPLES OF MONETARY ECONOMICS. Homewood, Ill.: Richard D. Irwin, 1975. 522 p.

Burger, Albert E. THE MONEY SUPPLY PROCESS. Belmont, Calif.: Wadsworth Publishing Co., 1971. 213 p. Paperbound.

The supply of money hypothesis developed in this book is based on the work of Brunner and Meltzer. It is a good "one stop" survey of money supply theory. The research of the Federal Reserve Bank of St. Louis has been integrated into this study.

Burstein, M.L. MONEY. Boston: Schenkman Publishing Co., 1963. 929 p.

An early attempt to integrate macroeconomic and monetary theory. Two especially good selections are on the index problem (pp. 12-14) and a critique of the quantity theory of money (pp. 729-36). Both selections are reprinted in [2].

Campbell, Colin D., and Campbell, Rosemary G. AN INTRODUCTION TO MONEY AND BANKING. New York: Holt, Rinehart and Winston, 1972. 413 p.

Chandler, Lester V. THE ECONOMICS OF MONEY AND BANKING. 6th ed. New York: Harper & Row Publishers, 1973. 624 p.

Cochran, John A. MONEY, BANKING, AND THE ECONOMY. 3d ed. New York: Macmillan, 1975. 649 p.

Culbertson, John M. MONEY AND BANKING. New York: McGraw-Hill Book Co., 1972. 599 p.

Dunkman, William E. MONEY, CREDIT, AND BANKING. New York: Random House, 1970. 487 p.

Fisher, Douglas. MONEY AND BANKING. Homewood, Ill.: Richard D. Irwin, 1971. 438 p.

An outstanding macro-monetary theoretical development for a money and banking text.

Fleming, Miles. MONETARY THEORY. London: Macmillan and Co., 1972. 63 p. Paperbound.

This is an excellent primer with a strong bibliography.

Frazer, William J., Jr. CRISIS IN ECONOMIC THEORY: A STUDY OF MONETARY POLICY, ANALYSIS, AND ECONOMIC GOALS. Gainesville: University Presses of Florida, 1973. 526 p.

> The crisis referred to in the title is in macro-monetary economics, not in microeconomics.

Goodhart, C.A.E. MONEY, INFORMATION AND UNCERTAINTY. New York: Barnes & Noble Books, 1975. 388 p.

> A microeconomic foundation is imposed on the usual general framework for macro-monetary analysis.

Harrod, Roy F. MONEY. New York: St. Martin's Press, 1969. 355 p.

> This is the book form of the lectures Sir Roy gave at Oxford University for forty years.

Hart, Albert Gailord, et al. MONEY, DEBT AND ECONOMIC ACTIVITY. 4th ed. Englewood Cliffs, N.J.: Prentice-Hall, 1969. 542 p.

> A standard undergraduate text--better than most.

Horvitz, Paul M. MONETARY POLICY AND THE FINANCIAL SYSTEM. 3d ed. Englewood Cliffs, N.J.: Prentice-Hall, 1974. 586 p.

Hutchison, Harry D. MONEY, BANKING AND THE U.S. ECONOMY. 3d ed. Englewood Cliffs, N.J.: Prentice-Hall, 1975. 560 p.

Kaufman, George G. MONEY, THE FINANCIAL SYSTEM, AND THE ECONOMY. Chicago: Rand McNally & Co., 1973. 518 p.

Klein, John J. MONEY AND THE ECONOMY. 3d ed. New York: Harcourt Brace Jovanovich, 1974. 574 p.

Klise, Eugene S. MONEY AND BANKING. 5th ed. Cincinnati: South-Western Publishing Co., 1972. 864 p.

Laidler, David. THE DEMAND FOR MONEY. New York: Intext Educational Publishers, 1969. 142 p. Paperbound.

> A good survey of work in monetary theory influenced by the GENERAL THEORY. The bibliography is worth the cost of the book.

McCulloch, J. Juston. MONEY AND INFLATION. New York: Academic Press, 1975. 120 p. Paperbound.

Marshall, Robert H., and Swanson, Rodney B. THE MONETARY PROCESS:

ESSENTIALS OF MONEY AND BANKING. Boston: Houghton Mifflin Co., 1974. 484 p.

Moore, Basil. AN INTRODUCTION TO THE THEORY OF FINANCE. New York: Free Press, 1968. 315 p.

A comprehensive textbook treatment of the Yale school's view of macro-monetary economics. The analytical framework is applied to real issues.

Newlyn, W.T. THEORY OF MONEY. 2d ed. Oxford: Clarendon Press, 1971. 232 p.

Use is made of partial equilibrium analysis in showing that money is a unique medium of exchange.

O'Bannon, Helen B., et al. MONEY AND BANKING: THEORY, POLICY, AND INSTITUTIONS. New York: Harper & Row Publishers, 1975. 608 p.

Pesek, Boris P., and Saving, Thomas R. THE FOUNDATIONS OF MONEY AND BANKING. New York: Macmillan, 1968. 552 p.

Pierce, D.G., and Shaw, D.M. MONETARY ECONOMICS. New York: Crane, Russak & Co., 1974. 454 p.

Polakoff, Murray E., et al. FINANCIAL INSTITUTIONS AND MARKETS. Boston: Houghton Mifflin Co., 1970. 655 p.

This is an advanced money and banking textbook-readings book. Over twenty experts wrote individual chapters. Flow of funds analysis is the central organizing device employed. An excellent selected bibliography is included at the end of each chapter.

Ritter, Lawrence S., and Silber, William L. MONEY. 2d enl. ed. New York: Basic Books, 1973. 303 p. Also paperbound.

A good, short introduction to the basics of money and banking. One of the best books with which to begin.

_____. PRINCIPLES OF MONEY, BANKING, AND FINANCIAL MARKETS. New York: Basic Books, 1974. 566 p.

Robertson, D[ennis]. H. MONEY. Rev., enl. ed. Chicago: University of Chicago Press, 1948. 241 p. Also paperbound.

This is perhaps the best known of the Cambridge Economic Handbooks. Originally published in 1922, it was revised in 1948 and additional chapters added. Sir Dennis was a master of coating the essentials with a bit of humor to make it all palatable.

Robinson, Roland I., and Wrightsman, Dwayne. FINANCIAL MARKETS: THE ACCUMULATION AND ALLOCATION OF WEALTH. New York: McGraw-Hill Book Co., 1974. 447 p.

Sayers, R.S. MODERN BANKING. 7th ed. London: Clarendon Press, 1967. 353 p. Also paperbound.

This is the classic British textbook treatment of money and banking.

Shapiro, Edward. UNDERSTANDING MONEY. New York: Harcourt Brace Jovanovich, 1975. 448 p.

Shapiro, Eli, et al. MONEY AND BANKING. 5th ed. New York: Holt, Rinehart and Winston, 1968. 733 p.

Thorn, Richard [S.]. INTRODUCTION TO MONEY AND BANKING. New York: Harper & Row Publishers, 1976. 544 p.

Timberlake, Richard H., Jr., and Selby, Edward B., Jr. MONEY AND BANKING. Belmont, Calif.: Wadsworth Publishing Co., 1972. 640 p.

Van Dahm, Thomas E. MONEY AND BANKING. Lexington, Mass.: D.C. Heath & Co., 1975. 542 p.

Wrightsman, Dwayne. AN INTRODUCTION TO MONETARY THEORY AND POLICY. New York: Macmillan, 1971. 255 p. Also paperbound.

MACROECONOMICS AND GROWTH

Ackley, Gardner. MACROECONOMIC THEORY. New York: Macmillan, 1961. 612 p.

The first important graduate text in macroeconomics. Badly in need of revision.

Allen, R.G.D. MACRO-ECONOMIC THEORY: A MATHEMATICAL TREATMENT. London: Macmillan and Co.; New York: St. Martin's Press, 1967. 432 p. Paperbound.

Most of the book is understandable with a minimum knowledge of calculus.

Ames, Edward. INCOME AND WEALTH. New York: Holt, Rinehart and Winston, 1969. 397 p.

Aschheim, Joseph, and Hsieh, Ching-Yao. MACROECONOMICS: INCOME AND MONETARY THEORY. Columbus, Ohio: Charles E. Merrill, 1969. 276 p.

Bailey, Martin J. NATIONAL INCOME AND THE PRICE LEVEL: A STUDY IN MACROECONOMIC THEORY. 2d ed. New York: McGraw-Hill Book Co., 1971. 285 p.

A graduate text out of the Chicago school.

Baird, Charles W. MACROECONOMICS: AN INTEGRATION OF MONETARY, SEARCH, AND INCOME THEORIES. Chicago: Science Research Associates, 1973. 334 p.

Barrett, Nancy S. THE THEORY OF MACROECONOMIC POLICY. 2d ed. Englewood Cliffs, N.J.: Prentice-Hall, 1975. 480 p.

Baumol, W[illiam]. J. ECONOMIC DYNAMICS. 2d ed. New York: Macmillan, 1959. 412 p.

Chapter 4 on growth theory, chapter 6 on price flexibility and equilibrium of the economy, and chapters 7 and 8 on different types of analysis should be of interest to all macro-monetary economists.

Bilas, Richard A., and Alessio, Frank J. THE ESSENTIALS OF MACROECONOMIC ANALYSIS. Dallas, Tex.: Business Publications, 1974. 356 p.

Blaug, Mark. ECONOMIC THEORY IN RETROSPECT. Rev. ed. Homewood, Ill.: Richard D. Irwin, 1968. 734 p.

The chapters of interest to the macro-monetarist are: (5) "Say's Law and Classical Monetary Theory"; (12) "The Austrian Theory of Capital and Interest"; (13) "General Equilibrium and Welfare Economics"; (14) "The Neoclassical Theory of Money, Interest, and Prices"; and (15) "Keynesian Economics."

Bowers, David A., and Baird, Robert N. ELEMENTARY MATHEMATICAL MACROECONOMICS. Englewood Cliffs, N.J.: Prentice-Hall, 1971. 319 p.

Branson, William H. MACROECONOMIC THEORY AND POLICY. New York: Harper & Row Publishers, 1972. 474 p.

This is a good graduate text.

Brooman, Frederick, and Jacoby, Henry A. MACROECONOMICS: AN INTRODUCTION TO THEORY AND POLICY. Chicago: Aldine Publishing Co., 1970. 434 p.

Brunhild, Gordon, and Burton, Robert H. MACROECONOMIC THEORY. Englewood Cliffs, N.J.: Prentice-Hall, 1974. 607 p.

Burmeister, Edwin, and Dobell, Rodney A. MATHEMATICAL THEORIES OF ECONOMIC GROWTH. New York: Macmillan, 1970. 464 p.

> An excellent book on economic growth theory written at an appropriate level for graduate courses. The authors begin with a one-sector model and progress right up to the frontier of modern economic theory.

Burrows, Paul, and Hitiris, Theodore. MACROECONOMIC THEORY. New York: John Wiley & Sons, 1974. 232 p.

Campagna, Anthony S. MACROECONOMICS: THEORY AND PRACTICE. Boston: Houghton Mifflin Co., 1974. 482 p.

Chambers, Edward J., et al. NATIONAL INCOME ANALYSIS AND FORECASTING. Glenview, Ill.: Scott, Foresman & Co., 1975. 516 p.

Cochrane, James L. MACROECONOMICS BEFORE KEYNES. Glenview, Ill.: Scott, Foresman & Co., 1970. 120 p. Paperbound.

> An attempt to develop physiocratic, classical, Marxian, and neo-classical macroeconomic models.

Cochrane, James L., et al. MACROECONOMICS: ANALYSIS AND POLICY. Glenview, Ill.: Scott, Foresman & Co., 1974. 411 p.

Cornford, John. GROWTH & STABILITY IN A MATURE ECONOMY. New York: John Wiley & Sons, 1972. Also paperbound.

> This growth text examines neoclassical and Keynesian growth models, as well as exploring the interaction between supply and demand theoretically and in the real world.

Crouch, Robert L. MACROECONOMICS. New York: Harcourt Brace Jovanovich, 1972. 440 p.

> The Patinkin approach to macroeconomics is used. The development is good but the presentation is marred by poor proofreading.

Culbertson, John M. MACROECONOMIC THEORY AND STABILIZATION POLICY. New York: McGraw-Hill Book Co., 1968. 561 p.

> A graduate text which is integrative rather than innovative.

Darby, Michael R. MACROECONOMICS. New York: McGraw-Hill Book Co., 1976. 480 p.

Daulen, Carl A., and Valentine, Lloyd M. BUSINESS CYCLES AND FORECASTING. 4th ed. Cincinnati: South-Western Publishing Co., 1974. 509 p.

Dernberg, Thomas F., and McDougall, Duncan, M. MACROECONOMICS: THE MEASUREMENT, ANALYSIS, AND CONTROL OF AGGREGATE ECONOMIC ACTIVITY. 4th ed. New York: McGraw-Hill Book Co., 1972. 503 p.

A best-selling undergraduate text.

Elliott, J. Walter. MACROECONOMIC ANALYSIS. Cambridge, Mass.: Winthrop Publishers, 1975. 500 p.

Evans, Michael K. MACROECONOMIC ACTIVITY. New York: Harper & Row Publishers, 1969. 645 p.

A graduate text that makes extensive use of econometric results.

Fair, Ray C. A MODEL OF MACROECONOMIC ACTIVITY. Vol. 1: THE THEORETICAL MODEL. Vol. 2: THE EMPIRICAL MODEL. Cambridge, Mass.: Ballinger Publishing Co., 1974 and 1976. 160 p. and 330 p.

The microfoundations of macroeconomic theory are emphasized.

Foley, Duncan K., and Sidrauski, Miguel. MONETARY AND FISCAL POLICY IN A GROWING ECONOMY. New York: Macmillan, 1971. 317 p.

This graduate text features a model that can be used interchangeably as a static equilibrium model and as a growth model. Investment is specified to influence both blades of Marshall's scissors.

Glahe, Fred R. MACROECONOMICS: THEORY AND POLICY. New York: Harcourt Brace Jovanovich, 1973. 351 p.

Hamberg, Daniel. MODELS OF ECONOMIC GROWTH. New York: Harper & Row Publishers, 1971. 246 p.

This book was written to be useful to undergraduates. It is still rather steep.

Hicks, J[ohn]. R. VALUE AND CAPITAL: AN INQUIRY INTO SOME FUNDAMENTAL PRINCIPLES OF ECONOMIC THEORY. 2d ed. New York: Oxford University Press, 1946. 352 p.

The plan of this book is a double inquiry. Parts 1 and 2 are concerned with value theory and general equilibrium, while parts 3 and 4 deal with the foundations and workings of dynamic economics. The microtheory then macrotheory approach was copied by Don Patinkin in his MONEY, INTEREST, AND PRICES. A brilliant attempt at integration. Parts 3 and 4 need to be reread again and again to be totally understood and fully appreciated.

Horwich, George. MONEY, CAPITAL, AND PRICES. Homewood, Ill.: Richard D. Irwin, 1964. 556 p.

Hosek, William R. MACROECONOMIC THEORY. Homewood, Ill.: Richard D. Irwin, 1975. 320 p.

Ireland, Thomas R., and Rutner, Jack L. PRINCIPLES OF MACROECONOMICS AND MONEY. Hinsdale, Ill.: Dryden Press, 1973. 381 p.

Johnson, Harry G. MACROECONOMICS AND MONETARY THEORY. Chicago, Ill.: Aldine Publishing Co., 1972. 213 p. Also paperbound.

> A lightly edited version of Johnson's lectures at the London School of Economics. A good review for graduate students.

Keiser, Norman F. MACROECONOMICS. 2d ed. New York: Random House, 1975. 539 p.

Kennedy, Peter E. MACROECONOMICS. Boston: Allyn & Bacon, 1975. 480 p. Paperbound.

Kogiku, K.C. AN INTRODUCTION TO MACROECONOMIC MODELS. New York: McGraw-Hill Book Co., 1968. 245 p.

Kregel, J.A. THE THEORY OF ECONOMIC GROWTH. London: Macmillan and Co., 1972. 96 p. Also paperbound.

> Both Cambridge schools are represented. A good current bibliography is included.

Kuh, Edwin, and Schmalensee, Richard L. AN INTRODUCTION TO APPLIED MACROECONOMICS. New York: American Elsevier Publishing Co., 1973. 245 p.

> This textbook is an attempt to provide students with some understanding of econometric models of national economics. It also provides a good survey of the relevant literature.

Lee, Maurice W. MACROECONOMICS: FLUCTUATIONS, GROWTH, AND STABILITY. 5th ed. Homewood, Ill.: Richard D. Irwin, 1971. 649 p.

Lindauer, John. MACROECONOMICS. 2d ed. New York: John Wiley & Sons, 1971. 472 p.

Lindsey, David, and Dolan, Edwin G. BASIC MACROECONOMICS: PRINCIPLES AND REALITY. Hinsdale, Ill.: Dryden Press, 1974. 327 p. Paperbound.

Lippitt, Vernon C. THE NATIONAL ECONOMIC ENVIRONMENT. New York: McGraw-Hill Book Co., 1975. 544 p.

Lovell, Michael C. MACROECONOMICS: MEASUREMENT, THEORY, AND POLICY. New York: John Wiley & Sons, 1975. 558 p.

McKenna, Joseph P. AGGREGATE ECONOMIC ANALYSIS. 4th ed. Hinsdale, Ill.: Dryden Press, 1972. 282 p.

Meade, James E. A NEO-CLASSICAL THEORY OF ECONOMIC GROWTH. 2d ed. New York: Oxford University Press, 1961. 198 p.

   Dynamic analysis is used to examine the behavior of a classical economic system during a process of equilibrium growth. One of the first textbooks in growth theory.

Merklein, Helmut. MACROECONOMICS. Belmont, Calif.: Wadsworth Publishing Co., 1972. 288 p.

Miller, Merton H., and Upton, Charles W. MACROECONOMICS: A NEO-CLASSICAL INTRODUCTION. Homewood, Ill.: Richard D. Irwin, 1974. 383 p.

   An undergraduate text with strong microfoundations in the Chicago school tradition.

Morishima, Michio. THE THEORY OF ECONOMIC GROWTH. New York: Oxford University Press, 1969. 310 p.

   This is a difficult, but impressive, graduate text.

Neher, Philip A. ECONOMIC GROWTH AND DEVELOPMENT: A MATHE-MATICAL INTRODUCTION. New York: John Wiley & Sons, 1971. 336 p.

   Neoclassical growth theory is developed and applied to open economies in underdeveloped and developed countries.

Ott, David J., et al. MACROECONOMIC THEORY. New York: McGraw-Hill Book Co., 1975. 400 p.

   This is a new graduate text.

Peterson, Wallace C. INCOME, EMPLOYMENT, AND ECONOMIC GROWTH. 3d ed. New York: W.W. Norton, 1974. 523 p.

Ross, Myron H. INCOME: ANALYSIS AND POLICY. 2d ed. New York: McGraw-Hill Book Co., 1968. 477 p.

Rowan, D.C., and Mayer, Thomas. INTERMEDIATE MACROECONOMICS: OUTPUT, INFLATION, AND GROWTH. New York: W.W. Norton, 1972. 437 p.

A standard English text now used in the United States.

Shapiro, Edward. MACROECONOMIC ANALYSIS. 3d ed. New York: Harcourt Brace Jovanovich, 1974. 519 p.

A best-selling undergraduate text.

Shaw, G.K. AN INTRODUCTION TO THE THEORY OF MACROECONOMIC POLICY. 2d ed. New York: Harper & Row Publishers, 1973. 209 p.

Siegal, Barry N. AGGREGATE ECONOMICS AND PUBLIC POLICY. 4th ed. Homewood, Ill.: Richard D. Irwin, 1974. 387 p.

Smith, Warren L. MACROECONOMICS. Homewood, Ill.: Richard D. Irwin, 1970. 557 p.

Solow, Robert M. GROWTH THEORY: AN EXPOSITION. New York: Oxford University Press, 1970. 109 p. Also paperbound.

Six lectures on the most important aspects of the one-sector theory of growth. These models do not lead directly to policy prescriptions nor are they just a game. "The job of building usable larger-scale econometric models on the basis of whatever analytical insights come from simple models is much more difficult and less glamorous. But it may be what God made graduate students for. Presumably He had something in mind." (p. 105.)

Sweeney, Richard J. A MACRO THEORY WITH MICRO FOUNDATIONS. Cincinnati: South-Western Publishing Co., 1974. 201 p.

Wan, Henry Y., Jr. ECONOMIC GROWTH. New York: Harcourt Brace Jovanovich, 1971. 441 p.

This is a difficult, but impressive, graduate text.

Wonnacott, Paul. MACROECONOMICS. Homewood, Ill.: Richard D. Irwin, 1974. 534 p.

One of the current favorites.

Zahn, Frank. MACROECONOMIC THEORY AND POLICY. Englewood Cliffs, N.J.: Prentice-Hall, 1975. 320 p.

LIBRARY SOURCES

Guides to Sources

Andreano, Ralph L., et al. THE STUDENT ECONOMIST'S HANDBOOK: A GUIDE TO SOURCES. Boston: Schenkman Publishing Co., 1967. 179 p.

> This worthwhile guide has been compiled with the undergraduate economics student studying in the United States in mind. Aside from describing how to find source materials in the library, this handbook discusses the major U.S. government documents, the major periodical and professional literature, and the major statistical sources.

Fletcher, John, ed. THE USE OF ECONOMICS LITERATURE. Hamden, Conn.: Archon Books, 1971. 320 p.

> This book is a very helpful guide to information sources useful to economists both in the United States and Great Britain. It covers a much wider range of topics in economics than does this bibliography. There is one chapter on business cycles and one on monetary economics. The most worthwhile chapters are those related to the use of economic literature. In the foreword, J.R. Sargent states a truism: "Libraries do not consist of books any more than the national income consists of the stock of capital. It is the flow of services, the highly-skilled labour of the graduate librarian specializing in a particular subject, that can do more than anything else."

Fundaburk, Emma Lila, ed. REFERENCE MATERIALS AND PERIODICALS IN ECONOMICS: AN INTERNATIONAL LIST IN FIVE VOLUMES. Vol. 2: GENERAL ECONOMICS, Metuchen, N.J.: Scarecrow Press, forthcoming.

> This handbook is selective. The book is divided into four parts and five indexes. Part 1 contains bibliographies, abstracts, digests, indexes, and catalogues. Part 2 contains dictionaries, directories, encyclopedias, almanacs, atlases, and bibliographies. Part 3 contains handbooks, manuals, guides, yearbooks, annuals, and services. Part 4 contains periodicals. It provides a quick way of learning the extent of the resource aids and the resources themselves.

Guides to Articles: Current

JOURNAL OF ECONOMIC LITERATURE. Nashville, Tenn.: American Economic Association, 1969-

> JOURNAL OF ECONOMIC LITERATURE is the most useful source of information on current books, monographs, and articles. The JOURNAL OF ECONOMIC ABSTRACTS, as it was originally named, began publishing in 1963. In 1969 the Journal's format was changed to include articles of general interest as well as the bibliographic information. (Each issue usually contains surveys of

two different areas of economics.) The title was also changed at that time to reflect the change in format.

The Journal is issued four times a year (March, June, September, and December). In each issue, besides the survey articles and communications, there are book reviews, an annotated listing of new books, the classification system for books, contents of current periodicals, classification system for articles and abstracts, subject index of articles in current periodicals, selected abstracts, and an index of authors of selected abstracts. The December issue also includes the general index for that year.

The classification system used for the new books and articles and abstracts is the same, with the article and abstract classification being more detailed. In the quarterly issues a three-digit basis is used. A compatible four-digit classification system is to be available in annual volumes.

At present, the volume for 1970 is in production. It will be followed by the volumes for 1971, 1969, and 1972 (presumably in that order).

Library and Documentation Center of the Economic Information Service (Ministry of Economic Affairs), ed. ECONOMIC ABSTRACTS. The Hague, Netherlands: Martinus Nijhoff, 1952/1953- .

A semimonthly review (with annual indexes) of a selection from the vast number of abstracts issued by the Library of Economic Information Service. It is most useful as a current source. The annotations are quite worthwhile. ECONOMIC ABSTRACTS selects its abstracts, since 1974, from the list published in ECONOMIC TITLES.

_____. ECONOMIC TITLES. The Hague, Netherlands: Martinus Nijhoff, 1974- .

This is a new semimonthly review (with annual index), providing annotated references from publications of interest to business, trade, industry, economic libraries, and research institutes. Each issue of ECONOMIC TITLES consists of approximately six hundred references arranged according to the Universal Decimal Classification (U.D.C.). The references consist of bibliographical data, one to three key words in English and a brief description of the contents in the original language of the publication.

Guides to Articles: Historic

American Economic Association, ed. ANNUAL VOLUMES OF THE JOURNAL OF ECONOMIC LITERATURE. Nashville, Tenn.: 1969- .

The forthcoming annual volumes of the JOURNAL OF ECONOMIC LITERATURE will include references to virtually all of the articles found in the quarterly issues, as well as to essays from books of collected articles. In addition, it will also include certain signed government documents, for example, testimony before the Joint Economic Committee. The annual volumes will continue from 1969 on, where the INDEX OF ECONOMIC ARTICLES IN JOURNALS AND COLLECTIVE VOLUMES ended.

_____. INDEX OF ECONOMIC ARTICLES IN JOURNALS AND COLLECTIVE VOLUMES, 10 vols., plus 2. Homewood, Ill.: Richard D. Irwin, 1961–72.

INDEX OF ECONOMIC ARTICLES IN JOURNALS AND COLLEC-TIVE VOLUMES began as the INDEX OF ECONOMIC JOURNALS. The articles indexed commenced with 1886 and concluded with 1968. From 1960 on articles in collective volumes (e.g., fest-schriften, Congressional committee reports) are included. (For the years 1960–63 and 1964–65, collective articles are contained in separate volumes VI A and VII A, respectively.)

This is the best source of historic English language articles in major professional journals and collective volumes. The introduction in each volume describes the coverage in detail and also how to use the index. This index is used also by the JOURNAL OF ECO-NOMIC LITERATURE.

Conover, Helen F., ed. MONEY AND BANKING: A SELECTED LIST OF REFERENCES. U.S. Library of Congress. Washington, D.C.: Government Printing Office, 1946. 13 p.

The references cover the period between World War I and World War II.

Griffin, Appleton P.C., ed. A LIST OF THE MORE IMPORTANT BOOKS IN THE LIBRARY OF CONGRESS ON BANKS AND BANKING. U.S. Library of Congress. Washington, D.C.: Government Printing Office, 1904. 55 p.

_____. A LIST OF WORKS RELATING TO THE FIRST AND SECOND BANKS OF THE UNITED STATES. U.S. Library of Congress. Washington, D.C.: Government Printing Office, 1908. 47 p.

_____. SELECTED LIST OF BOOKS WITH REFERENCES TO PERIODICALS RE-LATING TO CURRENCY AND BANKING. U.S. Library of Congress. Wash-ington, D.C.: Government Printing Office, 1908. 93 p.

The three bibliographies compiled by Griffin are summarized by H.H.B. Meyer and W.A. Slade, editors (below). These are the most complete bibliographies of pretwentieth-century money and banking.

International Committee for Social Science Documentation, ed. INTERNATIONAL BIBLIOGRAPHY OF THE SOCIAL SCIENCES: INTERNATIONAL BIBLIOGRAPHY OF ECONOMICS. London: Tavestock Publications; Chicago: Aldine Publish-ing Co., 1952– . [Early editions were prepared by the Foundation Nationale des Sciences Publiques (Paris) and published by UNESCO.]

> This bibliography is truly international; it includes the most important publications in every aspect of economics, whatever the country of origin or the language used. All scientific publications are included (books, articles in periodicals, duplicated reports, etc.), with the exception of newspaper articles and unpublished works (e.g., dissertations). Special attention is paid to the official publications of governments. The classification scheme is included in each volume. Because it is issued annually, it is primarily of historic interest.

Masui, Mitsuzo, ed. A BIBLIOGRAPHY OF FINANCE, 3 vols. Kobe, Japan: Kobe University School of Commerce, 1935. Reprint. New York: Burt Franklin & Co., 1969. 1,730 p.

> This bibliography contains references to articles and books on the various branches of monetary economics from the fifteenth century to the year 1933 in French, German, English, and American publications. It is a major source of historical material on all aspects of money. An author index has been added.

Meyer, Hermann H.B., and Slade, William Adams, eds. SELECTED LIST OF REFERENCES ON THE MONETARY QUESTION. U.S. Library of Congress. Washington, D.C.: Government Printing Office, 1913. 247 p.

> An excellent annotated bibliography of money and banking before World War I. Additional bibliographies are cited as well as other important sources.

Guides to Books and Monographs: Current

American Bibliographic Service, ed. QUARTERLY CHECK-LIST OF ECONOMICS AND POLITICAL SCIENCE. Darien, Conn.: 1958- .

> An alphabetical index by author of all (as complete as possible) recent nonperiodical publications in the major western languages. Beginning with the 1974 volume, it includes clarifying annotations to the entries whenever such notes are worthwhile to amplify or supplement relatively uninformative titles.

Ballabon, Maurice B., ed. ECONOMICS SELECTIONS: AN INTERNATIONAL BIBLIOGRAPHY. Series I: New Books in Economics. New York: Gordon and Breach, 1954- . [It was known as ECONOMICS LIBRARY SELECTIONS from 1954 through 1965, and as INTERNATIONAL ECONOMICS SELECTIONS BIBLIOGRAPHY in 1966.]

> New economics books in English, and selected titles in other languages, are annotated quarterly. "General Economic Theory" (02) and "Domestic Monetary and Fiscal Theory and Institutions" (30) are the sections of most interest.

JOURNAL OF ECONOMIC LITERATURE. (Annotated under Guides to Articles: Current.)

Library and Documentation Center of the Economic Information Service, ed. ECONOMIC ABSTRACTS. (Annotated under Guides to Articles: Current.)

_____. ECONOMIC TITLES. (Annotated under Guides to Articles: Current.)

Guides to Books and Monographs: Historic

Cohen, J., ed. SPECIAL BIBLIOGRAPHY IN MONETARY ECONOMICS AND FINANCE. Series II, no. 4. New York: Gordon and Breach, 1976. 216 p.

> A selection of money and banking books from ECONOMICS SE-LECTIONS: AN INTERNATIONAL BIBLIOGRAPHY. All the books are annotated.

Conover, Helen F., ed. MONEY AND BANKING: A SELECTED LIST OF REFERENCES. (Annotated under Guides to Articles: Historic.)

Department of Economics, University of Pittsburgh, ed. CUMULATIVE BIBLIOG-RAPHY OF ECONOMICS BOOKS, SERIES I AND II, 1954-1962. 2 vols. New York: Gordon and Breach, 1965. 352 p.

> This bibliography contains the citations (without annotation) of books contained in ECONOMICS LIBRARY SELECTIONS. (See above, Ballabon, Maurice B., ed., ECONOMIC SELECTIONS.) "General Economic Theory" (pp. 1-20) and "Money, Credit, and Banking" (pp. 122-34) have most of the citations of interest. However, pages 280-96 do list bibliographies, reference works, and journals. Helpful for a literature search but otherwise dated. This bibliography will be updated from time to time to include the Pittsburgh listings. The CUMULATIVE BIBLIOGRAPHY, 1963-1970 is currently in preparation.

Griffin, Appleton P.C., ed. A LIST OF THE MORE IMPORTANT BOOKS IN THE LIBRARY OF CONGRESS ON BANKS AND BANKING. (Annotated under Guides to Articles: Historic.)

_____. A LIST OF WORKS RELATING TO THE FIRST AND SECOND BANKS OF THE UNITED STATES. (Annotated under Guides to Articles: Historic.)

_____. SELECTED LIST OF BOOKS WITH REFERENCES TO PERIODICALS RELATING TO CURRENCY AND BANKS. (Annotated under Guides to Articles: Historic.)

International Committee for Social Science Documentation, ed. INTERNATIONAL BIBLIOGRAPHY OF THE SOCIAL SCIENCES: INTERNATIONAL BIBLIOGRAPHY

OF ECONOMICS. (Annotated under Guides to Articles: Historic.)

Masui, Mitsuzo, ed. A BIBLIOGRAPHY OF FINANCE. (Annotated under Guides to Articles: Historic.)

Meyer, Hermann H.B., and Slade, William Adams, eds. SELECTED LIST OF REFERENCES ON THE MONETARY QUESTION. (Annotated under Guides to Articles: Historic.)

Encyclopedias

Seligman, Edmund R.A., ed. ENCYCLOPEDIA OF THE SOCIAL SCIENCES. New York: Macmillan, 1930-35. Reprint. New York: Macmillan, 1951.

> The articles relating to money, banking, and macroeconomics are extremely dated but still of interest. Of more than general interest are the articles on unemployment, consumption, capital, distribution, interest, money, price stabilization, public finance, statics and dynamics, and wages.

Sills, David L., ed. INTERNATIONAL ENCYCLOPEDIA OF THE SOCIAL SCIENCES. New York: Macmillan, Free Press, 1968.

> If you want to learn about some area of economics, this is the place to start. All articles are written by experts in the field. This is only a sample of articles of interest: "Aggregation," "Business Cycles," "Capital," "Consumption," "Central Banking," "Distributed Lags," "Economic Equilibrium," "Economic Expectations," "Economic Growth," "Employment and Unemployment," "Financial Intermediaries," "Fiscal Policy," "Income and Employment Theory," "Inflation and Deflation," "Interest," "Inventories," "Investment," "Liquidity Preference," "Monetary Policy," "Money," "National Income and Product Accounts," "National Wealth," "Prediction and Forecasting Simulation," "Speculation, Hedging and Arbitrage," "Statics and Dynamics," "Stock-Flow Analysis," "Taxation," and "Wages."

> This Encyclopedia is a completely new reference work, designed to complement, not to supplant its predecessor, the ENCYCLOPEDIA OF THE SOCIAL SCIENCES.

Guide to Citations

Institute for Scientific Information, ed. SOCIAL SCIENCE CITATION INDEX. Philadelphia, 1973- .

> The SOCIAL SCIENCES CITATION INDEX, published annually, is an integrated search system consisting of three separate but related indexes: citation, source, and subject. Each covers exactly the same newly published articles but indexes them in different ways.

Depending on the search problem and the information already available on the topic, one of the three indexes can be the most effective starting point. Once some relevant articles are retrieved, the information they provide (title words, reference citations, authors, etc.) can be used to enter the other indexes to continue the search.

Guide to U.S. Government Documents

Morton, J.E. "A Student's Guide to American Federal Government Statistics." JOURNAL OF ECONOMIC LITERATURE 10 (June 1972): 371-97.

> Not only are the various publications discussed, but the means of collecting the data, the time period covered, and many other worthwhile and interesting facts are discussed.

U.S. Government Printing Office. CHECKLIST OF U.S. PUBLIC DOCUMENTS, 1789-1909. Washington, D.C.: 1911. 1,707 p.

> This is the major source for locating U.S. government publications before 1895.

_____. MONTHLY CATALOG OF U.S. GOVERNMENT PUBLICATIONS. Washington, D.C.: 1895- .

> This is the source for U.S. government publications since 1895.

MACRO-MONETARY BASIC LIBRARY

The greatest publishing explosion in economics in the past ten years has been in the area of macro-monetary economics. Although this book includes only important contributions to the macro-monetary literature, the list is still too lengthy for the general reader. Consequently, a basic library was selected. The following essay cites only the most important sources; it attempts to be both historically and ideologically accurate. The first two sections, "Before Keynes," and "Keynes," set the stage. The third section, "After Keynes," contains the bulk of the basic library.

Over Time and Through the Literature

John Maynard Keynes's GENERAL THEORY OF EMPLOYMENT, INTEREST AND MONEY, referenced by [47], has been almost universally regarded as the beginning of a new era in economics. It is only the breadth and nature of Keynes's inventive accomplishments which are in question; the writings his book has evoked have perhaps raised more questions than they have answered but the controversies have been intellectually, if not materially, rewarding. The Great Depression focused the interest of economists, as well as the general public, on the problem of cumulative involuntary unemployment of labor. Keynes believed the cause to be a lack of sufficient effective demand by the total populace--aggregate demand backed up by purchasing power. The reason for the lack of effective demand has been a continuing source of controversy ever since. Chicken-egg or egg-chicken riddles are never solved to everyone's complete satisfaction.

BEFORE KEYNES

To understand better the complexities of twentieth century macro-monetary economic problems, it is necessary to have a historic perspective. Adam Smith's WEALTH OF NATIONS, referenced by [69], was the first book (1776) devoted to national economic problems in the context of an economic order unencumbered by any restrictions on international trade. The optimal allocation of factors of production (e.g., labor and land) and optimal distribution of consumer and producer goods were made as if by an "invisible hand," through the unfettered operation of the market. After Smith, a number of economists in the classical tradition attempted to formalize his theory of competitive economies.

The world economy and the economies of individual nations were thought by Leon Walras (ELEMENTS OF PURE ECONOMICS, referenced by [76]) and most other classical economists to be in equilibrium or tending toward equilibrium. (The term "classical economists" is used here in Keynes's sense, i.e., anyone who wrote before the GENERAL THEORY.) For classical economists a state of equilibrium meant that the supply of and demand for each factor of production and for each good would be equal. While disequilibrium states were possible, they were believed to be only temporary. A system of simultaneous equations may be used to model such an economy in the same sense that a model plane may be built to resemble a Boeing 747. And so, mathematical luster and precision were added to French physiocrat J.-B. Say's Law of Markets: supply creates its own demand--which avers the impossibility of an excess demand for all goods and factors.[21]

As the power and wealth of the British Empire waxed during the nineteenth century, macroeconomic problems waned in importance--at least in the eyes of the English-speaking public and most economists. Consequently, economic interest shifted to the problem of explaining the process for determining equilibrium price (and quantity) levels of each good and factor in the microeconomy. Economists developed the assumptions necessary for Smith's "invisible hand" to operate among households and firms. These main assumptions, which comprise

---

[21]What Say meant or did not mean has provoked much current interest. See, for example, Thomas Sowell, SAY'S LAW (Princeton, N.J.: Princeton University Press, 1972); Robert Clower and Axel Leijonhufvud, "Say's Principle, What It Means and Doesn't Mean: Part I," INTERMOUNTAIN ECONOMIC REVIEW 4 (Fall 1973): 1-16; and W.H. Hutt, A REHABILITATION OF SAY'S LAW (Athens: Ohio University Press, 1974).

the very unrealistic doctrine of perfect competition, are: (1) Large number of buyers and sellers. This assures that no consumer or producer can influence the price of any good or factor; therefore, collusion between buyers and/or sellers is impossible. (2) Homogeneous goods and factors. This assures that all goods (or factors) are perfectly substitutable for each other. This also assumes that transport costs are zero. (3) Free entry to and exit from the market. This assures that buyers or sellers cannot be restricted by any type of constraint (e.g., excessive "start-up" costs, patents, etc.) from producing a good or selling a factor. (4) Perfect information and knowledge. This assures that there will be only one price for the homogeneous goods and factors at any one time. The emphasis within economic theory had changed from "Whither capitalism?" to "How does capitalism work?"

Alfred Marshall (PRINCIPLES OF ECONOMICS, referenced by [56]) along with other younger classical economists, wove the threads of nineteenth century economic thought--Say's Law, the economy as a simultaneous equation system, and perfect competition--into the cloth of classical economic theory. It was a theory suited to the ideology of the times: economic determination. As Keynes, his most brilliant student, would later write, "[Marshall created] a whole Copernican system, by which all the elements of the economic universe are kept in their places by mutual counterpoise and interaction."[22]

After a complete breakdown of international (and, in Europe, intranational) trade during the First World War, the vitality of the world economy appeared to be returning during the 1920s as predicted by classical theory. But reality and the predictions of classical theory were on a diverging course. Problems of "the price of a cup of tea" as Joan Robinson put it, counted for little against the macroeconomic problems of unemployment and inflation.[23] Six of the seven Victorian economists who were principal practitioners of classical theory (Menger, 1840-1921; Marshall, 1842-1924; Edgeworth, 1845-1926; Pareto, 1848-1923; Wicksell, 1851-1926; Wieser, 1851-1926; and Bohm-Bawerk, 1851-1914) died in the six years 1921-26. G.L.S. Shackle has, perhaps, said it best: "The great Victorian cohort had at last withdrawn into antiquity. A fresh start could be made without these giants peering over men's shoulders. Thus need and freedom beckoned."[24]

---

[22]John Maynard Keynes, THE COLLECTED WRITINGS OF JOHN MAYNARD KEYNES, ed. Elizabeth Johnson. (New York: St. Martin's Press, 1971-), vol. 10, ESSAYS IN BIOGRAPHY (1972), p. 205.

[23]As quoted in G.L.S. Shackle, THE YEARS OF HIGH THEORY (New York: Cambridge University Press, 1967), p. 289.

[24]Ibid., p. 296.

KEYNES

The worldwide depression of the 1930s provided the impetus necessary for a theoretic revolt, classical theory was incapable of explaining cumulative unemployment. For the so-called Keynesian Revolution (or any other economic revolution) to be successful, it had to meet certain criteria. It is Harry G. Johnson's belief that the most important criteria are: (1) the existence of an important social problem (e.g., unemployment), with which the classical theory could not cope given its theoretical construct, and (2) a unique appeal to the younger generation of that era.[25] The appeal might be the social relevance of the new theory, or the intellectual distinction with which it describes reality. The last chapter of Keynes's GENERAL THEORY is devoted to exploring the social philosophy toward which his theory might lead. The concern was not only with the world economy's failure to provide full employment but also with the inequitable distribution of wealth and income.

At first blush the intellectual distinction of Keynes's theoretical model lay in the fact that it was based on variables that have corresponding entries in the newly created national income accounting system. The new terminology of the national income accounts, along with the fact that a simplified version of his model was almost immediately summarized in mathematical jargon, made it incomprehensible to many of the older economists. It thereby provided a means by which the younger generation of economic scholars could bypass the system of academic seniority. But is this the extent of Keynes's contribution to economics and to the world at large? Was Keynes the greatest economist who ever lived or at least the best in the first half of the twentieth century, or was his name simply a catch-word for laymen and his work of relatively little interest to professional economists today?

This essay will attempt to muster the facts so that the extent of Keynes's influence may be seen and the first conjecture in the last sentence may be supported. But caution is advised. Even at this late date, it still may be impossible to assess completely the contributions of Keynes. Perhaps when the twenty-four volumes of THE COLLECTED WRITINGS OF JOHN MAYNARD KEYNES are all published by 1980, a final reassessment can be made.[26] However, as E.A.G. Robinson recently wrote, "If in the process of reappraisal Keynes does not emerge as a great man, something . . . will have gone sadly wrong with the criteria of greatness."[27]

---

[25] Harry G. Johnson, "The Keynesian Revolution and the Monetarist Counter-Revolutions," AMERICAN ECONOMIC REVIEW 61 (May 1971): 1-14, esp. p. 6.

[26] John Maynard Keynes, THE COLLECTED WRITINGS OF JOHN MAYNARD KEYNES, 24 vols. (New York: St. Martin's Press, 1971-).

[27] E.A.G. Robinson, "J.M. Keynes: Economist, Author, Statesman." ECONOMIC JOURNAL 82 (June 1972): 546.

To begin to understand Keynes as a personage, the place to start is R.F. Harrod's THE LIFE OF JOHN MAYNARD KEYNES, referenced by [37]. But to understand why he has been assessed so differently by professional economists, it is best to start with the preface to the GENERAL THEORY. "Those who are strongly wedded to what I shall call 'the classical theory,' will fluctuate, I expect, between a belief that I am quite wrong and in a belief that I am saying nothing new." And, "The difficulty lies, not in new ideas, but in escaping from the old ones, which ramify, for those brought up as most of us have been, into every corner of our minds." Referenced by [47, pp. v and viii].

AFTER KEYNES

To identify Keynes's contributions and how they have influenced other economists these past forty-odd years, this essay is organized chronologically: A. From the GENERAL THEORY to 1950; B. 1950 to 1960; and C. 1960 to the present. Readable commentaries on the main issues of each period can be found in survey articles written by Henry H. Villard and Harry G. Johnson.[28] Over the years both the issues and the answers have changed.

During the first period most of the books were other economists' interpretations of what Keynes had said. It took approximately fifteen years for the controversy over what Keynes actually meant to cease in professional journals and books. With the cessation of this controversy, the subtlety of Keynes's thought was gone and an orthodox consensus of his contribution to economic theory and policy emerged as a timeless and spaceless set of universal principles. All of which augured that the orthodox consensus itself would soon be ripe for a counterrevolution. Parenthetically, it must be remembered that after 1936 Keynes played little part in correcting faulty interpretations of his book, although he did provide a fine summary of his ideas in a 1937 QUARTERLY JOURNAL OF ECONOMICS article, referenced by [46]. Keynes suffered a severe heart attack in 1937 and became involved in the British war effort as soon as he was able

---

[28]Henry H. Villard, "Monetary Theory," in A SURVEY OF CONTEMPORARY ECONOMICS, ed. Howard S. Ellis. (Homewood, Ill.: Richard D. Irwin, 1948), 1: 314-51. Harry G. Johnson, "Monetary Theory and Policy," AMERICAN ECONOMIC REVIEW 52 (June 1962): 335-84; "Recent Developments in Monetary Theory," INDIAN ECONOMIC REVIEW 3 (February and August 1963): 29-69 and 1-28; "Recent Developments in Monetary Theory--A Commentary," in MONEY IN BRITAIN: 1959-1969, ed. D.R. Croome and H.G. Johnson. (New York: Oxford University Press, 1970), pp. 83-114; and "Major Issues in Monetary Economics." OXFORD ECONOMIC PAPERS 26 (July 1974): 212-25. The first two of the four Johnson articles are reprinted in Harry G. Johnson, ESSAYS IN MONETARY ECONOMICS (Cambridge, Mass.: Harvard University Press, 1967), pp. 15-72 and 73-103, and the third in Harry G. Johnson, FURTHER ESSAYS IN MONETARY ECONOMICS (Cambridge, Mass.: Harvard University Press, 1973), pp. 21-49.

to work again. He died in 1946 after being instrumental in setting up the International Bank for Reconstruction and Development and the International Monetary Fund, and before he could resume teaching at Kings College, Cambridge.

By the mid-1950s a neoclassical synthesis had been worked out between the classical theory and the orthodox consensus and much work was devoted to elaborating Keynes's ideas, especially with regard to consumption, investment, and monetary theory. Most recently the counterrevolution by the neoquantity theorists, or monetarists as they have come to be called; the criticism of revisionist theories by the neo-Keynesians; and the reappraisal of Keynes by Robert W. Clower, Axel Leijonhufvud et al., have caused most comment.

From the *GENERAL THEORY* to 1950

It has been said that Keynes owes a great deal to the fact that the GENERAL THEORY was published in English. For both Gunnar Myrdal (MONETARY EQUILIBRIUM, referenced by [60]), and Michal Kalecki (SELECTED ESSAYS ON THE DYNAMICS OF THE CAPITALIST ECONOMY, 1933-1970, referenced by [45]), have prior claim to some of the ideas in the GENERAL THEORY; their writings, however, have never approached its success.[29] In addition, the multiplier, one of the main ideas behind Keynes's theory, was worked out, not by Keynes, but by his pupil, R.F. Kahn.[30] The multiplier, which indicates how a change in private or public investment may have a multiplicative effect on income, became an integral part of Keynes's theory of cumulative unemployment.

Now that the Victorian cohort was dead, new approaches to economic problems were no longer intimidated. The complexities of Keynes's thought, however, had to be simplified to be understood. (Yet, simplifications can be interpretations.) Sir John Hicks in his world-famous article "Mr. Keynes and the 'Classics': A Suggested Interpretation" encapsulated the "static" essence of the

---

[29]Myrdal's book was published in Swedish in 1930; Kalecki's earlier essays were originally published in Polish. The even earlier work of Knut Wicksell should, perhaps, be mentioned here, referenced by [77]; it was originally published in Swedish in 1906.

[30]Richard [F.] Kahn, "The Relation of Home Investment to Unemployment," ECONOMIC JOURNAL 41 (June 1931): 173-98. Reprinted in Richard Kahn, SELECTED ESSAYS IN EMPLOYMENT AND GROWTH (New York: Cambridge University Press, 1972), pp.1-35.

GENERAL THEORY in the IS-LM nexus.[31]

Joan Robinson (INTRODUCTION TO THE THEORY OF EMPLOYMENT, referenced by [64]), and Alvin Hansen (A GUIDE TO KEYNES, referenced by [33]), have written the most enduring books explaining the GENERAL THEORY. Robinson's book has become the accepted interpretation among neo-Keynesians, while Hansen's book and his other writings, combined with Hicks's Keynesian-Walrasian model, have become the codex for the economists who are known simply as Keynesians. The basic difference between these two schools of thought is that the American Keynesians view the economy as a timeless stationary state where all the conclusions of classical theory hold except full employment, while the British (Cambridge University) neo-Keynesians view the economy in a setting where time is of importance: "the past cannot be changed and the future cannot be known." Referenced by [63, p. ix]. The Keynesian-Walrasian macroeconomic model has predominated, helped in no small way by the Nobel Prize-winning work of Hicks (VALUE AND CAPITAL, referenced by [42]), and Paul A. Samuelson (FOUNDATIONS OF ECONOMIC ANALYSIS, referenced by [65]).

The model which Hicks originated was not the only model of Keynes's system that has been developed; nevertheless it is the most used and abused.[32] However, it was Franco Modigliani, in a classic article, and Oscar Lange (PRICE FLEXIBILITY AND EMPLOYMENT, 1944, reprinted in [52]), who brought the Keynesian-Walrasian mathematical model to its fruition.[33] The Keynesian model of the GENERAL THEORY was evolving into the orthodox consensus.

---

[31]ECONOMETRICA 5 (April 1937): 147-59. Reprinted in [25; pp. 461-76, 41; pp. 126-42, 59; pp. 137-45, 73; pp. 255-67, and 78; pp. 245-58]. The essence is that equilibrium income and interest rate are determined by the interaction of the equilibrium values of saving and investment in the commodity market with the equilibrium values of money supply and demand in the money market. Keynes's approval of this interpretation was given in a letter to Hicks: John Hicks, "Recollections and Documents," ECONOMICA 40 (February 1973): 9-10.

[32]See, for example, Roy F. Harrod, "Mr. Keynes and Traditional Theory." ECONOMETRICA 5 (January 1937): 74-86; James E. Meade, "A Simplified Model of Mr. Keynes' System," REVIEW OF ECONOMIC STUDIES 4 (February 1937): 98-107; and W.B. Reddaway, "The General Theory of Employment, Interest, and Money," ECONOMIC RECORD 12 (June 1936): 28-36.

[33]Franco Modigliani, "Liquidity Preference and the Theory of Interest and Money." ECONOMETRICA 12 (January 1944): 45-88 and reprinted in [78; pp. 257-98]. A more recent article which corrects and extends the analysis is "The Monetary Mechanism and Its Interaction with Real Phenomena," REVIEW OF ECONOMICS AND STATISTICS 45, supplement (February 1963): 79-107.

In order to compare critically the thought processes of classical and Keynesian economists, classical beliefs are often reduced to five blanket assumptions: (1) that the invisible hand operates, (2) that all prices (labor wages, commodity prices, and interest rates) are flexible upwards or downwards, (3) that each individual knows the purchasing power of money is equal to the nominal quantity of money divided by the commodity price level (i.e., no money illusion), (4) that a change in current prices will change expected prices in the same direction and in the same proportion, and (5) that either the distribution of income and wealth does not affect anything, or, when income and wealth change the existing distributions are maintained. The classical economists held all five assumptions. In such an economy, involuntary unemployment of labor is unknown and the static neutral money proposition is held that money is simply "a veil." After full adjustment to a new nominal quantity of money has occurred, all the real variables in the system are independent of it and all the nominal variables in the system are proportionate to it.

Keynesians, on the other hand, rejected at least one of the classical assumptions and, consequently, the quantity of money does matter and cumulative involuntary unemployment is possible in their model. Most often the Keynesian argument is couched in terms of relaxing one or more of the first three assumptions. If the market does not allocate resources efficiently, or if nominal wages and prices are inflexible because there is imperfect competition in one or more of the sectors of the economy, or if individual suppliers of labor have money illusion, then money is nonneutral and unemployment may be possible.

Unemployment may be possible also, however, if saving and investment decisions are relatively uninfluenced by interest rates or if interest rates are inflexible. In the first case full employment may occur only at a negative interest rate. While in the second case, if interest rates are permanently held at a level above the equilibrium level but below a reasonable yield on securities, then money only will be held, and interest-bearing assets will be sold. This is the so-called liquidity trap. For these and many other reasons, full-employment output may be unattainable.

Although the static implications of the GENERAL THEORY received the initial interest, the dynamic aspects were also explored before World War II. R.F. Harrod (as retold in his TOWARDS A DYNAMIC ECONOMICS, referenced by [38]), was first (1939) to try to break the tethers of static classical "growth" theory. Keynesian growth theory educed much research and writing during the late 1940s and all through the 1950s. Most interest was focused on Harrod's equilibrium condition equating warranted and natural growth rates (s/C = n), where s is saving-output ratio, C is capital-output ratio, and n is the natural rate of growth of the "effective" labor force. The problem was how to "dull" Harrod's razor-edge equilibrium condition and still make economic sense.

J.R. Hicks blunted the edge of Harrod's equilibrium condition by hemming in the natural rate between a ceiling of maximal effective labor growth and a survival floor (A CONTRIBUTION TO THE THEORY OF THE TRADE CYCLE, referenced by [39], giving an "explosion-collapse" model of the business cycle.

Further attempts to reduce the peril of instability concentrated on the other two constants, s and C. Varying the saving-output and capital-output ratios reawakened interest in income distribution and differences between developing and developed economies. However, the Cambridge-Cambridge controversy that has arisen between the neo-Keynesians (Cambridge, England) and neo-neoclassicals (Cambridge, Massachusetts) did not flower until the 1960s and 1970s.[34]

The four best collections of essays and articles written during this period are: William Fellner and Bernard F. Haley, eds., READINGS IN THE THEORY OF INCOME DISTRIBUTION, referenced by [25]; Gottfried Haberler, ed., READINGS IN BUSINESS CYCLE THEORY, referenced by [32]; Friedrich A. Lutz and Lloyd W. Mints, eds., READINGS IN MONETARY THEORY, referenced by [55]; and S.E. Harris, ed., THE NEW ECONOMICS, referenced by [36]. The latter is especially important, for in it are collected the opinions of leading economists as to the initial and continuing impact of the GENERAL THEORY. The accuracy of their predictions, from a vantage point eleven years after its publication and only one year after the death of Keynes, is quite remarkable.

1950 to 1960

The principal writings of the 1950s seem to suggest that the GENERAL THEORY added absolutely nothing new to the pure theory of macro-monetary economics. Of course, Keynes had brought new insights to the theories of consumption, investment, and money, but they all fitted easily into the classical framework. Although there was no completely accepted interpretation of Keynes's model of the economy as set forth in the GENERAL THEORY, there was general agreement that the most important ideas have to do with the relationship of the interest rate to other variables in his model. Keynes thought that personal consumption expenditures were more dependent upon the level of income than upon the rate of interest (as the classics believed); that investment decisions were, in large part, determined by the interest rate (which was accepted by the classics); and that personal demand for money to hold was not only a function of the level of income (as the classics believed), but also of the rate of interest. The theories of consumption, investment, and money demand (or liquidity preference as it has come to be known because of the two-asset model of most of the GENERAL THEORY) are all indispensible to his doctrine of effective demand. Each of these three theories is reviewed below.

Both theoretically and empirically Keynes's consumption theory is normally regarded as his most important contribution. Whereas classical economists had emphasized saving decisions of households, Keynes, in a depression economy,

---

[34]Two recent and pertinent surveys of growth are: Ronald Britto, "Some Recent Developments in the Theory of Economic Growth: An Interpretation." JOURNAL OF ECONOMIC LITERATURE 11 (December 1973): 1343-66, and Edwin Burmeister, "Synthesizing the Neo-Austrian and Alternative Approaches to Capital Theory: A Survey." Ibid., 12 (June 1974): 413-56.

rightly stressed consumption decisions and relegated saving to the role of residual. Keynes's consumption theory was based on a psychological law: As income increases consumption will also increase, but not as rapidly. However, empirical and theoretical work on the consumption decision has added a microeconomic foundation to it. James Duesenberry (INCOME, SAVING, AND THE THEORY OF CONSUMER BEHAVIOR, referenced by [24]), and Franco Modigliani, reprinted in [51; pp. 388–436] did some of the earliest empirical and theoretical work. Milton Friedman, independently, reproduced much of Modigliani's earlier theory in his A THEORY OF THE CONSUMPTION FUNCTION, reprinted in [27]. Recently three good summaries of the relevant theoretical and empirical literature have appeared: M. Bruce Johnson's HOUSEHOLD BEHAVIOR: CONSUMPTION, INCOME AND WEALTH, referenced by [44], Thomas Mayer's PERMANENT INCOME, WEALTH AND CONSUMPTION, referenced by [57], and Robert Ferber's survey article.[35]

Investment theory has been the most demanding and the least fulfilling of Keynes's theoretical innovations. Some economic studies seemed to show that investment was not greatly influenced by the rate of interest, while Keynes assumed that it depended primarily on the interest rate.[36] There was also the wearisome problem of investment becoming part of the capital stock. Investment influenced both aggregate demand and aggregate supply; it did not just disappear as do consumable commodities. The books by J.R. Meyer and Edwin Kuh (THE INVESTMENT DECISION, referenced by [58]), and Vernon L. Smith (INVESTMENT AND PRODUCTION, referenced by [70]) try to make sense out of this most difficult area. The best recent book is Jack Hirshleifer's INVESTMENT, INTEREST, AND CAPITAL, referenced by [43]; the best recent survey article is by Dale Jorgenson.[37]

According to Keynes there were three motives for holding money: transactions, precautionary, and speculative. The transactions motive, which was carried over from the classical quantity theory of money, assumed that the amount of money needed to circulate income is technically fixed by the conditions and

---

[35]"Consumer Economics, A Survey," JOURNAL OF ECONOMIC LITERATURE 11 (December 1973): 1303–42.

[36]R.J. Hall and C.J. Hitch, "Price Theory and Business Behavior," OXFORD ECONOMIC PAPERS 2 (May 1939): 12–45.

[37]Dale W. Jorgenson, "Econometric Studies of Investment Behavior: A Survey," JOURNAL OF ECONOMIC LITERATURE 9 (December 1971): 1111–47. Four comments have been published: Lawrence R. Klein, "Issues in Econometric Studies of Investment Behavior," JOURNAL OF ECONOMIC LITERATURE 12 (March 1974): 43–49; Robert Eisner, "Comment," Ibid., 49–50; J.W. Elliott, "Theories of Corporate Investment Behavior Revisited," AMERICAN ECONOMIC REVIEW 63 (March 1973): 195–207; and Robert Eisner, "Econometric Studies of Investment Behavior: A Comment," WESTERN ECONOMIC JOURNAL 12 (March 1974): 91–104.

customs of society. The precautionary motive was to provide for contingencies requiring sudden expenditures and for unforeseen opportunities of advantageous purchase. The speculative motive was a sophisticated portfolio theory of the demand for money. If interest rates were rising, money would be increasingly invested in alternative assets which earn a return as well as a capital gain. But, if interest rates were falling, more money would be held, in spite of the zero return (assuming no price changes), because of the possible capital loss on interest-bearing assets.

The importance of the transactions and precautionary motives depends upon the cheapness and the reliability of methods of obtaining cash through temporary borrowing. The strength of the speculative motive is bound up with the level and stability of the rate of interest. All three motives have policy implications. If the monetarists are correct and the speculative motive is unimportant, then it follows that central bank control of the money supply will also control national income (given that commercial bank loans do not greatly influence money supply and that causation runs from money to income). Therefore, monetary policy could be tremendously effective. But, if the Keynesians are correct and the economy may become mired in the liquidity trap, there will be unemployment because the money needed to "grease the wheels of the economy" is held in the pockets and vaults of speculators who fear the worse. Only new expansionary fiscal policy, through its pump-priming effect on the economy, can provide the liquidity necessary to generate sufficient effective demand to assure full employment.

Except for the collection of original articles edited by Kenneth Kurihara (POST KEYNESIAN ECONOMICS, referenced by [51]), most of the important work regarding the demand and supply of money was originally published as journal articles. The best collection of these reprinted articles is R.S. Thorn's MONETARY THEORY AND POLICY, referenced by [73]. Most of the other important macro-monetary readings are to be found in Gordon and Klein's READINGS IN BUSINESS CYCLES, referenced by [29], Mueller's READINGS IN MACROECONOMICS, referenced by [59], and Williams and Huffnagle's MACROECONOMIC THEORY: SELECTED READINGS, referenced by [78].

The orthodox consensus appeared increasingly strong in the early 1950s, but in reality it was crumbling. It was not a general theory; it was a theory of unemployment while the classical theory had espoused full employment. The neoclassical synthesis was initiated by Don Patinkin's, "Price Flexibility and Full Employment" (reprinted with revisions in [55; pp. 252-83]). His monumental book MONEY, INTEREST, AND PRICES, referenced by [61] supplied the theoretic key that combined classical theory and Keynesian theory in such a way that money was neutral but the monetary and real sectors of the economy were not dichotomized.[38] The neoclassical synthesis matured rapidly.

---

[38]Dichotomy (real sector influences the monetary sector but not vice versa) and neutrality are propositions of classical theory but not of Keynesian theory.

Patinkin divided his book into two parts. The first is microeconomic and reiterates the static equation system ground-rules for households and firms. The second part is devoted to exploring the problems of a macroeconomy based upon a simultaneous equation system. Both parts stress the importance of the real balance effect in restoring the economy to full employment. Patinkin called it the sine qua non of macro-monetary theory. The technical argument is that as prices fall, the purchasing power of total new wealth increases; as people's real net wealth enlarges, they will save less and, consequently, spend more, which will create enough aggregate demand to restore full employment.[39] Real balances are equilibrating forces which help to drive the economy to equilibrium, and even the liquidity trap can be theoretically circumvented. But once the real balances' work is completed, their influence disappears and the neutrality of money will be maintained. As Don Patinkin remarked, "The wonders of the 'invisible hand' never cease." Referenced by [61, p. 191].

Classical theory, with the real balance effect, regained its preeminence as the more general comparative static equilibrium theory, for money was neutral and the real and monetary sectors were not dichotomized. It was necessary to loosen a classical assumption to get the Keynesian conclusion--unemployment. And, consequently, the neutrality of money was also lost. Hence, neoclassical theory was more general than Keynesian theory. Keynesian theory was reduced to a special case of the neoclassical synthesis.

Because they were forced to concede theoretical superiority, the Keynesians emphasized the greater pertinence of their theory to reality and thus to policy application. They stressed the lack of price flexibility and the insensitivity of investment and consumption expenditure decisions to the interest rate in the real world as reasons why monetary policy was useless in combating aggregate demand failures. Thus, they emphasized the novelty of Keynes's pump-priming economic policy, which proposed fiscal policy as the only rational way to move the economy toward full employment equilibrium. The novelty, although not the importance, of Keynes's proposals has been disputed by Herbert Stein's THE FISCAL REVOLUTION IN AMERICA, reprinted in [72]. Did Keynes really have nothing new to add as far as either economic policy or economic theory is concerned? This interpretation of the GENERAL THEORY would not go unchallenged.

Although the neoclassical synthesis was the new orthodoxy, the empirical relevance of its theoretical key was being questioned. To have a strong real balance effect, two conditions are necessary. Wages and prices must be flexible, and the money held in the economy must be an asset only and not at the same time a liability. Money added to a nation's money supply by the government's

---

[39]It is necessary that government, which does not allow wealth changes to affect its policy decisions, be the net debtor. A classic article by Lloyd A. Metzler, "Wealth, Saving, and the Rate of Interest," JOURNAL OF POLITICAL ECONOMY 59 (April 1951): 93-116, reprint in [78; pp. 335-65], deals with this point, as well as with others of importance.

printing press (outside money) meets the second condition, but money generated through the banking system (inside money) does not. This was the point of attack in Gurley and Shaw's MONEY IN A THEORY OF FINANCE, referenced by [31]. Moreover, empirical testing of the real balance effect seemed to indicate that it is usually weak and therefore only of theoretical importance; although, adjustment speeds cannot be determined by statistical manipulation of stock variables. Nevertheless, the position of real balances as the sine qua non of macro-monetary theory was somewhat weakened by these developments.

1960 to the Present

Notwithstanding these criticisms, the neoclassical synthesis was still riding high in the early 1960s. All the macroeconomic textbooks were written with Keynesian policy ideas subsumed in a classical general equilibrium system. Robert Lekachman (KEYNES' GENERAL THEORY: REPORTS OF THREE DECADES, referenced by [54]) edited a book with the message: "We are all Keynesians now." Controversies were not, however, obliterated by the synthesis. The inside-outside money controversy erupted again, the monetarist counterrevolution began in earnest, the Cambridge-Cambridge controversy flowered, and the GENERAL THEORY was being dissected by interpreters and re-interpreters. The best general readings book of this period was edited by Robert W. Clower (MONETARY THEORY, referenced by [22]).

The question of whether only government money contributes to the real balance effect was challenged by Pesek and Saving (MONEY, WEALTH, AND ECONOMIC THEORY, referenced by [62]). It was their contention that under certain circumstances bank money will also contribute to the strength of the real balance effect, i.e., if demand deposits are net worth. Patinkin, in his meticulous way, destroyed the magician's wand. Inside money will generate a real balance effect only as a short-run phenomenon and only if perfect competition is suspended.[40]

Even as Bent Hansen's A SURVEY OF GENERAL EQUILIBRIUM SYSTEMS, referenced by [34] seemed to acknowledge the supremacy of the neoclassical synthesis, three groups of dissenters--the monetarists, the neo-Keynesians, and the re-interpreters of Keynes--were launching their attacks. Milton Friedman, who is the chief spokesman of the monetarists, reduced his basic differences with the Keynesians to one of policy; he stressed the explanatory and controlling power of changes in the quantity of money, whereas the Keynesians stressed

---

[40]Don Patinkin, "Money and Wealth," STUDIES IN MONETARY ECONOMICS (New York: Harper & Row Publishers, 1972), pp. 168-94.

fiscal policy.[41] He and Anna Schwartz (A MONETARY HISTORY OF THE UNITED STATES, 1867-1960, referenced by [28]) studied the forces that mold our economy. The supply of money, in their view, is of great importance. Friedman's position has been criticized, amplified, and elucidated by publication of MILTON FRIEDMAN'S MONETARY FRAMEWORK, referenced by [30].[42]

Although Friedman originally traced the origins of his work to the quantity theorists, subsequently he has acknowledged his debt to Keynes's theory of money. His theory of the demand for money, like that of the Yale school (James Tobin, ESSAYS IN ECONOMICS, referenced by [74 and 75]), rests heavily on the idea that money is one of many assets an individual may choose to hold. However, the Yale school, which stems from the work of Tobin, Harry Markowitz, and Gurley and Shaw, regards the structure of interest rates, asset yields, and credit availabilities, rather than the quantity of money, as the linkage between financial institutions and the national economy.[43]

The long-awaited publication of Piero Sraffa's PRODUCTION OF COMMODITIES BY MEANS OF COMMODITIES, referenced by [71] in 1960, gave neo-Keynesians a theory of value and distribution based on an absolute rather than a marginal measure. The Cambridge-Cambridge controversy between the absolutists and marginalists has produced much of the interesting recent growth theory. The best articles have been reprinted in Amartya Sen, ed., GROWTH ECONOMICS, referenced in [66] and G.C. Harcourt and N.F. Laing, eds., CAPITAL AND GROWTH, referenced by [35].

The neo-Keynesians, dominated by Joan Robinson and other personal students of Keynes, have always thought they knew what was right (and wrong) with Keynes's theory. Joan Robinson has tried to refocus attention on real world problems without the interference of perfect competition and the rest of classical theory in her ECONOMIC HERESIES, referenced by [63]. She has referred to the Keynesians as "bastard" Keynesians for foisting on Keynes the argument that money

---

[41]See, for example, Milton Friedman, "A Theoretical Framework for Monetary Analysis," JOURNAL OF POLITICAL ECONOMY 78 (March/April 1970): 193-238, and "A Monetary Theory of Nominal Income," Ibid., 79 (March/April 1971): 323-37. Friedman's other articles are reprinted in [26].

[42]This book originated as Karl Brunner et al., "Symposium on Friedman's Theoretical Framework," JOURNAL OF POLITICAL ECONOMY 80 (September/October 1972): 837-950.

[43]See especially, James Tobin, "Commercial Banks as Creators of Money," in BANKING AND MONETARY STUDIES, ed. Deane Carson (Homewood, Ill.: Richard D. Irwin, 1963), pp. 408-19, reprinted in [74; pp. 272-82] and Harry Markowitz, PORTFOLIO SELECTION: EFFICIENT DIVERSIFICATION OF INVESTMENT (New York: John Wiley & Sons; New Haven, Conn.: Yale University Press, 1959).

wages are rigid for institutional reasons; rigidity of wages as the primary cause of unemployment was an interpretation of Alvin Hansen. Keynes's argument, as she sees it, is that a cut in wages would make the economic situation worse because of the expectation of further cuts, leading to falling prices and the discouraging of investment and ultimately the bankruptcy of the banking system. In Keynes's model, which adopted the classic tenet of flexible wages and prices, it was primarily hoarding on the part of investors (a sophisticated liquidity trap) --not rigid wages--which caused unemployment.

Since the early 1960s another appraisal of Keynes's work has been going on in the United States. In reappraising any author who has died, it is difficult to know how much of his originality and perceptiveness, or lack of it, is really that of his interpreters. For example, chapter 21 of the GENERAL THEORY stresses that the dichotomy between microeconomic theory and macro-monetary theory is a false one, but seems to provide no clue to their interrelationship. Subsequently, in 1963 Robert Clower published an article which interpreted Keynes to have found a way of linking macro-monetary and microtheory together through what Clower called the dual-decision hypothesis.[44] His key idea is that individuals' consumption behavior could not be predicated on each person being able to sell as much of his labor time at the going wage as he wishes (a premise of classical theory), but rather that firms make the decisions as to how much labor time they need. Moreover, from the standpoint of prospective employers, the offer of additional labor service by the unemployed is not directly connected with a demand for additional output as would be the case in a barter economy where such information is freely transmitted.

Therefore, since an employer bases his demand for labor on what he expects the future demand for his product to be, and since unemployed workers' demand is constrained by their limited income, persistent unemployment is possible; those who are unemployed are simply incapable of expressing their real product demands and hence are not hired. Consequently, if the objective of firms is to maximize profits, there is no reason to believe that individuals are likewise maximizing their satisfaction as classical microeconomic theory would predict.

In 1968 a complete reinterpretation of the GENERAL THEORY, in the Walrasian framework of the Keynesians, was begun by Axel Leijonhufvud. In ON KEYNESIAN ECONOMICS AND THE ECONOMICS OF KEYNES, referenced by [53], Keynes's economic policy, as well as his theory, is shown to be one for all seasons. As Leijonhufvud interprets Keynes, Keynes would recommend monetary policy as the best way to handle economic slowups if entrepreneurs' expectations are positive, i.e., potential investments should be profitable and monetary controls are expected to work. The use of open market operations, especially to

---

[44]Robert W. Clower, "The Keynesian Counter-Revolution: A Theoretical Appraisal," in THE THEORY OF INTEREST RATES, ed. F.H. Hahn and F. Brechling (London: Macmillan and Co., 1965), pp. 103-25, and reprinted in [22; pp. 270-97].

reduce interest rates, would encourage entrepreneurs to invest and cause owners of long-lived assets to perceive an increase in their wealth, which consequently affects their actual consumption decisions (second psychological law of consumption). Of course, if entrepreneurs' expectations are negative, it is necessary to use fiscal policy to reverse them; this was the problem in the Great Depression.

While the interest of the monetarists is in Leijonhufvud's reinterpretation of Keynes's economic policy, Keynes's greatness must be judged on the basis of his contributions to economic theory as explained above. Leijonhufvud contends that Keynes's "long struggle to escape" from the classical (static, full employment, and perfect information) tradition of economic theory ensued because he had created a better and more general model (dynamic, less than full employment, and less than perfect information) of how the economic system operates. Leijonhufvud feels that in an uncertain world it is perfectly plausible for the economy to react to disturbances (from equilibrium) by adjusting the quantity of labor employed and goods produced rather than by adjusting prices, which is the classical view. Here Keynes's multiplier enters as a deviation-amplifying process, whereas, in Walrasian analysis only deviation-counteracting forces are at work.

Keynes, it is argued by Leijonhufvud, was comparatively little concerned that absolute prices (especially money wages) were slow to adjust. The most important problem in the economy, as he saw it, was that relative prices were out of kilter (especially interest rates) rather than absolute prices (especially money wages). For it is easier to reduce errant absolute prices by merely contracting the money supply through monetary policy, than by trying to reduce wage rates. The virtue of a falling interest rate in Keynes's view is that both investors and consumers should be stimulated to spend money: investors, because the present value of income streams of long-lived capital assets would rise and, hence, the demand price offered for them; consumers, because of the second psychological law of consumption.

In a barter economy there will never be a deviation-amplifying, information-distorting process. Only in a monetary economy, where goods and factors are exchanged for money and money for goods and factors, is Keynes's effective demand doctrine of importance. It is the lack of liquidity, emphasized by Clower and Leijonhufvud, that causes depressions which are exacerbated by the multiplier.[45] This is why, says Leijonhufvud, the real balance effect was depreciated by Keynes and why depressions tend to persist for prolonged periods of time; reductions of wages and prices, of course, make products cheaper to buy, but if the economy is sucked dry of liquidity for transactions (due to people holding money and other assets only for speculative purposes) and wages also are reduced, this will tend to restrict buying rather than increase it.

---

[45]Liquidity is defined here as both physical and financial "buffer-stocks" (e.g., input and output inventories, salable assets, money, and so forth).

Leijonhufvud was not the only economist who thought that the mysteries of the GENERAL THEORY could be penetrated. The number of contributors to the "reconstruction" grows continuously without any idea of when the blizzard will cease. The main contributors besides Robinson, Clower, and Leijonhufvud, are Paul Davidson, J. A. Kregel, G.L.S. Shackle, and Sir John Hicks.

In MONEY AND THE REAL WORLD, referenced by [23], Davidson, like Leijon-hufvud, believes that Keynes can be adequately understood only if some sort of amalgamation of Keynes's A TREATISE ON MONEY, referenced by [48], and the GENERAL THEORY is made. The TREATISE emphasizes the monetary aspects of the economy, while the GENERAL THEORY emphasizes the world of physical commodities. Davidson uses a Marshallian microtheoretical framework, as did Keynes, in contrast to Leijonhufvud.

The two essential properties of a money economy to Davidson are: (1) the existence of uncertainty in the Knight-Keynes sense, and (2) the existence of irreversible time.[46] These two properties have been the life work of G.L.S. Shackle. In his splendid work EPISTEMICS AND ECONOMICS, referenced by [67], Shackle expounds on the interdependency of uncertainty and time in a money economy.[47] Keynes is shown to be deeply Marshallian, i.e., distrustful of calendar time. Consequently, in the GENERAL THEORY he moved away from the Stockholm-type period analysis to what Shackle calls the kaleidic method, after the way a kaleidoscope works. In Keynes's 1937 exegesis of his own thought, reprinted in [46], he integrated the two essences of a monetary economy--uncertainty and time--emphasizing the main ground of his departure from classical theory: (1) orthodox theory assumes knowledge of a calculable future and, consequently, (2) it has no need for a macro-monetary theory of supply and demand.

J. A. Kregel's THE RECONSTRUCTION OF POLITICAL ECONOMY, referenced by [50], re-emphasizes the positions held by Robinson and Davidson and by Shackle. His reconstruction is based primarily on the works of Robinson and Sraffa on growth and the distribution of income.[48] As with Shackle, Kregel

---

[46]Davidson uses the definition of a monetary economy given by Robert W. Clower, "Goods buy money and money buys goods--but goods do not buy goods in any organized market." Referenced by [22; p. 14] and "A Reconsideration of the Microfoundations of Monetary Theory," WESTERN ECONOMIC JOURNAL 6 (December 1967): 1-8, reprinted in [22; pp. 202-11].

[47]The theme of chapter 37, "Kaleidic-Economics," has subsequently been elaborated in his KEYNESIAN KALEIDICS (Chicago: Aldine Publishing Co., 1974).

[48]In the foreword to Kregel's book, Joan Robinson stresses that Michal Kalecki, not Keynes, is the father of the British Keynesian theory of distribution, referenced by [50; p. x].

believes that economics is bound up with general equilibrium analysis and needs to be set free.[49] Economics is about human relations over time, not "interchanges between atomic particles." Referenced by [50; p. 209].

Sir John Hicks was the first and the last interpreter of the GENERAL THEORY cited here. His original interpretation (IS-LM model) has been extensively criticized as being too simple. In his latest retrospective reconstruction (THE CRISIS IN KEYNESIAN ECONOMICS, referenced by [40]), he makes a strong defense of the model--but only as the core and not as Keynes's complete theory. He does so by re-examining the three basic parts of Keynes's theory: (1) multiplier theory, (2) marginal efficiency of capital, and (3) liquidity preference. Hicks changes his earlier ground rules by using a stock-flow dynamic economy and comparing situations when markets are "flexprice" or "fixprice"--when price has an allocative or a social function. Under such an interpretation the generality of the GENERAL THEORY is discernible.

THE GENERAL THEORY OF EMPLOYMENT, INTEREST AND MONEY is the phoenix bird of economic literature, constantly reborn. Only the length of each "life" is in question, since each interpreter believes he has brought about a resurrection. This is possible because the macroeconomy is neither fully controllable nor fully knowable, because of the time element. The passage of time means there is uncertainty, and with time and uncertainty money has utility. Additional complexities emerge with the introduction of money as a medium of exchange into the matrix of claims (i.e., how trades are proposed and settled). Hence, money is in some ways like the little girl with the curl in the middle of her forehead. When money is good it is very, very good, but when it is bad, it is horrid!

The influence of John Maynard Keynes has increased, rather than diminished, over the years. The reasons have been catalogued above. Keynes is a great man. Macro-monetary economics was founded by Keynes; his ideas are still of primary interest. However, the time has come for new ideas and approaches.

---

[49]The pros and cons of general equilibrium theory are referenced by [21] and [49], respectively.

References

[21] Arrow, Kenneth J., and Hahn, Frank H. GENERAL COMPETITIVE
ANALYSIS. San Francisco: Holden-Day; Edinburgh: Oliver and
Boyd, 1971. 452 p.

[22] Clower, Robert W., ed. MONETARY THEORY. Baltimore:
Penguin Books, 1970. 360 p. Paperbound.

[23] Davidson, Paul. MONEY AND THE REAL WORLD. New York:
John Wiley & Sons, 1972. 384 p.

[24] Duesenberry, James S. INCOME, SAVING AND THE THEORY
OF CONSUMER BEHAVIOR. Cambridge, Mass.: Harvard University
Press, 1949. 128 p.

[25] Fellner, William [J.], and Haley, Bernard F. READINGS IN THE
THEORY OF INCOME DISTRIBUTION. Homewood, Ill.: Richard
D. Irwin, 1946. 734 p.

[26] Friedman, Milton. THE OPTIMUM QUANTITY OF MONEY AND
OTHER ESSAYS. Chicago: Aldine Publishing Co., 1969. 296 p.

[27] _____. A THEORY OF THE CONSUMPTION FUNCTION.
Princeton, N.J.: Princeton University Press, 1957. 259 p.

[28] Friedman, Milton, and Schwartz, Anna Jacobson. A MONETARY
HISTORY OF THE UNITED STATES, 1867-1960. Princeton, N.J.:
Princeton University Press, 1963. 884 p. Also paperbound.

[29] Gordon, Robert Aaron, and Klein, Lawrence R. READINGS IN
BUSINESS CYCLES. Homewood, Ill.: Richard D. Irwin, 1965.
741 p.

[30] Gordon, Robert J., ed. MILTON FRIEDMAN'S MONETARY
FRAMEWORK. Chicago: University of Chicago Press, 1975.
192 p. Also paperbound.

[31] Gurley, John G., and Shaw, Edward S. MONEY IN A THEORY
OF FINANCE. Washington, D.C.: Brookings Institution Press, 1960.
371 p.

[32] Haberler, Gottfried, ed. READINGS IN BUSINESS CYCLE THEORY.
Homewood, Ill.: Richard D. Irwin, 1944. 510 p.

[33]   Hansen, Alvin H. A GUIDE TO KEYNES. New York: McGraw-Hill Book Co., 1953. 250 p. Also paperbound.

[34]   Hansen, Bent. A SURVEY OF GENERAL EQUILIBRIUM SYSTEMS. New York: McGraw-Hill Book Co., 1970. 251 p.

[35]   Harcourt, G.C., and Laing, N.F., eds. CAPITAL AND GROWTH. Baltimore: Penguin Books, 1971. 383 p. Paperbound.

[36]   Harris, Seymour E. THE NEW ECONOMICS: KEYNES' INFLUENCE ON THEORY AND POLICY. New York: Augustus M. Kelley, 1947. 717 p.

[37]   Harrod, Roy F. THE LIFE OF JOHN MAYNARD KEYNES. New York: St. Martin's Press, 1951. 690 p. Also paperbound.

[38]   _____. TOWARDS A DYNAMIC ECONOMICS. London: Macmillan and Co., 1948. 169 p.

[39]   Hicks, John R. A CONTRIBUTION TO THE THEORY OF THE TRADE CYCLE. New York: Oxford University Press, 1950. 217 p.

[40]   _____. THE CRISIS IN KEYNESIAN ECONOMICS. New York: Basic Books, 1974. 85 p.

[41]   _____. CRITICAL ESSAYS IN MONETARY THEORY. New York: Oxford University Press, 1967. 233 p.

[42]   _____. VALUE AND CAPITAL: AN INQUIRY INTO SOME FUNDAMENTAL PRINCIPLES OF ECONOMIC THEORY. 2d ed. New York: Oxford University Press, 1946. 340 p.

[43]   Hirshleifer, Jack. INVESTMENT, INTEREST, AND CAPITAL. Englewood Cliffs, N.J.: Prentice-Hall, 1970. 330 p.

[44]   Johnson, M. Bruce. HOUSEHOLD BEHAVIOUR: CONSUMPTION, INCOME AND WEALTH. Baltimore: Penguin Books, 1971. 159 p. Paperbound.

[45]   Kalecki, Michal. SELECTED ESSAYS ON THE DYNAMICS OF THE CAPITALIST ECONOMY: 1933-1970. New York: Cambridge University Press, 1971. 198 p.

[46] Keynes, John Maynard. "The General Theory of Employment." QUARTERLY JOURNAL OF ECONOMICS 51 (February 1937): 209-23. Reprinted in [22; pp. 215-25].

[47] _____. THE GENERAL THEORY OF EMPLOYMENT, INTEREST AND MONEY. New York: St. Martin's Press, 1936. 415 p. Paperbound ed. New York: Harcourt Brace, 1936.

[48] _____. A TREATISE ON MONEY. Vol. 1: THE PURE THEORY OF MONEY, vol. 2: THE APPLIED THEORY OF MONEY. New York: St. Martin's Press, 1930. 381 and 424 p.

[49] Kornai, Janos. ANTI-EQUILIBRIUM: ON ECONOMIC SYSTEMS THEORY AND THE TASKS OF RESEARCH. New York: American Elsevier Publishing Co., 1971. 422 p. Also paperbound.

[50] Kregel, J. A. THE RECONSTRUCTION OF POLITICAL ECONOMY. New York: John Wiley & Sons, 1973. 236 p.

[51] Kurihara, Kenneth K., ed. POST KEYNESIAN ECONOMICS. New Brunswick, N.J.: Rutgers University Press, 1954. 460 p.

[52] Lange, Oscar. PRICE FLEXIBILITY AND EMPLOYMENT. San Antonio, Tex.: Trinity University Press, 1944. 126 p.

[53] Leijonhufvud, Axel. ON KEYNESIAN ECONOMICS AND THE ECONOMICS OF KEYNES. New York: Oxford University Press, 1968. 445 p.

[54] Lekachman, Robert, ed. KEYNES' GENERAL THEORY: REPORTS OF THREE DECADES. New York: St. Martin's Press, 1964. 361 p.

[55] Lutz, Friedrich A., and Mints, Lloyd W., eds. READINGS IN MONETARY THEORY. Homewood, Ill.: Richard D. Irwin, 1951. 524 p.

[56] Marshall, Alfred. PRINCIPLES OF ECONOMICS. 8th ed. New York: Macmillan, 1920. 763 p. Paperbound ed. London: Macmillan and Co., 1962.

[57] Mayer, Thomas. PERMANENT INCOME, WEALTH, AND CONSUMPTION. Berkeley and Los Angeles: University of California Press, 1972. 428 p.

[58] Meyer, John R., and Kuh, Edwin. THE INVESTMENT DECISION: AN EMPIRICAL STUDY. Cambridge, Mass.: Harvard University Press, 1957. 300 p.

[59] Mueller, M.G. READINGS IN MACROECONOMICS. 2d ed. New York: Holt, Rinehart and Winston, 1971. 491 p. Paperbound.

[60] Myrdal, Gunnar. MONETARY EQUILIBRIUM. New York: Augustus M. Kelley, 1939. 226 p.

[61] Patinkin, Don. MONEY, INTEREST, AND PRICES. 2d ed. New York: Harper & Row Publishers, 1965. 733 p.

[62] Pesek, Boris P., and Saving, Thomas R. MONEY, WEALTH, AND ECONOMIC THEORY. New York: Macmillan, 1967. 464 p.

[63] Robinson, Joan. ECONOMIC HERESIES. New York: Basic Books, 1971. 170 p. Also paperbound.

[64] _____. INTRODUCTION TO THE THEORY OF EMPLOYMENT. New York: St. Martin's Press, 1937. 112 p.

[65] Samuelson, Paul A. FOUNDATIONS OF ECONOMIC ANALYSIS. Cambridge, Mass.: Harvard University Press, 1947. 459 p. Also paperbound.

[66] Sen, Amartya, ed. GROWTH ECONOMICS. Baltimore: Penguin Books, 1970. 549 p. Paperbound.

[67] Shackle, G.L.S. EPISTEMICS AND ECONOMICS. New York: Cambridge University Press, 1972. 500 p.

[68] _____. THE YEARS OF HIGH THEORY. New York: Cambridge University Press, 1967. 328 p.

[69] Smith, Adam. THE WEALTH OF NATIONS. New York: Modern Library, 1937. 976 p. Also paperbound.

[70] Smith, Vernon [L.]. INVESTMENT AND PRODUCTION. Cambridge, Mass.: Harvard University Press, 1961. 340 p.

[71] Sraffa, Piero. PRODUCTION OF COMMODITIES BY MEANS OF COMMODITIES. New York: Cambridge University Press, 1960. 99 p. Also paperbound.

[72] Stein, Herbert. THE FISCAL REVOLUTION IN AMERICA. Chicago: University of Chicago Press, 1969. 526 p. Also paperbound.

[73] Thorn, Richard S., ed. MONETARY THEORY AND POLICY. New York: Random House, 1966. 684 p.

[74] Tobin, James. ESSAYS IN ECONOMICS. Vol. 1: MACROECONOMICS. Chicago: Markham, 1971. 542 p.

[75] _____. ESSAYS IN ECONOMICS. Vol. 2: CONSUMPTION AND ECONOMETRICS. New York: American Elsevier Publishing Co., 1975. 492 p.

[76] Walras, Leon. ELEMENTS OF PURE ECONOMICS. Translated by William Jaffe. Homewood, Ill.: Richard D. Irwin, 1954. 620 p.

[77] Wicksell, Knut. LECTURES ON POLITICAL ECONOMY, 2 vols. Translated by E. Classen. Vol. 2: MONEY. London: Routledge and Kegan Paul, 1935. 238 p.

[78] Williams, Harold R., and Huffnagle, John D. MACROECONOMIC THEORY: SELECTED READINGS. New York: Prentice-Hall, 1969. 537 p. Paperbound.

Chapter 2

FINANCIAL INTERMEDIATION
AND COMMERCIAL BANKING

INTRODUCTION

Financial intermediaries are those organizations that attract deposits through offering services or some kind of financial yield. The deposits are then loaned out to generate income.

The more important financial intermediaries are commercial banks, mutual savings banks, savings and loan associations, life and other insurance companies, credit unions, pension funds, investment companies, and finance companies. The reason one often hears the term "commercial banks and other financial intermediaries" is that traditionally commercial banks have been considered different from the other institutions because of their holdings of demand deposits. This difference has been tempered somewhat in the past quarter century. The money and banking textbooks annotated in chapter 1 give a survey of the material covered here.

SOURCES

History

Clower, Robert W. "Monetary History and Positive Economics." JOURNAL OF ECONOMIC HISTORY 24 (September 1964): 364-79. Reprinted in [4].

    This is a critical review of Friedman, Milton, and Schwartz, Anna Jacobson. A MONETARY HISTORY OF THE UNITED STATES, 1867-1960. Princeton, N.J.: Princeton University Press, 1963. The importance of the stock of money as the prime mover of economic activity is investigated.

Friedman, Milton, and Schwartz, Anna Jacobson. A MONETARY HISTORY OF THE UNITED STATES, 1867-1960. Princeton, N.J.: Princeton University Press, 1963. 884 p. Also paperbound.

    A monetarist history that is filled with graphs and statistics but is

still interesting reading. The importance of money supply to national income is stressed.

_____ . MONETARY STATISTICS OF THE UNITED STATES. ESTIMATES,
SOURCES, METHODS. New York: National Bureau of Economic Research,
1970. 649 p.

The Friedman and Schwartz survey of the construction of estimates
of the quantity of money in the United States is thorough, and
carefully documented. They critically assess the estimates of other
scholars and official agencies to be able to refute them.

Krooss, Herman E., ed. DOCUMENTARY HISTORY OF BANKING IN THE
UNITED STATES. 4 vols. New York: Chelsea House, 1969. 3,274 p.

Besides the introduction by Paul Samuelson and section comments by
Krooss, all the rest consists of some three hundred documents covering more than three hundred years. The first document of 1627
describes the introduction of wampum into the Plymouth Colony.
The last document is a June 1968 report by the Joint Economic
Committee. These four volumes constitute a gold mine for the
serious scholar.

Pringle, Robin. BANKING IN BRITAIN. New York: Harper & Row Publishers,
1975. 196 p. Paperbound.

The development of British banking owes much to a lack of detailed
banking legislation.

Sayers, R.S. GILLETTS IN THE LONDON MONEY MARKET: 1867-1967.
New York: Oxford University Press, 1968. 204 p.

This is the history of a large London "bill-broker." A companion
volume records the family's earlier history as a country banker.
See, Taylor, Audrey M. GILLETTS: BANKERS AT BANBURY AND
OXFORD. New York: Oxford University Press, 1964. 260 p.
Stone's map of "Ten Miles Round Banbury" (c. 1855) is included
in a pocket.

Shaw, Edward S. "Financial Intermediaries." In INTERNATIONAL ENCYCLO-
PEDIA OF THE SOCIAL SCIENCES, edited by D.L. Sills, vol. 5, pp. 432-38.
New York: Macmillan-Free Press, 1968.

Shaw discusses in depth those intermediaries which issue indirect
debt of their own to buy the primary debt of others.

Tobin, James. "The Monetary Interpretations of History." AMERICAN ECO-
NOMIC REVIEW 55 (June 1965): 646-85. Reprinted in [4].

This is a critical review of Friedman, Milton and Schwartz, Anna
Jacobson. A MONETARY HISTORY OF THE UNITED STATES,
1867-1960. His concluding remark is "This is one of those rare

books that leave their mark on all future research on the subject."

Wadsworth, J.E., ed. THE BANKS AND THE MONETARY SYSTEM IN THE U.K., 1959-1971. London: Methuen; New York: Barnes & Noble, 1973. 527 p. Also paperbound.

Developments from the Radcliffe Report to the monetary reforms of 1971 from a banking viewpoint, comprising articles selected from the MIDLAND BANK REVIEW.

Theory

PORTFOLIO THEORY

Alhadeff, David A., and Alhadeff, Charlotte P. "An Integrated Model for Commercial Banks." JOURNAL OF FINANCE 12 (March 1957): 24-35.

An attempt to integrate internal bank management and monetary theory and policy.

Andersen, Leonall C., and Burger, Albert E. "Asset Management and Commercial Bank Portfolio Behavior: Theory and Practice." JOURNAL OF FINANCE 24 (May 1969): 207-22. Reprinted in [1].

Are banks profit maximizers or do they simply accommodate to loan demand? In addition, has there been a significant change in bank portfolio behavior in recent years? Their answer is that the profit nature of banks has caused a change in their portfolio behavior.

Arrow, Kenneth J. "Alternative Approaches to the Theory of Choice In Risk-Taking Situations." ECONOMETRICA 19 (October 1951): 404-37.

This is a survey essay which is reprinted as the first essay in Arrow, Kenneth J. ESSAYS IN THE THEORY OF RISK-BEARING. Chicago: Markham, 1971. Although there have been advances in the theory of choice since 1951, this is the article with which to begin. A large number of useful references is included.

_____. ESSAYS IN THE THEORY OF RISK-BEARING. Chicago: Markham, 1971. 278 p.

Some of the essays in this volume are dated. However, it is the best source for anyone doing work in this area. It contains the Yrjo Jahnsson lectures, delivered on December 16-18, 1963, in Helsinki, Finland, previously published as ASPECTS OF THE THEORY OF RISK-BEARING. Helsinki: Yrjo Jahnssonin Saatio, 1965.

Baumol, William J. PORTFOLIO THEORY: THE SELECTION OF ASSETS. Morristown, N.J.: General Learning Press, 1970. 32 p. Paperbound.

This is a quick and quite clear introduction to portfolio theory. The coverage is broad and gives a good survey of the basic principles.

Baumol, William J., and Malkiel, Burton [G.]. "The Firm's Optimal Debt-Equity Combination and the Cost of Capital." QUARTERLY JOURNAL OF ECONOMICS 81 (November 1967): 547-78.

Baumol and Malkiel show that there is an optimal capital structure that is consistent with the precepts of economic theory. The Modigliani and Miller analysis is used and supplemented by some institutional observations.

Bicksler, James L., and Samuelson, Paul A., eds. INVESTMENT PORTFOLIO DECISION-MAKING. Lexington, Mass.: Lexington Books, 1974. 384 p.

This collection of recent articles stresses two major areas of importance: normative portfolio decision making, and understanding the empirical structure of financial markets.

Bierwag, G.O., and Grove, M.A. "Indifference Curves in Asset Analysis." ECONOMIC JOURNAL 76 (June 1966): 337-43.

It is shown that the theory of asset choice is a special case of demand theory, where consumers' preferences are variable.

Brunner, Karl, and Meltzer, Allan H. "Economies of Scale in Cash Balances Reconsidered." QUARTERLY JOURNAL OF ECONOMICS 81 (August 1967): 422-36.

The Baumol and Tobin transactions demand theories assert that economies of scale exist in holding money, while the quantity theory must be irrational or without general validity because it implies an absence of scale economies. The authors show that the quantity theory of money does explain the demand for cash to a first approximation.

Catt, A.J.L. "Idle Balances and the Motives for Liquidity." OXFORD ECONOMIC PAPERS 14 (June 1962): 124-37.

The Radcliffe Report raised many questions regarding the size and nature of liquidity.. Catt is not for controls; he wants the market to work. His conclusions are the opposite of those reached by Gaskin, M. "Liquidity and the Money Mechanism." OXFORD ECONOMIC PAPERS 12 (October 1960): 274-93.

Christ, Carl F. "Interest Rates and 'Portfolio Selection' among Liquid Assets in the U.S." In MEASUREMENT IN ECONOMICS: STUDIES IN MATHEMATICAL

ECONOMICS AND ECONOMETRICS IN MEMORY OF YEHIRDA GRUNFELD, edited by Carl Christ et al., pp. 201-18. Stanford, Calif.: Stanford University Press, 1963.

> The ratio between currency and demand deposits is fairly stable and a function of the long-term corporate bond rate. The results when time deposits are included are poor; this suggests substitution between demand and time deposits.

Demsetz, Harold. "The Cost of Transacting." QUARTERLY JOURNAL OF ECONOMICS 82 (February 1968): 33-53.

> A neglected aspect, at that time, of economic market behavior is analyzed. Transactions are costly.

Duesenberry, James [S.]. "The Portfolio Approach to the Demand for Money and Other Assets." REVIEW OF ECONOMICS AND STATISTICS 45, supplement (February 1963): 9-24. Reprinted in [16] [19].

> The household demand for money and other assets has no single explanation. The major factors that explain money demand are distribution of income and extent of confidence in income stability. Note the discussions by K.J. Arrow, P. Cagan, and I. Friend in the same supplement.

Foley, Duncan K., and Sidrauski, Miguel. "Portfolio Choice, Investment and Growth." AMERICAN ECONOMIC REVIEW 60 (March 1970): 44-63.

> In their two-sector growth model of the economy, the level of investment is jointly determined by the flow supply of investment goods and the stock demand for capital. The demand for capital is just one of many demands in the portfolio.

Friedman, Milton, and Savage, L.J. "The Utility Analysis of Choices Involving Risk." JOURNAL OF POLITICAL ECONOMY 56 (August 1948): 279-304.

> Their major contribution is to apply an idea from von Neumann and Morganstern: among alternatives involving risk, choose the one with largest expected utility. Also, see Friedman and Savage's article "The Expected Utility Hypothesis and the Measurability of Utility." JOURNAL OF POLITICAL ECONOMY 60 (December 1952): 463-74; and Marschak, J. "Rational Behavior, Uncertain Prospects, and Measurable Utility." ECONOMETRICA 18 (April 1950): 111-41.

Guarnieri, Raymond L. "A Suggestion for Rigorizing the Theory of Prediction." WESTERN ECONOMIC JOURNAL 11 (June 1973): 147-49.

> "Prediction is possible if one conceives of a futures market lying within a general equilibrium model assuming perfect certainty. All that is needed is a serendipitously constructed data base."

Guthrie, Harold W. "Consumers' Propensities to Hold Liquid Assets." JOURNAL OF THE AMERICAN STATISTICAL ASSOCIATION 55 (Summer 1960): 469-90.

> An attempt was made to isolate the precautionary demand for money. The relationships between liquid balances, age, size of consumer unit, level of income, and home ownership were tested.

Hester, D[onald]. D., and Tobin, James, eds. RISK AVERSION AND PORTFOLIO CHOICE. New York: John Wiley & Sons, 1967. 180 p.

> This volume contains seven essays, of which three were previously published. Tobin's paper "Liquidity Preference as Behavior Towards Risk." REVIEW OF ECONOMIC STUDIES 25 (February 1958): 65-86; and a previously unpublished paper by G.J. Feeney and D.D. Hester. "Stock Market Indices: A Principal Component Analysis," are the pick of the crop. This is monetary theory as taught by the Yale school.

_____. STUDIES OF PORTFOLIO BEHAVIOR. New York: John Wiley & Sons, 1967. 258 p.

> This volume is one of three by the same editors dealing with "theoretical and empirical monetary economics." The six essays are institutionally oriented. The portfolio choices of households, nonfinancial corporations, banks, and life insurance companies are studied.

Hicks, John R. "The Pure Theory of Portfolio Selection." In his CRITICAL ESSAYS IN MONETARY THEORY, pp. 103-25. New York: Oxford University Press, 1967.

> Hicks suggests that the third and fourth moments of the probability distribution be looked at when selecting a portfolio, and not only the first and second moments.

Latane, Henry A., and Tuttle, Donald L. "Criteria for Portfolio Building." JOURNAL OF FINANCE 22 (September 1967): 359-73.

> Not only do portfolio managers make repeated choices among risky ventures, but these choices also have cumulative effects. Their model considers the questions of leverage, diversification, transaction costs, and length of holding period.

Markowitz, Harry. PORTFOLIO SELECTION: EFFICIENT DIVERSIFICATION OF INVESTMENT. New York: John Wiley & Sons, 1959. 332 p. Hardbound; New Haven, Conn.: Yale University Press, 1970. 344 p. Paperbound.

> Markowitz is the father of modern portfolio selection. The paperbound edition of this important book offers a new preface which brings it up to date. It also includes an extensive new annotated bibliography.

Melnik, Arie. "Short Run Determinants of Commercial Bank Investment Portfolios." JOURNAL OF FINANCE 25 (June 1970): 639-49.

The investment portfolios of the sample banks proved to be sensitive to changes in wealth, relative yield, and deposit stability.

Moore, Basil. AN INTRODUCTION TO THE THEORY OF FINANCE. New York: Free Press, 1968. 315 p.

A comprehensive textbook treatment of the Yale school's view of macro-monetary economics. The analytical framework is applied to real issues.

Morrison, George R. LIQUIDITY PREFERENCES OF COMMERCIAL BANKS. Chicago: University of Chicago Press, 1966. 174 p.

Even though banks appear to respond slowly to liquidity changes, the Federal Reserve is not "pushing on a string."

Parkin, M[ichael]. "Discount House Portfolio and Debt Selection." REVIEW OF ECONOMIC STUDIES 37 (October 1970): 469-97.

The theory of portfolio selection is applied to discount houses.

Patinkin, Don. "An Indirect-Utility Approach to the Theory of Money, Assets and Saving." In THE THEORY OF INTEREST RATES, edited by F.H. Hahn and F.P.R. Brechling, pp. 52-79. New York: St. Martin's Press, 1966.

The approach used is that of Baumol, Markowitz, and Tobin relative to the demand for money. Essentially the same approach is used in his second edition of MONEY, INTEREST, AND PRICES.

Peltzman, Sam. "Capital Investment in Commercial Banking and Its Relationship to Portfolio Regulation." JOURNAL OF POLITICAL ECONOMY 78 (January/February 1970): 1-26.

Bankers know how to maximize their objective function under the constraints imposed by government regulation of bank capital. Given the constraints, bankers do substitute deposit insurance for capital.

Sharpe, William F. "Capital Asset Prices: A Theory of Market Equilibrium Under Conditions of Risk." JOURNAL OF FINANCE 19 (September 1964): 425-42.

There is a trade-off between risk and return. The analysis is focused both on the individual and on the capital market.

_____. PORTFOLIO THEORY AND CAPITAL MARKETS. New York: McGraw-Hill Book Co., 1970. 350 p.

Markets operating under certainty and uncertainty are covered.

Silber, William L. PORTFOLIO BEHAVIOR OF FINANCIAL INSTITUTIONS: AN EMPIRICAL STUDY WITH IMPLICATIONS FOR MONETARY POLICY, INTEREST-RATE DETERMINATION, AND FINANCIAL MODEL-BUILDING. New York: Holt, Rinehart and Winston, 1970. 153 p.

> The subtitle is a good annotation.

Tobin, James. "The Theory of Portfolio Selection." In THE THEORY OF IN-TEREST RATES, edited by F.H. Hahn and F.P.R. Brechling, pp. 3-51. New York: St. Martin's Press, 1966.

> Tobin, in forty-nine pages, has reviewed portfolio selection with regard to predictable and imperfectly predictable assets. The second section is where his true interest lies.

Woodworth, G. Walter. THE MANAGEMENT OF CYCLICAL LIQUIDITY OF COMMERCIAL BANKS. Boston: Bankers Publishing, 1967. 140 p.

> Because the management of bank liabilities can have only a small effect on cyclical liquidity, it is necessary to manage bank assets.

_____. "Theories of Cyclical Liquidity Management of Commercial Banks." NATIONAL BANKING REVIEW 4 (June 1967): 377-95.

> The historical evolution and development of equity management theory, as it applies to commercial banking practice, is surveyed.

INSIDE-OUTSIDE MONEY

Buchanan, James M. "An Outside Economist's Defense of Pesek and Saving." JOURNAL OF ECONOMIC LITERATURE 1 (September 1969): 812-14.

> Accounting conventions always "prove" that gains from exchange are impossible. Wealth measures can only be objectified if this elementary fact is ignored.

Crick, W.F. "The Genesis of Bank Deposits." ECONOMICA o.s. 7 (June 1927): 191-202. Reprinted in [11].

> A good introduction to the whole "commercial banks as creators of money" controversy.

Culbertson, John M. "Intermediaries and Monetary Theory: A Criticism of the Gurley-Shaw Theory." AMERICAN ECONOMIC REVIEW 48 (March 1958): 119-31. Gurley, John G., and Shaw, E.S. "Reply." Ibid., pp. 132-38.

> This is a review and defense of Gurley and Shaw's "Financial As-pects of Economic Development." AMERICAN ECONOMIC REVIEW 45 (September 1955): 515-38; and "Financial Intermediaries and the Saving-Investment Process." JOURNAL OF FINANCE 11 (May 1956): 157-76.

Gurley, John G., and Shaw, Edward S. "Financial Intermediaries and the Saving-Investment Process. JOURNAL OF FINANCE 11 (May 1956): 257-76. Reprinted in [10] [17] [19].

> Substitutability of money created by banks with financial assets created by other financial intermediaries, is a major determinant of the supply of money, no matter what level of income.

_____. MONEY IN A THEORY OF FINANCE. Washington, D.C.: Brookings Institution, 1960. 371 p.

> A study of the influence of financial intermediaries on economic growth and monetary policy. It reopened the inside-outside money controversy, causing a rewriting of the macroeconomic section of Patinkin's MONEY, INTEREST, AND PRICES.

Hester, Donald D., and Tobin, James, eds. FINANCIAL MARKETS AND ECONOMIC ACTIVITY. New York: John Wiley & Sons, 1967. 266 p.

> A collection of the Yale school's "portfolio-balance" approach to monetary analysis. The first essay is most famous, James Tobin's "Commercial Banks as Creators of 'Money'." This is one of three volumes by the same editors; it stresses macroeconomics.

Johnson, Harry G. "Inside Money, Outside Money, Income, Wealth and Welfare in Contemporary Monetary Theory." JOURNAL OF MONEY, CREDIT AND BANKING 1 (February 1969): 30-45.

> This is a critique of Pesek, Boris, and Saving, Thomas R. MONEY, WEALTH, AND ECONOMIC THEORY. New York: Macmillan, 1967. An additional critique is Johnson, Harry G. "A Comment on Pesek and Saving's Theory of Money and Wealth." JOURNAL ON MONEY, CREDIT AND BANKING 1 (August 1969): 535-37.

Marty, Alvin L. "Gurley and Shaw on Money in a Theory of Finance." JOURNAL OF POLITICAL ECONOMY 69 (February 1961): 56-59. Reprinted in [2].

> A critical review of Gurley and Shaw's MONEY IN A THEORY OF FINANCE. For instance, Gurley and Shaw try to carry over comparative static results to a growing economy.

Patinkin, Don. "Financial Intermediaries and the Logical Structure of Monetary Theory." AMERICAN ECONOMIC REVIEW 51 (March 1961): 95-116.

> This is a review of Gurley and Shaw's MONEY IN A THEORY OF FINANCE. The review is an extremely critical one--well worth reading. Gurley and Shaw brought to the fore the distinction between "inside" and "outside" money. Patinkin's model in the first edition (1956) of MONEY, INTEREST, AND PRICES was only an outside money model.

_____. "Money and Wealth: A Review Article." JOURNAL OF ECONOMIC LITERATURE 7 (December 1969): 1140-60.

> Patinkin's review of Pesek and Saving's MONEY, WEALTH, AND ECONOMIC THEORY sets out clearly what is necessary for a real balance effect to occur. Saving commented on this article and Patinkin replied, with little additional light shed on the problem. See both Saving, Thomas R. "Outside Money, Inside Money, and the Real Balance Effect." JOURNAL OF MONEY, CREDIT AND BANKING 2 (February 1970): 83-100; and Patinkin, Don. "Inside Money, Monopoly Bank Profits, and the Real-Balance Effect." Ibid., 3 (May 1971): 271-75. Patinkin's definitive word appears in his book STUDIES IN MONETARY ECONOMICS (New York: Harper & Row Publishers, 1972), pp. 168-94.

Pesek, Boris P., and Saving, Thomas R. MONEY, WEALTH, AND ECONOMIC THEORY. New York: Macmillan, 1967. 464 p.

> An expansion of the real balance effect literature, challenging the validity of the distinction between inside and outside money. If demand deposits are net wealth rather than liabilities, their case is won. Don Patinkin critically reviews this book in "Money and Wealth: A Review Article." JOURNAL OF ECONOMIC LITERATURE 7 (December 1969): 1140-60.

Phillips, Chester Arthur. BANK CREDIT. New York: Macmillan, 1921. 388 p.

> This book is thought to provide the classical exposition of the multiple expansion of money: the beginning of inside money and the "old view." However, Alfred Marshall may have been the originator. See Clower, Robert W. "Marshall on Deposit Multipliers." ECONOMIC INQUIRY 13 (June 1975): 252.

Tobin, James. "Commercial Banks as Creators of Money." In BANKING AND MONETARY STUDIES, edited by Deane Carson, pp. 408-19. Homewood, Ill.: Richard D. Irwin, 1963. Reprinted in [17].

> Commercial banks do not possess a "widow's cruse" I Kings 17:14-16. There is substitutability of money for other assets and the law of supply and demand does operate in financial markets: the "new view."

OPTIMAL QUANTITY OF MONEY

Clower, Robert W. "Is there an Optimal Money Supply?" JOURNAL OF FINANCE 25 (May 1970): 425-33.

> Like most questions in welfare economics, what is important is the stimulus to study, not the answers. Why is money a unique medium of exchange? See also Johnson, H.G. "Is there an Optimal

Money Supply?" JOURNAL OF FINANCE 25 (May 1970): 435–42; and the "Discussion," pp. 443-53.

Feige, Edgar I., and Parkin, M[ichael]. "The Optimal Quantity of Money, Bonds, Commodity Inventories, and Capital." AMERICAN ECONOMIC REVIEW 61 (June 1971): 335–49.

Their analysis shows that the paying of interest on real money balances is socially optimal. The simplicity of their results is called into question by Russell, Thomas. "Feige and Parkin on the Optimal Quantity of Money." AMERICAN ECONOMIC REVIEW 64 (December '1974): 1074-76.

Friedman, Milton. THE OPTIMUM QUANTITY OF MONEY. Chicago: Aldine Publishing Co., 1969. 296 p.

A collection of recent articles by the leader of not only the Chicago school but of all monetarists. The title essay is original with this volume.

Johnson, Harry G. "Is there an Optimal Money Supply?" JOURNAL OF FINANCE 25 (May 1970): 435-42.

The complete question is: Is there an optimal real money supply such that there is a continuous full employment of resources? As Johnson would restate the title question: Is there an optimal money supply policy? The answer is yes, if many real world considerations are ignored.

———. "Problems of Efficiency in Monetary Management." JOURNAL OF POLITICAL ECONOMY 76 (September/October 1968): 971-90. Reprinted in [13].

Three aspects of the problem of efficiency are distinguished: (1) structural efficiency of the banking system, (2) efficiency in stabilization policy, and (3) efficiency in secular economic policy.

Marty, Alvin L. "The Optimal Rate of Growth of Money." JOURNAL OF POLITICAL ECONOMY 76, supplement (July/August 1968): 860-73.

An additional article in the same issue was written by Tobin, James. "Notes on Optimal Monetary Growth," pp. 833-59. The comments are equally as good, pp. 874-92.

Pesek, B[oris]. P. "Banks' Supply Function and Equilibrium Quantity of Money." CANADIAN JOURNAL OF ECONOMICS 3 (August 1970): 357-85.

An attempt to use the theory of value in an area of economics where there is doubt about its relevance.

Stein, Jerome L. "The Optimum Quantity of Money." JOURNAL OF MONEY, CREDIT AND BANKING 2 (November 1970): 397-419.

> This is a review of Milton Friedman's THE OPTIMUM QUANTITY OF MONEY. Stein's critique refers only to the title essay, the only one not previously published.

Tobin, James. "Notes on Optimal Monetary Growth." JOURNAL OF POLITICAL ECONOMY 76, supplement (July/August .1968): 833-59.

> Optimal monetary growth is examined in terms of the central government's deadweight debt to its citizens. Choices between the present and future are difficult to make.

Tsiang, S.C. "A Critical Note on the Optimal Supply of Money." JOURNAL OF MONEY, CREDIT AND BANKING 1 (May 1969): 266-80.

> The idea behind optimal supply theory is that the opportunity cost of holding money should be reduced to the zero cost of creating it. Tsiang raises a cry against the hidden dangers of this idea.

Practice

Alhadeff, David A. COMPETITION AND CONTROLS IN BANKING. A STUDY OF THE REGULATIONS OF BANK COMPETITION IN ITALY, FRANCE, AND ENGLAND. Berkeley and Los Angeles: University of California Press, 1968. 398 p.

> Alhadeff measures competition among banks and other financial intermediaries, the effectiveness of government policy in regulating bank competition, and the relationship between banking regulation and national monetary policies.

American Bankers Association. THE COMMERCIAL BANKING INDUSTRY. Englewood Cliffs, N.J.: Prentice-Hall, 1962. 395 p. Also paperbound.

> This monograph is the result of an invitation from the Commission on Money and Credit. Seven similar monographs were written by other financial trade associations.

_____. THE ECONOMIC POWER OF COMMERCIAL BANKS. Washington, D.C.: 1970. 189 p.

> The Association's position is expounded with regard to the extent to which commercial banks control, or are controlled by, other banks and nonbank corporations.

Andersen, Leonall C., and Burger, Albert E. "Asset Management and Commercial Bank Portfolio Behavior: Theory and Practice." JOURNAL OF FINANCE 24 (May 1969): 207-22. Reprinted in [1].

Are banks profit maximizers or do they simply accommodate to loan demand? In addition, has there been a significant change in bank portfolio behavior in recent years? Their answer is that the profit nature of banks has caused a change in their portfolio behavior.

Aschheim, Joseph. "Commercial Bank Uniqueness." JOURNAL OF POLITICAL ECONOMY 78 (March/April 1970): 353-55.

Commercial banks are different in degree but not in kind from non-bank intermediaries.

Baumol, William J. THE STOCK MARKET AND ECONOMIC EFFICIENCY. New York: Fordham University Press, 1965. 108 p.

The book consists of discussions of: (1) the role of the specialist, (2) the determinants of stock prices, and (3) the efficiency of the capital allocation process. Also included is an appendix discussion of the effect of stock options on the decisions of managers and on their sense of identification with stockholders.

Benston, George J. "Savings Banking and the Public Interest." JOURNAL OF MONEY, BANKING AND CREDIT 4, supplement (February 1972): 133-226.

The whole issue is devoted to this study commissioned by the Committee on Industry Objectives of the Savings Bank Association of New York State. Is the specialization of savings banks in the public interest? Benston's answer is that the public interest is best served in a free competitive market. Also see his article "Economies of Scale of Financial Institutions." JOURNAL OF MONEY, CREDIT AND BANKING 4 (May 1972): 312-41.

Brainard, William C. "Financial Intermediaries and the Theory of Monetary Control." In FINANCIAL MARKETS AND ECONOMIC ACTIVITY, edited by D. Hester, and J. Tobin, pp. 94-141. New York: John Wiley & Sons, 1967.

This essay is a reprint from YALE ECONOMIC ESSAYS 4 (Fall 1964): 431-82. A general equilibrium model of financial and capital markets is devised to study the "new view" of monetary theory.

Brill, Daniel H., and Ulrey, Ann P. "The Role of Financial Intermediaries in U.S. Capital Markets." FEDERAL RESERVE BULLETIN 53 (January 1967): 18-31.

Financial intermediaries are the middlemen in accepting and holding "unlikely" assets and supplying loans to long-term borrowers.

Bryan, William R., and Carleton, Willard T. "Short-Run Adjustments of an Individual Bank." ECONOMETRICA 35 (April 1967): 321-47.

This article argues that micro models of the short-run balance sheet adjustments are untested and perhaps misspecified. An improved experimental model is specified and estimated.

Chase, Samuel B., Jr. "Financial Structure and Regulation: Some Knotty Problems." JOURNAL OF FINANCE 26 (May 1971): 585-97.

> The removal of restrictions on rates of interest payable on demand, time, and savings deposits is of utmost importance in improving the performance of deposit intermediaries.

Clayton, George. "British Financial Intermediaries in Theory and Practice." ECONOMIC JOURNAL 72 (December 1962): 869-86.

> Empirical evidence is used to determine to what degree nonbank financial intermediaries complicate the implementation of monetary policy. They are seen as doing little more than fulfilling an intermediary role between savers and borrowers.

Cohen, Kalman J., and Hammer, Frederick S. "Deposit Turnover, Innovations, and Bank Profitability." BANKERS MAGAZINE 151 (Spring 1968): 76-82.

> Innovative banks have benefited themselves as well as their customers.

Comptroller of the Currency, U.S. Treasury Department, ed. STUDIES IN BANKING COMPETITION AND THE BANKING STRUCTURE. Washington, D.C.: 1966. 426 p. Paperbound.

> This volume contains reprints of articles related to banking structure and competition that have appeared in NATIONAL BANKING REVIEW. The articles are grouped under five headings: (1) "Merger Policy," (2) "Branch Banking," (3) "New Bank Entry," (4) "Bank Competition and Bank Regulation," and (5) "Bank Costs and the Banking Structure."

Fischer, Gerald C. AMERICAN BANKING STRUCTURE. New York: Columbia University Press, 1968. 441 p.

> This historical survey of American banking was supported by the American Bankers Association; however, the book is not tainted. It is a good, detailed analysis.

Flannery, Mark J., and Jaffee, Dwight M. THE ECONOMIC IMPLICATIONS OF AN ELECTRONIC MONETARY TRANSFER SYSTEM. Lexington, Mass.: D.C. Heath & Co., 1973. 225 p.

> What will be the characteristics of a cashless society? This short book gives one view. It is not a treatise on EMTS but rather an analysis of transfer systems, past, present, and future. The title is misleading.

Frost, P.A. "Banks' Demand for Excess Reserves." JOURNAL OF POLITICAL ECONOMY 79 (July/August 1971): 805-25.

Inventory theory is used to derive a demand function for excess reserves which is kinked at very low interest rates.

Galbraith, J.A. "Monetary Policy and Nonbank Financial Intermediaries." NATIONAL BANKING REVIEW 4 (September 1966): 53-60. Reprinted in [10] [14].

The destabilizing effect of shifts of funds from banks to near banks and vice versa are discussed.

Goldfeld, Stephen M. COMMERCIAL BANK BEHAVIOR AND FINANCIAL ACTIVITY. New York: North-Holland, 1966. 212 p.

Goldfeld attempts to examine commercial bank portfolio behavior, relating investment and consumption directly to financial variables and to investigate the impact of monetary policies.

Goldsmith, R.W. FINANCIAL INTERMEDIARIES IN THE AMERICAN ECONOMY SINCE 1900. Princeton, N.J.: Princeton University Press, 1958. 450 p.

Goldsmith's study of the changing roles of the financial intermediaries provides a wealth of data on the growth in total assets of these institutions from 1900 to 1952. Goldsmith also attempts to contribute to "a much needed general theory of financial institutions."

Goodman, Oscar R. "Antitrust and Competitive Issues in the United States Banking Structure." JOURNAL OF FINANCE 26 (May 1971): 615-46.

The bank regulatory agencies and the Antitrust Division of the Department of Justice have differing opinions as to what constitutes illegality by banks. A good list of references is included.

Gramley, Lyle E., and Chase, Samuel B., Jr. "Time Deposits in Monetary Analysis." FEDERAL RESERVE BULLETIN 51 (October 1965): 1380-406. Reprinted in [4].

The NATIONAL BANKING REVIEW 3 (June 1966): 509-22; and Ibid., 4 (December 1966): 205-13 contain further comments on this article. Gramley and Chase's conclusions are anti-monetarist; the behavior of the financial market is too complex for simple monetary rules to work.

Greenbaum, Stuart I. "Competition and Efficiency in the Banking System: Empirical Research and Its Policy Implications." JOURNAL OF POLITICAL ECONOMY 75 (August 1967): 461-78.

This article is noteworthy for three reasons. It is a concise summary of all the important previous studies on banking structure; it provides a pioneer effort in defining a sociably optimal banking structure; and, it contains a bibliography of over fifty references.

Guttentag, Jack M., and Herman, Edward S. "Banking Structure and Performance." THE BULLETIN, no. 41/43 (February 1967), pp. 1-200.

> The study uses the industrial organization approach of structure, practice, and performance. The impact of branch versus unit banking is emphasized.

Guttentag, Jack M., and Lindsay, Robert. "The Uniqueness of Commercial Banks." JOURNAL OF POLITICAL ECONOMY 76 (September/October 1968): 991-1014.

> They attempt to establish the uniqueness of commercial banks by showing that banks have a greater capacity for varying the total volume of credit than nonbank intermediaries. Their position is challenged in Aschheim, Joseph. "Commercial Bank Uniqueness." JOURNAL OF POLITICAL ECONOMY 78 (March-April) 1970): 353-55.

Hendershott, Patric H., and de Leeuw, Frank. "Free Reserves, Interest Rates and Deposits." JOURNAL OF FINANCE 25 (June 1970): 599-613.

> Their study shows a strong link between central bank operations and the money stock. Open market operations influence both deposits and short-term interest rates with little, if any, lag.

Jaffee, D[wight].M. CREDIT RATIONING AND THE COMMERCIAL LOAN MARKET: AN ECONOMETRIC STUDY OF THE COMMERCIAL LOAN MARKET. New York: John Wiley & Sons, 1971. 195 p.

> Jaffee focuses his attention on developing empirical evidence to show the existence of credit rationing in the commercial loan market.

Jaffee, D[wight].M., and Modigliani, Franco. "A Theory and Test of Credit Rationing." AMERICAN ECONOMIC REVIEW 59 (December 1969): 850-72.

> The size of the bank's loan is independent of the firms' end of period value. Note also the more recent generalizations by Smith, Vernon. "A Theory and Test of Credit Rationing: Some Generalizations," and Jaffee, D.M. "A Theory and Test of Credit Rationing: Further Notes." AMERICAN ECONOMIC REVIEW 62 (June 1972): 477-83 and 484-88, respectively.

Katona, George. BUSINESS LOOKS AT BANKS. Ann Arbor: University of Michigan Press, 1957. 184 p.

> This book is the result of a nationwide sample interview survey. On the whole, business executives have favorable attitudes toward commercial banks.

Lawrence, Robert, and Lougee, Duane. "Determinants of Correspondent Banking Relationships." JOURNAL OF MONEY, CREDIT AND BANKING 2 (August 1970): 358-69. Reprinted in [1].

> The number of correspondent ties or their geographic distribution is not related to Federal Reserve membership, although correspondent balances are. Bank size is the key variable.

Lee, Tong Hun. "Substitutability of Non-Bank Intermediary Liabilities for Money: The Empirical Evidence." JOURNAL OF FINANCE 21 (September 1966): 441-57.

> This article uses empirical data to substantiate unequivocally the substitution hypothesis of Gurley and Shaw. Citations are given for both proponents and opponents of this hypothesis.

Luckett, D.G. "Credit Standards and Tight Money." JOURNAL OF MONEY, CREDIT AND BANKING 2 (November 1970): 420-35.

> The view of bank operations held by those who believe the credit-rationing thesis is valid. Restrictive monetary policy will hit loans of "venture capital"--loans most conducive to economic growth-- hardest.

Morrison, George R. LIQUIDITY PREFERENCES OF COMMERCIAL BANKS. Chicago: University of Chicago Press, 1966. 174 p.

> Even though banks appear to respond slowly to liquidity changes, the Federal Reserve is not "pushing on a string."

Robinson, Roland I. MANAGEMENT OF BANK FUNDS. New York: McGraw-Hill Book Co., 1962. 453 p.

> Sections include: (1) introduction (mainly methodological considerations), (2) liquidity management, (3) loan management, (4) policies for specific types of loans, (5) investment management, and (6) profit management.

_____. MONEY AND CAPITAL MARKETS. New York: McGraw-Hill Book Co., 1964. 380 p.

> Expository treatment of financial markets in a united design. Places financial markets at center of saving-investment system. Then discusses inter-workings of markets.

Smith, Vernon L. "Bidding Theory and the Treasury Bill Auction: Does Price Discrimination Increase Bill Prices?" REVIEW OF ECONOMICS AND STATISTICS 48 (May 1966): 141-46.

> Smith suggests that the Treasury reduces its revenue from bill offerings because it uses price discrimination rather than a competitive auction.

. "A Theory and Test of Credit Rationing: Some Generalizations."
AMERICAN ECONOMIC REVIEW 62 (June 1972): 477-83.

Smith suggests some extentions to an article by Jaffee, D.M.,
and Modigliani, Franco. "A Theory and Test of Credit Rationing."
Ibid., 59 (December 1969): 850-72. A note by Jaffee follows
Smith's article, Ibid., 62 (June 1972): 484-88.

Smith, Warren L. "Financial Intermediaries and Monetary Control." QUAR-
TERLY JOURNAL OF ECONOMICS 73 (November 1959): 533-53.

Smith is an "old view" man. Financial intermediaries are different
from banks. The activities of financial intermediaries have not
destabilized the economy. Consequently, there is no good reason
why they should be brought under the control of the Federal Reserve.

Stone, Robert W. "The Changing Structure of the Money Market." JOURNAL
OF FINANCE 20 (May 1965): 229-38.

At the time Stone wrote, money market rates had shown very little
variation.

Tobin, James. "Deposit Interest Ceilings as a Monetary Control." JOURNAL
OF MONEY, CREDIT AND BANKING 2 (February 1970): 4-14.

The small saver has been discriminated against. Tobin says, "A
government that fails to provide purchasing power bonds is in a
poor moral position to deny savers competitive interest rates during
an inflationary period."

Tobin, James, and Brainard, William [C.]. "Financial Intermediaries and the
Effectiveness of Monetary Controls." AMERICAN ECONOMIC REVIEW 53
(May 1963): 383-400.

This is one of the early articles that formulated the Yale school
view of monetary economics. See its fruition in Tobin, James.
"A General Equilibrium Approach to Monetary Theory." JOUR-
NAL OF MONEY, CREDIT AND BANKING 1 (February 1969):
15-29.

Tucker, Donald. "Credit Rationing, Interest Rate Lags, and Monetary Policy
Speed." QUARTERLY JOURNAL OF ECONOMICS 82 (February 1968): 54-84.

If a valid argument is to be made about the speed of the effects
of monetary policy, credit rationing must be included in the empirical economic model. See also his earlier article "Dynamic
Income Adjustment to Money Supply Changes." AMERICAN ECO-
NOMIC REVIEW 56 (June 1966): 433-49.

Vernon, Jack. "Ownership and Control Among Large Member Banks." JOUR-
NAL OF FINANCE 25 (June 1970): 651-57.

Management control, rather than owner control, has been dominant in most large member banks in recent years.

Weiss, Steven J. "Commercial Bank Price Competition: The Case of 'Free' Checking Accounts." NEW ENGLAND ECONOMIC REVIEW 1 (September/ October 1969): 3-22.

A discussion of one of the few price competitive aspects of commercial banking.

Wood, John H. "Two Notes on the Uniqueness of Commercial Banks." JOURNAL OF FINANCE 25 (March 1970): 99-108.

The "old view" of commercial banks is stressed. Banks can cause greater changes, not only in total credit extended, but also in price level, employment, and output where wage rigidities exist.

Yohe, William P. "A Study of Federal Open Market Voting, 1955-64." SOUTHERN ECONOMIC JOURNAL 32 (April 1966): 396-405.

The roll call voting information on Open Market Committee decisions was used to: (1) summarize the character of the voting, (2) examine whether "behavioral persuasion" was used, and (3) explore why there is such a high rate of unanimity in decisions.

Chapter 3

MACRO-MONETARY THEORY

INTRODUCTION

This chapter would not have been written if it had not been for John Maynard Keynes. National income accounting, disequilibrium analysis, and aggregation are only a few of the many concepts and techniques that he originated or elaborated.

This is the heart of all macroeconomic and growth courses, whether at the undergraduate or graduate level. The macroeconomic and growth textbooks annotated in chapter 1 give a survey of the material covered here, and the essay on economic organization elucidates the problems. The sections covering post-Keynes analysis and aggregation in this chapter are the ones that have ignited the most theoretical and empirical interest recently.

SOURCES

Early Theory

QUANTITY THEORY OF MONEY: CLASSICAL

Allais, Maurice. "A Restatement of the Quantity Theory of Money." AMERICAN ECONOMIC REVIEW 56 (December 1966): 1123-57.

> An attempt to show that human behavior is invariant in space and over time, at least in its collective aspect. A comparison of Cagan's and Allais's earlier views are also given.

Dean, Edwin, ed. THE CONTROVERSY OVER THE QUANTITY THEORY OF MONEY. New York: D.C. Heath & Co., 1965. 140 p. Paperbound.

> Selections from the writings of R. Cantillon, I. Fisher, A. C. Pigou, J.M. Keynes, A.H. Hansen, M. Friedman, and J. Tobin are included. It serves well as a primer.

Encarnacion, Jose. "Consistency Between Say's Identity and the Cambridge Equation." ECONOMIC JOURNAL 68 (December 1958): 827-30.

It is important to remember which are the independent and the dependent variables in a system.

Fisher, Irving. THE PURCHASING POWER OF MONEY. Rev. ed. New York: Augustus M. Kelley, 1922. 539 p.

The purchasing power of money depends exclusively on the volume of money and velocity of circulation, the volume and velocity of bank deposits subject to check, and the volume of trade.

Samuelson, Paul A. "What Classical and Neoclassical Monetary Theory Really Was." CANADIAN JOURNAL OF ECONOMICS 1 (February 1968): 1-15. Reprinted in [2] [13].

It is not necessary to have real balances in the utility function to have a correctly specified model of a "monetary" economy. It is only necessary that the utility function contain, along with the physical quantities of goods consumed, the stock of money and all money prices being homogeneous of degree zero (i.e., no money illusion). A comment and a reply of interest are: Clower, R.W. "What Traditional Monetary Theory Really Wasn't." CANADIAN JOURNAL OF ECONOMICS 2 (May 1969): 299-302; and Samuelson, Paul A. "Nonoptimality of Money Holdings under Laissez Faire." Ibid, pp. 303-8.

QUANTITY THEORY OF MONEY: FRIEDMANITE

Brunner, Karl, and Meltzer, Allan H. "Predicting Velocity: Implications for Theory and Policy." JOURNAL OF FINANCE 18 (May 1963): 319-54.

This is an attempt to make the quantity theory relevant to the short run. Their results emphasize that the supply and demand functions for money provide more stable relationships than alternative approaches.

Brunner, Karl, et al. "Symposium on Friedman's Theoretical Framework." JOURNAL OF POLITICAL ECONOMY 80 (September/October 1972): 837-950.

The symposium includes articles by Brunner and Allan H. Meltzer, "Friedman's Monetary Theory"; James Tobin, "Friedman's Theoretical Framework"; Paul Davidson, "A Keynesian View of Friedman's Theoretical Framework for Monetary Analysis"; Don Patinkin, "Friedman on the Quantity Theory and Keynesian Economics"; and Milton Friedman, "Comments on the Critics."

It is not definitively determined whether or not Friedman is a Keynesian. This symposium has been issued as a book: Gordon, Robert J., ed. MILTON FRIEDMAN'S MONETARY FRAMEWORK. Chicago: University of Chicago Press, 1974. 192 p.

Friedman, Milton. "A Monetary and Fiscal Framework for Economic Stability." AMERICAN ECONOMIC REVIEW 38 (June 1948): 245-64. Reprinted in [10] [11] [15].

No private creation or destruction of money, a balanced budget, and a reformed net tax policy--all in all, a modest proposal.

_____. "The Quantity Theory of Money." In INTERNATIONAL ENCYCLO-PEDIA OF THE SOCIAL SCIENCES, edited by D.L. Sills, vol. 10, pp. 427-38. New York: Macmillan-Free Press, 1968.

This is basically a restatement and updating of his "The Demand for Money: Some Theoretical and Empirical Results." JOURNAL OF POLITICAL ECONOMY 67 (August 1959): 327-51.

_____. "The Quantity Theory of Money: A Restatement." In his STUDIES IN THE QUANTITY THEORY OF MONEY, pp. 3-11. Chicago: University of Chicago Press, 1956. Reprinted in [2] [15] [19].

"The quantity theory of money is a term evocative of a general approach rather than a label for a well-defined theory." So starts Friedman's defense of the quantity theory of money--a theory of the demand for money.

_____. "The Role of Monetary Policy." AMERICAN ECONOMIC REVIEW 58 (March 1968): 1-17. Reprinted in [4] [8] [16] [17].

Friedman's position is that monetary authorities should publicly adopt the policy of achieving a steady rate of growth of the money supply. The leading spokesman of the monetarists uses price flexibility as his "can opener." See Lerner, Abba P. "The Economists' Can Opener." WESTERN ECONOMIC JOURNAL 6 (March 1968): 94-96.

_____. "A Theoretical Framework for Monetary Analysis." JOURNAL OF POLITICAL ECONOMY 78 (March/April 1970): 193-238.

The short-run difference between the quantity theory and the Keynesian theory rests on whether income or price is exogenously determined. The long run belongs to the quantity theory. An addendum is "A Monetary Theory of Nominal Income." Ibid., 79 (March/April 1971): 323-37.

_____, ed. STUDIES IN THE QUANTITY THEORY OF MONEY. Chicago: University of Chicago Press, 1956. 263 p.

The most significant book in the rebirth of the quantity theory of money as conceived by the Chicago school. The initial essay by Milton Friedman, "The Quantity Theory of Money--A Restatement," is the first and only systematic statement of his position, which became the Chicago tradition.

Hahn, Frank. "Professor Friedman's Views on Monetary Theory." ECONOMICA 38 (February 1971): 61-80.

> This is a review article of Friedman, Milton. THE OPTIMUM QUANTITY OF MONEY. Chicago: Aldine Publishing Co., 1969. Friedman has no theory of money and, in fact, does not claim to have one. His understanding of how money works is based entirely on his empirical studies of historical data.

Meigs, A. James. MONEY MATTERS. New York: Harper & Row Publishers, 1972. 430 p.

> This was the hoped for definitive word on monetarism. It has not achieved that distinction.

Patinkin, Don. "The Chicago Tradition, the Quantity Theory and Friedman." JOURNAL OF MONEY, CREDIT AND BANKING 1 (February 1969): 46-70.

> Patinkin's position is that Friedman's work is not part of any Chicago tradition--oral or written. He has made similar charges elsewhere: "On the Short-Run Non-Neutrality of Money in the Quantity Theory." BANCA NAZIONALE DEL LAVORO: QUARTERLY REVIEW, no. 100 (March 1972): 3-22; and "Friedman on the Quantity Theory and Keynesian Economics." JOURNAL OF POLITICAL ECONOMY 80 (September/October 1972): 883-905. Friedman's reply is "Comments on the Critics." Ibid., pp. 906-50.

Sprinkel, Beryl Wayne. MONEY AND MARKETS. Homewood, III.: Richard D. Irwin, 1971. 328 p. Also paperbound.

> Sprinkel is a monetarist commercial banker and economist. This book does an excellent job of explaining the monetarist position to intelligent and interested laypersons.

Tobin, James. "Money and Income: Post Hoc Ergo Propter Hoc?" Friedman, Milton. "Comment on Tobin." Tobin, James. "Rejoinder." QUARTERLY JOURNAL OF ECONOMICS 84 (May 1970): 301-17, 318-27, and 328-29.

> Tobin's concluding point is that Friedman has two monetary theories: one that accounts for the procyclical movement of velocity and the other that is consistent with timing evidence.

CONTRA-QUANTITY THEORY OF MONEY

The quantity and contra-quantity theories of money are different interpretations of where the break between cause and effect exists in the stream of monetary history. Of course, in an economic model the determination is simpler: whether money supply or commodity price is exogenous. The sources which give the implications for monetary history--banking and currency schools, etc.--are found in chapter 4.

Davidson, Paul, and Weintraub, Sidney. "Money as Cause and Effect." ECO-NOMIC JOURNAL 83 (December 1973): 1117-32.

> Because the nominal wage is exogenously determined, monetary policy is impotent in regard to inflation. Incomes policy may be the only effective way to accomplish price stability.

Sen, S.R. "Sir James Steuart's General Theory of Employment, Interest, and Money." ECONOMICA 14 (February 1947): 19-36.

> Steuart and Keynes thought along similar lines according to this article. Also see Skinner, A.S. "Money and Prices: A Critique of the Quantity of Money." SCOTTISH JOURNAL OF POLITICAL ECONOMY 14 (November 1967): 275-90.

Later Thought: Theoretical and Applied

CONTEMPORARIES OF KEYNES: RIVALS AND FRIENDS

Feiwel, G.R. THE INTELLECTUAL CAPITAL OF MICHAL KALECKI. Knoxville: University of Tennessee Press, 1974. 576 p.

> This is a complete appraisal of the many contributions of Kalecki. The independent codiscovery of the "general theory" by Kalecki and Keynes is stressed. It becomes the Kalecki-Keynes revolution.

Haberler, Gottfried. PROSPERITY AND DEPRESSION. 4th ed. Cambridge: Harvard University Press, 1958. Reprint in paperbound. New York: Atheneum Publishers, 1963.

> A pre-World War II look at what causes business fluctuations. An early version of the real balance effect was included in the first edition (1939).

Hagen, Everett E. "The Classical Theory of the Level of Output and Employment." In READINGS IN MACROECONOMICS, edited by M.G. Mueller, 2d ed., pp. 3-15. New York: Holt, Rinehart and Winston, 1971.

> A good summary of why the "invisible hand" should work.

Kahn, Richard [F.]. "The Relation of Home Investment to Unemployment." ECONOMIC JOURNAL 41 (June 1931): 173-98.

> This is where the multiplier made famous by Keynes was initially specified.

Kalecki, Michal. SELECTED ESSAYS ON THE DYNAMICS OF THE CAPITALIST ECONOMY, 1933-1970. New York: Cambridge University Press, 1971. 198 p.

> Three papers are included which were published in Polish before

the GENERAL THEORY appeared and include many of its essentials.
The economics taught at Cambridge University is, in many ways,
closer to the writings of Kalecki than to those of Keynes.

Marshall, Alfred. PRINCIPLES OF ECONOMICS. 8th ed. New York: St.
Martin's Press, 1920. 763 p. Paperbound edition. London: Macmillan and Co.

This book was the approach used to teach all economics in Britain
from the turn of the century to the GENERAL THEORY. Marshall
was Keynes's mentor.

Myrdal, Gunner. MONETARY EQUILIBRIUM. New York: Augustus M. Kelley,
1939. 226 p.

Basically Keynes's approach in the GENERAL THEORY, but published in Swedish in 1931 and in German in 1933. This is the
last classic the Swedish school has produced.

Ohlin, Bertil. "Some Notes on the Stockholm Theory of Savings and Investment
I." ECONOMIC JOURNAL 47 (March 1937): 53-69. Reprinted in [6].
"Some Notes on the Stockholm Theory of Savings and Investment II." ECO-
NOMIC JOURNAL 47 (June 1937): 221-40.

Ohlin points out the differences and similarities between the Swedish
school and Keynes's GENERAL THEORY. Also note: Keynes,
John Maynard. "Alternative Theories of the Rate of Interest."
ECONOMIC JOURNAL 47 (June 1937): 241-52; and Ohlin,
Bertil, Hawtrey, R.G., Robertson, D.H. "Alternative Theories of
the Rate of Interest: Three Rejoinders." ECONOMIC JOURNAL
47 (September 1937): 423-43. Of additional interest is Keynes,
John Maynard. "The 'Ex-Ante' Theory of the Rate of Interest."
ECONOMIC JOURNAL 47 (December 1937): 663-69; and Lerner,
A.P. "Alternative Formulations of the Theory of Interest."
ECONOMIC JOURNAL 48 (June 1938): 211-30.

Pigou, A.C. EMPLOYMENT AND EQUILIBRIUM: A THEORETICAL DISCUS-
SION. New York: Augustus M. Kelley, 1941. 283 p.

This volume is Pigou's first reply to Keynes's GENERAL THEORY.
Price flexibility combined with the real balance effect is the easy
answer to the difficulties of unemployment. A review article by
Nicholas Kaldor, in ECONOMIC JOURNAL 51 (December 1941):
458-73 is well worth reading.

_____. THE THEORY OF UNEMPLOYMENT. New York: Augustus M. Kelley,
1933. 344 p.

This is the book that Keynes used as his classical theory straw man.
The analysis is correct for an economy that is at equilibrium or
returning to it. The market works perfectly. Problems relating
to liquidity, unemployment, and information never arise.

_____. THE VEIL OF MONEY. London: Macmillan and Co., 1949. 150 p.

A further attempt by Pigou to investigate the importance of money in economic theorizing. Money is only a wrapper around the real gross national product. However, changes in the wrapper may have very substantial effects on the real substance within.

Robertson, Dennis H. "A Survey of Modern Monetary Controversy." MANCHESTER SCHOOL OF ECONOMIC AND SOCIAL STUDIES 9 (January 1938): 1-19. Reprinted in [6].

Robertson finds at least eight differences of opinion, in either emphasis or expression. The quantity theory versus Keynesian theory and loanable funds versus liquidity preference are only part of the problem. The state must still solve policy problems.

Shackle, G.L.S. THE YEARS OF HIGH THEORY. New York: Cambridge University Press, 1967. 328 p.

A survey of invention and tradition in economic thought from 1926-39. Every one of the eighteen chapters is worth reading. Chapters 9 through 16 deal with the Keynesian revolution.

Wicksell, Knut. LECTURES ON POLITICAL ECONOMY. Vol. 2: MONEY. Translated by E. Classen. London: Routledge & Kegan Paul, 1935. 238 p.

The second volume was originally published in Swedish in 1906. An introduction by Lord Robbins is very helpful in understanding Wicksell's relative anonymity. Wicksell was far ahead of the times. When the translation was published in 1935, the book was already almost thirty years old, and yet it still anticipated many of the ideas in Keynes's GENERAL THEORY. Keynes had been forced to do a lot of unnecessary original thinking.

CONTEMPORARIES OF KEYNES: UNDERGROUND

The underground consisted of those who worried about the sufficiency or insufficiency of effective aggregate demand, in contrast to most classical economists. The sources with which to begin are: Keynes, John Maynard. THE GENERAL THEORY OF EMPLOYMENT, INTEREST AND MONEY. New York: Harcourt, Brace, 1936. Chapter 23; and Haberler, Gottfried, ed. READINGS IN BUSINESS CYCLE THEORY. Homewood, Ill.: Richard D. Irwin, 1944. Pt. 5.

Hansen, Alvin H. "Economic Progress and Declining Population Growth." AMERICAN ECONOMIC REVIEW 29 (March 1939): 1-15. Reprinted in [15].

The best presentation in an article of the secular stagnation thesis. This is the long-run version of the underconsumption thesis.

In addition consult Keynes, John Maynard. "Some Economic Consequences of a Declining Population." EUGENICS REVIEW 29

(April 1937): 13-17; and Higgins, Benjamin. "Concepts and Criteria of Secular Stagnation." In INCOME, EMPLOYMENT, AND PUBLIC POLICY, edited by Lloyd A. Metzler, pp. 82-107. New York: W.W. Norton, 1948.

Neisser, Hans. "General Overproduction." JOURNAL OF POLITICAL ECONOMY 42 (August 1934): 433-65. Reprinted in [6].

A discussion of Marxian and older doctrines of the underconsumption thesis.

BUSINESS CYCLES: THEORY, ECONOMETRIC MODELS, AND FORECASTING

Abramovitz, Moses. "The Nature and Significance of Kuznets Cycles." ECONOMIC DEVELOPMENT AND CULTURAL CHANGE 9 (April 1961): 225-48. Reprinted in [5].

The fifteen to twenty-five year general waves in economic changes are called Kuznets cycles. Also see Abramovitz, Moses. "The Passing of the Kuznets Cycle." ECONOMICA 35 (November 1968): 349-67.

_____. "Resource and Output Trends in the U.S. Since 1870." AMERICAN ECONOMIC REVIEW 46 (May 1956): 5-23.

The long-swing hypothesis is supported by the data available to Abramovitz. Our past experience shows that long upswings are always terminated by a severe depression.

Adams, F. Gerard, and Rowe, David M. FORECASTS AND SIMULATIONS FROM THE WHARTON ECONOMETRIC MODEL, 1974-1975 EDITION. Morristown, N.J.: General Learning Press, 1974. 45 p. Paperbound.

Very simply, the conclusions are that "a policy of recession is not a quick means to solve the inflation problem."

Adelman, Irma, and Adelman, Frank L. "The Dynamic Properties of the Klein-Goldberger Model." ECONOMETRICA 27 (October 1959): 596-625. Reprinted in [5].

They used a computer to test the propagation and impulse problems named by Ragnar Frisch. Also see Adelman, Irma. "Business Cycles--Endogenous or Stochastic?" ECONOMIC JOURNAL 70 (December 1960): 783-96.

Alexander, Sidney S. "Rate of Change Approaches to Forecasting: Diffusion Indexes and First Differences." ECONOMIC JOURNAL 68 (June 1958): 288-301. Reprinted in [5].

The diffusion indexes and first differences are defined and compared.

Alexander concludes that the choice is one of convenience with regard to predicting turning points.

Andersen, Leonall C., and Carlson, Keith M. "A Monetarist Model for Economic Stabilization." Federal Reserve Bank of St. Louis REVIEW 52 (April 1970): 7-25.

A small model is developed to analyze economic stabilization issues. One of its virtues is that it primarily depends on only two variables: money stock and high employment expenditures.

Ando, Albert, and Modigliani, Franco. "Econometric Analysis of Stabilization Policies." AMERICAN ECONOMIC REVIEW 59 (May 1969): 296-314.

This is an interim performance report on the FRB-MIT quarterly econometric model. Policy simulations have been bothered by shortcomings in the treatment of imports, capital gains, and un-filled orders.

Bronfenbrenner, Martin, ed. IS THE BUSINESS CYCLE OBSOLETE? New York: John Wiley & Sons, 1969. 579 p.

These papers were given at a conference of the Social Science Research Council Committee on Economic Stability. Three main observations emerged: (1) nowhere in the industrialized world has a country suffered a major contraction since World War II, (2) minor fluctuations have persisted, and (3) in the industrialized countries of Western Europe and Japan, the cycles of the postwar period have not involved significant declines in aggregate output.

Burmeister, Edwin, ed. "Symposium. Econometric Model Performance: Comparative Simulation Studies of Models of the U.S. Economy." INTERNATIONAL ECONOMIC REVIEW 15 and 16 (June and October 1974 and February 1975): 265-414, 541-653, and 3-111, respectively.

Over one hundred pages in each of these three issues were devoted to papers given at the Conference on Econometrics and Mathematical Economics sponsored by the National Bureau of Economic Research and the National Science Foundation.

Burns, Arthur F. "Hicks and the Real Cycle." JOURNAL OF POLITICAL ECONOMY 6 (February 1952): 1-24.

This is a review article of Hicks's A CONTRIBUTION TO THE THEORY OF THE TRADE CYCLE. Burns feels Hicks's book is too far removed from reality (i.e., the work of the National Bureau of Economic Research).

_____. "Progress Towards Economic Stability." AMERICAN ECONOMIC REVIEW 50 (March 1960): 1-19.

There has been governmental pressure (e.g., Employment Act of 1946) to calm down the business cycle. However, cycles have not been eliminated.

Burns, Arthur F., and Mitchell, Wesley C. MEASURING BUSINESS CYCLES. Studies in Business Cycles, vol. 2. New York: National Bureau of Economic Research, 1946. 587 p.

Impressive in scope and executed with painstaking care, the work presents a detailed, technical analysis of a method for studying the cyclical behavior of individual series of data.

Christ, Carl F. "Aggregate Econometric Models." AMERICAN ECONOMIC REVIEW 46 (June 1956): 385-408. Reprinted in [5].

This is a review article of Klein, Lawrence R., and Goldberger, Arthur S. AN ECONOMETRIC MODEL OF THE UNITED STATES 1929-1952. New York: North-Holland, 1955. Christ is unwilling to be as objective as he should be--a glowing review.

_____. "Econometric Models of the Financial Sector." JOURNAL OF MONEY, CREDIT AND BANKING 3 (May 1971): 419-49.

This is a survey of the theory and the results of nine important econometric models of the U.S. economy. Also see Christ, Carl F. "A Model of Monetary and Fiscal Policy Effects on the Money Stock, Price Level and Real Output." JOURNAL OF MONEY, CREDIT AND BANKING 1 (November 1969): 683-705.

Clark, John Maurice. STRATEGIC FACTORS IN BUSINESS CYCLES. New York: Augustus M. Kelley, 1934. 253 p.

This is an early, theoretical approach to business cycles. Each cycle is divided into eight different stages.

Cooper, J. Phillip. DEVELOPMENT OF THE MONETARY SECTOR, PREDICTION AND POLICY ANALYSIS IN THE FRB-MIT-PENN MODEL. Lexington, Mass.: Lexington Books, 1974. 256 p.

Chapter 2 was written with F. Modigliani and R.H. Rasche, chapter 3 with C.R. Nelson, and chapter 5 with S. Fischer. In this model a steady expansion of the money supply is harmful to the economy-- of course.

Cooper, J. Phillip, and Fischer, Stanley. "Monetary and Fiscal Policy in the Fully Stochastic St. Louis Econometric Model." JOURNAL OF MONEY, CREDIT AND BANKING 6 (February 1974): 1-22.

This question is asked of the St. Louis model: Is stability gained by actively using monetary and fiscal policy? The answer is an econometric yes. Also see their article, "Simulations of Monetary

Rules in the FRB–MIT–Penn Model." JOURNAL OF MONEY,
CREDIT AND BANKING 4 (May 1972): 384–96.

de Leeuw, Frank, and Gramlich, Edward M. "The Channels of Monetary Policy."
FEDERAL RESERVE BULLETIN 55 (June 1969): 472–90. Also printed in JOUR-
NAL OF FINANCE 24 (May 1969): 265–90. Reprinted in [1] [4].

The Federal Reserve–MIT econometric model of the economy is put
through its paces. Its monetary multipliers are much larger than
those of most other econometric models but smaller than those ob-
tained by the staff of the St. Louis Federal Reserve Bank.

_____. "The Federal Reserve–MIT Econometric Model." FEDERAL RESERVE
BULLETIN 54 (January 1968): 11–40.

This is the first report on the FRB–MIT model.

Duesenberry, James S. BUSINESS CYCLES AND ECONOMIC GROWTH. New
York: McGraw-Hill Book Co., 1958. 352 p.

The core of Duesenberry's contribution to dynamic economics is a
modification of the accelerator-multiplier interaction which he
labels a capital-income adjustment process.

_____. "A Simulation of the U.S. Economy in Recession." ECONOMETRICA
28 (October 1960): 749–809. Reprinted in [5].

The Duesenberry-Eckstein-Fromm model used quarterly data to simu-
late the U.S. economy in the recession phase of the business cycle.

Duesenberry, James S., et al. THE BROOKINGS MODEL: SOME FURTHER
RESULTS. New York: American Elsevier Publishing Co., 1969. 540 p.

This third volume of the Brookings Quarterly Econometric model
contains an introduction by Edwin Kuh, nine chapters chiefly de-
voted to the presentation of new estimation results, and four chap-
ters on solutions of the complete model. The earlier volumes are:
James Duesenberry et al., eds. THE BROOKINGS QUARTERLY
ECONOMETRIC MODEL OF THE UNITED STATES; and Gary
Fromm and Paul Taubman. POLICY SIMULATIONS WITH AN
ECONOMETRIC MODEL.

_____, eds. THE BROOKINGS QUARTERLY ECONOMETRIC MODEL OF THE
UNITED STATES. Chicago: Rand McNally, 1965. 791 p.

It was the first attempt to build a model of the macroeconomy sector-
by-sector. A continuation of this study may be found in Gary Fromm
and Paul Taubman. POLICY SIMULATIONS WITH AN ECONOME-
TRIC MODEL and James Duesenberry et al. THE BROOKINGS MODEL:
SOME FURTHER RESULTS.

Evans, Michael K., and Klein, Lawrence R. THE WHARTON ECONOMETRIC FORECASTING MODEL. Philadelphia: University of Pennsylvania Press, 1967. 161 p.

> This book is simply an explanation of how the model was constructed and some of the results obtained.

Ezekiel, Mordecai. "The Cobweb Theorem." QUARTERLY JOURNAL OF ECONOMICS 52 (February 1938): 255-80. Reprinted in [6].

> A discussion of other mechanisms, in addition to the cobweb, as an explanation of commodity cycles.

Fisher, Gordon, and Sheppard, David. "Effects of Monetary Policy on the United States Economy: A Survey of Econometric Evidence." OECD ECONOMIC OUTLOOK: OCCASIONAL STUDIES, December 1972, pp. 1-128.

> This study assesses and reviews the results of the econometric research done in the United States. The bibliography contains 153 references.

Friedman, Milton, and Schwartz, A[nna]. J[acobson]. "Money and Business Cycles." REVIEW OF ECONOMICS AND STATISTICS 45, supplement (February 1963): 32-65. Reprinted in [14].

> Two important generalizations are made: (1) a one-to-one relation between monetary changes and changes in money income and prices exists, and (2) changes in money stock can generally be attributed to specific historical circumstances.

Frisch, Ragnar. "Propagation Problems and Impulse Problems in Dynamic Economics." In ECONOMIC ESSAYS IN HONOR OF GUSTAV CASSEL, edited by J.W. Angell et al., pp. 171-205. New York: Augustus M. Kelley, 1933. Reprinted in [5].

> If we assume that most economic oscillations are free oscillations, then the length of cycle is determined endogenously while the amplitude is determined exogenously.

Fromm, Gary, and Taubman, Paul. POLICY SIMULATIONS WITH AN ECONOMETRIC MODEL. Washington, D.C.: Brookings Institution, 1968. 194 p.

> This is the second preliminary study of the Brookings model. The simulations were done before the 1947-65 revisions of the national income and product accounts were made. Consequently, the results are not of great interest empirically. Both the other volumes are edited or written by James S. Duesenberry et al. THE BROOKINGS QUARTERLY ECONOMETRIC MODEL OF THE UNITED STATES; and THE BROOKINGS MODEL: SOME FURTHER RESULTS.

Goldberger, Arthur S.   IMPACT MULTIPLIERS AND DYNAMIC PROPERTIES OF
THE KLEIN-GOLDBERGER MODEL.   New York: North-Holland, 1959.   138 p.

> This is an up-date of Klein, L.R., and Goldberger, A.S.   AN
> ECONOMETRIC MODEL OF THE UNITED STATES, 1929-1952.
> New York: North-Holland, 1955.   180 p.

Goldfeld, Stephen M., and Blinder, Alan S.   "Some Implications of Endogenous
Stabilization Policy."   BROOKINGS PAPERS ON ECONOMIC ACTIVITY   3,
no. 3 (1972):   585-640.

> Goldfeld and Blinder suggest that reduced-form estimation may
> create problems when policy reaction functions exist, even if the
> rest of the model was specified correctly.   Fiscal multipliers tend
> to be substantially underestimated.

Goodwin, R.M.   "A Model of Cyclical Growth."   In THE BUSINESS CYCLE
IN THE POST-WAR WORLD, edited by Erik Lundberg, pp. 203-21.   New York:
St. Martin's Press, 1955.   Reprinted in [5].

> Goodwin is concerned with the "simultaneous existence and mutual
> conditioning of economic growth and economic cycles."   Two assump-
> tions are made: economic progress is not steady and the cycle is
> dominated by economic growth.

Gordon, Robert A[aron].   "The Brookings Model in Action: A Review Article."
JOURNAL OF POLITICAL ECONOMY   78 (May/June 1970):   489-525.

> This is a review of all the work done with the Brookings Model,
> with special emphasis on Fromm, Gary, and Taubman, Paul.
> POLICY SIMULATIONS WITH AN ECONOMETRIC MODEL.
> Washington, D.C.:   Brookings Institution, 1968.

_____.   ECONOMIC STABILITY AND GROWTH: THE AMERICAN RECORD.
New York: Harper & Row Publishers, 1974.   216 p.   Paperbound.

> A historical survey of the American economy since World War I.

Gordon, Robert A., and Klein, Lawrence R., eds.   READINGS IN BUSINESS
CYCLES.   Homewood, Ill.:   Richard D. Irwin, 1965.   731 p.

> This is the second volume to appear in the American Economic
> Association's series of republished business cycle articles.   This
> volume has more mathematical and econometrical articles.   Eight
> areas of interest are covered: (1) "Theory," (2) "Methodology,"
> (3) "Econometric Models," (4) "Studies of Particular Variables,"
> (5) "Long Cycles," (6) "International Aspects," (7) "Forecasting,"
> and (8) "Policy."

Haberler, Gottfried.   "Monetary and Real Factors Affecting Economic Stability:
A Critique of Certain Tendencies in Modern Economic Theory."   BANCA

NAZIONALE DEL LAVORO: QUARTERLY REVIEW, no. 9 (September 1956), pp. 85-99. Reprinted in [5].

The explanation of what causes cycles is heavily weighted toward real factors. Haberler feels that monetary factors have not been given their due as creators of instability.

_____, ed. READINGS IN BUSINESS CYCLE THEORY. Homewood, III.: Richard D. Irwin, 1944. 510 p.

The best articles in business cycle theory published before 1944 as selected by a committee of the American Economic Association. The articles were divided into six parts: (1) "Over-all Picture of the Business Cycle and Method of Analysis," (2) "Saving, Invest- ment and National Income," (3) "The Multiplier, Acceleration Principle and Government Spending," (4) "Monetary Theory of the Business Cycle," (5) "Underconsumption Theory and Secular Stagna- tion Thesis," and (6) "Special Commodity Cycles." An extensive bibliography is included.

Hansen, Alvin H. BUSINESS CYCLES AND NATIONAL INCOME. Enl. ed. New York: W.W. Norton, 1964. 741 p.

Sections include: (1) "The Nature of Business Cycles," (2) "The Theory of Income and Employment," (3) "The Business-Cycle Theory" (contains selected readings), (4) "Business Cycles and Public Policy," and (5) "Prosperity and Recession since the Second World War." A superb bibliography by R.V. Clemence is included.

Hendershott, Patric H. "Recent Development of the Financial Sector of Econo- metric Models." JOURNAL OF FINANCE 23 (March 1968): 41-66.

The FRB-MIT Penn model is used by Hendershott. He did some of the major work in deriving its financial sector. In addition he empirically analyzes those segments of the financial market that have not been examined in detail before.

Hickman, B[ert].G. GROWTH AND STABILITY OF THE POSTWAR ECONOMY. Washington, D.C.: Brookings Institution, 1960. 444 p.

Part 1 of the book deals with the concept and significance of economic stability and compares American business cycles in the postwar and prewar period. Part 2 describes, in detail, the U.S. cycles between 1946 and 1958. Part 3 discusses the role of key factors in the postwar cycles (i.e., federal spending, consumption, investment, residential construction, monetary policy, and price movements).

Hicks, John R. A CONTRIBUTION TO THE THEORY OF THE TRADE CYCLE. New York: Oxford University Press, 1950. 217 p.

The first attempt to use Harrod's growth theory to build a sophisticated model of the business cycle. Hicks believes monetary reform,
to re-establish monetary security and moderate use of fiscal controls
and public investment, is an alternative that would hold out hope
for the 1950s. After twenty-five years, the cure is still being
sought.

Klein, L[awrence].R., and Goldberger, A[rthur].S. AN ECONOMETRIC MODEL
OF THE UNITED STATES, 1929-1952. Amsterdam: North-Holland, 1955. 180 p.

For its time this was the best aggregate econometric model of the
United States.

Kondratieff, Nikolai D. "The Long Waves in Economic Life." REVIEW OF
ECONOMIC STATISTICS 17 (November 1935): 105-15. Reprinted in [6].

The person after whom the fifty-year waves in capitalistic economies
are named explains their existence. In addition the interested
reader should consult Garvy, George. "Kondratieff's Theory of
Long Cycles." REVIEW OF ECONOMIC STATISTICS 25 (November 1943): 203-20.

Koopmans, Tjalling C. "Measurement Without Theory." REVIEW OF ECONOMIC
STUDIES 29 (August 1947): 161-72. Reprinted in [5].

This is a review article of Burns, Arthur F., and Mitchell, Wesley
C. MEASURING BUSINESS CYCLES. New York: National Bu-
reau of Economic Research, 1946. Koopmans's position is that you
should have a theory before you begin measuring and testing. The
debate is interesting. See Vining, Rutledge. "Koopmans on the
Choice of Variables to be Studied and of Methods of Measurement."
REVIEW OF ECONOMICS AND STATISTICS 31 (May 1949): 77-
86. Reprinted in [5]; Koopmans, Tjalling C. "A Reply." REVIEW
OF ECONOMICS AND STATISTICS 31 (May 1949): 86-91.
Reprinted in [5]; and Vining, Rutledge. "A Rejoinder." REVIEW
OF ECONOMICS AND STATISTICS 31 (May 1949): 91-94.
Reprinted in [5].

Matthews, R.C.O. THE BUSINESS CYCLE. Cambridge Economic Handbook.
Chicago: University of Chicago Press, 1959. 316 p.

The business cycle is caused by the variability of private investment. The history, theory, and policy implications of business
cycles are examined. The supply side is given short shrift.

Metzler, Lloyd A. "The Nature and Stability of Inventory Cycles." REVIEW
OF ECONOMICS AND STATISTICS 23 (August 1941): 113-29. Reprinted in
[5].

Business cycles are either a cumulative process with certain limiting
stabilizers or movements of employment and income which adapt to

cyclical changes in the parameters of an otherwise stable system.

Minsky, Hyman P. "A Linear Model of Cyclical Growth." REVIEW OF ECO-
NOMICS AND STATISTICS 41 (May 1959): 133-45. Reprinted in [5].

   Minsky's model combines an explosive accelerator-multiplier hypothesis with an exogenously determined ceiling on the rate of
   growth of income.

Mitchell, Wesley C. "Business Cycles." In BUSINESS CYCLES AND UNEM-
PLOYMENT, edited by National Bureau of Economic Research, pp. 5-18. New
York: McGraw-Hill Book Co., 1923. Reprinted in [6].

   The head of the bureau defines business cycles for the President's
   Conference on Unemployment.

_____. BUSINESS CYCLES: THE PROBLEM AND ITS SETTING. New York:
National Bureau of Economic Research, 1927. 511 p.

   The dean of the cycle men shows his encyclopedic knowledge of
   the field. The book is mainly of historic value now. This book
   is an up-dating of his 1913 book BUSINESS CYCLES.

Moore, G.H., ed. BUSINESS CYCLE INDICATORS. Vol. 1. Princeton,
N.J.: Princeton University Press, 1961. 792 p.

   Mainly designed as a reference guide, not to be read completely,
   the number and repetition of authors being the limiting parameters.

National Bureau of Economic Research, ed. BUSINESS CYCLES AND UNEM-
PLOYMENT. New York: McGraw-Hill Book Co., 1923. 405 p.

   The bureau explains the interrelationships of business cycles and
   unemployment. Each of the twenty-odd chapters in the book
   examines a different phase of the problem.

Schumpeter, Joseph A. "The Analysis of Economic Change." REVIEW OF
ECONOMIC STATISTICS 17 (May 1935): 2-10. Reprinted in [6].

   What causes business cycles? There is more than one valid way by
   which an innovation and its monetary complement are related.

Smithies, Arthur. "Economic Fluctuations and Growth." ECONOMETRICA 25
(January 1957): 1-52. Reprinted in [5].

   Smithies attempts both mathematically and nonmathematically to
   weld together the business cycle theory of Tinbergen and Harrod's
   growth theory.

Stekler, H.O. "Forecasting with Econometric Models: An Evaluation."
ECONOMETRICA 36 (July/October 1968): 437-63.

The predictive performance of the following models is analyzed: (1) Klein quarterly model, (2) OBE (Office of Business Economics) model, (3) Fromm model, (4) Friend and Jones model, (5) Friend and Taubman model, and (6) Liu model. The Klein-Goldberger and Suits models are analyzed elsewhere.

Suits, Daniel B. "Forecasting and Analysis with an Econometric Model." AMERICAN ECONOMIC REVIEW 52 (March 1962): 104-32. Reprinted in [5].

Suits builds an econometric model of the U.S. economy. He demonstrates its use as a forecaster and, consequently, its implications for policy analysis. Also see Stekler, H.O. "Forecasting and Analysis with an Econometric Model: Comment." AMERICAN ECONOMIC REVIEW 56 (December 1966): 1241-48.

Tinbergen, Jan. "Econometric Business Cycle Research." REVIEW OF ECONOMIC STUDIES 7 (1939-40): 73-90. Reprinted in [6].

A survey of econometric research by a Nobel Laureate. His explanation of the logic employed is especially interesting. Also see Koopmans, T.C. "Logic of Econometric Business Cycle Research." REVIEW OF ECONOMIC STATISTICS 25 (November 1943): 203-20.

_____. STATISTICAL TESTING OF BUSINESS CYCLE THEORIES. New York: Agathon Press, 1938. 244 p.

This study, done for the League of Nations, is the first to employ econometric analysis. Tinbergen was awarded the Nobel Prize chiefly for this ground-breaking work.

Tobin, James, and Brainard, William [C.]. "Pitfalls in Financial Model Building." AMERICAN ECONOMIC REVIEW 58 (May 1968): 99-122.

Econometric and theoretical models which do not specify the essential interdependences of markets (especially financial) will fall on infertile ground and give sterile results.

Warburton, Clark. "The Misplaced Emphasis on Contemporary Business-Fluctuation Theory." JOURNAL OF BUSINESS 19 (October 1946): 199-220.

An early monetarist speaks out against the investment-savings relationship as the cause of the Great Depression.

Zarnowitz, Victor, ed. THE BUSINESS CYCLE TODAY, 1ST. Economic Research: Retrospect and Prospect. Fiftieth Anniversary Colloquiums, 7 vols. New York: Columbia University Press, 1972. 345 p.

THE BUSINESS CYCLE TODAY was one of seven colloquiums in honor of the National Bureau of Economic Research's (NBER) fiftieth anniversary in 1970. The moderators were P.A. Samuelson and F.T. Juster, with presentations by I. Mintz, S. Fabriant, G.E. Moore, V. Zarnowitz, and Y. Haitovsky and N. Wallace. The other six colloquiums also were published by Columbia University Press in 1972: NBER, ed. FINANCE AND CAPITAL MARKETS, 2D. 84 p.; Fuchs, Victor, ed. POLICY ISSUES AND RESEARCH OPPORTUNITIES IN INDUSTRIAL ORGANIZATION, 3D. 80 p.; NBER, ed. PUBLIC EXPENDITURES AND TAXATIONS, 4TH. 91 p.; NBER, ed. ECONOMIC GROWTH, 5TH. 109 p.; Schultz, Theodore W. HUMAN RESOURCES, 6TH. 114 p.; and Kuznets, Simon. QUANTITATIVE ECONOMIC RESEARCH: TRENDS AND PROBLEMS, 7TH. 115 p.

NATIONAL INCOME AND FLOW OF FUNDS ACCOUNTS: THEORY AND APPLICATION

Chow, Gregory C. "Multiplier, Accelerator, and Liquidity Preference in the Determination of National Income in the United States." REVIEW OF ECONOMICS AND STATISTICS 49 (February 1967): 1-15. Reprinted in [15].

All three relations are useful in predicting national income. Liquidity preference was the least important, although money stock had a larger dollar-for-dollar effect on private expenditures than government expenditures.

Cohen, Jacob. "Copeland's Moneyflows After Twenty-five Years: A Survey." JOURNAL OF ECONOMIC LITERATURE 10 (March 1972): 1-25.

The impact has not been as great as originally thought. But, perhaps, the fault lies in the uses made of the flow-of-funds, not in the idea.

Copeland, Morris A. A STUDY OF MONEY-FLOWS IN THE UNITED STATES. New York: National Bureau of Economic Research, 1952. 600 p.

This is the seminal work on flow-of-funds accounting.

Harris, Seymour E., ed. "Budgetary Concepts: A Symposium." REVIEW OF ECONOMICS AND STATISTICS 45 (May 1963): 113-47.

This is an analysis of the U.S. budgetary accounting and policies. Fifteen well-known economists expressed their views.

Kendrick, John W. ECONOMIC ACCOUNTS AND THEIR USES. New York: McGraw-Hill Book Co., 1972. 351 p.

The history of conceptual and statistical work in national income accounts is covered, along with the latest developments in this field.

Kuznets, Simon S. "National Income." In INTERNATIONAL ENCYCLOPEDIA OF THE SOCIAL SCIENCES, edited by Edmund R.A. Seligman, vol. 11, pp. 205-24. New York: Macmillan, 1937. Reprinted in [3].

It is necessary that the gap between what can be and is measured, and what ought to be measured, be recognized. Some of the early work of a recent Nobel Laureate.

Lekachman, Robert. NATIONAL INCOME AND THE PUBLIC WELFARE. New York: Random House, 1972. 149 p. Paperbound.

Why is it that voluntary and involuntary expenditures are lumped together? What is needed is a more sophisticated deflation of national income data.

Parker, R.H., and Harcourt, G.C., eds. READINGS IN THE CONCEPT AND MEASUREMENT OF INCOME. New York: Cambridge University Press, 1969. 410 p. Also paperbound.

This readings book has collected the most important literature in accounting and economics concerning the concept and measurement of income.

Powelson, John P. NATIONAL INCOME AND FLOW-OF-FUNDS ANALYSIS. New York: McGraw-Hill Book Co., 1960. 561 p.

This is a textbook treatment of national income accounting and flow-of-funds accounts--as published by the Federal Reserve Board in August 1959.

Ruggles, Richard, and Ruggles, Nancy D. NATIONAL INCOME ACCOUNTS AND INCOME ANALYSIS. 2d ed. New York: McGraw-Hill Book Co., 1956. 460 p.

The general trend in economics follows the idea that economists should concern themselves more with observed facts. To this end the development of national income accounting has been instrumental. This book tries to set forth the basic concepts of national income accounting without giving detailed empirical and theoretical material.

Sharp, Carl S. "Development and Use of National Income Data." In A SURVEY OF CONTEMPORARY ECONOMICS, edited by Howard S. Ellis, vol. 1, pp. 288-313. Homewood, Ill.: Richard D. Irwin, 1948.

This essay covers the first decade of developments in the field of national income.

U.S. Department of Commerce, Office of Business Economics. "The Economic Accounts of the United States: Retrospect and Prospect." SURVEY OF CURRENT BUSINESS 51, supplement (July 1971): 1-230.

This is the fiftieth anniversary issue of SURVEY OF CURRENT
BUSINESS. Over forty economists gave their views on the economic accounts.

Keynes

HIS WORKS AND WORKS ABOUT HIM

Harrod, R[oy].F. THE LIFE OF JOHN MAYNARD KEYNES. New York: St.
Martin's Press, 1951. 690 p. Also paperbound.

Written by a well-known economist at the behest of Keynes's family.
It is so complete a biography that no other has been written. This
is the book to begin with if the "true" John Maynard Keynes is to
be known.

Keynes, John Maynard. THE COLLECTED WRITINGS OF JOHN MAYNARD
KEYNES. 24 vols. New York: St. Martin's Press, 1971-- .

The COLLECTED WRITINGS are a necessity for any research library.
All twenty-four volumes will be published by the end of this decade.
The titles of the individual volumes with their original dates of
publication are: 1, INDIAN CURRENCY AND FINANCE (1913);
2, THE ECONOMIC CONSEQUENCES OF THE PEACE (1919);
3, A REVISION OF THE TREATY (1922); 4, TRACT ON MONE-
TARY REFORM (1923); 5, TREATISE ON MONEY, VOL. I (1930);
6, TREATISE ON MONEY, VOL. II; 7, THE GENERAL THEORY
(1936); 8, TREATISE ON PROBABILITY (1921); 9, ESSAYS ON
PERSUASION (1931); 10, ESSAYS IN BIOGRAPHY (1933); 11,
ECONOMIC ARTICLES AND CORRESPONDENCE; 12, ECONOMIC
ARTICLES AND CORRESPONDENCE; 13, THE GENERAL THEORY
AND AFTER, PART I; 14, THE GENERAL THEORY AND AFTER,
PART II; 15, ACTIVITIES 1906-1914: INDIA AND CAMBRIDGE;
16, ACTIVITIES 1914-1919: THE TREASURY AND VERSAILLES;
17, ACTIVITIES AND ASSOCIATED WRITINGS: TREATY REVISION
AND RECONSTRUCTION, 1920-22; 18, ACTIVITIES AND ASSO-
CIATED WRITINGS: THE END OF REPARATIONS, 1922-32; 19,
ACTIVITIES AND ASSOCIATED WRITINGS: THE RETURN TO
GOLD AND INDUSTRIAL POLICY, 1924-29; 20, ACTIVITIES AND
ASSOCIATED WRITINGS: RETHINKING EMPLOYMENT AND UN-
EMPLOYMENT POLICIES, 1929-31; 21, ACTIVITIES AND ASSO-
CIATED WRITINGS: WORLD CRISES AND POLITICS IN BRITAIN
AND AMERICA, 1931-39; 22, ACTIVITIES AND ASSOCIATED
WRITINGS: WAR FINANCE, 1940-45; 23, ACTIVITIES AND
ASSOCIATED WRITINGS: SHAPING THE POST-WAR WORLD,
1940-46; and 24, BIBLIOGRAPHY AND INDEX.

_____ . "The General Theory of Employment." QUARTERLY JOURNAL OF
ECONOMICS 51 (February 1937): 209-23. Reprinted in [2] [7].

This article is the best way to begin to understand his GENERAL THEORY. Keynes felt his main grounds of departure from the orthodox theory were: (1) the future is uncalculable, and (2) Say's law is, consequently, wrong. This article is Keynes's reply to the symposium on the GENERAL THEORY which appeared in the QUARTERLY JOURNAL OF ECONOMICS 51 (November 1936): 147-203.

_____. THE GENERAL THEORY OF EMPLOYMENT, INTEREST AND MONEY. Vol. 7 COLLECTED WRITINGS OF JOHN MAYNARD KEYNES, distributed by St. Martin's Press, N.Y. New York: Harcourt Brace, 1936. 415 p. Also paperbound.

The locus classicus of modern macro-monetary economics. This book caused a revolution in economic thought that is a continuing phenomenon.

_____. A TREATISE ON MONEY. 2 vols. New York: St. Martin's Press, 1930. 381 p. and 424 p.

Keynes said, "The relation between [the GENERAL THEORY and this book] is probably clearer to myself than it will be to others." Volume 1 is the pure theory of money while volume 2 is concerned with the application of the theory.

Keynes, Milo, ed. ESSAYS ON JOHN MAYNARD KEYNES. New York: Cambridge University Press, 1975. 324 p.

A nephew has attempted to recapture each of the interests of Lord Keynes through over twenty-five essays by his friends and associates. Seventeen illustrations are included.

Lekachman, Robert. THE AGE OF KEYNES. New York: Random House, 1966. 324 p. Also paperbound.

A historical narrative about Keynes's influence on the political economy of his era. According to Lekachman, the American Keynesians are the true decendants of Keynes.

Minsky, Hyman P. JOHN MAYNARD KEYNES. New York: Columbia University Press, 1975. 192 p. Also paperbound.

A current recapitulation of Keynes's greatness. A neo-Keynesian approach is taken.

Patinkin, Don. KEYNES' MONETARY THOUGHT: A STUDY OF ITS DEVELOPMENT. Durham, N.C.: Duke University Press, 1976. 162 p.

A central issue is the change that took place in Keynes's monetary thinking between the TREATISE ON MONEY (1930) and the GENERAL THEORY (1936). Axel Leijonhufvud, in contrast, places the break between the TRACT ON MONETARY REFORM (1923) and the TREATISE ON MONEY in his ON KEYNESIAN ECONOMICS

AND THE ECONOMICS OF KEYNES.

Robinson, E.A.G. "John Maynard Keynes 1883-1946." ECONOMIC JOURNAL 57 (March 1947): 1-68. Reprinted in [9].

> A lengthy obituary about Keynes by a former student, coeditor, and friend.

Robinson, Joan, ed. AFTER KEYNES. New York: Barnes & Noble, 1973. 202 p.

> These are papers presented to the economics section at the 1972 annual meeting of the British Association for the Advancement of Science. Joan Robinson's "What has become of the Keynesian Revolution?" and Elizabeth Johnson's "John Maynard Keynes-- Scientist or Politician," are the most worthwhile contributions. The Johnson article is also in JOURNAL OF POLITICAL ECON- OMY 82 (January/February 1974): 99-111.

Schumpeter, Joseph A. "John Maynard Keynes, 1883-1946." AMERICAN ECONOMIC REVIEW 36 (September 1946): 495-518. Reprinted in [7].

> A charming obituary; nevertheless, Schumpeter wonders why Keynes sought to show that unemployment was possible even with perfect competition and no rigidities.

INTERPRETATIONS OF THE *GENERAL THEORY* BEFORE 1956

Champernowne, D.G. "Unemployment, Basic and Monetary: the Classical Analysis and the Keynesian." REVIEW OF ECONOMIC STUDIES 3 (June 1936): 201-16. Reprinted in [9].

> Keynes says the wage bargain determines the money wage, not the real wage. Perhaps his view is convincing in the short run--temporary money illusion.

Dillard, Dudley. THE ECONOMICS OF JOHN MAYNARD KEYNES. Engle- wood Cliffs, N.J.: Prentice-Hall, 1948. 382 p.

> The first rigorous attempt by an American to explain the GENERAL THEORY in layman's language.

_____. "The Theory of a Monetary Economy." In POST KEYNESIAN ECO- NOMICS, edited by Kenneth K. Kurihara, pp. 3-30. New Brunswick, N.J.: Rutgers University Press, 1955.

> An early attempt to differentiate Keynes's own theory (primary emphasis on money) from Keynesian economics (real income and employment theory), which uses Keynes's tools. The primary tool, of course, is pump-priming fiscal policy.

Haberler, Gottfried. "The General Theory After Ten Years." In THE NEW ECONOMICS, edited by Seymour E. Harris, pp. 161-80. New York: Augustus M. Kelley, 1947. Reprinted in [9].

> The GENERAL THEORY caused no revolution. A milestone, perhaps, but no break in the development of economic theory.

_____. "Mr. Keynes' Theory of the 'Multiplier': A Methodological Criticism." ZEITSCHRIFT FUER NATIONALOKONOMIE 7 (August 1936): 299-305. Reprinted in [6].

> Keynes used two different concepts of the marginal propensity to consume, an empirical statement and a barren algebraic relation.

Hahn, L. Albert. THE ECONOMICS OF ILLUSION. New York: Squire Publishing, 1949. 270 p.

> This is a damning critique of Keynes. In Hahn's own words, "All that is wrong and exaggerated in Keynes I said much earlier and more clearly."

Hansen, Alvin H. "The General Theory." In THE NEW ECONOMICS, edited by Seymour E. Harris, pp. 133-44. New York: Augustus M. Kelley, 1947. Reprinted in [15].

> Keynes may in the end rival Adam Smith because of his influence on both theory and policy.

_____. A GUIDE TO KEYNES. New York: McGraw-Hill Book Co., 1953. 251 p. Also paperbound.

> The ultimate Keynesian exposition of the GENERAL THEORY. This book is perhaps the main reason why the GENERAL THEORY is not read and properly understood.

Harris, Seymour E. "Introduction: Keynes' Attack on Laissez Faire and Classical Economics and Wage Theory." In his THE NEW ECONOMICS, pp. 541-57. New York: Augustus M. Kelley, 1947. Reprinted in [20].

> Harris points out that Keynes was not in favor of rising wage rates; however, he did not believe unemployment was associated with excessive wage rates as did the classics. His emphasis was on effective demand in a free market economy.

_____, ed. THE NEW ECONOMICS: KEYNES' INFLUENCE ON THEORY AND PUBLIC POLICY. New York: Augustus M. Kelley, 1947. 717 p.

> A superb collection of articles analyzing the economics of Keynes. Almost all of the well-known economists are represented. Seymour E. Harris has done a masterful job of editing and introducing the various chapters. Some of his introductions to the writings of others have become classics in their own right.

Harrod, Roy F. "Mr. Keynes and Traditional Theory." ECONOMETRICA 5 (January 1937): 74-86. Reprinted in [7] [9].

> The GENERAL THEORY is not general; it is merely a shift on emphasis in traditional theory. It is a static readjustment of the system.

Hazlitt, Henry. THE FAILURE OF THE "NEW ECONOMICS." Princeton, N.J.: D. Van Nostrand, 1959. 470 p.

> This is the primary Keynes baiter in action. He analyzes the GENERAL THEORY sentence by sentence, pointing out, for example, the misquotation of Voltaire by Keynes. ("It was not Candide who was the incurable optimist, but Pongloss.")

_____, ed. THE CRITICS OF KEYNESIAN ECONOMICS. Princeton, N.J.: D. Van Nostrand, 1960. 427 p.

> An interesting collection of anti-Keynes essays. They range from the sublime (F. Modigliani and W.H. Hutt) to the ridiculous (G. Garrett).

Hicks, J[ohn].R. "Mr. Keynes and the 'Classics': A Suggested Interpretation." ECONOMETRICA 5 (April 1937): 147-59. Reprinted in [3] [10] [15] [16] [19] [20].

> In this article Hicks formulated the IS-LM macroeconomic model that is used in almost all intermediate theory textbooks. Hicks has said that Keynes gave his approval to this comparative static model ("Recollections and Documents." ECONOMICA 40 [February 1973]: 2-11). This article (the "Holy Writ" of the so-called "bastard Keynesians") and an extension, "The 'Classics' Again," are reprinted in Hicks, John R. CRITICAL ESSAYS IN MONETARY THEORY. New York: Oxford University Press, 1967.

Hutt, W.H. KEYNESIANISM: RETROSPECT AND PROSPECT. Chicago: Henry Regnery, 1963. 458 p.

> A reevaluation of Keynes by the first man to emphasize the theory of idle resources. Keynes's GENERAL THEORY is thought by Hutt to be only random thoughts. The "conservative" viewpoint (no government intervention in the marketplace) is prevalent.

_____. THE THEORY OF IDLE RESOURCES. London: Jonathan Cape, 1939. 193 p.

> Hutt stresses the idea that wasteful idleness (a term in place of unemployment to mean idleness of capital also) arises through the restriction of competition.

Klein, Lawrence R. "The Empirical Foundations of Keynesian Economics." In POST KEYNESIAN ECONOMICS, edited by Kenneth K. Kurihara, pp. 277-319. New Brunswick, N.J.: Rutgers University Press, 1955.

Econometric testing has shown Keynes's original intuition to stand up well before the facts of economic life. See also Klein, Lawrence R. "Theories of Effective Demand and Employment." JOURNAL OF POLITICAL ECONOMY 55 (April 1947): 108-32.

_____. THE KEYNESIAN REVOLUTION. 2d ed. New York: Macmillan, 1966. 304 p. Also paperbound.

Klein develops only the assumptions necessary to obtain the theoretical results usually claimed by Keynesians.

_____. "Theories of Effective Demand and Employment." JOURNAL OF POLITICAL ECONOMY 55 (April 1947): 108-31. Reprinted in [20].

He compares and contrasts three theories of employment: (1) classical, (2) Keynesian, and (3) Marxian, in terms of the stagnation thesis and the redistribution of income.

Kurihara, Kenneth K., ed. POST KEYNESIAN ECONOMICS. New Brunswick, N.J.: Rutgers University Press, 1954. 460 p.

A collection of original articles dedicated to the memory of John Maynard Keynes, each taking the GENERAL THEORY as a frame of reference. The articles are divided into three groups (1) "Monetary Theory and Policy," (2) "Economic Fluctuations and Growth," and (3) "Aggregative Economics and Testing." Articles by Martin Bronfenbrenner, Don Patinkin, L.R. Klein, and Franco Modigliani, among others, are of enduring value.

Lange, Oscar. PRICE FLEXIBILITY AND EMPLOYMENT. San Antonio, Tex.: Trinity University Press, 1944. 126 p.

The earliest book to set forth the neoclassical resurgence. Lange's book is built upon the then-recent works of Keynes, Hicks, and Samuelson.

_____. "The Rate of Interest and the Optimum Propensity to Consume." ECONOMICA 5 (February 1938): 12-32. Reprinted in [6].

Lange sets up an equation system of Keynes's GENERAL THEORY to handle a problem which has bothered the under-consumption theorists. If the interest-elasticity of the demand for liquidity is positive, the interest rate remaining constant, "the optimum propensity to consume is when the expenditure on consumption is such that a further increase does not any more increase the marginal efficiency of investment." If the interest-elasticity of the demand for liquidity is zero, any drop in the marginal propensity to consume will cause the rate of interest to fall and, consequently, stimulate investment.

Leontief, Wassily. "Postulates: Keynes' General Theory and the Classicists." In THE NEW ECONOMICS, edited by Seymour E. Harris, pp. 232-42. New York: Augustus M. Kelley, 1947. Reprinted in [20].

> Leontief feels that the supply of labor, the demand for money, and the distributive aspects of economic change are the most important differences between Keynes and the classics. Nevertheless, he believes that Keynes over emphasized the importance of the weak points in classical theory. "He seemed to press . . . for reconstruction of the whole foundation in order to mend a leaky roof."

Lerner, Abba P. "Mr. Keynes' General Theory of Employment, Interest and Money." INTERNATIONAL LABOUR REVIEW 34 (October 1936): 435-54. Reprinted in [7] [9].

> We can spend ourselves rich! Keynes takes the high road of reducing interest rates rather than the "devious, dark, difficult, and unreliable path" of reducing money wages.

_____. "Saving and Investment: Definitions, Assumptions, Objectives." QUARTERLY JOURNAL OF ECONOMICS 53 (August 1939): 611-19. Reprinted in [7].

> Five of the best known definitions of saving and investment are given: GENERAL THEORY, TREATISE ON MONEY, D.H. Robertson's, Swedish school, and R.G. Hawtrey's. See these other articles on the rate of interest by A.P. Lerner: "Alternative Formulations of the Theory of Interest." ECONOMIC JOURNAL 48 (June 1938): 211-30. Reprinted in [7]; and "Saving and Investment." QUARTERLY JOURNAL OF ECONOMICS 52 (February 1938): 297-309. Reprinted in [7].

Lutz, F[riedrich].A. "The Outcome of the Saving-Investment Discussion." QUARTERLY JOURNAL OF ECONOMICS 52 (August 1938): 588-614. Reprinted in [6].

> He discusses a number of definitions of saving and investment to consider their usefulness. Abba P. Lerner objects to Lutz's championing of Robertson's definitions over those of Keynes. He feels both sets of definitions are consistent. See "Saving and Investment: Definitions, Assumptions, Objectives." QUARTERLY JOURNAL OF ECONOMICS 53 (August 1939): 611-19. Reprinted in [7].

Machlup, Fritz. "Period Analysis and Multiplier Theory." QUARTERLY JOURNAL OF ECONOMICS 54 (November 1939): 1-27. Reprinted in [6].

> The multiplier operates over time, which means that uncertainty interferes. If the multiplier is to be of use in the real world, it must renounce an appearance of neatness and precision.

Marget, Arthur W. THE THEORY OF PRICES. 2 vols. New York: Augustus M. Kelley, 1939 and 1942. 649 p. and 827 p.

This is an attempt to integrate monetary theory with the general theory of value. These two volumes exhibit scholarship at its highest level. His criticism of Keynes's theory is the clearest of compliments. His criticism of Keynes's doctrinal history is made to show Keynes's misinterpretation of received doctrine.

Meade, James E. "A Simplified Model of Mr. Keynes' System." REVIEW OF ECONOMIC STUDIES 4 (February 1937): 98-107. Reprinted in [7].

An early model of the GENERAL THEORY in which the equilibrium and stability conditions are carefully specified.

Metzler, Lloyd A. "Keynes and the Theory of Business Cycles." In THE NEW ECONOMICS, edited by Seymour E. Harris, pp. 436-49. New York: Augustus M. Kelley, 1947.

As long as aggregate demand was always effective demand, Keynes has nothing to say about business cycles. Also see Metzler's article "Business Cycles and the Modern Theory of Employment." AMERI-CAN ECONOMIC REVIEW 36 (June 1946): 278-91.

Modigliani, Franco. "Liquidity Preference and the Theory of Interest and Money." ECONOMETRICA 12 (January 1944): 45-88. Reprinted in [11] [20].

The first complete and rigorous statement of comparative static macrotheory--both Keynesian and classical. An improved model was published by Modigliani in "The Monetary Mechanism and Its Interaction with Real Phenomena." REVIEW OF ECONOMICS AND STATISTICS 45, supplement (February 1963): 79-107.

Pigou, A.C. KEYNES'S "GENERAL THEORY": A RETROSPECTIVE VIEW. New York: St. Martin's Press, 1953. 76 p.

This short book of Pigou's is an attempt to clarify the Keynes and Keynesian debate and to provide a guide for additional reading. Each chapter (nineteen chapters) is only a few pages long. All in all, a complimentary view of Keynes's GENERAL THEORY.

_____. LAPSES FROM FULL EMPLOYMENT. London: Macmillan and Co., 1945. 73 p.

The argument is whether demand need be expanded (Beveridge policy) or stabilized (White Paper policy). Pigou is for stabilization but gives no hint as to how it will help unemployment. However, his thesis is that there is always a tendency towards full employment in a free market.

Polanyi, Michael. FULL EMPLOYMENT AND FREE TRADE. 2d ed. New York: Cambridge University Press, 1948. 171 p.

Keynes's doctrine is criticized by a world-renowned physical chemist turned social scientist. "In my opinion, few contributions from that period stand up as well in retrospect as Polanyi's book" (Axel Leijonhufvud).

Reddaway, W.B. "The General Theory of Employment, Interest, and Money." ECONOMIC RECORD 12 (June 1936): 28-36. Reprinted in [9].

A review of the GENERAL THEORY, in which Reddaway models it.

Robinson, Joan. INTRODUCTION TO THE THEORY OF EMPLOYMENT. 2d ed. New York: St. Martin's Press, 1969. 112 p.

A British Keynesian's account of the main principles of the GENERAL THEORY.

Samuelson, Paul A. "The General Theory." ECONOMETRICA 14 (July 1946): 187-200. Reprinted in [7] [9].

The GENERAL THEORY is an obscure book; it needs a key. The key is the denial of the implicit classical axiom that "motivated investment is indefinitely expandible or contractable."

_____. "The Simple Mathematics of Income Determination." In INCOME, EMPLOYMENT, AND PUBLIC POLICY, edited by Lloyd A. Metzler et al., pp. 133-55. New York: W.W. Norton, 1948. Reprinted in [8] [15].

A discussion of the "black art" of calculating different income multipliers. This is the graphical Keynesian cross (C+I=C+S) in mathematical terms.

Shackle, G.I.S. EXPECTATIONS, INVESTMENT, AND INCOME. 2d ed. New York: Oxford University Press, 1968. 166 p.

Shackle has written a critical examination of the GENERAL THEORY and Myrdal's MONETARY EQUILIBRIUM. The second edition includes a new essay of twenty-eight pages describing the intellectual circumstances which lead to writing the original text.

Smith, Warren L. "A Graphical Exposition of a Complete Keynesian System." SOUTHERN ECONOMIC JOURNAL 23 (October 1956): 115-25. Reprinted in [8] [15] [17].

The title serves as a complete annotation.

Streeten, Paul P. "Keynes and the Classical Tradition." In POST KEYNESIAN ECONOMICS, edited by Kenneth K. Kurihara, pp. 345-64. New Brunswick, N.J.: Rutgers University Press, 1955. Reprinted in [20].

An essay comparing Keynes's value premises with those of the British classical tradition.

Sweezy, Paul M. "John Maynard Keynes." SCIENCE AND SOCIETY 10 (Fall 1946): 399-405. Reprinted in [7] [9].

Keynes should be remembered for having shown that Say's Law is a fraud and a delusion--a negative rather than a positive contribution.

Timlin, M.F. KEYNESIAN ECONOMICS. Toronto: University of Toronto Press, 1942. 207 p.

Basically a reformulation and expansion of portions of Keynes's analysis, using the more recent works of Lange, Hicks, Lerner, Robertson, and Ohlin.

Viner, Jacob. "Mr. Keynes on the Causes of Unemployment." QUARTERLY JOURNAL OF ECONOMICS 51 (November 1936): 147-67. Reprinted in [9].

Although Keynes is a stylist of the first order, his book is hard to read, to master, or to appraise. His ideas, methods of manipulation, and language are all new. There is, however, ample reward for even partial mastery of the argument. Short-run analysis is necessary when dealing with unemployment.

Wright, David McCord. "Future of Keynesian Economics." AMERICAN ECONOMIC REVIEW 35 (June 1945): 284-307.

The challenge to the old orthodoxy was the lack of aggregate demand and the implications for intervention in the market system.

_____. THE KEYNESIAN SYSTEM. New York: Fordham University Press, 1962. 101 p.

Wright believes that the GENERAL THEORY can only be understood in a time perspective. Keynes has not adequately coped with the problems of today. But he is still a great man, "Keynes the man, as distinguished from Keynes the myth, would have recognized all these problems, and re-interpreted his system towards growth rather than simple spending."

Post-Keynes Analysis

EQUILIBRIUM THEORY: ORTHODOX CONSENSUS AND NEOCLASSICAL SYNTHESIS

Archibald, G.C., and Lipsey, R[ichard].G. "Monetary and Value Theory: A Critique of Lange and Patinkin." REVIEW OF ECONOMIC STUDIES 26 (October 1958): 1-22. Reprinted in [2] [19].

Patinkin's first edition of MONEY, INTEREST, AND PRICES did not include a long-run analysis. Archibald and Lipsey provide it.

A long-run analysis is included in Patinkin's second edition. This controversy over long-run analysis led to Baumol, W.J., et al. "A Symposium on Monetary Theory." REVIEW OF ECONOMIC STUDIES 28 (October 1960): 29-56. An article in the symposium by Clower, R.W., and Burstein, M.L. "On the Invariance of Demand for Cash and Other Assets," pp. 32-36, is reprinted in [2].

Arrow, Kenneth J. "Economic Equilibrium." In INTERNATIONAL ENCYCLOPEDIA OF THE SOCIAL SCIENCES, edited by David L. Sills, vol. 4, pp. 376-88. New York: Macmillan-Free Press, 1968.

A good historical development that leads right up to the frontier.

_____. "Toward a Theory of Price Adjustment." In THE ALLOCATION OF ECONOMIC RESOURCES, edited by Moses Abramovitz et al., pp. 41-51. Palo Alto, Calif.: Stanford University Press, 1959.

The question is asked, Who determines price under competitive conditions? The answer, No one. Price adjustment under perfect and imperfect competition is discussed. The implications for the speed of adjustment are also examined.

Arrow, Kenneth J., and Hahn, F[rank].H. GENERAL COMPETITIVE ANALYSIS. San Francisco: Holden-Day, 1971. 464 p.

A mathematical analysis of this area of economics. Chapters 12, 13, and 14 are mostly macroeconomic in nature.

Baird, C[harles].W. "Knut Wicksell on the Integration of Monetary and Value Theory." SWEDISH JOURNAL OF ECONOMICS 72 (June 1970): 101-10.

Wicksell was not guilty of the invalid dichotomy (i.e., divorcing real and monetary economic analysis when real balance variables appear in the equations of the real sector) and his exposition of the real balance effect is more forceful than Patinkin's.

Barro, Robert J. "A Theory of Monopolistic Price Adjustment." REVIEW OF ECONOMIC STUDIES 39 (January 1972): 17-26.

The results of K.J. Arrow ("Toward a Theory of Price Adjustment") are expanded beyond a competitive model.

Baumol, W[illiam].J., et al. "A Symposium on Monetary Theory." REVIEW OF ECONOMIC STUDIES 28 (October 1960): 29-56.

The participants were: W.J. Baumol, R.W. Clower and M.L. Burstein, F.H. Hahn, R.J. Ball and Ronald Bodkin, G.C. Archibald and R.C. Lipsey. A personal editorial note gave the reason why Don Patinkin did not answer these charges: "The Editors regret that it has not been possible to include a contribution from Professor Patinkin, owing to [an] inability to agree on a suitable length." The papers were

in response to Archibald and Lipsey's critique of Patinkin's first
edition of MONEY, INTEREST, AND PRICES.

Beckmann, Martin, and Ryder, Harl. "Simultaneous Price and Quantity Adjustment in a Single Market." ECONOMETRICA 37 (July 1969): 470-84.

> The Walrasian paradigm has been expanded to include the interac-
> tion of quantity and price adjustments in a single nonclearing
> market--a seminal paper.

Christ, Carl [F.]. "A Simple Macroeconomic Model with a Government Budget Restraint." JOURNAL OF POLITICAL ECONOMY 76 (January/February 1968):
53-67.

> When governments choose a mix of monetary and fiscal policies,
> they must take into account the government budget restraint. This
> restraint is somewhat flexible because the government can issue
> fiat money.

Clower, Robert W., and Burstein, M.L. "On the Invariance of Demand for
Money and Other Assets." REVIEW OF ECONOMIC STUDIES 28 (October
1960): 32-36. Reprinted in [2].

> Assuming the uniqueness of equilibrium states, invariance propositions
> hold not only for a bond-and-money economy but also for more
> general systems. Also, see Rakshit, M.K. "Invariance of the
> Demand for Cash and Other Assets: A Comment." OXFORD
> ECONOMIC PAPERS 16 (July 1964): 291-96; and Liviatan, N.
> "On the Long-Run Theory of Consumption and Real Balances."
> OXFORD ECONOMIC PAPERS 17 (July 1965): 205-18.

Clower, Robert W., and Leijonhufvud, Axel. "Say's Principle, What It Means
and Doesn't Mean: Part I." INTERMOUNTAIN ECONOMIC REVIEW 4 (Fall
1973): 1-16.

> The planned trades of individual transactors (and all transactors)
> in nominal terms must sum identically to zero. However, this says
> nothing at all about whether the excess demand of any commodity
> is zero. It is known, of course, that the sum of all excess demands
> must be zero if equilibrium is ever to be achieved.

Galloway, Lowell E., and Smith, Paul E. "Real Balances and the Permanent
Income Hypothesis." QUARTERLY JOURNAL OF ECONOMICS 75 (May 1961):
302-13.

> The real balance effect is given low marks as a substitute for fiscal
> and monetary policy.

Grossman, Herschel I. "The Nature of Quantities in Market Disequilibrium."
AMERICAN ECONOMIC REVIEW 64 (June 1974): 509-14.

Grossman criticizes the quantity adjustment mechanisms of Beckmann and Ryder and of Veendorp. Quantity is a multifaceted concept. Veendorp takes exception to this analysis in Veendorp, E.C.H. "The Nature of Quantities in Market Disequilibriums." Ibid., pp. 515-17.

Haberler, Gottfried. "The Pigou Effect Once More." JOURNAL OF POLITICAL ECONOMY 60 (June 1952): 240-46.

This is a good summary of articles by Hansen, Alvin H. "The Pigouian Effect." JOURNAL OF POLITICAL ECONOMY 59 (December 1951): 535-36; Metzler, Lloyd A. "Wealth, Saving, and the Rate of Interest." Ibid., 59 (April 1951): 93-116; and Patinkin, Don. "Price Flexibility and Full Employment." In READINGS IN MONETARY THEORY, edited by F.A. Lutz and L.W. Mints, pp. 252-83. Homewood, Ill.: Richard D. Irwin, 1951. Reprinted in [10] [13] [15] [16] [20].

Hahn, Frank H. "On Some Problems of Proving the Existence of an Equilibrium in a Monetary Economy." In THE THEORY OF INTEREST RATES, edited by F.H. Hahn and F.P.R. Brechling, pp. 126-35. London: Macmillan and Co., 1965. Reprinted in [2].

In a monetary economy where contracts are written in money terms and recontracting is not possible, an equilibrium solution may not exist. The real balance effect does not prove existence.

_____. ON THE NOTION OF EQUILIBRIUM IN ECONOMICS: AN INAUGURAL LECTURE. New York: Cambridge University Press, 1973. 44 p. Paperbound.

In his inaugural lecture as a Cambridge professor, Hahn discusses the importance of equilibrium in economics and at the same time castigates his colleague, N. Kaldor ("The Irrelevance of Equilibrium Economics." ECONOMIC JOURNAL 82 [December 1972]: 1237-55) for his view of equilibrium economics as "barren and irrelevant." An essay well worth reading, especially for the non-mathematician.

_____. "The Rate of Interest and General Equilibrium Analysis." ECONOMIC JOURNAL 65 (March 1955): 52-66.

Hahn shows that money is not neutral in Franco Modigliani's 1944 classic article ("Liquidity Preference and the Theory of Interest and Money." ECONOMETRICA 12 [January 1944]: 45-88). He also demonstrates that the only difference between the liquidity preference and loanable funds theories is the period chosen for consideration.

Hansen, Alvin H. "Keynes After Thirty Years." WELTWIRTSCHAFTLICHES ARCHIV 97 (December 1966): 213-312. Reprinted in [8].

The head of the American Keynesians discusses Keynes.

Hansen, Bent. A SURVEY OF GENERAL EQUILIBRIUM SYSTEMS. New York: McGraw-Hill Book Co., 1970. 254 p.

Currently the best theoretical survey of the most important general equilibrium systems encountered in contemporary economic literature.

Hicks, J[ohn].R. "Recollections and Documents." ECONOMICA 40 (February 1973): 2-11.

Sir John recalls the era between the TREATISE ON MONEY and the GENERAL THEORY in terms of his own writings. In his eyes the TREATISE is the great book.

_____. VALUE AND CAPITAL: AN INQUIRY INTO SOME FUNDAMENTAL PRINCIPLES OF ECONOMIC THEORY. 2d ed. Oxford University Press, 1946. 340 p.

A classic in which Keynes's GENERAL THEORY is converted into neo-Walrasian theory.

Hutt, W.H. A REHABILITATION OF SAY'S LAW. Athens: Ohio University Press, 1974. 150 p.

Insufficient supply is the cause of depression and unemployment. Supply is insufficient because potential inputs or outputs are being priced above market-clearing values in noncompeting sectors of the economy. The contributions of A. Leijonhufvud, R. Clower, L. Yeager, and T. Sowell are examined and criticized.

Hynes, J. Allan. "On the Theory of Real Balances." JOURNAL OF MONEY, CREDIT AND BANKING 6 (February 1974): 65-83.

A good survey article of the liquidity trap, as well as the real balance effect. Assets do have substitutes in the real world.

Jaffe, William. "Walras' Theory of Tatonnement: A Critique of Recent Interpretations." JOURNAL OF POLITICAL ECONOMY 75 (February 1967): 1-19.

Tatonnement (reaching equilibrium price through an auctioneer calling out relevant prices) has come a long way. So far in fact that it hardly resembles what Walras had in mind.

Johnson, Harry G. "The GENERAL THEORY After Twenty-five Years." AMERICAN ECONOMIC REVIEW 51 (May 1961): 1-17.

This is a review which was more a survey than a critique. This understanding of what the GENERAL THEORY had to say was not shaken completely until the publication of Leijonhufvud, Axel. ON KEYNESIAN ECONOMICS AND THE ECONOMICS OF KEYNES.

New York: Oxford University Press, 1968.

_____. "Monetary Theory and Keynesian Economics." PAKISTAN ECONOMIC JOURNAL 8 (June 1958): 56-70. Reprinted in [2].

A good summary of Keynesian theory using the IS-LM model with a factor market attached. Keynes's theory is looked on as a great advance over the quantity theory, especially with regard to depression conditions. The IS-LM model is thought to play down the influence of monetary conditions, contrary to Keynes.

Kuenne, R.E. THE THEORY OF GENERAL ECONOMIC EQUILIBRIUM. Princeton, N.J.: Princeton University Press, 1963. 605 p.

Review of general equilibrium theory from Walras to Arrow-Debreu.

Kurihara, Kenneth K. "Contributions and Limitations of Keynesian Theory." ECONOMIC STUDIES QUARTERLY 20 (April 1969): 34-49. Reprinted in [13].

The contributions and limitations are briefly described. A good Keynesian summary.

Lange, Oscar. "Say's Law: A Restatement and Criticism." In STUDIES IN MATHEMATICAL ECONOMICS AND ECONOMETRICS, edited by Oscar Lange et al., pp. 49-68. Chicago: Chicago University Press, 1942.

This is where the confusion over Walras's law and Say's law began. This was supposed to be an article of clarification.

Leijonhufvud, Axel. "Notes on the Theory of Markets." INTERMOUNTAIN ECONOMIC REVIEW 1 (Fall 1970): 1-13.

Information flows in the market are examined using feedback control systems. A recent article by Rock, James M., et al. "What Good Are Supply Functions in Classical Economics." INTERMOUNTAIN ECONOMIC REVIEW 5 (Spring 1974): 85-91, extends and clarifies the exposition.

Lekachman, Robert. THE AGE OF KEYNES. New York: Random House, 1966. 324 p. Also paperbound.

A historical narrative about Keynes's influence on the political economy of his era. The explanation of the GENERAL THEORY is pure Keynesianism.

_____, ed. KEYNES' GENERAL THEORY: REPORTS OF THREE DECADES. New York: St. Martin's Press, 1964. 359 p. Also paperbound.

Nine distinguished economists have each written two essays about John M. Keynes and his GENERAL THEORY: E.A.G. Robinson, W.B. Reddaway, R.F. Harrod, D.G. Champernowne, Abba P. Lerner,

Jacob Viner, Gottfried Haberler, Paul M. Sweezy, and Paul A. Samuelson. Six wrote their first essay within one or two years of the GENERAL THEORY's publication; three wrote ten years later at Keynes's death; and they all wrote again during 1962-63 for this volume.

Lerner, Abba P. ECONOMICS OF EMPLOYMENT. New York: McGraw-Hill Book Co., 1951. 413 p. Also paperbound.

A somewhat different presentation of the Keynes-classics synthesis utilizing Lerner's theories of functional finance and burden of the debt.

Liviatan, Nissan. "On the Long-Run Theory of Consumption and Real Balances." OXFORD ECONOMIC PAPERS 17 (July 1965): 205-18.

The "invariance principle" of Archibald and Lipsey is not a useful economic concept when applied to more complex models.

Lloyd, Cliff [L.]. "The Real Balance Effect: Sine Qua What? OXFORD ECONOMIC PAPERS 14 (October 1962): 267-74.

The real balance effect is the sine qua non of the classical quantity theory of money but not of monetary theory in general.

_____. "The Real Balance Effect and the Slutsky Equation." JOURNAL OF POLITICAL ECONOMY 72 (June 1964): 295-99.

The invariance principle of Archibald and Lipsey is shown to be valid and in full equilibrium, the real balance effect does not vanish.

_____. "Two Classical Monetary Models." In VALUE, CAPITAL AND GROWTH, edited by J.N. Wolfe, pp. 305-17. Chicago: Aldine Publishing Co., 1968.

The empirical implications of Clower's demand for money model are spelled out. Clower's constraint model ("Permanent Income and Transitory Balances: Hahn's Paradox." OXFORD ECONOMIC PAPERS 15 [July 1963]: 177-90) is shown to be rich in implications.

Marty, Alvin L. "The Real Balance Effect: An Exercise in Capital Theory." CANADIAN JOURNAL OF ECONOMICS AND POLITICAL SCIENCE 30 (August 1964): 360-67.

The desired stock of balances and flow of commodities should be deduced from initial assumptions and not assumed.

Mayer, Thomas. "The Empirical Significance of the Real Balance Effect." QUARTERLY JOURNAL OF ECONOMICS 73 (May 1959): 275-91.

The Keynes and Pigou effects are joined by Mayer to form the real balance effect. The empirical evidence is not strong. The real balance effect is only of theoretical importance.

Meinich, Per. "Money Illusion and the Real Balance Effect." STATSOKOVO-MISK TIDDSKRIFT 78 (March 1964): 8-33.

This article critically analyzes the Patinkin and Lloyd models with regard to their rationality, and the effect of money illusion on the substitution, income, and real balance effects.

Metzler, Lloyd A. "Three Lags in the Circular Flow of Income." In INCOME, EMPLOYMENT AND PUBLIC POLICY, edited by Lloyd A. Metzler et al., pp. 11-32. New York: W.W. Norton, 1948.

This is an early critique of static macro-monetary theory. The three lags are: (1) consumers' expenditures lag behind income payments, (2) production lags behind sales, and (3) dividends lag behind profits. The household-expenditure lag is short relative to the lag in output. An empirical foundation is provided for the theory of inventory and, consequently, business cycles.

_____. "Wealth, Saving and the Rate of Interest." JOURNAL OF POLITICAL ECONOMY 59 (April 1951): 93-116. Reprinted in [19] [20].

The real balance effect has kept money neutral but the interest rate implicit in neoclassical macroeconomics is at least partly determined by monetary forces. A classic article on the wealth effect, as it is influenced by changes in the interest rate.

Modigliani, Franco. "Liquidity Preference and the Theory of Interest and Money." ECONOMETRICA 12 (January 1944): 45-88. Reprinted in [11] [20].

The first complete and rigorous statement of comparative static macrotheory--both Keynesian and classical. An improved model was published by Modigliani in the next article cited below.

_____. "The Monetary Mechanism and Its Interaction with Real Phenomena." REVIEW OF ECONOMICS AND STATISTICS 45, supplement (February 1963): 79-107.

This is Modigliani's mid-1950 model of the macroeconomy. He compares and contrasts it with his seminal 1944 article (above). The argument is difficult to follow because the published version of the mid-1950 model is less than one-third of the original contribution.

Mundell, Robert A. "An Exposition of Some Subleties in the Keynesian System." WELTWIRSCHAFTLICHES ARCHIV 93 (December 1964): 301-13. Reprinted in [8] [16].

The supply sector is examined in the interest rate-real wage plane. An extention of the IS-LM model, where prices and wages are allowed to be flexible or rigid.

_____. "A Fallacy in the Interpretation of Macroeconomic Equilibrium." JOURNAL OF POLITICAL ECONOMY 73 (February 1965): 61-66. Reprinted in [8] [10].

The flows that change stocks may not be infinitesimally small with regard to the size of the stock; consequently, they should not be disregarded. However, these flows are not dimensionally equivalent to the rate of interest as Mundell claims.

Patinkin, Don. "Keynesian Economics and the Quantity Theory." In POST KEYNESIAN ECONOMICS, edited by Kenneth K. Kurihara, pp. 123-52. New Brunswick, N.J.: Rutgers University Press, 1955.

The neutrality of changes in money stock is dependent on the absence of money illusion. An equilibrium model is assumed.

_____. MONEY, INTEREST, AND PRICES. 2d ed. New York: Harper & Row Publishers, 1965. 733 p.

The definitive statement that, as a comparative static equilibrium model, neoclassical theory is more general than the GENERAL THEORY. The real balance effect is the linchpin that preserves neutrality and discards the invalid dichotomy (i.e., divorcing real and monetary economic analysis when real balance variables appear in the equations of the real sector).

This book is the culmination of a series of articles by Patinkin all cited therein. The first and most important is "Price Flexibility and Full Employment." In READINGS IN MONETARY THEORY, edited by F.A. Lutz and L.W. Mints, pp. 252-83. Homewood, Ill.: Richard D. Irwin, 1951. Reprinted in [10] [13] [15] [16] [20].

Pigou, A.C. "The Classical Stationary State." ECONOMIC JOURNAL 53 (December 1943): 343-51. Reprinted in [20].

A classical stationary state (consumption equals income) will always prevail if flexible wages and prices are assumed, money illusion is disallowed, and real balance effects are positive.

_____. "Economic Progress in a Stable Environment." ECONOMICA 14 (August 1947): 180-88. Reprinted in [11].

An economy in market equilibrium is moved along by saving, which is always equal to investment. The problem is this: Will a final (thorough-going) equilibrium be established before the rate of interest falls to zero? It all depends on the assumptions you make.

Ritter, Lawrence S. "The Role of Money in Keynesian Theory." In BANKING AND MONETARY STUDIES, edited by Deane Carson, pp. 134-50. Homewood, Ill.: Richard D. Irwin, 1963. Reprinted in [10] [14] [15] [16].

Does money matter in the Keynesian system? The central question is velocity. If money is to be important, velocity must either remain constant or move with money supply. Quantity theorists believe this, while the Radcliffe Report finds velocity neither to be consistent nor to move with money supply. Keynesian theory is in between.

Silber, William L. "Fiscal Policies in IS-LM Analysis: A Correction." JOURNAL OF MONEY, CREDIT AND BANKING 2 (November 1970): 461-72.

Traditional IS-LM analysis often does not take the monetary effects of debt financing into account. Even if this is done, bond-finance and new money-finance cases are not to be treated symmetrically.

Somers, Harold M. "A Theory of Income Determination." JOURNAL OF POLITICAL ECONOMY 58 (December 1950): 523-41. Reprinted in [13].

This is an integration of the Keynesian, Robertsonian, and Swedish school theories of income determination.

Sowell, Thomas. SAY'S LAW. Princeton, N.J.: Princeton University Press, 1972. 247 p.

With regard to the controversies over Say's Law, this is the place to start. An annotated bibliography is included.

Stein, Jerome L. "A Method of Identifying Disturbances which Produce Changes in Money National Income." JOURNAL OF POLITICAL ECONOMY 68 (February 1960): 1-16. Reprinted in [16].

An extension of the IS-LM model. Exogenous disturbances are classified as being either real, monetary, or liquidity.

Valavanis, Stefan. "A Denial of Patinkin's Contradiction." KYKLOS 8, no. 4 (1955): 351-68.

Who is guilty of the invalid dichotomy? Valavanis shows that semantics are always of importance. A very useful chronological bibliography is included.

Weintraub, Sidney. A GENERAL THEORY OF THE PRICE LEVEL, OUTPUT, INCOME DISTRIBUTION AND ECONOMIC GROWTH. Philadelphia: Chilton Books, 1959. 123 p.

This is an attempt to generalize the GENERAL THEORY. Weintraub's starting point is the "magic constant": the observed stability of the ratio of the value of social product or output or income to the wage bill.

Witte, James G., Jr. "Walras' Law and the Patinkin Paradox: A Qualitative Calculus for Macroeconomics." JOURNAL OF POLITICAL ECONOMY 74 (February 1966): 72-76.

> A clear understanding of Walras's law reduces significantly the ambiguity with regard to a change in the equilibrium in Patinkin's model values of interest rate and price level.

DISEQUILIBRIUM THEORY

Alchian, Armen A. "Information Costs, Pricing, and Resource Unemployment." WESTERN ECONOMIC JOURNAL 7 (June 1969): 109-28.

> Collecting information about potential exchange opportunities is costly. Economic theory can be consistent and also relevant to problems of unemployment and price stability, if information costs are taken into account.

Arrow, Kenneth J. "Limited Knowledge and Economic Analysis." AMERICAN ECONOMIC REVIEW 64 (March 1974): 1-10.

> Until the economics of uncertainty is better understood, the uncertainties about economics will remain. This is also the theme of his Nobel lecture which is reprinted in "General Economic Equilibrium: Purpose, Analytic Techniques, Collective Choice." AMERICAN ECONOMIC REVIEW 64 (June 1974): 253-72.

Barro, R[obert].J., and Grossman, H.I. "A General Disequilibrium Model of Income and Employment." AMERICAN ECONOMIC REVIEW 64 (June 1974): 82-93.

> This is an attempt to do disequilibrium analysis in a comparative static framework by operating off the supply and demand curves. Work by Clower and Patinkin is joined to formulate a model of an economy experiencing excessive aggregate demand. See also Patinkin, Don. MONEY, INTEREST, AND PRICES. 2d ed. New York: Harper & Row Publishers, 1965, chapter 13; and Clower, Robert. "The Keynesian Counter-Revolution: A Theoretical Appraisal." In THE THEORY OF INTEREST RATES, edited by F.H. Hahn and F.P.R. Brechling, pp. 103-25. New York: St. Martin's Press, 1966. Reprinted in [2].

Benassy, Jean-Pascal. "Disequilibrium Exchange in Barter and Monetary Economies." ECONOMIC INQUIRY 13 (June 1975): 131-56.

> Ostroy's model has been extended to compare the relative performances of barter and monetary arrangements at fixed disequilibrium prices.

Benavie, Arthur. "The Dual Decision Process in Disequilibrium." ATLANTIC ECONOMIC JOURNAL 2 (November 1974): 48-57.

This is a critical review of the dual-decision literature. A number of important references are included.

Boulding, K[enneth E.]. "The Economics of Knowledge and the Knowledge of Economics." AMERICAN ECONOMIC REVIEW 56 (May 1966): 1-13.

Knowledge is not, necessarily, truth. There is great danger in the rationalization of decision-making processes. A powerful critique of current (1966) economics and the importance of correct information.

Burstein, M.L. "Some More Keynesian Economics." ECONOMIC INQUIRY 13 (March 1975): 39-54.

The importance of the GENERAL THEORY lies in the fact that it can be interpreted in so many ways.

Clower, Robert W. "The Keynesian Counter-Revolution: A Theoretical Appraisal." In THE THEORY OF INTEREST RATES, edited by F.H. Hahn and F.P.R. Brechling, pp. 103-25. London: Macmillan and Co., 1965. Reprinted in [2].

The dual decision hypothesis is formulated herein; only effective demand (motivational demand backed up by purchasing power) influences employment decisions.

_____. "A Reconsideration of the Microfoundations of Monetary Theory." WESTERN ECONOMIC JOURNAL 6 (December 1967): 1-8. Reprinted in [2].

"Money buys goods and goods buy money; but goods do not buy goods." Clower's aphorism points out the uniqueness of money as the sole medium of exchange in a monetary economy. In "Comment." WESTERN ECONOMIC JOURNAL 10 (September 1971): 304-5, Clower demonstrates the differences between a one constraint barter economy and a two constraint monetary economy in graphical terms.

_____. "Reflections on the Keynesian Perplex." ZEITSCHRIFT FUER NATIONALOKONOMIE 35 (1975): 1-24.

"It would be wrong to regard established microtheory as a suitable foundation for macrotheory, for the central if not sole object of macrotheory is to enhance our understanding of short-run disequilibrium adjustment processes." Sir John Hicks gets his due. A bibliography of over seventy-five items is included.

Clower, Robert W., and Leijonhufvud, Axel. "Say's Principle, What It Means and Doesn't Mean: Part I." INTERMOUNTAIN ECONOMIC REVIEW 4 (Fall 1973): 1-16.

The planned trades of individual transactors (and all transactors) in nominal terms must sum identically to zero. However, this says nothing at all about whether the excess demand of any commodity is zero. It is known, of course, that the sum of all excess demands must be zero if equilibrium is ever to be achieved.

Coddington, Alan. "What Did Keynes Really Mean?" CHALLENGE: THE MAGAZINE OF ECONOMIC AFFAIRS 16 (November/December 1974): 13-19.

"In its brazen pursuit of paradox and perverse logic, the book [GENERAL THEORY] has far more in common with CATCH-22 than with THE WEALTH OF NATIONS."

Davidson, Paul. "A Keynesian View of Patinkin's Theory of Employment." ECONOMIC JOURNAL 77 (September 1967): 559-78.

This is a comparison of Patinkin's model with that of Davidson and other British Keynesian writers. The basic difference has to do with the formulation of the aggregate supply and demand for labor and, consequently, the aggregate output supply function.

_____. MONEY AND THE REAL WORLD. New York: John Wiley & Sons, 1972. 384 p.

This book is a critique of the GENERAL THEORY along British Keynesian lines. Keynes's essential properties of money are made the keystone of the analysis, especially the Finance Motive that Davidson has elucidated elsewhere.

Feyerabend, Paul. AGAINST METHOD. Atlantic Highlands, N.J.: Humanities Press, 1975. 339 p.

Feyerabend argues that Karl Popper, Thomas Kuhn, and Imre Lakatos are wrong: "The only principle of [scientific inquire] which does not inhibit progress is anything goes." Another interesting book in the general area of the theory of knowledge is: Hollis, Martin and Nell, Edward. RATIONAL ECONOMIC MAN: A PHILO-SOPHICAL CRITIQUE OF NEO-CLASSICAL ECONOMICS. New York: Cambridge University Press, 1975. 279 p.

Frisch, Ragnar. "On the Notion of Equilibrium and Disequilibrium." REVIEW OF ECONOMIC STUDIES 3 (1935/36): 100-106.

This short article arose out of a discussion of Wicksell's "natural" (or equilibrium) interest rate as opposed to a market rate.

Hayek, Friedrich A. "Price Expectations, Monetary Disturbances and Maladjustments." NATIONALOKONOMISK TIDSCHRIFT 73, no. 3 (1935): 171-91. Reprinted in [6].

The main difficulty of equilibrium theory is its complete abstraction from time.

Hines, A.G. ON THE REAPPRAISAL OF KEYNESIAN ECONOMICS. New York: Humanities Press, 1971. 68 p. Paperbound.

> An extension of the work of Clower and Leijonhufvud to determine Keynes's real contribution. The fifth and final section on research problems which are suggested by the reappraisal should raise some eyebrows and generate some ideas.

Hirshleifer, Jack. "Where Are We in the Theory of Information?" AMERICAN ECONOMIC REVIEW 83 (May 1973): 31-39.

> Only the problems of the production, dissemination, and manipulation of information in a market context are discussed. Information theory is an outgrowth of the economic theory of uncertainty. A good bibliography is included.

Howitt, P.W. "Stability and the Quantity Theory." JOURNAL OF POLITICAL ECONOMY 82 (January/February 1974): 133-51.

> In this model recontracting is not utilized. Nevertheless, the stability of the model is demonstrated even though transactions take place during the period of price adjustment.

Kaldor, Nicholas. "The Irrelevance of Equilibrium Economics." ECONOMIC JOURNAL 82 (December 1972): 1237-55.

> Arrow-Debreu-Walrasian equilibrium economics is berated because it does not handle effective demand along with increasing returns and imperfect competition. Kaldor's statements are somewhat unjust. Should be read in conjunction with Hahn, F.H. ON THE NOTION OF EQUILIBRIUM IN ECONOMICS. Cambridge: At the University Press, 1973. 44 p.

Kalecki, Michal. "The Principle of Increased Risk." ECONOMICA 4 (November 1937): 440-47.

> An entrepreneur's rate of investment decisions is shown to be a function of his capital accumulation and the rate of change of net marginal productivity.

Kornai, Janos. ANTI-EQUILIBRIUM. New York: American Elsevier Publishing Co., 1971. 422 p. Also paperbound.

> This is an in-depth critique of the simultaneous equation model as a model of the economic system. This is an exciting book that points the way to more interesting economic theories but does little to push forward the frontier. As Kornai says, "Time is ripe for a synthesis of economic systems theory."

Kregel, J.A. THE RECONSTRUCTION OF POLITICAL ECONOMY: AN INTRODUCTION TO POST-KEYNESIAN ECONOMICS. Foreword by Joan

Robinson. New York: John Wiley & Sons, 1973. 236 p.

The British Keynesian approach to problems of growth and distribution is summarized. Those Walrasian neoclassicals who realize that their theory is unrealistic (Debreu, Arrow, and Hahn) are playing a "harmless, though expensive, intellectual game." This book is aimed at neoclassicals who think their theory is representative of the real world.

The same approach is followed in a survey article Kregel wrote with A.S. Eishner: "An Essay on Post-Keynesian Theory: A New Paradigm in Economics." JOURNAL OF ECONOMIC LITERATURE 13 (December 1975): 1293-314.

Kuhn, Thomas. THE STRUCTURE OF SCIENTIFIC REVOLUTIONS. 2d ed., enl. INTERNATIONAL ENCYCLOPEDIA OF UNIFIED SCIENCE, vol. 2, no. 2. Chicago: University of Chicago Press, 1970. 222 p. Also paperbound.

Scientific progress is made through radical changes in theory, not by a continuous stockpiling of facts and techniques. Can this viewpoint be applied to social sciences--especially economics? It has been; how well is still being questioned. If no paradigm is ever completely correct, revolutions are perhaps necessary to bring in the new ideas.

Lachmann, L.M. MACRO-ECONOMIC THINKING AND THE MARKET ECONOMY: AN ESSAY ON THE NEGLECT OF THE MICRO-FOUNDATIONS AND ITS CONSEQUENCES. Hobart Paper 56. London: Institute of Economic Affairs, 1973. 56 p. Paperbound.

Another call for macroeconomists to look more closely to their microeconomic foundations. The stress is on allocation theories within the context of the Cambridge controversy.

Lakatos, Imre. "Proofs and Refutations (I), (II), (III), and (IV)." BRITISH JOURNAL FOR THE PHILOSOPHY OF SCIENCE 14 (May, August, November, 1963, February 1964): 1-25, 120-39, 221-45, 296-342.

The problem of the relationship between polyhedra and polygons is used to attack the dogmatic position that by the power of our human intellect and/or senses truth can be attained and known that it is attained. See also, his "Falsification and the Methodology of Scientific Research Programmes." In CRITICISM AND THE GROWTH OF KNOWLEDGE, edited by Imre Lakatos and Alan Musgrave, pp. 91-196. New York: Cambridge University Press, 1970, and the preface to this volume.

The economic applications and a good bibliography are given in Latsis, Spiro J. "Situational Determination in Economics." BRITISH JOURNAL FOR THE PHILOSOPHY OF SCIENCE 23 (August 1972): 207-45.

Leijonhufvud, Axel. "Effective Demand Failures." SWEDISH ECONOMIC JOURNAL 75 (February 1973): 27-48.

Is the market system self-regulating or not? Effective demand failures can destroy the self-regulating capacity of the market system if buffer stocks (liquid assets, especially money) have been depleted. Expectations of the future are exceedingly important, especially because they are constantly being revised.

———. KEYNES AND THE CLASSICS: TWO LECTURES. New York: Transatlantic Arts, 1969. 46 p. Paperbound.

A useful book to start with for those who find his ON KEYNESIAN ECONOMICS AND THE ECONOMICS OF KEYNES too prolix.

———. "Keynes and the Keynesians: A Suggested Interpretation." AMERICAN ECONOMIC REVIEW 57 (May 1967): 401-10.

A suggested interpretation of Keynes's thought based on Walrasian price theory. He castigates the static IS-LM model as a completely inadequate representation of Keynes's macroeconomy.

———. ON KEYNESIAN ECONOMICS AND THE ECONOMICS OF KEYNES. New York: Oxford University Press, 1968. 445 p.

It attempts to show how the Keynesians have misinterpreted the GENERAL THEORY--certain to be a classic. The analysis has been criticized because Keynes is interpreted as a Walrasian, rather than as a Marshallian, price theorist.

Lerner, Abba P. "From 'The Treatise on Money' to 'The General Theory'." JOURNAL OF ECONOMIC LITERATURE 12 (March 1974): 38-42.

Another elder statesman gives his opinion on the development of Keynes's thought from the TREATISE to the GENERAL THEORY. He feels that most of the confusion has arisen out of ambiguities in the concept of "saving." His interpretation is at some odds with those of Shackle, Leijonhufvud, and Davidson.

Ostroy, Joseph M. "The Informational Efficiency of Monetary Exchange." AMERICAN ECONOMIC REVIEW 63 (September 1973): 597-610.

How long does it take for an economy to go from a state in which the sum of individual excess demands is zero to a state in which all individual excess demands are zero for each commodity? The comparison is between barter and monetary economics.

Richardson, G.B. "Equilibrium, Expectations and Information." ECONOMIC JOURNAL 69 (June 1959): 223-37.

The conditions necessary for an entrepreneur to have adequate

information are "incompatible with perfect competition." Consequently, a hypothetical perfectly competitive economy has no re-
quirement to gravitate towards general equilibrium or, once at
equilibrium, to remain at rest.

Robinson, Joan. ECONOMIC HERESIES. New York: Basic Books, 1971.
170 p. Also paperbound.

The leader of the British Keynesians railing at the American Keynesians (whom she calls "bastard Keynesians") and others who cling
to false ideas.

Roll, Eric. THE WORLD AFTER KEYNES: AN EXAMINATION OF THE ECO-
NOMIC ORDER. New York: Frederick A. Praeger, 1968. 206 p.

The influences of Keynes's ideas since World War II as seen by a
Britisher.

Shackle, G.L.S. "Economic Expectations." In INTERNATIONAL ENCYCLO-
PEDIA OF THE SOCIAL SCIENCES, edited by D.L. Sills, vol. 4, pp. 389-95.
New York: Macmillan-Free Press, 1968.

The master lists and discusses the determinants of expectations and
the role they play in the human and social world.

_____. EPISTEMICS AND ECONOMICS: A CRITIQUE OF ECONOMIC
DOCTRINES. New York: Cambridge University Press, 1972. 501 p.

Epistemics is defined by Shackle as the theory of thoughts. Economics is, consequently, an application of epistemics. There must
be some way of making time and reason compatible; expectations
are the halfway house. This is a very lucid but cynical book,
in the sense that economics is not as useful or hopeful as one
might wish. This book will be a classic.

_____. "Keynes and Today's Establishment in Economic Theory: A View."
JOURNAL OF ECONOMIC LITERATURE 11 (June 1973): 516-19.

This is Shackle's critique of Axel Leijonhufvud's ON KEYNESIAN
ECONOMICS AND THE ECONOMICS OF KEYNES. His differences with Leijonhufvud's view are not as great as he makes out.

_____. KEYNESIAN KALEIDICS. Chicago: Aldine Publishing Co., 1974.
92 p.

Shackle feels Keynes wrote three versions of his theory of money
and employment: (1) A TREATISE ON MONEY, (2) THE GENERAL
THEORY, and (3) his 1937 QUARTERLY JOURNAL OF ECONOMICS
article. As Keynes progressed his answers were clearer and he was
better able to explain why "the ideas which are here expressed are
extremely simple."

Starr, Ross M. "Exchange in Barter and Monetary Economics." QUARTERLY JOURNAL OF ECONOMICS 86 (May 1972): 290-302.

> As long as a monetary economy is costless, it can do everything better, or as well as, a barter economy. A selected number of sources is included.

Stewart, Michael. KEYNES AND AFTER. 2d ed. Gloucester, Mass.: Peter Smith. Hardbound; Baltimore: Penguin Books, 1972. 317 p. Paperbound.

> A competent and easy-to-read British Keynesian view of macro-monetary economics since 1936.

Tucker, Donald. "Macroeconomic Models and the Demand for Money under Market Disequilibrium." JOURNAL OF MONEY, CREDIT AND BANKING 3 (February 1971): 57-83.

> This author devotes his primary attention to a world where market disequilibrium prevails. He looks at estimation problems and the demand for money in this context. Also see his article, "Credit Rationing, Interest Rate Lags, and Monetary Policy Speed." QUARTERLY JOURNAL OF ECONOMICS 82 (February 1968): 54-84.

Post-Keynes Aggregation

INCOME, CONSUMPTION, AND SAVING

Ando, Albert, and Modigliani, Franco. "The 'Life Cycle' Hypothesis of Saving: Aggregate Implications and Tests." AMERICAN ECONOMIC REVIEW 53 (March 1963): 55-84. Reprinted in [5].

> This is the first consumption theory that uses a dynamic hypothesis explicitly stated as specifications of the consumer's utility function. Otherwise, it is similar to the earlier Duesenberry-Modigliani hypothesis. A good bibliography is included.

Bailey, M[artin].J. "Saving and the Rate of Interest." JOURNAL OF POLITICAL ECONOMY 65 (August 1957): 279-305.

> The influence of the rate of interest on saving has been an open question. The question is fully explored.

Brady, Dorothy S., and Friedman, Rose D. "Saving and the Income Distribution." In STUDIES IN INCOME AND WEALTH, edited by National Bureau of Economic Research, vol. 10, pp. 247-65. New York: 1947.

> They suggest that an individual's consumption behavior is a function of the ratio of current income to average community income--"keeping up with the Joneses."

Davis, T.E. "The Consumption Function as a Tool for Prediction." REVIEW OF ECONOMICS AND STATISTICS 34 (August 1952): 270-77.

He substitutes previous-peak consumption for previous-peak income in Duesenberry's relative income hypothesis.

Duesenberry, James S. "Income-Consumption Relations and Their Implications." In INCOME, EMPLOYMENT AND PUBLIC POLICY, edited by Lloyd A. Metzler et al., pp. 54-81. New York: W.W. Norton, 1948. Reprinted in [8] [10] [15] [16] [20].

Part of this paper was presented at the January 1949 meeting of the Econometric Society where Franco Modigliani presented a paper containing an almost identical income-consumption relation. This is the relative income hypothesis.

_____. INCOME, SAVING AND THE THEORY OF CONSUMER BEHAVIOR. Cambridge, Mass.: Harvard University Press, 1949. 128 p.

This is Duesenberry's dissertation. It expounds the relative income hypothesis. His dissertation chairman was Arthur Smithies, an exponent of the absolute income hypothesis. An excellent bibliography of consumption literature prior to 1948 is included.

Farrell, M.J. "The New Theories of the Consumption Function." ECONOMIC JOURNAL 69 (December 1959): 678-96. Reprinted in [5] [15].

This is a survey article that is not all that successful because of the additional jargon invented by the author. He distinguishes between different general hypotheses rather than the theories of particular economists.

Ferber, Robert. "Consumer Economics, A Survey." JOURNAL OF ECONOMIC LITERATURE 11 (December 1973): 1303-42.

This is the most recent survey of the macro aspects of consumer economics. There are 203 references included. Most were written during the past ten years. In six sections it covers: "General Theories of the Consumption Function," "Ceteris Paribus Variables," "Asset Functions," "Extensions of Consumer Theory," "Considerations from Other Social Sciences," and "Future Directions." Ferber's general directions for future work are: (1) unification of the different theories of the consumption function, (2) development of a theory for the role of ceteris paribus variables, particularly socioeconomic factors, in consumption, (3) incorporation of knowledge about consumer behavior from other social sciences, (4) determination of human and nonhuman capital, including the interrelation of the two categories, and (5) application of consumer economics analysis to the public sector. The major data limitation is the lack of relevant "lifetime" panel data (consumption data overtime for a specific universe).

_____. "Research on Household Behavior." AMERICAN ECONOMIC REVIEW 52 (March 1962): 19-63. Reprinted in [16].

A study of the most important empirical research concerning consumer behavior at the microeconomic level. Some space is devoted to the theoretical development of the relative and permanent income hypotheses.

_____. A STUDY OF AGGREGATE CONSUMPTION. New York: National Bureau of Economic Research, 1953. 72 p.

A review of the literature on aggregate consumption functions. The studies surveyed by Ferber tended to verify the absolute income hypothesis.

Friedman, Milton. A THEORY OF THE CONSUMPTION FUNCTION. Princeton, N.J.: Princeton University Press, 1957. 259 p.

An attempt to integrate his permanent income hypothesis into the microeconomic theory of the household. The difference between measured and permanent magnitudes is crucial.

Gorman, W.M., et al. "Symposium on Aggregation." REVIEW OF ECONOMIC STUDIES 35 (October 1968): 367-442.

The main emphasis is aggregation of capital goods. The participants were W.M. Gorman, "The Structure of Utility Functions"; F.M. Fisher, "Embodied Technology and the Existence of Labor and Output Aggregates"; B.P. Stigum, "On a Property of Concave Functions"; F.M. Fisher, "Embodied Technology and the Aggregation of Fixed and Movable Capital Goods"; and J.K. Whitaker, "Capital Aggregation and Optimality Conditions."

Green, H.A. John. AGGREGATION IN ECONOMIC ANALYSIS. Princeton, N.J.: Princeton University Press, 1964. 139 p.

Green states that the economist's attitude toward aggregation resembles that of the Scottish preacher whom Sir Dennis Robertson quotes as saying to his flock, "Brethren, here is a gr-reat difficulty; let us look it firmly in the face and pass on." Green examines how aggregation is done and the problems that arise from it.

Guthrie, Harold W. "An Empirical Evaluation of Theories of Saving." REVIEW OF ECONOMICS AND STATISTICS 45 (November 1963): 430-33. Reprinted in [16].

The Keynes, Duesenberry, and Friedman theories were submitted to similar statistical tests. Given the specifications Guthrie levies, no theory was found to be obviously superior to the others on empirical grounds.

Hamburger, Michael J. "Interest Rates and the Demand for Consumer Durable Goods." AMERICAN ECONOMIC REVIEW 57 (December 1967): 1131-53.

Contrary to the Keynesian position that consumption is insensitive to interest rates, Hamburger shows that the demand for durable goods is indeed sensitive. The question may be raised, however, where the division should be made between consumption and investment goods.

Houthakker, H.S. "The Present State of Consumption Theory: A Survey Article." ECONOMETRICA 29 (October 1961): 704-40.

The survey is devoted primarily to the logical foundations of consumer choice. Only the final section deals with problems of aggregation and the possible interactions among consumers' preferences.

Houthakker, H.S., and Taylor, Lester D. CONSUMER DEMAND IN THE UNITED STATES: ANALYSIS AND PROJECTIONS. 2d enl. ed. Cambridge, Mass.: Harvard University Press, 1970. 333 p.

The authors have put together a dynamic state adjustment model relating consumer demand to inventories and to income. In the second edition the data and projects are updated and revised.

Hymans, Saul H. "The Cyclical Behavior of Consumers' Income and Spending: 1921-61." SOUTHERN ECONOMIC JOURNAL 32 (July 1965): 23-34. Reprinted in [10].

Since World War II fiscal stabilizers have replaced the dividend stabilizer in its role as a strong anticyclical payment.

Johnson, M. Bruce. HOUSEHOLD BEHAVIOR: CONSUMPTION, INCOME AND WEALTH. Baltimore: Penguin Books, 1971. 159 p. Paperbound.

Johnson provides a critical analysis of the essentials of consumption theory. The theories of Keynes, Modigliani, Duesenberry, Friedman, Clower and Johnson, and others are examined in light of the empirical evidence. Currently the best introduction to the subject.

Katona, George. THE POWERFUL CONSUMER. New York: McGraw-Hill Book Co., 1960. 276 p.

This book is the result of a sample interview survey. The two basic propositions are: (1) demand depends on income and confidence, and (2) changes in confidence are measurable.

Katona, George, and Mueller, E. CONSUMER RESPONSE TO INCOME INCREASES. Washington, D.C.: Brookings Institution, 1968. 262 p.

The authors were asked to measure consumers' responses to the tax reduction in 1964. Sample data indicate that increases in income are not immediately allocated proportionally to existing consumer budgets, but used to move consumer units closer to specific goals.

Kuznets, Simon [S.]. NATIONAL PRODUCT SINCE 1869. New York: National Bureau of Economic Research, 1946. 253 p.

Kuznets's estimates of the equality of the average and marginal propensities to consume contradicted the absolute income hypothesis. The estimates were from 1869 to 1929.

Lee, Thomas A. INCOME AND VALUE MEASUREMENT. Baltimore: Park Press, 1975. 160 p.

The age-old index problem is tackled again. The analysis is for economists and accountants. An extensive bibliography is provided.

Lubell, Harold. "Effects of Redistribution of Income on Consumers' Expenditures." AMERICAN ECONOMIC REVIEW 37 (March 1947): 157-70. Reprinted in [15].

It is recommended that a national survey be made to test Keynes's hypothesis that redistribution of income will influence aggregate consumption. His sample survey revealed little effect.

Mack, Ruth P. "Economics of Consumption." In A SURVEY OF CONTEMPORARY ECONOMICS, vol. 2, edited by Bernard F. Haley, pp. 39-78. Homewood, Ill.: Richard D. Irwin, 1952.

Ruth Mack's survey of consumption concentrates on the "dynamics of consumer buying and saving." It follows the pattern expected of an economist from the National Bureau of Economic Research, that is, welfare and distribution theory, along with choice theory, are not included. Note the comments by Joseph S. Davis and Jacob Marschak, Ibid., pp. 78-80 and 80-82, respectively.

Mayer, Thomas. PERMANENT INCOME, WEALTH, AND CONSUMPTION: A CRITIQUE OF THE PERMANENT INCOME THEORY, THE LIFE-CYCLE HYPOTH-ESIS AND RELATED THEORIES. Berkeley and Los Angeles: University of California Press, 1972. 428 p.

Both the measured income theories on the one hand and the life cycle and permanent income theories on the other hand perform poorly. His standard income theory only specifies that truth lies somewhere in between.

Modigliani, Franco. "Fluctuations in the Saving-Income Ratio: A Problem in Economic Forecasting." In STUDIES IN INCOME AND WEALTH, edited by National Bureau of Economic Research, vol. 2, pp. 371-441. New York: 1949.

His forecasts made with a relative income hypothesis approach demonstrate a good statistical fit with aggregate data.

_____. "The Life Cycle Hypothesis of Saving, the Demand for Wealth and the Supply of Capital." SOCIAL RESEARCH 33 (Summer 1966): 160-208.

Aggregative implications of the model are exhibited with regard to both the long and short-run behavior of the saving-income and wealth-income ratios. Empirical tests of some of the implications are provided.

Modigliani, Franco, and Brumberg, Richard. "Utility Analysis and the Consumption Function." In POST KEYNESIAN ECONOMICS, edited by Kenneth K. Kurihara, pp. 388-436. New Brunswick, N.J.: Rutgers University Press, 1954. Reprinted in [20].

The starting point is the accepted theory of consumer choice. They depart from Keynes, however, by claiming that the proportion of an individual's income saved is essentially independent of current income.

Perry, George L. "Consumer Demand in the United States: A Review Article." AMERICAN ECONOMIC REVIEW 57 (September 1967): 832-40.

This is a review of Houthakker, H.S. and Taylor, Lester D. CONSUMER DEMAND IN THE UNITED STATES, 1929-1970. Cambridge, Mass.: Harvard University Press, 1966. 224 p. A dynamic model was used to estimate a system of demand functions, based on time series data, from an eighty-three commodity breakdown of total consumption expenditures. The model was used to project 1970 consumption expenditures.

Rasche, Robert H. "Impact of the Stock Market on Private Demand." AMERICAN ECONOMIC REVIEW 62 (May 1972): 220-28.

The impact of the stock market with regard to consumption on the macroeconomy is studied. The comments by Franco Modigliani (Ibid., pp. 229-33) are especially suggestive of research which needs to be done.

Rudra, Ashok. MEASUREMENT IN ECONOMICS. New York: Paragon Book, 1969. 82 p.

The first essay, "Aggregation and Index Numbers," pp. 1-10, should be of interest to all macro-monetary economists.

Smithies, Arthur. "Forecasting Postwar Demand." ECONOMETRICA 13 (January 1945): 1-14.

Based on the absolute income hypothesis, Smithies forecasted a depression after World War II.

Spiro, Alan. "Wealth and the Consumption Function." JOURNAL OF POLITICAL ECONOMY 70 (August 1962): 339-54.

An interesting theory of consumption that has not received as much attention as it should have because of its close kinship to the better-known theories of Modigliani and Friedman.

Suits, Daniel B. "The Determinants of Consumer Expenditure: A Review of Present Knowledge." In IMPACTS OF MONETARY POLICY, edited by Commission on Money and Credit, pp. 1–57. Englewood Cliffs, N.J.: Prentice-Hall, 1963.

A survey of consumption literature, especially of the definition of consumption and the empirical literature.

Tarshis, Lorie. "The Flow of Business Funds, Consumption and Investment." In POST KEYNESIAN ECONOMICS, edited by Kenneth K. Kurihara, pp. 365–87. New Brunswick, N.J.: Rutgers University Press, 1955.

Business can have a greater impact on the level of aggregate income than normally thought, through retained earnings.

Theil, Henri. LINEAR AGGREGATION OF ECONOMIC VARIABLES. New York: North-Holland, 1954. 205 p.

Once it has been determined that the use of macromodels is necessary, the problems of aggregation surface. Theil finds theoretical analysis, empirical findings, and intuition to be necessary for successful macroanalysis. The exposition has a mathematical appearance, but, as Theil says, "The reader is advised not to be frightened."

Thurow, Lester C. "The Optimum Lifetime Distribution of Consumption Expenditures." AMERICAN ECONOMIC REVIEW 59 (June 1969): 324–30.

There is no symmetry with regard to the lifetime redistribution of income. Income can be redistributed to the future by saving; however, redistribution to the present is far more difficult. Oh, for the advantages of a slave market. . . .

Tobin, James. "Asset Holdings and Spending Decisions." AMERICAN ECONOMIC REVIEW 42 (May 1952): 109–23.

This is one of Tobin's early articles on portfolio theory, especially with regard to wealth. It is difficult to state a simple hypothesis relating spending to wealth. For an attempt to apply the same theoretical tools to a wide range of assets, see his article "A Dynamic Aggregation Model." JOURNAL OF POLITICAL ECONOMY 63 (April 1955): 103–15.

_____. "Consumption Function." In INTERNATIONAL ENCYCLOPEDIA OF THE SOCIAL SCIENCES, edited by D.L. Sills, vol. 3, pp. 358–68. New York: Macmillan-Free Press, 1968.

The best short introduction available to the propensity to consume and multiplier analysis.

Tobin, James, and Swan, Craig. "Money and Permanent Income: Some Empirical Tests." AMERICAN ECONOMIC REVIEW 59 (May 1969): 285-95.

> The permanent income hypothesis does not fit postwar data very well. The short-run fluctuations in the demand for money are interpreted as well by a Keynesian model.

Zellner, Arnold, et al. "Further Analysis of the Short-Run Consumption Function with Emphasis on the Role of Liquid Assets." ECONOMETRICA 33 (July 1965): 571-81.

> Their tests show inertia and habit persistence effects are not operative in addition to the income expenditure effect. Some support is shown, however, for the real balance effect. The role of distributed lags is dismissed in a later article. Zellner, Arnold, and Geisel, Martin S. "Analysis of Distributed Lag Models with Applications to Consumption Function Estimation." ECONOMETRICA 38 (November 1970): 865-88.

INVESTMENT AND INVENTORY THEORY

Almon, Shirley. "The Distributed Lag between Capital Appropriations and Expenditures." ECONOMETRICA 33 (January 1965): 178-96.

> The assumption used is that weights of this independent variable assume the pattern of an inverted vee. See also de Leeuw, Frank. "The Demand for Capital Goods by Manufacturers: A Study of Quarterly Time Series." ECONOMETRICA 30 (July 1962): 407-23.

Anderson, W.H. Locke. "Business Fixed Investment: A Marriage of Fact and Fancy." In THE DETERMINANTS OF INVESTMENT BEHAVIOR. National Bureau of Economic Research. New York: Columbia University Press, 1967. Reprinted in [15].

> "The basic position of the accelerationists is that capital goods must be loved to be worth purchasing. The basic position of the profiteers is that capital goods cannot be bought for love, alas, but only for money." The decision-making process is found to be interrelated--both love and money are important.

Bailey, M[artin].J. "Formal Criteria for Investment Decisions." JOURNAL OF POLITICAL ECONOMY 67 (October 1959): 476-88.

> Present-value analysis is to be viewed with caution. The only safe rule is that the investment portfolio should be selected so that the ratio of the marginal utilities of consumption over time is equal to the ratio of the marginal opportunity costs of consumption over time.

Baumol, W[illiam].J., and Malkiel, Burton [G.]. "The Firm's Optimal Debt-Equity Combination and the Cost of Capital." QUARTERLY JOURNAL OF ECONOMICS

81 (November 1967): 547-78.

> Baumol and Malkiel show that there is an optimal capital structure that is consistent with the precepts of economic theory. The Modigliani and Miller analysis is used, supplemented by some institutional observations.

Baumol, William J., et al. "Earnings Retention, New Capital and the Growth of the Firm." REVIEW OF ECONOMICS AND STATISTICS 52 (November 1970): 345-55.

> Ploughback has little effect on growth. The return is small, especially with regard to new equity capital. Questions are raised about the efficiency of the investment process.

Bischoff, C.W. "Business Investment in the 1970's: A Comparison of Models." BROOKINGS PAPERS ON ECONOMIC ACTIVITY 1, no. 1 (1970): 13-58.

> Five models are examined. Although economists have not reached an unanimous agreement as to the factors influencing business investment, the ones emphasized are: output, costs of internal and external finance, capital goods prices, and tax policies.

Brems, Hans. "What Induces Induced Investment." KYKLOS 16, fasc. 4 (1963): 569-82. Reprinted in [20].

> The better producers' goods of a Schumpeterian model are compared to the more producers' goods of a Harrod theory of growth or a Samuelson interaction model as inducements of investment. Brems looks on net profits per year as the best explanation for investment.

Chenery, Hollis. "Overcapacity and the Acceleration Principle." ECONOMETRICA 20 (January 1952): 1-28.

> This is an attempt to formalize a theory of investment behavior from a more generalized production function that takes economies of scale into account. The simple production function previously used with the acceleration principle did not. Some empirical work was also done.

Dasgupto, Ajit K., and Pearce, D.W. COST-BENEFIT ANALYSIS: THEORY AND PRACTICE. New York: Barnes & Noble, 1972. 270 p.

> The most recent survey of this field.

Eisner, Robert. "The Aggregate Investment Function." In INTERNATIONAL ENCYCLOPEDIA OF THE SOCIAL SCIENCES, edited by D.L. Sills, vol. 8, pp. 185-94. New York: Macmillan-Free Press, 1968.

> The relation of the marginal efficiency of investment and capital is defined. In addition the components of investment demand are presented.

_____. "Capacity, Investment, and Profits." QUARTERLY REVIEW OF ECO-NOMICS AND BUSINESS 4 (Autumn 1964): 7-12. Reprinted in [16].

Profits are the carrot that keeps the economy running. But only if the carrot is elusive will investment continue.

_____. "A Distributed Lag Investment Function." ECONOMETRICA 28 (January 1960): 1-29.

The estimation of parameters of an investment function is attempted through the use of a distributed lag accelerator which incorporates a world of risk and uncertainty.

_____. "Investment: Fact or Fancy." AMERICAN ECONOMIC REVIEW 53 (May 1963): 237-46.

The acceleration principle is the right fancy (theory), and the right facts (econometric tests) are those that relate investment to permanent changes in demand.

_____. "A Permanent Income Theory for Investment: Some Empirical Explorations." AMERICAN ECONOMIC REVIEW 57 (June 1967): 363-90.

Cross-section and time-section slices of the McGraw-Hill capital expenditure surveys from 1949 through 1958 were used to ascertain why businessmen invest. Decisions are made on how permanent components of the variables under consideration influence expectations of the future. Bygones are bygones.

Eisner, Robert, and Nadiri, M.I. "Investment Behavior and Neo-Classical Theory." REVIEW OF ECONOMICS AND STATISTICS 50 (August 1968): 369-82.

Eisner and Nadiri argue for an investment function based upon an accelerator. They attack the neoclassical theory of optimal accumulation of capital put forth by D.W. Jorgenson and C.D. Siebert. Also, see Eisner, R., and Nadiri, M.I. "Neo-Classical Theory of Investment Behavior: A Comment." REVIEW OF ECONOMICS AND STATISTICS 52 (May 1970): 216-22.

Eisner, Robert, and Strotz, Robert H. "Determinants of Business Investment." In IMPACTS OF MONETARY POLICY, edited by Commission on Money and Credit, pp. 59-337. Englewood Cliffs, N.J.: Prentice-Hall, 1963.

This is a critical review of all the previous work on determinants of business investment. A comprehensive bibliography by George R. Post is included.

Elliott, J.W[alter]. "Theories of Corporate Investment Behavior Revisited." AMERICAN ECONOMIC REVIEW 63 (March 1973): 195-207.

The Jorgenson-Siebert and Eisner-Nadiri investment models are summarized and tested. Eisner's permanent income theory for investment gains most support. As important background, see Jorgenson, D.W. "Capital Theory and Investment Behavior." AMERICAN ECONOMIC REVIEW 53 (May 1963): 247-59; and Eisner, Robert. "A Permanent Income Theory for Investment: Some Empirical Explorations." AMERICAN ECONOMIC REVIEW 57 (June 1967): 363-90.

Ferber, Robert, ed. THE DETERMINANTS OF INVESTMENT BEHAVIOR. National Bureau of Economic Research. New York: Columbia University Press, 1967. 622 p.

The basic inputs to this conference were twelve papers, grouped under five headings, which were scrutinized by some fourteen discussants.

Haavelmo, Trygve. A STUDY IN THE THEORY OF INVESTMENT. Chicago: University of Chicago Press, 1960. 229 p.

The modern approach is to regard investment as a process of accumulating capital stock--of adjusting an actual level of capital to the level desired. The difficulty in formulating an equilibrium theory of investment is that the demand side is a stock magnitude while the supply side is a flow.

Harcourt, G.C. "Investment-Decision Criteria, Investment Incentives and the Choice of Technique." ECONOMIC JOURNAL 78 (March 1968): 77-95.

Harcourt shows that investment decisions are extremely complex even when all the "relevant" information is known. The impact of three different tax systems on investment-decision criteria is analyzed.

Hawkins, C.J., and Pearce, D.W. CAPITAL INVESTMENT APPRAISAL. London: Macmillan and Co., 1971. 88 p. Paperbound.

The survey is rapid but worthwhile. A two-page bibliography is included.

Hayek, Friedrich A. PROFITS, INTEREST AND INVESTMENT. New York: Augustus M. Kelley, 1939. 266 p.

The essays in this collection, by a Nobel Laureate, retain their importance because of the emphasis on investment and, especially, the effect of expectations on investment. "The 'Paradox' of Saving" pp. 199-263, first published in 1929, is of current importance.

Hirshleiffer, Jack. "The Investment Decision." In INTERNATIONAL ENCYCLOPEDIA OF THE SOCIAL SCIENCES, edited by D.L. Sills, vol. 8, pp. 194-202. New York: Macmillan-Free Press, 1968.

The theory of the investment decision is developed from the viewpoint of the individual consumer. The treatment of risk and uncertainty is particularly good.

_____ . "Investment Decision Under Uncertainty." QUARTERLY JOURNAL OF ECONOMICS 79 (November 1965): 509-36.

Investment decisions are always made under uncertainty because it is a present sacrifice for a future benefit. He develops a theory of uncertain choice over time given different possible dated contingencies. A succeeding article is "Investment Decision Under Uncertainty: Applications of the State-Preference Approach." QUARTERLY JOURNAL OF ECONOMICS 80 (May 1966): 252-77.

_____ . INVESTMENT, INTEREST, AND CAPITAL. Englewood Cliffs, N.J.: Prentice-Hall, 1970. 330 p.

The overall treatment here follows Irving Fisher in spirit and in form. The analysis goes beyond Fisher's treatment in these main respects: (1) in introducing the firm, in addition to individuals, as a decision-making agent, (2) in studying capital as a factor of production, and most importantly, (3) in providing a rigorous treatment of intertemporal decisions under uncertainty.

_____ . "On the Theory of the Optimum Investment Decision." JOURNAL OF POLITICAL ECONOMY 66 (August 1958): 329-52.

The problem of capital budgeting is approached theoretically through the use of isoquant analysis.

Janankar, P. INVESTMENT: THEORIES AND EVIDENCE. London: Macmillan and Co., 1972. 78 p. Paperbound.

A very worthwhile survey of investment, including capital investment. A three-page bibliography has been selected.

Jorgenson, Dale W. "Capital Theory and Investment Behavior." AMERICAN ECONOMIC REVIEW 53 (May 1963): 247-59. Reprinted in [5].

Jorgenson believes the neoclassical theory of capital should be the accepted theory; however, the econometric literature on business investment consists of ad hoc descriptive generalizations. He attempts to show that the demand for capital responds to the relative factor prices or the ratio of factor prices to the price of output.

_____ . "Econometric Studies of Investment Behavior: A Survey." JOURNAL OF ECONOMIC LITERATURE 9 (December 1971): 1111-47.

The point of departure used by Jorgenson is the flexible accelerator model of Chenery and Koyck. The bibliography is extensive.

There have been three comments published about this survey: Klein, Lawrence R. "Issues in Econometric Studies of Investment Behavior." JOURNAL OF ECONOMIC LITERATURE 12 (March 1974): 43-49; Eisner, Robert. "Comment." Ibid., pp. 49-50; and Eisner, Robert. "Econometric Studies of Investment Behavior: A Comment." WESTERN ECONOMIC JOURNAL 12 (March 1974): 91-104.

_____. "The Theory of Investment Behavior." In THE DETERMINANTS OF INVESTMENT BEHAVIOR, National Bureau of Economic Research, pp. 129-55. New York: Columbia University Press, 1967. Reprinted in [13].

Jorgenson compares the neoclassical theory of investment with a number of Keynesian theories. He believes that decisions are made at the margin.

Jorgenson, Dale W., and Siebert, C.D. "A Comparison of Alternative Theories of Corporate Investment Behavior." AMERICAN ECONOMIC REVIEW 58 (September 1968): 681-712.

This article develops and tests five investment function models. It compares the accelerator and neoclassical model. A rather meager sample of fifteen firms was used. Elliott, J.W. "Theories of Corporate Investment Behavior Revisited." AMERICAN ECONOMIC REVIEW 63 (March 1973): 195-207, also, tests the conflicting investment function models.

_____. "Issues in the Development of the Neo-Classical Theory of Investment Behavior." REVIEW OF ECONOMICS AND STATISTICS 51 (August 1969): 346-53.

The authors defend the neoclassical investment model against the attacks of Eisner and Nadiri.

Knox, A.D. "The Acceleration Principle and the Theory of Investment: A Survey." ECONOMICA 19 (August 1952): 269-97. Reprinted in [15] [16].

The acceleration principle with fixed coefficients is not an adequate theory of investment. Economic life is not as constant as economists would like.

Koyck, L.M. DISTRIBUTED LAGS AND INVESTMENT ANALYSIS. New York: North-Holland, 1954. 111 p.

Empirical analysis is difficult because of the time-shape of reactions. Koyck is especially interested in distributed lags of considerate length--a formulation that has taken his name.

Kuh, Edwin. "Theory and Institutions in the Study of Investment Behavior." AMERICAN ECONOMIC REVIEW 53 (May 1963): 260-68.

He sketches accepted capital and investment theory, and the present state of empirical information about the relative importance of profit and acceleration determinants of investment. A good bibliography of the early literature is included.

Kuznets, Simon [S.]. "Proportion of Capital Formation to National Product." AMERICAN ECONOMIC REVIEW 42 (May 1952): 507-26.

Time-series data are used to see if there is a relation between investment and income.

Lerner, Abba P. "On the Marginal Product of Capital and the Marginal Efficiency of Investment." JOURNAL OF POLITICAL ECONOMY 61 (February 1953): 1-14.

It is the index problem, in a profound sense, all over again. The comparison of the rates of return of stocks and flows may lead to invalid suppositions.

Lund, Phillip J. INVESTMENT: THE STUDY OF AN ECONOMIC AGGREGATE. San Francisco: Holden-Day, 1971. 167 p.

The theories and econometric testing of investment are surveyed. A reasonably good bibliography is included.

Lutz, F[riedrich].A., and Lutz, Vera. THE THEORY OF INVESTMENT OF THE FIRM. Princeton, N.J.: Princeton University Press, 1951. 263 p.

Systematic account of the formal theory of investment decisions of the firm. Essentially an examination of profit-maximizing behavior when interest rates enter into firms' decisions.

Marglin, S.A. "Investment and Interest: A Reformulation and Extension of Keynesian Theory." ECONOMIC JOURNAL 80 (December 1970): 910-31.

The "reformulation" is an investment function that intersects the investment axis and the "extension" is a monopolistic investment function that has a kink in it.

Metzler, Lloyd A. "The Rate of Interest and the Marginal Product of Capital." JOURNAL OF POLITICAL ECONOMY 58 (August 1950): 289-306; and "The Rate of Interest and the Marginal Product of Capital: A Correction." JOURNAL OF POLITICAL ECONOMY 59 (February 1951): 67-68.

William Hamburger and Edmund Malinvaud called Metzler's attention to the fact that the social rate of substitution between present and future is equal to the rate of interest and not to the marginal product of social capital.

Meyer, J.R. and Kuh, Edwin. THE INVESTMENT DECISION. Cambridge, Mass.: Harvard University Press, 1957. 299 p.

This book is an attempt to justify theoretically the expenditures on capital equipment. A review of econometric studies of investment in fixed capital through 1953 is given.

Modigliani, Franco, and Miller, Merton [H.]. "The Cost of Capital, Corporation Finance, and the Theory of Investment." AMERICAN ECONOMIC REVIEW 48 (June 1958): 261-97.

This is a classic article on the cost of capital. Three propositions are developed: (1) the market value of any firm is independent of its capital structure and is given by capitalizing its expected return at the rate Q appropriate to its class; (2) the market price of any share of stock is its capitalized expected return, etc.; and (3) the cutoff point for investment in the firm will in all cases be Q and will be entirely unaffected by the type of security used to finance the investment.

Nadiri, M.I. "An Alternative Model of Business Investment Spending." BROOKINGS PAPERS ON ECONOMIC ACTIVITY 3, no. 3 (1972): 547-73.

Nadiri separates the relative price and quantity determinants in the neoclassical investment model. He concludes that the neoclassical model results in excess emphasis being placed on monetary and fiscal policy.

Prest, A.R., and Turvey, R[alph]. "Cost-Benefit Analysis: A Survey." ECONOMIC JOURNAL 75 (December 1965): 683-735.

The problem of adding up benefits and costs is discussed along with various applications. The bibliography is not complete but it is a good beginning.

Robinson, Joan. THE ACCUMULATION OF CAPITAL. 3d ed. Homewood, Ill.: Richard D. Irwin, 1956. 460 p.

Basically a discussion of the theory of value. Robinson discusses the accumulation of capital, assuming there is only one technique available with fixed coefficients between labor and equipment. Since there is only one technique available, new laborers will require the same tools as existing workers. Therefore, the new production function is dependent on accumulated capital. As long as the increase in capital follows this trend, a stable state will exist.

Smith, Vernon L. INVESTMENT AND PRODUCTION. Cambridge, Mass.: Harvard University Press, 1961. 340 p.

A good example of how the differences between stock and flow items should be explicitly integrated into theory.

Solow, Robert M. "On a Family of Lag Distributions." ECONOMETRICA 28 (April 1960): 393-406.

This article is a generalization of Koyck's method for distributed lags. Solow uses the Pascal distributions, of which the geometric is a special case.

Thurow, Lester C. "A Disequilibrium Neoclassical Investment Function." REVIEW OF ECONOMICS AND STATISTICS 51 (November 1969): 431-35.

Thurow tests a Jorgenson neoclassical investment function but allows the cost of capital and the marginal product of capital to diverge. Both are based on the same theory but they yield very different results.

Treadway, Arthur B. "On Rational Entrepreneurial Behaviour and the Demand for Investment." REVIEW OF ECONOMIC STUDIES 36 (April 1969): 227-39.

Treadway extends the "cost of adjustment" analysis to: (1) regions of increasing returns, (2) behavior with a variable stock, and (3) production functions which are not linearly homogeneous.

Trivedi, P.K. "Inventory Behaviour in U.K. Manufacturing, 1956-67." REVIEW OF ECONOMIC STUDIES 37 (October 1970): 517-36.

This is an almost virgin area of inquiry in Britain. Abramovitz's distinction between production to order and production for stocks is taken into account. This is especially important because there exists a strong causal relationship between U.K. imports and inventory charges.

Wells, Paul. "Output and the Demand for Capital in the Short Run." SOUTHERN ECONOMIC JOURNAL 32 (October 1965): 146-52. Reprinted in [8] [10].

Wells feels that no adequate theory of the level of aggregate investment exists in a "one good" model of the economy.

White, W[illiam].H. "Interest Elasticity of Investment Demand--The Case from Business Attitude Surveys Re-examined." AMERICAN ECONOMIC REVIEW 46 (September 1956): 565-87. Reprinted in [15 revised].

This is a review of various surveys to determine the influence of the interest rate on investment. His conclusion is "the middle ground of relative interest elasticity."

Witte, James G., Jr. "The Microfoundations of the Social Investment Function." JOURNAL OF POLITICAL ECONOMY 71 (October 1963): 441-56. Reprinted in [8] [20].

Firm investment is a flow; consequently, comparative static analysis

is useless. "I question the usefulness of the stationary state as a
beginning or terminal point of macroeconomic theory."

REAL AND MONETARY MULTIPLIERS AND THE ACCELERATOR RELATION

Ackley, Gardner. "The Multiplier Time Period: Money, Inventories, and
Flexibility." AMERICAN ECONOMIC REVIEW 41 (June 1951): 350-68.
Reprinted in [17].

> The theory of the multiplier is only true as a first approximation
> under ideal conditions.

Ando, Albert, and Modigliani, Franco. "The Relative Stability of Monetary
Velocity and the Investment Multiplier."; DePrano, Michael, and Mayer, Thomas.
"Autonomous Expenditures and Money."; Friedman, Milton, and Meiselman, David.
"Reply to Ando and Modigliani and DePrano and Mayer."; Ando, Albert, and
Modigliani, Franco. "Rejoinder."; DePrano, Michael, and Mayer, Thomas.
"Rejoinder." AMERICAN ECONOMIC REVIEW 55 (September 1965): 693-
792.

> An acrimonious exchange that changed none of the opinions of the
> bellicose participants.

Barrett, C.R., and Walters, A[lan].A. "The Stability of Keynesian and Monetary Multipliers in the United Kingdom." REVIEW OF ECONOMICS AND STA-
TISTICS 48 (November 1966): 395-405.

> The importance that both money and autonomous expenditures have
> on the determination of aggregate consumption depends very much
> on economic conditions.

Baumol, W[illiam].J., and Peston, M.H. "More on the Multiplier Effects of a Balanced Budget." AMERICAN ECONOMIC REVIEW 45 (March 1955): 140-48.

> The balance budget (unit) multiplier is perhaps only an irrelevant
> tautology.

Brunner, Karl, and Meltzer, Allan H. "Predicting Velocity: Implications for
Theory and Policy." JOURNAL OF FINANCE 18 (May 1963): 319-54.

> This is an attempt to make the quantity theory relevant to the short
> run. Their results emphasize that the supply and demand functions
> for money provide more stable relationships than alternative ap-
> proaches.

Caff, J.T. "A Generalization of the Multiplier-Accelerator Model." ECO-
NOMIC JOURNAL 71 (March 1961): 36-52.

> There is comfort to be found in the knowledge that the generalized
> model yields results not greatly different from the simpler lagged
> models. The performance of possible extensions can now be known

and it is shown that recurrence relation models can explain growth as well as cycles.

Clark, John Maurice. "Business Acceleration and the Law of Demand: A Technical Factor in Economic Cycles." JOURNAL OF POLITICAL ECONOMY 25 (March 1917): 217-35. Reprinted in [6].

The accelerator was initially formulated in this article.

Eckaus, Richard S. "The Acceleration Principle Reconsidered." QUARTERLY JOURNAL OF ECONOMICS 67 (May 1953): 209-30. Reprinted in [20].

When the acceleration principle is rewritten as the velocity principle, investment is influenced by future output and present capital stock.

Evans, Michael K. "Reconstruction and Estimation of the Balance Budget Multiplier." REVIEW OF ECONOMICS AND STATISTICS 51 (February 1969): 14-25.

This is a survey of the balance budget literature with ample references. The Wharton model is used to determine numerical estimates of the balance budget multiplier over time. The estimate is closer to zero than to unity.

Freidman, Milton, and Meiselman, David. "The Relative Stability of Monetary Velocity and the Investment Multiplier in the United States, 1897-1958." In STABILIZATION POLICIES, edited by Commission on Money and Credit, pp. 165-268. Englewood Cliffs, N.J.: Prentice-Hall, 1963.

Their result is that the quantity theory is a better description of U.S. economic history than Keynesian theory. This provoked a number of comments. Ando and Modigliani and DePrano and Mayer in the AMERICAN ECONOMIC REVIEW 55 (September 1965): 693-792; and D.D. Hester in the REVIEW OF ECONOMICS AND STATISTICS 46 (November 1964): 364-77.

Goodwin, R.M. "The Non-Linear Accelerator and the Persistence of Business Cycles." ECONOMETRICA 19 (January 1951): 1-17.

The roles of lags and secular evolution are shown. The equilibrium position of each complex system is unstable but there exists a stable limit cycle. Also see, Goodwin, R.M. "The Business Cycle as a Self-Sustaining Oscillation." ECONOMETRICA 17 (April 1949): 184-85, which is an earlier summary of this paper.

_____. "Secular and Cyclical Aspects of the Multiplier and the Accelerator." In INCOME, EMPLOYMENT AND PUBLIC POLICY, edited by Lloyd A. Metzler et al., pp. 108-32. New York: W.W. Norton, 1948.

The multiplier and accelerator govern the cyclical behavior, and in a more complex fashion the secular response of the economy to technology and population growth.

Haavelmo, Trygve. "Multiplier Effects of a Balanced Budget." ECONOMET-RICA 13 (October 1945): 311-18. Reprinted in [18].

The first explicit demonstration that a "balanced budget" produces a unit multiplier.

Hester, Donald D. "Keynes and the Quantity Theory: A Comment on the Friedman-Meiselman CMC Paper."; Friedman, Milton, and Meiselman, David. "Reply."; Hester, Donald D. "Rejoinder." REVIEW OF ECONOMICS AND STATISTICS 46 (November 1964): 364-68, 369-76, 376-77.

The stability of the multipliers is again at issue. Hester tests the quantity theory and the Keynesian theory and shows why Friedman-Meiselman tests are misleading, i.e., inconclusive.

Kahn, R[ichard].F. "The Relation of Home Investment to Unemployment." ECO-NOMIC JOURNAL 41 (June 1931): 173-98.

It is in this article that Lord Kahn formulated the idea of the multiplier.

Kaufman, George G. "More on an Empirical Definition of Money." AMERI-CAN ECONOMIC REVIEW 59 (March 1969): 78-87. Reprinted in [4].

This is a further critique of the Friedman-Meiselman thesis on the relative stability of real and monetary multipliers. Kaufman's main point is that demand deposits or time deposits should not be in-cluded in money when relating to earlier observations of income. Also see Timberlake, Richard H., Jr., and Fortson, James. "Time Deposits in the Definition of Money." AMERICAN ECONOMIC REVIEW 57 (March 1967): 190-94. Reprinted in [4].

Peston, M.H. "Generalizing the Balanced Budget Multiplier."; Salant, W.A. "Comment." REVIEW OF ECONOMICS AND STATISTICS 40 (August 1958): 288-93.

These two comments are more or less the last words on the balanced budget multiplier. All of the relevant citations are included in the footnotes.

Salant, William A. "Taxes, Income Determination, and the Balanced Budget Theorem." REVIEW OF ECONOMICS AND STATISTICS 39 (May 1957): 152-61. Reprinted in [5] [16].

The balance budget theorem is closer to reality than the view it superseded, that the balance budget multiplier is zero.

Samuelson, Paul A. "Dynamic Process Analysis." In A SURVEY OF CON-
TEMPORARY ECONOMICS, vol. 1, edited by Howard S. Ellis, pp. 352-87.
Homewood, Ill.: Richard D. Irwin, 1948.

> Besides Marshallian and Walrasian notions of stability, process
> analysis has burst forth mainly in macroeconomics. The principle
> of acceleration, the multiplier, their interaction, and cobweb
> analysis are the main areas of rudimentary dynamics.

_____. "Interactions between the Multiplier Analysis and the Principle of
Acceleration." REVIEW OF ECONOMIC STATISTICS 21 (May 1939): 75-78.
Reprinted in [6] [10] [15] [20].

> Although Samuelson states that the interactions are "strictly a
> marginal analysis to be applied to the study of small oscillations,"
> his caveat has gone unheeded.

Strotz, Robert H. "Empirical Evidence on the Impact of Monetary Variables
on Aggregate Expenditure." In MONETARY PROCESS AND POLICY, edited
by George Horwich, pp. 295-329. Homewood, Ill.: Richard D. Irwin, 1967.

> This survey article is restricted to studies that Strotz finds interest-
> ing. A discussion by David Meiselman in the same volume (pp. 322-
> 29) is of interest.

Tsiang, S.C. "Accelerator, Theory of the Firm, and the Business Cycle."
QUARTERLY JOURNAL OF ECONOMICS 65 (August 1951): 325-41.

> An early attempt at building an explanation of business cycles not
> based on the multiplier-accelerator mechanical interaction. His
> alternative is a "realistic" explanation of what causes excess ca-
> pacity coupled with a Kaldor-Kalecki type of trade cycle.

Turvey, Ralph. "Some Notes on Multiplier Theory." AMERICAN ECONOMIC
REVIEW 58 (June 1953): 275-95.

> The multiplier can only be understood if a sharp distinction is
> drawn between households and firms. The unit multiplier, ex post
> versus ex ante, and saving as the residual are other issues touched
> upon. Also see his article, "The Multiplier." ECONOMICA 15
> (November 1948): 259-69.

Walters, Alan A. "Monetary Multipliers in the U.K. 1880-1962." OXFORD
ECONOMIC PAPERS 18 (November 1966): 270-83.

> This paper explores the linkages between money, prices, and in-
> come. After 1955 money stock is a poor predictor of the level
> or change in income. But a simple Keynesian model does no
> better. "The monetary chaos of the late 50s early 60s remains
> inexplicable."

LABOR MARKET

Edwards, Edgar O. "Classical and Keynesian Employment Theories: A Reconciliation." QUARTERLY JOURNAL OF ECONOMICS 73 (August 1959): 407-28.

   Edwards feels the differences have been maximized.

Fisher, Malcolm R. THE ECONOMIC ANALYSIS OF LABOUR. New York: St. Martin's Press, 1971. 317 p.

   A good theoretical and empirical study of both sides of this market. A good list of references is included in the notes.

Hicks, John R. THE THEORY OF WAGES. 2d ed. London: Macmillan and Co., 1963. 407 p.

   The first edition was published in 1932 and had been out of print for more than twenty years, primarily because of Gerald Shove's review. The new edition is divided into three sections. Section 1 is a reprint of the first edition. Section 2 includes a couple of Hicks's articles written within a few years of the publication of the first edition and Gerald Shove's review. Section 3 tells the story of the book, "its pre-natal as well as post-natal vicissitudes."

Long, Clarence D. "The Illusion of Wage Rigidity." REVIEW OF ECONOMICS AND STATISTICS 42 (May 1960): 140-51.

   There is no evidence of wages being rigid in the downturns of business and employment. On the other hand, wages are highly sensitive to long and short-run economic cycles.

Mishan, E.J. "The Demand for Labor in a Classical and Keynesian Framework." JOURNAL OF POLITICAL ECONOMY 72 (December 1964): 610-16. Reprinted in [8] [10].

   The marginal productivity of labor is not the demand for labor curve of either the classical or Keynesian framework. Demand for labor is derived from an effective demand for goods.

Stigler, George J. "Information in the Labor Market." JOURNAL OF POLITICAL ECONOMY 70, supplement (October 1962): 94-105.

   The article stimulated a good deal of the interest in the costs of information. Searches by both sides of the market are costly. There is no reason to suppose that social capital should be equal to the sum of private capital(s). Where is the "invisible hand" when you need it most?

Tobin, James. "Money Wage Rates and Employment." In THE NEW ECONOMICS,

Macro-Monetary Theory

edited by S.E. Harris, pp. 572-87. New York: Augustus M. Kelley, 1947.
Reprinted in [15] [20].

Tobin summarizes how money wage rates may alter the level of
employment. His solution is greatly advanced by Keynes's analysis
of effective demand.

OUTPUT RELATIONS

Brown, M. ON THE THEORY AND MEASUREMENT OF TECHNOLOGICAL
CHANGE. New York: Cambridge University Press, 1966. 228 p.

Brown uses a microeconomic approach, but the book is of importance to macroeconomists as well.

Brubaker, Earl R. "Multi-Neutral Technical Progress: Compatibilities, Conditions, and Consistency with Some Evidence." AMERICAN ECONOMIC REVIEW
62 (December 1972): 997-1003.

The combinations of nine types of single neutrality results in only
nine dual combinations and one triple (Hicks-Harrod-Solow) that
are logically consistent.

Cobb, Charles W., and Douglas, Paul H. "A Theory of Production." AMERI-
CAN ECONOMIC REVIEW 18 (March 1928): 139-65.

The famous Cobb-Douglas production function was developed and
tested in this article.

Fellner, William [J.]. "Two Propositions in the Theory of Induced Innovations."
ECONOMIC JOURNAL 71 (June 1961): 305-8.

The "learning process" in a competitive firm may be negated to
some extent by market imperfections.

Jorgenson, Dale W., and Griliches, Zvi. "The Explanation of Productivity
Change." REVIEW OF ECONOMIC STUDIES 34 (July 1967): 249-83.

Before productivity can be accurately measured, it is necessary
that errors of measurement be corrected.

Kendrick, John W. POSTWAR PRODUCTIVITY TRENDS IN THE UNITED STATES.
New York: Columbia University Press, 1973. 389 p.

High real wages breed lower productivity.

Kennedy, Charles. "Induced Bias in Innovations and the Theory of Distribution."
ECONOMIC JOURNAL 74 (September 1964): 541-47.

To get around the problems in Sir John Hicks's theory of induced
inventions (changes in relative factor prices), a model is constructed

in which technical progress takes place only in the consumption sector. Kennedy shows that his innovation possibility function is really a disguised form of N. Kaldor's technical progress function ("A Model of Economic Growth." ECONOMIC JOURNAL 67 [December 1957]: 591-624).

Kuh, Edwin. "Unemployment, Production Functions, and Effective Demand." JOURNAL OF POLITICAL ECONOMY 74 (June 1966): 238-49.

Kuh shifts the emphasis of Keynesian unemployment theory. Money illusion is discarded, having been replaced by technical conditions of production and imperfect competition.

Leon, Paolo. STRUCTURAL CHANGE AND GROWTH IN CAPITALISM. Baltimore: Johns Hopkins Press, 1967. 176 p.

The structure and development process is examined, with the neoclassical production function coming under heavy attack.

Lipsey, Richard G., ed. "Symposium on Production Functions and Economic Growth." REVIEW OF ECONOMIC STUDIES 29 (June 1962): 155-266.

The articles are by Kenneth J. Arrow; Nicholas Kaldor and James A. Mirrlees; Paul A. Samuelson; Robert M. Solow; Joan Robinson; J.E. Meade; D.G. Champernowne; J. Black; and Richard Stone and J.A.C. Brown. Although the M.I.T. versus Cambridge, England, battle appears to be evenly fought, logic is with England.

Marty, Alvin [L.]. "The Aggregate Supply Function." METROECONOMICA 11 (December 1959): 179-87.

The aggregate supply function of Keynes is really more than a forty-five degree line. See also, Leijonhufvud, Axel. "Keynes' Employment Function: Comment." HISTORY OF POLITICAL ECONOMY 6 (Summer 1974): 164-70.

Nelson, Richard R. "Aggregate Production Functions and Medium-Range Growth Projections." AMERICAN ECONOMIC REVIEW 54 (September 1964): 575-606. Reprinted in [8].

The projections of Edward F. Denison, Robert M. Solow, and others are compared. See, for example, Denison, Edward F. THE SOURCES OF ECONOMIC GROWTH IN THE UNITED STATES AND THE ALTERNATIVES BEFORE US. Committee for Economic Development, Supplementary Paper, no. 13. New York: 1962. 297 p.; Solow, R.M. "Technical Progress, Capital Formation, and Economic Growth." AMERICAN ECONOMIC REVIEW 52 (May 1962): 76-86.

Nelson, Richard R., et al. TECHNOLOGY, ECONOMIC GROWTH, AND PUBLIC POLICY. Washington, D.C.: Brookings Institution, 1967. 251 p.

An attempt to focus explicitly on technological knowledge with physical inputs as determinants. Also see Mansfield, Edwin. "Rates of Return from Industrial Research and Development." AMERICAN ECONOMIC REVIEW 55 (May 1965): 312-22; Griliches, Zvi. "Research Expenditures, Education, and the Aggregate Agricultural Production Function." AMERICAN ECONOMIC REVIEW 54 (December 1964): 961-74.

Robinson, Joan. "The Classification of Inventions." REVIEW OF ECONOMIC STUDIES 5 (February 1938): 139-42.

In this short note, Joan Robinson defines explicitly what is meant by Hicks and Harrod neutral inventions.

Samuelson, Paul A. "A Theory of Induced Innovation Along Kennedy-Weizsacker Lines." REVIEW OF ECONOMICS AND STATISTICS 47 (November 1965): 343-56.

Samuelson is willing to accept a Kennedy-Weizsacker-Samuelson hyphenation. But he will not part with the traditional production function. The Harrod-neutral labor augmentation result is possible with a variety of exogenous assumptions. See these additional notes: Kennedy, Charles. "Samuelson on Induced Innovation."; Samuelson, Paul A. "Rejoinder: Agreements, Disagreements, Doubts, and the Case of Induced Harrod-Neutral Technological Change." REVIEW OF ECONOMICS AND STATISTICS 48 (November 1966): 442-44; 444-48.

Schmookler, Jacob. INVENTION AND ECONOMIC GROWTH. Cambridge, Mass.: Harvard University Press, 1966. 346 p.

Schmookler determined that the rate of technological change is not exogenous to the economic system. His results show a high correlation between patent rate and investment rate.

Solow, Robert M. "Investment and Technical Progress." In MATHEMATICAL METHODS IN THE SOCIAL SCIENCES, 1959, Stanford Mathematical Studies in the Social Sciences, vol. 4, edited by Kenneth J. Arrow et al., pp. 89-104. Palo Alto, Calif.: Stanford University Press, 1960.

Solow investigates the proposal that, of the observed increase in output per head, by far the largest share is a consequence of technical progress rather than of increased capital per head. A Cobb-Douglas aggregate production function is used.

_____. "Technical Progress and the Aggregate Production Function." REVIEW OF ECONOMICS AND STATISTICS 39 (August 1957): 312-20. Reprinted in [10] [15].

This is a simple way of separating movements along the aggregate production function from shifts in it, (i.e., relative shares attributable to capital and technical change, respectively). A correction and response are: Hogan, Warren P. "Technical Progress and Production Functions"; Solow, Robert M. "Reply." REVIEW OF ECONOMICS AND STATISTICS 40 (November 1958): 407-11; 411-13.

Uzawa, Hirofumi. "Neutral Inventions and the Stability of Growth Equilibrium." REVIEW OF ECONOMIC STUDIES 28 (February 1961): 117-24.

A comparison of Hicks and Harrod neutral inventions is made. A Cobb-Douglas production function with technical invention is both Harrod and Hicks neutral. Harrod neutrality is proved to exist in a stable growth equilibrium.

MONEY DEMAND: DEFINITION AND VALUE

Archibald, G.C., and Lipsey, R.G. "Monetary and Value Theory: A Critique of Lange and Patinkin." REVIEW OF ECONOMIC STUDIES 26 (October 1958): 1-22. Reprinted in [2] [19].

Patinkin's first edition of MONEY, INTEREST, AND PRICES did not include a long-run analysis. Archibald and Lipsey provided it. Patinkin included their work in the second edition of his book. This controversy led to Baumol, W.J., et al. "A Symposium on Monetary Theory." REVIEW OF ECONOMIC STUDIES 28 (October 1960): 29-56. An article in the symposium by Clower, R.W., and Burstein, M.L. "On the Invariance of Demand for Cash and Other Assets." (Ibid., pp. 32-36) is reprinted in [2].

Baumol, W[illiam].J. "Stocks, Flows and Monetary Theory." QUARTERLY JOURNAL OF ECONOMICS 76 (February 1962): 46-56.

The problems of stock-flow equilibrium, invalid dichotomy, and determination of the equilibrium rate of interest are discussed in straightforward language. Solutions are reached.

_____. "The Transactions Demand for Cash: An Inventory Theoretic Approach." QUARTERLY JOURNAL OF ECONOMICS 66 (November 1952): 545-56. Reprinted in [16] [19].

This note is an application of inventory control analysis to monetary theory. In a very simple situation, the rational individual, with a constant price level, will demand cash in proportion to the square root of the value of his transactions. There are obvious implications with regard to policy decisions.

Baumol, W[illiam].J., et al. "A Symposium on Monetary Theory." REVIEW OF ECONOMIC STUDIES 28 (October 1960): 29-56.

The participants were: W.J. Baumol, R.W. Clower and M.L. Burstein, F.H. Hahn, R.J. Ball and Ronald Bodkin, G.C. Archibald

and R.C. Lipsey. In a personal editorial note the reason is given
why Don Patinkin did not reply: "The Editors regret that it has
not been possible to include a contribution Professor Patinkin, owing
to [an] inability to agree on a suitable length." The papers were in
response to Archibald and Lipsey's critique of Patinkin's first edition
of MONEY, INTEREST, AND PRICES.

Becker, Gary S., and Baumol, William J. "The Classical Monetary Theory:
The Outcome of the Discussion." ECONOMICA 19 (November 1952): 355-
76.

An interesting article, although it set theoretical advancement
back at least ten years because of the continuing confusion between Say's and Walras's laws.

Bierwag, G.O., and Grove, M.A. "Indifference Curves in Asset Analysis."
ECONOMIC JOURNAL 76 (June 1966): 337-43.

It is shown that the theory of asset choice is a special case of
demand theory, where consumers' preferences are variable.

Bilkes, Gerrit, and Ames, Edward. "Monetary Theory and Economic Consoli-
dations." In TRADE, STABILITY, AND MACROECONOMICS: ESSAYS IN
HONOR OF LLOYD A. METZLER, edited by George Horwich and Paul A.
Samuelson, pp. 455-84. New York: Academic Press, 1974.

Consolidations used by Leijonhufvud, Patinkin, Gurley and Shaw,
Pesek and Saving, and Friedman are examined and criticized.
Disaggregation is the essence of monetary theory.

Bronfenbrenner, Martin, and Mayer, Thomas. "Liquidity Functions in the American Economy." ECONOMETRICA 28 (October 1960): 810-34. Reprinted in
[15].

An interesting study of the demand for money. Besides the level
of income and the interest rate, a number of other variables were
investigated. No support was found for the liquidity traps.

Brunner, Karl. "Inconsistency and Indeterminacy in Classical Economics."
ECONOMETRICA 19 (April 1951): 152-73.

This article is a critical survey of Patinkin's articles on the properties of classical systems. It also takes into account the comments
of a number of other economists, both published and unpublished.
Brunner's conclusion is that classical theory is composed of two
unrelated segments--one real, the other monetary.

Brunner, Karl, and Meltzer, Allan H. "Liquidity Traps for Money, Bank Credit,
and Interest Rates." JOURNAL OF POLITICAL ECONOMY 76 (January/February
1968): 1-37.

They deny the existence of liquidity traps in the 1930s or in the present. Monetary policy is not akin to "pushing on a string"; it can be effective if policy makers would watch the change in money supply rather than the rate of change of bank credit. Brunner and Meltzer also cast doubt on the importance of the real balance effect.

_____. "Some Further Investigations of Demand and Supply Functions for Money." JOURNAL OF FINANCE 19 (May 1964): 240-83.

It is suggested that monetary theory, using the work of Brunner and Meltzer, may be useful in furnishing a framework for monetary policy.

_____. "The Uses of Money: Money in the Theory of an Exchange Economy." AMERICAN ECONOMIC REVIEW 61 (December 1971): 784-805.

Why is money held? Once we leave the world of certainty combined with costless information, money has utility and is productive.

Cannan, Edwin. "The Application of the Theoretical Apparatus of Supply and Demand to Units of Currency." ECONOMIC JOURNAL 31 (December 1921): 453-61. Reprinted in [11].

Too much supply of or demand for money will cause it to go out of use--substitutes will appear. An important requisite of useful currency is stability of value.

Catt, A.J.L. "Idle Balances and the Motives for Liquidity." OXFORD ECONOMIC PAPERS 14 (June 1962): 124-37.

The Radcliffe Report raised many questions regarding the size and nature of liquidity. Catt is not for controls; he wants the market to work. His conclusions are opposite to those reached by Gaskin, M. "Liquidity and the Money Mechanism." OXFORD ECONOMIC PAPERS 12 (October 1960): 274-93.

Chetty, V. Karuppan. "On Measuring the Nearness of Near Moneys." AMERICAN ECONOMIC REVIEW 59 (June 1969): 270-81. Reprinted in [4].

Statistical tests were made to test the degree of substitution between money and other financial assets. Time deposits, deposits in mutual savings banks, and deposits in savings and loan associations, in that order, were found to be good substitutes for money. Hypotheses by Friedman, and Gurley and Shaw were substantiated. A good list of references is provided. Also see Lee, T.H. "On Measuring the Nearness of Near Moneys: Comment."; Steinhaur, L., and Chang, J.; Chetty, V.K. "Reply." AMERICAN ECONOMIC REVIEW 62 (March 1972): 217-20; 221-25; 226-29.

Chow, Gregory C. "On the Long-run and Short-run Demand for Money."
JOURNAL OF POLITICAL ECONOMY 74 (April 1966): 111-31.

It is possible to treat the demand for money as a special case of
the demand for durable goods. Permanent income is more important
than durable goods in short-run transactions demand for money.

Clower, Robert W. "Classical Monetary Theory Revisited." ECONOMICA 30
(May 1963): 165-70.

An introduction to the confusion between Walras's law, Say's law,
classical dichotomy, and other mysteries of classical monetary theory.

_____. "Permanent Income and Transitory Balances: Hahn's Paradox." OX-
FORD ECONOMIC PAPERS 15 (July 1963): 177-90.

Hahn's Paradox was brought about when Hahn defined "permanent"
with reference to both a fixed and an infinite horizon in the same
paper.

_____. "A Reconsideration of the Microfoundations of Monetary Theory."
WESTERN ECONOMIC JOURNAL 6 (December 1967): 1-8. Reprinted in [2].

"Money buys goods and goods buy money; but goods do not buy
goods." Clower's aphorism points out the uniqueness of money as
the sole medium of exchange in a monetary economy. In "Comment." WESTERN ECONOMIC JOURNAL 10 (September 1971):
304-5, Clower demonstrates the differences between a one constraint barter economy and a two constraint monetary economy in
graphical terms.

Clower, Robert W., and Burstein, M.L. "On the Invariance of Demand for
Money and Other Assets." REVIEW OF ECONOMIC STUDIES 28 (October
1960): 32-36. Reprinted in [2].

Assuming the uniqueness of equilibrium states, invariance propositions hold not only for a bond-and-money economy but also for
more general systems. Also, see Rakshit, M.K. "Invariance of
the Demand for Cash and Other Assets: A Comment." OXFORD
ECONOMIC PAPERS 16 (July 1964): 291-96; Liviatan, N. "On
the Long-Run Theory of Consumption and Real Balances." OXFORD
ECONOMIC PAPERS 17 (July 1965): 205-18.

Davidson, Paul. "Keynes's Finance Motive." OXFORD ECONOMIC PAPERS
17 (March 1965): 47-65.

This is an explanation of Keynes's fourth demand for money.
Money will be held by entrepreneurs to insure that they will be
able to carry out their plans. The IS-LM dynamic analysis done
by Davidson is heavily criticized in Horwich, George. "Keynes's
Finance Motive: Comment." OXFORD ECONOMIC PAPERS 18

(July 1966): 242-51. Davidson's response is "The Importance of the Demand for Finance." OXFORD ECONOMIC PAPERS 19 (July 1967): 245-53.

de Leeuw, Frank. "Demand for Money--Speed of Adjustment, Interest Rates and Wealth." In MONETARY PROCESS AND POLICY: A SYMPOSIUM, edited by George Horwich, pp. 167-86. Homewood, Ill.: Richard D. Irwin, 1967.

> Quarterly postwar data show that there is a considerable lag in the adjustment of the quantity of money demanded to the interest rate and scale-variables; this is a departure from traditional theory. Of interest is Johnson, Harry G. "Comment on the de Leeuw Findings on Demand for Money." Ibid., pp. 368-70.

Demsetz, Harold. "The Cost of Transacting." QUARTERLY JOURNAL OF ECONOMICS 82 (February 1968): 33-53.

> A neglected aspect, at that time, of economic market behavior is analyzed. Transactions are costly.

Ellis, Howard S. "Notes on the Demand for Money." KYKLOS 15, fasc. 1 (1962): 216-30.

> Ellis feels the rectangular hyperbola demand for money is naive, as is the liquidity trap. He also says a word about active and idle balances and the costs of demanding money.

_____. "Some Fundamentals in the Theory of Velocity." QUARTERLY JOURNAL OF ECONOMICS 52 (May 1938): 431-72. Reprinted in [11].

> Does the effective quantity of money (money supply multiplied by velocity) determine prices or does liquidity demand determine the rate of interest? Causality is influenced by time.

Feige, Edgar I. THE DEMAND FOR LIQUID ASSETS: A TEMPORAL CROSS-SECTION ANALYSIS. Englewood Cliffs, N.J.: Prentice-Hall, 1964. 103 p.

> This is a doctoral dissertation with three basic hypotheses Feige considers particularly relevant to the effectiveness of monetary policy: (1) the liabilities of nonbank financial intermediaries are close substitutes for money, (2) the demand for money is a stable function of a limited number of variables, and (3) the demand for money is independent of the supply of money.

_____. "Expectations and Adjustment in the Monetary Sector." AMERICAN ECONOMIC REVIEW 57 (May 1967): 462-73.

> This article is the first real attempt to distinguish between adaptive expectations and distributed lag adjustments in the demand for money. See the critical discussions by Gary Fromm, Thomas R. Saving, and George R. Morrison. Ibid., pp. 474-77, 477-79, 479-81.

Fleming, Miles. MONETARY THEORY. London: Macmillan and Co., 1972. 63 p. Paperbound.

This is an excellent primer with a strong bibliography.

_____. "The Timing of Payments and the Demand for Money." ECONOMICA 31 (May 1964): 132-57.

Studying the demand for money with comparative static systems has emphasized an error of classical thought. There has been little or no analysis of the factors which determine the timing of financial transactions.

Friedman, Milton. "The Demand for Money: Some Theoretical and Empirical Results." JOURNAL OF POLITICAL ECONOMY 67 (August 1959): 327-51. Reprinted in [5] [19].

The importance of changes in the stock of money on the economy should not be underestimated. For another view see Duesenberry, James. "Discussion." JOURNAL OF POLITICAL ECONOMY 67 (August 1959): 528-30.

_____. "Interest Rates and the Demand for Money." JOURNAL OF LAW AND ECONOMICS 9 (October 1966): 71-86. Reprinted in [8].

What is important for monetary theory and policy is known if the demand for money function is reasonably stable, is determined by a fairly small number of variables, and can be empirically specified with some accuracy.

_____. "A Monetary Theory of Nominal Income." JOURNAL OF POLITICAL ECONOMY 79 (March/April 1971): 323-37.

Current nominal income is a function of current and prior nominal quantities of money. The problem of the division of a change in nominal income between prices and output is bypassed. Also see, "A Theoretical Framework for Monetary Analysis." Ibid., 78 (March/April 1970): 193-238.

_____. "The Quantity Theory of Money: A Restatement." In his STUDIES IN THE QUANTITY THEORY OF MONEY, pp. 3-21. Chicago: Chicago University Press, 1956. Reprinted in [2] [15] [19].

"The quantity theory of money is a term evocative of a general approach rather than label for a well-defined theory." So starts Friedman's defense of the quantity theory of money--a theory of the demand for money.

Friedman, Milton, and Schwartz, Anna J[acobson]. "The Definition of Money: New Wealth and Neutrality." JOURNAL OF MONEY, CREDIT AND BANK-ING 1 (February 1969): 1-14.

A critique of the definitions of money made by Pesek and Saving, Newlyn, Yeager, and Gramley and Chase.

Gilbert, J.C. "The Demand for Money: The Development of an Economic Concept." JOURNAL OF POLITICAL ECONOMY 61 (April 1953): 144-59.

The analysis of the demand for money should be based on the two fundamental causes: time and uncertainty.

Guthrie, Harold W. "Consumers' Propensities to Hold Liquid Assets." JOURNAL OF THE AMERICAN STATISTICAL ASSOCIATION 55 (Summer 1960): 469-90.

An attempt was made to isolate the precautionary demand for money. The relationships between liquid balances and age, size of consumer unit, level of income, and home ownership were tested.

Hahn, F[rank].H. "The General Equilibrium Theory of Money--A Comment." REVIEW OF ECONOMIC STUDIES 19, no. 3 (1952-53): 179-85.

In this review of Patinkin's work, Hahn points out a couple of errors: the real value of bonds should be taken as a dependent variable and, consequently, the rate of interest no longer appears as a separate variable. Patinkin in a reply shows that the basic argument of his original paper is not affected. Patinkin, Don. "Further Considerations of the General Equilibrium Theory of Money." Ibid., pp. 186-95.

_____. "Real Balances and Consumption." OXFORD ECONOMIC PAPERS 15 (June 1962): 117-23.

If our model has constant prices, positive marginal propensity to consume, and perfect capital markets, the asset effect will most surely not be transitory. However, if a small amount of realism is allowed to enter, the real balance effect may well be transitory. See Clower, Robert W. "Permanent Income and Transitory Balances: Hahn's Paradox." OXFORD ECONOMIC PAPERS 15 (June 1963): 177-90.

Hicks, J[ohn].R. "A Suggestion for Simplifying the Theory of Money." ECONOMICA 2 (February 1935): 1-19. Reprinted in [11].

A classic article. Hicks's suggestion is that a marginal revolution is needed in monetary theory. Marshall and his followers were so dominated by the classical concept of money as a "veil" that they regarded the demand for money as a demand for real balances-- for the things money can buy.

Hirshleifer, Jack. "Exchange Theory: The Missing Chapter." WESTERN ECONOMIC JOURNAL 11 (June 1973): 129-46.

Money enters into exchange theory both as a medium of exchange and as a temporary store of value. Even in a competitive economy with certainty and simple pricing, money lowers transaction costs.

Jevons, W.S. "Barter." In his MONEY AND THE MECHANISM OF EXCHANGE, 23d ed., pp. 1-7. London: Kegan Paul, 1910. Reprinted in [2].

The three "wants" of barter are: (1) want of coincidence, (2) want of a measure of value, and (3) want of a means of subdivision.

Johnson, Harry G., ed. "Issues in Monetary Research, 1966." JOURNAL OF POLITICAL ECONOMY 75, supplement (August 1967): 431-654.

This is the proceedings of a conference of university professors of monetary economics. The papers by Thomas R. Saving, "Monetary-Policy Targets and Indicators," pp. 446-56; Allan H. Meltzer, "Major Issues in the Regulation of Financial Institutions," pp. 482-500; and L.G. Telser, "A Critique of Some Recent Empirical Research on the Explanation of the Term Structure of Interest Rates," pp. 546-60, are of most continuing interest.

_____, "Issues in Monetary Research, 1967." JOURNAL OF POLITICAL ECONOMY 76, supplement (July/August 1968): 661-952.

Phillips curve trade-offs, the effects of monetary and credit policies, and optimal monetary growth were the issues which generated the most interest, then and now. This supplement is the proceedings of a conference.

Kane, Edward J. [Martial, Alfred]. "Biological Analogies for Money: A Crucial Breakthrough." JOURNAL OF FINANCE 24 (March 1969): 111-12. Reprinted in [4] [12].

Money's biological analogue is not found. Six near-misses are discovered: fat, spirit, blood, muck, muscle, and bile.

Klein, Benjamin. "Competitive Interest Payments on Bank Deposits and the Long-Run Demand for Money." AMERICAN ECONOMIC REVIEW 64 (December 1974): 931-49.

Two assumptions are tested: (1) the interest rate is the opportunity cost of holding money, and (2) the current ban on demand deposit interest payments is fully effective. A good list of references is given.

Laidler, David. "The Definition of Money: Theoretical and Empirical Problems." JOURNAL OF MONEY, CREDIT AND BANKING 1 (August 1969): 508-25. Reprinted in [1] [4].

According to the empirical data available to Laidler, it does not seem to matter if the authorities try to control only demand deposits or both demand and time deposits together. The demand for money defined either way is stable. See the comments by Case M. Sprinkle and Ronald L. Teigen, Ibid., pp. 526-30; 531-34.

_____. THE DEMAND FOR MONEY. New York: Intext Educational Publishers, 1969. 142 p. Paperbound.

A good survey of work in monetary theory influenced by the GENERAL THEORY. The bibliography is worth the cost of the book.

_____. "The Rate of Interest and the Demand for Money: Some Empirical Evidence." JOURNAL OF POLITICAL ECONOMY 74 (December 1966): 543-55.

The main conclusions are these: (1) there is a stable relationship between the demand for money and the interest rate, (2) the relevant interest rate is a short one, and (3) there is little evidence of the existence of a liquidity trap.

_____. "Some Evidence on the Demand for Money." JOURNAL OF POLITICAL ECONOMY 74 (February 1966): 55-68.

This empirical evidence seems to suggest that permanent income is a better explanatory variable than measured income or non-human wealth. Also, the definition of money should include time deposits.

Latane, Henry A. "Cash Balances and the Interest Rate--A Pragmatic Approach." REVIEW OF ECONOMICS AND STATISTICS 36 (November 1954): 456-60. Reprinted in [16] [19].

Quantitative relationships are developed to determine how changes in the interest rate influence the demand for cash balances. It appears that the interest rate and velocity are directly related. In a sequel to this article, "Income Velocity and Interest Rates: A Pragmatic Approach." REVIEW OF ECONOMICS AND STATISTICS 42 (November 1960): 443-49, Latane concluded his results were "consistent with the hypothesis that there has been a rather constant interest elasticity of demand for cash balances of approximately eighty-five over this period."

Laumas, G.S. "Savings Deposits in the Definition of Money." JOURNAL OF POLITICAL ECONOMY 77 (November/December 1969): 892-96.

Laumas finds that for the postwar period $M_2^* = M_1 + 0.5785 (M_2 - M_1)$ is a more appropriate stock of money for theoretical and empirical analysis. Also see Laumas. "The Degree of Moneyness of Savings Deposits." AMERICAN ECONOMIC REVIEW 58 (June 1968): 501-3.

Lee, Tong Hun. "Alternative Interest Rates and the Demand for Money: The Empirical Evidence." AMERICAN ECONOMIC REVIEW 57 (December 1967): 1168-81.

Which rate of interest exerts the most influence on the demand for money? Lee claims that the yield on nonbank intermediary liabilities should claim the honor. However, see also Hamburger, M.J. "Alternative Interest Rates and the Demand for Money: Comment." Lee, Tong Hun. "Reply." AMERICAN ECONOMIC REVIEW 59 (June 1969): 407-11; 412-17.

_____. "Income, Wealth and the Demand for Money: Some Evidence from Cross-Section Data." JOURNAL OF THE AMERICAN STATISTICAL ASSOCIA-TION 59 (September 1964): 746-62.

Both income and wealth have a significant positive effect on the demand for money. The either/or constraint hypothesis is not supported.

Lerner, Abba P. "The Essential Properties of Interest and Money." QUARTERLY JOURNAL OF ECONOMICS 66 (May 1952): 172-93.

This article attempts to straighten out chapter 17 of Keynes's GENERAL THEORY, which has the same title. The rigidity of wages and prices is necessary to maintain stability of purchasing power.

Leser, C.E.V. "The Consumer's Demand for Money." ECONOMETRICA 11 (April 1943): 123-40.

Leser was the first to show that a trader's equilibrium demand for cash balances is independent of the general price level and of initial balances, and is governed solely by tastes and real income.

McKean, Roland N. "Liquidity and a National Balance Sheet." JOURNAL OF POLITICAL ECONOMY 57 (December 1949): 506-22. Reprinted in [11].

If we are to be able to gauge effective demand, it is important to understand more about liquidity.

Marschak, Jacob. "The Rationale of the Demand for Money and of 'Money Illusion'." METROECONOMICA 2 (August 1950): 71-100.

If positive stocks of money are present, so is money illusion. The importance of money as a medium of exchange is emphasized as a prime reason for holding money. Rationality condones it; consequently, illusion is a misnomer.

Melitz, Jacques, and Martin, George. "Financial Intermediaries, Money Definition and Monetary Control." JOURNAL OF MONEY, CREDIT AND BANKING 3 (August 1971): 693-701.

The conclusion they reach is that the Federal Reserve can control M3 at least as closely, though not necessarily better than, M1 and M2. This is not to imply that the Federal Reserve can set money stock at will.

Meltzer, Allan H. "The Demand for Money: The Evidence from the Time Series." JOURNAL OF POLITICAL ECONOMY 71 (June 1963): 219-46. Reprinted in [19].

A clear division is sought between the quantity theory and the "new view." The income-expenditure approach is give short shrift.

———. "Money, Intermediation and Growth." JOURNAL OF ECONOMIC LITERATURE 1 (March 1969): 27-40.

This survey article is divided into two subsections: (1) "The Definition of Money and the Role of Intermediaries," and (2) "Money and Growth." Most pages are spent on the "old view" versus "new view" and the optimal quantity of money. These are issues that have not generated a lot of subsequent interest.

Miller, M[erton].H., and Orr, D[avid]. " A Model of the Demand for Money by Firms." QUARTERLY JOURNAL OF ECONOMICS 80 (August 1966): 413-35.

This article is a critique and extension of the inventory approach to the demand for money. Economies of scale are found in cash holdings.

Mishan, E.J. "A Fallacy in the Interpretation of the Cash Balance Effect." ECONOMICA 25 (May 1958): 106-18.

A distinction is made between the so-called Pigou effect and the cash balance effect. Patinkin is shown to be inconsistent.

Modigliani, Franco. "Liquidity Preference." In INTERNATIONAL ENCYCLO-PEDIA OF THE SOCIAL SCIENCES, edited by D.L. Sills, vol. 9, pp. 394-409. New York: Macmillan-Free Press, 1968.

Liquidity preference (the relation between the quantity of money demanded and the interest rate) is viewed from a historic perspective.

Morgan, E.V[ictor]. "The Essential Qualities of Money." MANCHESTER SCHOOL OF ECONOMICS AND SOCIAL STUDIES 37 (September 1969): 237-48.

The essential difference between money and money substitutes is that the supply of bank deposits is determined exogenously.

Negishi, Takashi. "Conditions for Neutral Money." REVIEW OF ECONOMIC STUDIES 31 (April 1964): 147-48.

The conditions are: (1) all utility functions are identical, (2) they are homogeneous, and (3) the utility of money is separable from that of goods.

Niehaus, Jurg. "Money and Barter in General Equilibrium with Transactions Costs." AMERICAN ECONOMIC REVIEW 61 (December 1971): 773-83.

The neoclassical system is extended to include transactions and storage costs. Time preference is neglected. An earlier article is also of interest "Money in a Static Theory of Optimal Payments Arrangements." JOURNAL OF MONEY, CREDIT AND BANKING 1 (November 1969): 706-26.

Ostroy, Joseph M. "The Informational Efficiency of Monetary Exchange." AMERICAN ECONOMIC REVIEW 63 (September 1973): 597-610.

How long does it take for an economy to go from the sum of individual excess demands is zero to all individual excess demands are zero for each commodity? The comparison is between barter and monetary economies.

Patinkin, Don. "Dichotomies of the Pricing Process in Economic Theory." ECONOMICA 21 (May 1954): 113-28.

Patinkin tries to separate the valid from the invalid dichotomy in neoclassical and classical literature. Neither school provides clear and explicit guidance on the dichotomization issue.

_____. "Financial Intermediaries and the Logical Structure of Monetary Theory." AMERICAN ECONOMIC REVIEW 51 (March 1961): 95-116.

This is a review article of Gurley, John G. and Shaw, Edward S. MONEY IN A THEORY OF FINANCE. Washington, D.C.: Brookings Institution, 1960. The review is an extremely critical one-- well worth reading. Gurley and Shaw brought to the fore the distinction between "inside" and "outside" money. Patinkin's model in the first edition of MONEY, INTEREST, AND PRICES (1956) was only an outside money model.

_____. "The Indeterminacy of Absolute Prices in Classical Economic Theory." ECONOMETRICA 17 (January 1949): 1-27.

This is where Patinkin's quarrel with the classical dichotomy begins. The real balance effect is introduced to determine the equilibrium value of the absolute price level.

_____. "Price Flexibility and Full Employment." In READINGS IN MONETARY THEORY, edited by Friedrich A. Lutz and Lloyd W. Mints, pp. 252-83. Homewood, Ill.: Richard D. Irwin, 1951. Reprinted in [10] [11] [13] [15] [16] [20].

This is a corrected reprint of an article by the same title which appeared in AMERICAN ECONOMIC REVIEW 38 (September 1948): 543-64. If the problem of unemployment is discussed dynamically rather than comparative statically, wage rigidity is no longer necessary for involuntary unemployment. Consequently, there is no longer any basic issue separating the Keynesians and the classics.

Rakshit, M.K. "Invariance of the Demand for Cash and Other Assets." OXFORD ECONOMIC PAPERS 16 (July 1964): 291-96.

This is a critique of the Clower-Burstein invariance analysis. Once individuals purchase and sell bonds, it becomes difficult to conceive of one-week maximizers.

Samuelson, Paul A. "What Classical and Neoclassical Monetary Theory Really Was." CANADIAN JOURNAL OF ECONOMICS 1 (February 1968): 1-15. Reprinted in [2] [13].

It is not necessary to have real balances in the utility function to have a correctly specified model of a "monetary" economy. It is only necessary that the utility function contain, along with the physical quantities of goods consumed, the stock of money and all money prices and that they be homogeneous of degree zero. A comment and a reply of interest are: Clower, R.W. "What Traditional Monetary Theory Really Wasn't."; Samuelson, Paul A. "Nonoptimality of Money Holdings under Laissez Faire." CANADIAN JOURNAL OF ECONOMICS 2 (May 1969): 299-302, 303-8.

Schumpeter, Joseph A. "Money and the Social Product." INTERNATIONAL ECONOMIC PAPERS. Translations prepared for the International Economic Association, no. 6. Edited by Alan T. Peacock et al. New York: Macmillan, 1956. pp. 148-211.

In monetary economics, especially, "theory is all the more necessary as a prerequisite of practical decisions."

Senior, Nassau W. "On the Quantity and Value of Money." In his THREE LECTURES ON THE VALUE OF MONEY, pp. 5-31. London: B. Fellows, 1840. Reprinted in [2].

The value of money depends permanently only on the cost of its production.

Simmons, Edward C. "The Relative Liquidity of Money and Other Things." AMERICAN ECONOMIC REVIEW 37 (May 1947): 308-11. Reprinted in [11].

The fewer the substitutes there are for money the better can be monetary management.

Starr, Ross M. "Exchange in Barter and Monetary Economies." QUARTERLY JOURNAL OF ECONOMICS 86 (May 1972): 290-302.

As long as a monetary economy is costless, it can do everything better or at least as well as a barter economy. A selected number of sources is included.

Teigen, Ronald L. "Demand and Supply Functions for Money in the United States: Some Structural Estimates." ECONOMETRICA 32 (October 1964): 476-509.

To determine the money stock, inside money as well as outside money must be taken into account. Without inside money, elasticities are biased downward.. Also see Teigen, Ronald L. "The Demand for and Supply of Money." In READINGS IN MONEY, NATIONAL INCOME, AND STABILIZATION POLICY, edited by W.L. Smith and Ronald L. Teigen, pp. 68-103. 3d ed. Homewood, Ill.: Richard D. Irwin, 1974.

Thompson, Earl A. "The Theory of Money and Income Consistent with Orthodox Value Theory." In TRADE, STABILITY, AND MACROECONOMICS: ESSAYS IN HONOR OF LLOYD A. METZLER, edited by George Horwich and Paul A. Samuelson, pp. 427-53. New York: Academic Press, 1974.

The view is expounded that many of the "logical fallacies" in the classical view of a money economy are caused by modern monetary economists, because money supply is introduced into the classical model as being exogenous rather than endogenous. The argument is persuasive; however, much of Thompson's case rests on his unpublished manuscripts.

Tobin, James. "A General Equilibrium Approach to Monetary Theory." JOURNAL OF MONEY, CREDIT AND BANKING 1 (February 1969): 15-29.

Tobin reviews the Yale school's approach to monetary economics. Aggregate demand is perversely affected when the valuations of physical assets change relative to their replacement costs.

_____. "The Interest Elasticity of Transactions Demand for Cash." REVIEW OF ECONOMICS AND STATISTICS 38 (August 1956): 241-47.

The direct and opportunity costs of going into and out of the market are analyzed with regard to an optimal inventory. The classic article is Baumol, W.J. "The Transactions Demand for Cash--An Inventory Theoretic Approach." QUARTERLY JOURNAL OF ECONOMICS 66 (November 1952): 545-56.

_____. "Liquidity Preference as Behavior towards Risk." REVIEW OF ECONOMIC STUDIES 25 (February 1958): 65-86. Reprinted in [15] [19] [20].

A classic article describing a risk aversion theory of liquidity preference. The inverse relation between the demand for money and the rate of interest is supported.

_____ . "Money, Capital and Other Stores of Value." AMERICAN ECONOMIC REVIEW 51 (May 1961): 26-37. Reprinted in [14].

Some of the difficulties of analyzing the real and monetary aspects of a stock-flow economy are explored.

Wallace, Neil. "An Approach to the Study of Money and Nonmoney Exchange Situations." JOURNAL OF MONEY, CREDIT AND BANKING 4 (November 1972): 838-47.

The costs of transactions are compared between money and nonmoney economies. Just the tip of the iceberg is showing.

Wonnacott, Paul. "Neutral Money in Patinkin's Money, Interest, and Prices." REVIEW OF ECONOMIC STUDIES 26 (October 1958): 70-71.

In his first edition, Patinkin defined a barter economy by altering the unit of account. The possibility of nonneutral money was eliminated.

Yeager, Leland B. "Essential Properties of the Medium of Exchange." KYKLOS 21 (February 1968): 45-68. Reprinted in [1] [2].

The important point is made that what makes money unique is that it is the only universally accepted medium of exchange in the real world.

MONEY SUPPLY

Bain, A.D. CONTROL OF THE MONEY SUPPLY. Baltimore: Penguin Books, 1971. 175 p. Paperbound.

A short survey of the importance of controlling the money supply written by an Englishman. Does the stock of money influence the flow of income or vice versa? A selected bibliography is included.

Brunner, Karl. "A Schema for the Supply Theory of Money." INTERNATIONAL ECONOMIC REVIEW 2 (January 1961): 79-109.

A framework is built for further study of empirical money supply theory. Money stock is explained in terms of the public's demand functions for currency and time deposits, the monetary base (adjusted for the cumulated reserve limitations), the interbank deposit structure, and a bank's demand for Federal Reserve money.

_____ . "Some Major Problems in Monetary Theory." AMERICAN ECONOMIC REVIEW 51 (May 1961): 47-56. Reprinted in [10].

This is an outline of a long neglected approach to money supply theory.

Brunner, Karl, and Meltzer, Allan H. "The Uses of Money: Money in the Theory of an Exchange Economy." AMERICAN ECONOMIC REVIEW 61 (December 1971): 784-805.

Why is money held? Once the world of certainty combined with costless information is left, money has utility and is productive.

Burger, Albert E. THE MONEY SUPPLY PROCESS. Belmont, Calif.: Wadsworth Publishing Co., 1971. 213 p. Paperbound.

The supply of money hypothesis developed in this book is based on the work of Brunner and Meltzer. It is a good "one stop" survey of money supply theory. The research of the Federal Reserve Bank of St. Louis has been integrated into this study.

Burger, Albert E., and Balbach, Anatal. "Measurement of the Domestic Money Stock." Federal Reserve Bank of St. Louis REVIEW 54 (May 1972): 10-23.

Burger and Balbach construct a domestic money stock series which takes account of international capital flows.

Burger, Albert E., and Jordan, Jerry L. "The Revised Money Stock: Explanations and Illustrations." Federal Reserve Bank of St. Louis REVIEW 53 (January 1971): 6-15.

The 1970 revision of money stock data is reviewed.

Burger, Albert E., et al. "Money Stock Control and Its Implications for Monetary Policy." Federal Reserve Bank of St. Louis REVIEW 53 (October 1971): 6-22.

The St. Louis bank's attempt to formulate a procedure to control money stock and evaluate the results. If money stock control becomes a policy of the Federal Reserve, this procedure may prove useful.

Cagan, Phillip. "The Demand for Currency Relative to the Total Money Supply." JOURNAL OF POLITICAL ECONOMY 66 (August 1958): 303-28.

No one variable can account for the fluctuations in the ratio of currency to total money supply. The three most important are: expected net rate of interest on deposits, expected real income per capita, and income taxes as a percentage of personal income.

_____. DETERMINANTS AND EFFECTS OF CHANGES IN THE STOCK OF MONEY, 1875-1960. New York: Columbia University Press, 1965. 408 p.

The book begins with an excellent description of the major issues. The material is systematically organized with the aid of an analytic framework which reduces variations in the money stock to changes in high-powered money, the bank reserve ratio, and the currency ratio. This is a companion volume to Friedman and Schwartz, A MONETARY HISTORY OF THE UNITED STATES, 1867-1960.

_____ . "The Non-Neutrality of Money in the Long Run." JOURNAL OF MONEY, CREDIT AND BANKING 1 (May 1969): 207-27.

"In the final analysis, if there are no lagged adjustments, if expectations are perfect, if the banking system is perfectly competitive, and if redistributive effects of government expenditures are ignored, money will be neutral."

Dacey, W.M. "Treasury Bills and the Money Supply." LLOYDS BANK REVIEW 70 (January 1960): 1-16.

This article was written after the Radcliffe Report was issued. Dacey shows that monetary policy must always take into account debt management. Neither control of money supply nor control of the rate of interest alone will give an effective monetary policy.

Fand, David I. "Some Implications of Money Supply Analysis." AMERICAN ECONOMIC REVIEW 57 (May 1967): 380-400. Reprinted in [4].

As long as there are no free reserves and banks and the public do not change their portfolios, money supply is of little interest. This is not the case in the real world, however.

Friedman, Milton, and Schwartz, Anna Jacobson. A MONETARY HISTORY OF THE UNITED STATES, 1867-1960. Princeton, N.J.: Princeton University Press, 1963. 884 p. Also paperbound.

A monetarist history that is filled with graphs and statistics but still is interesting reading. The importance of money supply to national income is stressed.

Hawtrey, R.G. "Money and Index-Numbers." JOURNAL OF THE ROYAL STATISTICAL SOCIETY 93, pt. 1 (1930): 64-85. Reprinted in [11].

What are the monetary causes that affect prices? "They are causes affecting the amount of the consumers' income and outlay otherwise than in proportion to the factors of production."

Jordan, Jerry L. "Elements of Money Stock Determination." Federal Reserve Bank of St. Louis REVIEW 51 (October 1969): 10-19. Reprinted in [1] [4].

Does the quantity theory of money hold and, if so, can monetary authorities control the stock of money? Control is difficult because money supply is influenced by many things besides the wishes of the authorities. Also see Jordan, Jerry L. "Relations Among Monetary Aggregates." Federal Reserve Bank of St. Louis REVIEW 51 (March 1969): 8-9.

Kareken, John H. "Commercial Banks and the Supply of Money: A Market Determined Demand Deposit Rate." FEDERAL RESERVE BULLETIN 53 (October 1967): 1699-712.

The "new view" of monetary economics is espoused.

Meade, James E. "The Amount of Money and the Banking System." ECONOMIC JOURNAL 44 (March 1934): 77-83. Reprinted in [11].

A statistical and theoretical study done to show how the supply of money would be affected by changes in the banking system.

Meigs, A. James. FREE RESERVES AND THE MONEY SUPPLY. Chicago: University of Chicago Press, 1962. 134 p.

There is no way that an outside observer can deduce from the level of free reserves what the Federal Reserve wants commercial banks to do or what they are doing. There are just too many influences at work.

Meltzer, Allan H. "Money Supply Revisited: A Review Article." JOURNAL OF POLITICAL ECONOMY 75 (April 1967): 169-82.

The article is a review of Cagan, Phillip. DETERMINANTS AND EFFECTS OF CHANGES IN THE STOCK OF MONEY, 1875-1960. New York: Columbia University Press, 1965. Meltzer is a monetarist, as is Cagan; consequently, they are very much in agreement that money stock is not merely a passive factor in income determination.

Newlyn, W.T. "The Supply of Money and Its Control." ECONOMIC JOURNAL 74 (June 1964): 327-47.

It is shown that the "old orthodoxy" and the "new orthodoxy," with regard to the basic postulates of monetary and banking theory, are not all that different. What is needed is a correct and unambiguous restatement.

Phillips, Chester Arthur. BANK CREDIT. New York: Macmillan, 1921. 388 p.

This book is thought to provide the classical exposition of the multiple expansion of money, the beginning of "inside" money and the "old view." However, Alfred Marshall may have been the originator. See Clower, Robert W. "Marshall on Deposit Multipliers." ECONOMIC INQUIRY 13 (June 1975): 252.

Pigou, A.C. "The Value of Money." QUARTERLY JOURNAL OF ECONOMICS 32 (November 1917): 38-65. Reprinted in [11].

Monetary theory is too complex; consequently, a model is needed.

Pigou feels he has invented the superior mousetrap. A correction of the original article was made, Ibid., 32 (February 1918): 209.

Robertson, Dennis H. "British Monetary Policy." LLOYDS BANK MONTHLY REVIEW 10 (May 1939): 146-57. Reprinted in [12].

The interesting and short conversation between Socrates and Oeconomist about the nature of money is still of value.

_____. "A Note on the Theory of Money." ECONOMICA 13 (August 1933): 243-47. Reprinted in [11].

Robertson shows that two propositions Keynes makes in his TREATISE ON MONEY are not well founded.

Teigen, Ronald L. "Demand and Supply Functions for Money in the United States: Some Structural Estimates." ECONOMETRICA 32 (October 1964): 476-509.

To determine the money stock, inside money as well as outside money must be taken into account. Without inside money, elasticities are biased downward. Also see Teigen, Ronald L. "The Demand for and Supply of Money." In READINGS IN MONEY, NATIONAL INCOME, AND STABILIZATION POLICY, edited by W.L. Smith and Ronald L. Teigen, 3d ed., pp. 68-103. Homewood, Ill.: Richard D. Irwin, 1974.

Tolly, G.S. "Providing for Growth of the Money Supply." JOURNAL OF POLITICAL ECONOMY 65 (December 1957): 477-84. Reprinted in [19].

The range of ways that money supply may be increased is discussed. The effects on policy goals of the various alternatives are considered.

Tucker, Donald. "Dynamic Income Adjustment to Money-Supply Changes." AMERICAN ECONOMIC REVIEW 56 (June 1966): 433-49.

The speed with which investment responds to changes in the interest rate and other variables will influence directly the speed at which the economy responds to changes in money supply.

INTEREST RATE: THEORY

Alchian, Armen A. "The Rate of Interest, Fisher's Rate of Return Over Cost and Keynes' Internal Rate." AMERICAN ECONOMIC REVIEW 45 (December 1955): 938-43.

Fisher's marginal rate of return over cost and Keynes's marginal efficiency of capital are not identical, as Keynes alleged in the GENERAL THEORY.

Cassel, Gustav. "The Rate of Interest, the Bank Rate, and the Stabilization of Prices." QUARTERLY JOURNAL OF ECONOMICS 42 (August 1928): 511-29. Reprinted in [11].

The difference between the rate of interest as a price and as a value is discussed.

Clower, Robert W. "Productivity, Thrift and the Rate of Interest." ECONOMIC JOURNAL 64 (March 1954): 107-15.

Stock-flow analysis is used to come to grips with interest theory.

Conard, Joseph W. AN INTRODUCTION TO THE THEORY OF INTEREST. Berkeley and Los Angeles: University of California Press, 1959. 395 p.

This is not an introduction for the layperson. It is a seminal work. All aspects of the theory of interest are discussed.

Fellner, William [J.], and Somers, Harold M. "Alternative Monetary Approaches to Interest Theory." REVIEW OF ECONOMIC STATISTICS 23 (February 1941): 43-48. Reprinted in [19].

The liquidity preference-loanable funds theories are compared. They hold them to be equivalent in general equilibrium because all demand and supplies become interrelated.

_____. "Note on 'Stocks' and 'Flows' in Monetary Interest Theory." REVIEW OF ECONOMICS AND STATISTICS 31 (May 1949): 145-46.

This note expands the thesis that stock and flow theories of the rate of interest are equivalent. For an exchange of views see the discussion by Karl Brunner, Lawrence R. Klein, and Fellner and Somers in ECONOMETRICA 18 (July 1950): 236-52.

Fisher, Irving. THE NATURE OF INCOME AND CAPITAL. New York: Augustus M. Kelley, 1906. 448 p.

Fisher wishes to bring attention to the role of income in all economic problems. "It is income for which labor is exerted; and it is the distribution of income which constitutes the disparity between rich and poor."

_____. THE THEORY OF INTEREST. New York: Augustus M. Kelley, 1930. 587 p.

This book was begun as a revision of his THE RATE OF INTEREST (1907). His interest theory is summed up by his subtitle to this volume: AS DETERMINED BY IMPATIENCE TO SPEND INCOME AND OPPORTUNITY TO INVEST IT.

Freeman, Jo Fisher. "Liquidity Preference versus Loanable Funds: A New Approach to the Problem." ECONOMIC JOURNAL 73 (December 1963): 681–88.

> The determination of the equilibrium rate of interest is a function of the model used. It is also necessary to distinguish between long and short-term interest rates.

Gibson, William E. "Price-Expectations Effects on Interest Rates." JOURNAL OF FINANCE 25 (March 1970): 19–34. Reprinted in [4].

> There is a positive correlation between expected rates of price change and nominal interest rates. Monetary policy authorities must realize the ramifications of maintaining interest rates below their equilibrium levels.

Guttentag, Jack M., ed. ESSAYS ON INTEREST RATES. 2 vols. New York: Columbia University Press, 1969 and 1971. 296 p. and 482 p.

> An assortment of essays dealing with all aspects of interest rates. The essays are mostly older reprints and not articles at the frontier.

Hahn, Frank H. "The Rate of Interest and General Equilibrium Analysis." ECONOMIC JOURNAL 65 (March 1955): 52–66.

> Hahn shows that money is not neutral in Franco Modigliani's 1944 classic article ("Liquidity Preference and the Theory of Interest and Money." ECONOMETRICA 12 [January 1944]: 45–88). He also demonstrates that the only difference between the liquidity preference and loanable funds theories is the period chosen for consideration.

Homer, Sidney. A HISTORY OF INTEREST RATES. New Brunswick, N.J.: Rutgers University Press, 1963. 633 p.

> Homer's book covers the history of interest rates on every continent from 2000 B.C. to the present; a massive compilation of data is made available to the serious student of interest rate history.

Knight, Frank H. "Capital and Interest." ENCYCLOPAEDIA BRITANNICA, vol. 3, pp. 779–801. Chicago: Encyclopaedia Britannica, 1946. Reprinted in [3].

> A good defense of the Chicago school's theory of capital. Compare this to Boulding, Kenneth E. "Capital and Interest." ENCYCLOPAEDIA BRITANNICA, vol. 3, pp. 799–803. Chicago: Encyclopaedia Britannica, 1974.

_____. "Capital and Interest." IN ENCYCLOPEDIA OF THE SOCIAL SCIENCES, edited by E.R.A. Seligman, vol. 7, pp. 131–43. New York: Macmillan, 1932.

> A classic essay by one of the Chicago school.

Lerner, Abba P. "The Essential Properties of Interest and Money." QUARTERLY JOURNAL OF ECONOMICS 66 (May 1952): 172-93.

> This article attempts to straighten out chapter 17 of Keynes's GENERAL THEORY, which has the same title. The rigidity of wages and prices is necessary to maintain stability of purchasing power.

_____. "Interest Theory: Supply and Demand for Loans or Supply and Demand for Cash." REVIEW OF ECONOMIC STATISTICS 26 (May 1944): 88-91.

> One of the early shots in the liquidity preference-loanable funds war.

Lloyd, Cliff L. "The Equivalence of the Liquidity Preference and Loanable Funds Theories and the New Stock-Flow Analysis." REVIEW OF ECONOMIC STUDIES 27 (June 1960): 206-9.

> If bonds and/or money are stock-flow goods, it takes more than Walras's law to prove their equivalence.

Lutz, Friedrich A. THE THEORY OF INTEREST. Chicago: Aldine Publishing Co., 1968. 346 p.

> A good survey of the various theories of interest. The theories of the rate of interest and the term structure are integrated and critiqued.

Patinkin, Don. "Interest." In INTERNATIONAL ENCYCLOPEDIA OF THE SOCIAL SCIENCES, edited by D.L. Sills, vol. 7, pp. 471-85. New York: Macmillan-Free Press, 1968.

> The history of the word interest is only one of the interesting aspects of this survey.

_____. "Liquidity Preference and Loanable Funds: Stock and Flow Analysis." ECONOMICA 25 (November 1958): 300-307.

> There are differences among the various theories of the rate of interest. However, they should not be attributed to the equations selected for analysis or to the choice of stock versus flow analysis.

Robertson, Dennis H. "Mr. Keynes and the Rate of Interest." In his ESSAYS IN MONEY AND INTEREST, pp. 150-87. London: William Collins, 1966.

> More or less the summing up of a rather heated argument by two Cambridge dons. Still a topic of continuing interest.

_____. "Some Notes on the Theory of Interest." In MONEY, TRADE AND ECONOMIC GROWTH, edited by D. McCord Wright et al., pp. 193-209. New York: Macmillan, 1951.

Robertson calls this essay "pedantic footnotes" to two of his en-
deavors to synthesize the old and new theories of interest. See
also: "Mr. Keynes and the Rate of Interest." In his ESSAYS IN
MONEY AND INTEREST, pp. 150-87. London: William Collins,
1966; and "What Has Happened to the Rate of Interest?" THREE
BANKS REVIEW, no. 1 (March 1949): 15-31.

Sargent, Thomas J. "Commodity Price Expectations and the Interest Rate."
QUARTERLY JOURNAL OF ECONOMICS 83 (February 1969): 127-40. Reprinted in [4].

This is an inquiry into the Gibson paradox. Irving Fisher's explanation by means of distributed lags is shown to hold up. Incredibly
long lags are estimated.

Shackle, G.L.S. "Recent Theories Concerning the Nature and Role of Interest."
ECONOMIC JOURNAL 71 (June 1961): 209-54. Reprinted in [19].

A survey article financed by the Rockefeller Foundation. Three
general areas are covered: (1) criticism and defense of Keynes's
position, (2) the flow, stock, and stock-flow aspects of interest
rate determination, and (3) interest as a regulator of the growth
(investment demand) of society. The term structure controversies
are not touched upon.

Somers, Harold M. "Monetary Policy and the Theory of Interest." QUARTERLY
JOURNAL OF ECONOMICS 55 (May 1941): 488-507. Reprinted in [3].

A clear distinction is drawn between the liquidity preference and
loanable-funds theories of interest. Of course, it settled no arguments.

Tsiang, S.C. "Liquidity Preference and Loanable Funds Theories, Multiplier
and Velocity Analysis: A Synthesis." AMERICAN ECONOMIC REVIEW 46
(September 1956): 539-64.

This article provides a good survey of the literature. It also attempts to reconcile the multiplier and velocity analysis of income
expansion.

Turvey, Ralph. "Consistency and Consolidation in the Theory of Interest."
ECONOMICA 21 (November 1954): 300-307.

The main point made is that ceteris paribus assumptions should be
made explicit rather than implicit. Recent papers on the theory
of interest are more confusing than constructive.

_____. INTEREST RATES AND ASSET PRICES. London: Allen and Unwin,
1960. 109 p.

Sections are entitled: "Bond Preferences and Liquidity Preference,"

"Transactions Motive for Holding Money," "The Influence of Income and of Real Assets," "The Consolidation of the Private Indebtedness," "Long and Short-Term Rates of Interest," and "Further Developments."

Wicksell, Knut. "The Influence of the Rate of Interest on Prices." ECONOMIC JOURNAL 17 (June 1907): 213-20.

Wicksell, the founder and leader of the Swedish school, is critical of the quantity theory which holds that interest rates are only natural rates. Wicksell's theory is based on the equating of the market and natural rates of interest.

Yohe, William P., and Karnosky, Denis. "Interest Rates and Price Level Changes, 1962-69." Federal Reserve Bank of St. Louis REVIEW 51 (December 1969): 19-36. Reprinted in [4].

They report on the response of interest rates to price expectations. The lags are not as long as those reported by other studies; however, the period covered was longer and different statistical techniques were used.

INTEREST RATE: TERM STRUCTURE

Buse, A. "Interest Rates, the Meiselman Model and Random Numbers." JOURNAL OF POLITICAL ECONOMY 75 (February 1967): 49-62.

The empirical content of Meiselman's model is reexamined and found wanting.

Culbertson, John M. "The Term Structure of Interest Rates." QUARTERLY JOURNAL OF ECONOMICS 71 (November 1957): 485-517.

Rates on short-term and long-term U.S. government securities are tied to each other and to other securities through substitutability. However, substitutability is limited to some extent by the maturity structure of the debt.

Dodds, J.C., and Ford, J.W. EXPECTATIONS, UNCERTAINTY AND THE TERM STRUCTURE OF INTEREST RATES. New York: Harper & Row Publishers, 1974. 314 p.

A theoretical and econometric study of term structure for Britain, Italy, and the United States is done based on current data. All the current hypotheses are tested.

Fama, Eugene F. "Efficient Capital Markets: A Review of Theory and Empirical Work." JOURNAL OF FINANCE 25 (May 1970): 383-417.

Remembering that "efficient" in this context means that prices are determined under the assumption of full information, the title tells it all. Forty-seven references are included.

Feldstein, Martin [S.], amd Eckstein, Otto. "The Fundamental Determinants of the Interest Rate." REVIEW OF ECONOMICS AND STATISTICS 52 (November 1970): 363-75.

> The result of their analysis is a synthesis of Keynes's theory of liquidity preference and Fisher's model of the role of anticipated inflation.

Hamburger, Michael [J.], and Latta, Cynthia. "The Term Structure of Interest Rates: Some Additional Evidence." JOURNAL OF MONEY, CREDIT AND BANKING 1 (February 1969): 71-83.

> Their reexamination supports Wood's theory in comparison to Modigliani and Sutch's preferred habitat theory. Open market operations either in short or long-run securities influence the yield curve in a very prompt and predictable way.

Kane, Edward J. "The Term Structure of Interest Rates: An Attempt to Reconcile Teaching with Practice." JOURNAL OF FINANCE 25 (May 1970): 361-74.

> This article is a comparison of the expectations theory used by academicians and the segmentation theories used by policymakers and financial analysts.

Kane, Edward J., and Malkiel, Burton G. "The Term Structure of Interest Rates: An Analysis of a Survey of Interest-Rate Expectations." REVIEW OF ECONOMICS AND STATISTICS 49 (August 1967): 343-55.

> This is an attempt to measure market expectations directly by means of a mail survey of banks, life insurance companies, and nonfinancial corporations. Their conclusion is that the market does work.

Kessel, Reuben A. THE CYCLICAL BEHAVIOR OF THE TERM STRUCTURE OF INTEREST RATES. Occasional Paper, no. 91. New York: National Bureau of Economic Research, 1965. 124 p.

> The term structure of interest rates has been divided into three theories for the purpose of this study. They are: (1) expectations theory, (2) liquidity preference, and (3) one based on the premise that the market for default-free securities is segmented.

Lutz, Friedrich A. "The Structure of Interest Rates." QUARTERLY JOURNAL OF ECONOMICS 55 (November 1940): 36-63. Reprinted in [3].

> The first clear exposition of the term structure problem. A topic which continues to attract academicians and others.

Malkiel, Burton G. THE TERM STRUCTURE OF INTEREST RATES: EXPECTA-TIONS AND BEHAVIOR PATTERNS. Princeton, N.J.: Princeton University Press, 1966. 292 p.

> Malkiel develops an expectations theory of term structure using hedging pressure and segmentation theories.

_____. THE TERM STRUCTURE OF INTEREST RATES: THEORY, EMPIRICAL EVIDENCE AND APPLICATIONS. New York: General Learning Press, 1970. 26 p. Paperbound.

> A short and to-the-point survey of term structure. A worthwhile bibliography is appended.

Masera, R.S. THE TERM STRUCTURE OF INTEREST RATES. New York: Oxford University Press, 1972.

> As the subtitle indicates, this book is AN EXPECTATIONS MODEL TESTED ON POST-WAR ITALIAN DATA. The beginning explana-tion of the current theories of the term structure is a good intro-ductory survey.

Meiselman, David. THE TERM STRUCTURE OF INTEREST RATES. Englewood Cliffs, N.J.: Prentice-Hall, 1962. 87 p.

> Meiselman up-dates the expectations theory by constructing an error-learning model--expectations change as new information is received. This is a major work in an area fraught with competing theories and controversies.

Michaelsen, Jacob B. THE TERM STRUCTURE OF INTEREST RATES: FINAN-CIAL INTERMEDIARIES AND DEBT MANAGEMENT. New York: Intext Educa-tional Publishers, 1973. 188 p.

> An important summary of recent work on term structure. It is in-tended for undergraduate instruction. An excellent bibliography is included which will be of interest to graduate students and pro-fessionals as well.

Modigliani, Franco, and Sutch, Richard. "Debt Management and Term Structure of Interest Rates." JOURNAL OF POLITICAL ECONOMY 75, supplement (August 1967): 569-89.

> The preferred habitat theory is applied to U.S. Treasury securities in the postwar period. Their approach is critiqued by Wallace, Neil. "Comment"; and Kessel, Reuben A. "Comment." Ibid., pp. 590-95. Their most recent study is Sutch, Richard and Modig-liani, Franco. "The Term Structure of Interest Rates." JOURNAL OF MONEY, CREDIT AND BANKING 1 (February 1969): 112-20.

———. "Innovations in Interest Rate Policy." AMERICAN ECONOMIC RE-
VIEW 56 (May 1966): 178-97.

Operation Twist is shown to have little effect on the term structure.
Their expectations model accounts for the term structure remarkably
well: the so-called "preferred habitat theory." Also see the "Discussion." Ibid., pp. 198-207, by W.L. Smith, R.R. Koch, and
B.G. Malkiel.

Nelson, Charles R. THE TERM STRUCTURE OF INTEREST RATES. New York:
Basic Books, 1972. 139 p.

This book is the winner of the second "Irving Fisher Award,"
sponsored by Omicron Delta Epsilon.

Pierson, Gail. "Effect of Economic Policy on the Term Structure of Interest
Rates." REVIEW OF ECONOMICS AND STATISTICS 52 (February 1970):
1-11.

A general "unrestricted" model is specified to estimate the interest
rates based on the supply and demand equations for each maturity
classification of debt. Various government policies are examined
as to their influence on term structure of government securities and
the usefulness of the expectations hypothesis is assessed.

Roll, Richard. THE BEHAVIOR OF INTEREST RATES: AN APPLICATION OF
THE EFFICIENT MARKET MODEL TO U.S. TREASURY BILLS. New York:
Basic Books, 1970. 157 p.

The pure expectations hypothesis performed poorly, while the time-
dependent market segmentation hypothesis performed well.

Sutch, Richard, and Modigliani, Franco. "The Term Structure of Interest Rates:
A Re-Examination of the Evidence." JOURNAL OF MONEY, CREDIT AND
BANKING 1 (February 1969): 112-20.

This is the third article by Modigliani and Sutch bearing on the
explanatory power of their preferred habitat theory. This comment
is in response to Hamburger, Michael J., and Latta, Cynthia M.
"The Term Structure of Interest Rates." Ibid., pp. 71-83.

Telser, Lester G. "A Critique of Some Recent Empirical Research on the Explanation of the Term Structure of Interest Rates." JOURNAL OF POLITICAL
ECONOMY 75, supplement (August 1967): 546-60.

Telser's survey article is a necessity if valuable time is not to be
wasted in understanding the controversies in term structure.

Terrell, William T., and Frazer, William J., Jr. "Interest Rates, Portfolio
Behavior, and Marketable Government Securities." JOURNAL OF FINANCE
27 (March 1972): 1-36.

This study of term structure emphasizes the demand side for government securities rather than the supply side.

Wood, John H. "Expectations, Errors, and the Term Structure of Interest Rates."
JOURNAL OF POLITICAL ECONOMY 71 (April 1963): 160-71. Reprinted in
[19].

This is a review article of Meiselman, David. THE TERM STRUC-
TURE OF INTEREST RATES. Englewood Cliffs, N.J.: Prentice-
Hall, 1962. Meiselman has tested the expectations theory versus
the institutional and other theories. Woods is impressed with his
handling of the empirical data with regard to the expectations
theory, but not with the other theories. Also see Wood, John H.
"The Expectations Hypothesis, the Yield Curve and Monetary Policy."
QUARTERLY JOURNAL OF ECONOMICS 78 (August 1964): 457-
70.

GROWTH, ACCUMULATION, AND DISTRIBUTION

Abramovitz, Moses. "Economics of Growth." In A SURVEY OF CONTEMPO-
RARY ECONOMICS, vol. 2, edited by Bernard F. Haley, pp. 132-78. Homewood, Ill.: Richard D. Irwin, 1952.

Abramovitz's survey stresses the scope and content of economic
growth with heavy emphasis on capital formation. Consequently,
Harrod-Domar growth theories were neglected because "they make
no assertions with respect to the likely development of capital
formation over time."

Arrow, Kenneth J. "The Economic Implications of Learning by Doing." REVIEW
OF ECONOMIC STUDIES 29 (June 1962): 155-73.

Discusses the "boot strap" theory in economics. It is a fundamental
contribution.

Bliss, C.J. CAPITAL THEORY AND THE DISTRIBUTION OF INCOME. New
York: American Elsevier Publishing Co., 1975. 392 p. Also paperbound.

"When economists reach agreement on the theory of capital they
will shortly reach agreement on everything else." Small chance!
All of the topics covered are central to capital theory plus some
others. The first systematic treatment of this area.

Boulding, Kenneth E. "The Concept of Economic Surplus." AMERICAN ECO-
NOMIC REVIEW 35 (December 1945): 851-69. Reprinted in [3].

Economic surplus is the basis of the Ricardian theory of economic
rent and the Marxian theory of surplus-value. It arises whenever
elasticities of demand and supply are not perfectly elastic.

Britto, Ronald. "Some Recent Developments in the Theory of Economic Growth: An Interpretation." JOURNAL OF ECONOMIC LITERATURE 11 (December 1973): 1343-66.

> The author says this paper can be considered as an attempt to bring Hahn and Matthews's 1964 survey of economic growth up to date. Consequently, most of the 145 references are to current work. The section headings are: "The Two-Class Model," "Savings Behavior Determined by Utility Maximization," "Technical Progress," "Money," "Heterogeneous Capital Goods," and "Optimal Growth."

Bronfenbrenner, Martin. INCOME DISTRIBUTION THEORY. Chicago: Aldine Publishing Co., 1971. 502 p.

> A complete view of the field by an authority.

Burmeister, Edwin. "Synthesizing the Neo-Austrian and Alternative Approaches to Capital Theory: A Survey." JOURNAL OF ECONOMIC LITERATURE 12 (June 1974): 413-56.

> This article is in part a critical review of J.R. Hicks's CAPITAL AND TIME: A NEO-AUSTRIAN THEORY. Burmeister compares the neo-Austrian approach to the von Neumann approach with the latter proving to be more worthwhile; Hicks reached the opposite conclusion. Extremely interesting with a long, but selected, bibliography.

Burmeister, Edwin, and Phelps, Edmund [S.]. "Money, Public Debt, Inflation and Real Interest." JOURNAL OF MONEY, CREDIT AND BANKING 3 (May 1971): 153-82.

> The "neutrality" of changes in money and public debt are clarified with regard to three neoclassical growth models.

Cass, David, and Stiglitz, Joseph E. "Implications of Alternative Savings and Expectations Hypotheses for Choices of Techniques and Patterns of Growth." JOURNAL OF POLITICAL ECONOMY 77 (July/August 1969): 586-627.

> The problem is attacked in terms of a machine that is "clay" once it is constructed, i.e., its production characteristics are fixed. The conclusions reached are only in terms of balanced growth. This article is an extension of the article by Solow, R., et al. "Neoclassical Growth Fixed Factor Proportions." REVIEW OF ECONOMIC STUDIES 33 (April 1966): 79-115.

Cass, David; Stiglitz, Joseph E.; and Yaari, Menahem E. "A Reexamination of the Pure Consumption Loan Model." JOURNAL OF POLITICAL ECONOMY 74 (August 1966): 353-67.

> This article is a reexamination of Samuelson, Paul A. "An Exact Consumption-Loan Model of Interest." JOURNAL OF POLITICAL

ECONOMY 66 (December 1958): 467-82. It is not the only re-evaluation as is obvious from the references in the Cass-Yaari paper. Samuelson's very difficult problem is to determine the intertemporal interest rates in a competitive market, where the population is either stationary or growing in any prescribed fashion, and there is no capital. However, Samuelson's article is of interest to capital theorists because it incorporates ideas needed in a model of capital accumulation with decentralized decision making.

David, Paul A., and Reder, Melvin W., eds. NATIONS AND HOUSEHOLDS IN ECONOMIC GROWTH: ESSAYS IN HONOR OF MOSES ABRAMOVITZ. New York: Academic Press, 1974. 414 p.

Fifteen original papers by the well known and not so well known. A superb collection for a festschrift. The second section on "Macro-economic Performance: Growth and Stability" is of special interest.

Denison, Edward F. ACCOUNTING FOR UNITED STATES ECONOMIC GROWTH, 1929-1969. Washington, D.C.: Brookings Institution, 1974. 355 p. Also paperbound.

This is his third study of this topic. Although there is no longer the shock the first two studies generated, the analysis is more interesting. This is especially true of the discussion and measurement of the gap between actual and potential output.

_____. THE SOURCES OF ECONOMIC GROWTH IN THE UNITED STATES AND THE ALTERNATIVES BEFORE US. Committee for Economic Development. Supplementary Paper, no. 13. New York: 1962. 297 p.

Denison introduces an average labor quality variable into the Solow-type production function.

Diamond, Peter A. "National Debt in a Neoclassical Economy." AMERICAN ECONOMIC REVIEW 55 (December 1965): 1126-50.

The influence of internal and external debt, and possible substitution between them, in a neoclassical growth model is explored. Other approaches along these same lines are discussed and integrated.

Domar, Evsey [D.]. "Capital Expansion, Rate of Growth, and Employment." ECONOMETRICA 14 (April 1946): 137-47.

This is the Domar growth model. The focal point is the dual role of investment over time--influencing both aggregate demand and aggregate supply.

_____. ESSAYS IN THE THEORY OF ECONOMIC GROWTH. New York: Oxford University Press, 1957. 272 p.

The best essays written by the other half of the Harrod–Domar growth theory duo. Domar has written a very informative foreword which puts his essays in perspective.

Easterlin, R.A. POPULATION, LABOR FORCE, AND LONG SWINGS IN ECONOMIC GROWTH: THE AMERICAN EXPERIENCE. New York: Columbia University Press, 1968. 318 p.

The author delves into a broad range of macroanalytic relations among demographic and economic phenomena.

Eisner, Robert. "On Growth Models and the Neo–Classical Resurgence." ECONOMIC JOURNAL 68 (December 1958): 707-21.

This article is an attack on recent articles by a number of authors, especially Robert Solow and James Tobin. Eisner feels that the knife-edge approach of Harrod-Domar-Hicks is a closer approxima- tion of reality. Of additional interest are Tobin, James. "Reply to Professor Eisner." ECONOMIC JOURNAL 68 (September 1959): 599-600; and Solow, Robert. "Is Factor Substitution a Crime, and if so, How Bad? Reply to Professor Eisner." ECONOMIC JOUR- NAL 68 (September 1959): 597-99.

Enthoven, Alain C. "A Neo–Classical Model of Money, Debt, and Economic Growth." In MONEY IN A THEORY OF FINANCE, by Gurley, J.G. and Shaw, E.S., pp. 303-59. Washington, D.C.: Brookings Institution, 1960.

This is an early attempt to bring money into the theory of economic growth. Enthoven's logic is tighter than that of Gurley and Shaw.

Fellner, William [J.]. "Two Propositions in the Theory of Induced Innovations." ECONOMIC JOURNAL 71 (June 1961): 305-8.

The "learning process" in a competitive firm may be negated to some extent by "market imperfections."

Ferguson, C.E. "The Simple Analytics of Neoclassical Growth Theory." QUAR- TERLY REVIEW OF ECONOMICS AND BUSINESS 8 (Spring 1968): 69-83. Reprinted in [8].

A simple graphical method is presented for sorting out the various forms of technical progress. This is a good article with which to start if you have any interest at all in growth theory.

Gorman, W.M., et al. "Symposium on Aggregation." REVIEW OF ECONOMIC STUDIES 35 (October 1968): 367-442.

The main emphasis is aggregation of capital goods. The participants were W.M. Gorman, "The Structure of Utility Functions"; F.M. Fisher, "Embodied Technology and the Existence of Labor and Out- put Aggregates"; B.P. Stigum, "On a Property of Concave Func- tions"; F.M. Fisher, "Embodied Technology and the Aggregation of

Fixed and Movable Capital Goods"; and J.K. Whitaker, "Capital Aggregation and Optimality Conditions."

Griliches, Zvi, and Jorgenson, Dale W. "The Explanation of Productivity Change." REVIEW OF ECONOMIC STUDIES 34 (July 1967): 249-83.

A survey and advancement of the literature. Their corrected results show that movements along a production function (rate of growth of input) explain 96.7 percent of the observed changes in the pattern of productive activity. Shifts in the production function account for the rest.

Haberler, Gottfried, ed. "Paradoxes in Capital Theory: A Symposium." QUARTERLY JOURNAL OF ECONOMICS 80 (November 1966): 503-83.

The symposium contains contributions by Luigi L. Pasinetti; Paul A. Samuelson and David Levhari; Michio Morishima; Michael Bruno, Edwin Burmeister, and Eytan Sheshinski; P. Garegnani; and a summary by Samuelson. Levhari and Samuelson confirm that the non-switching theorem is false.

Hahn, Frank H., and Matthews, R.C.O. "The Theory of Economic Growth: A Survey." ECONOMIC JOURNAL 74 (December 1964): 779-902.

This is a complete survey of all the theoretical literature on economic growth before and since Abramovitz, M. "Economics of Growth." In A SURVEY OF CONTEMPORARY ECONOMICS, vol. 2, edited by B.F. Haley. Homewood, Ill.: Richard D. Irwin, 1952. There are over 150 references in the bibliography.

Harcourt, G.C. SOME CAMBRIDGE CONTROVERSIES IN THE THEORY OF CAPITAL. New York: Cambridge University Press, 1972. 272 p. Also paperbound.

This book is an expansion of his survey article under the same title [JOURNAL OF ECONOMIC LITERATURE 7 (June 1969): 369-405]. Capital theory is controversial because it is difficult and because value systems and rival ideologies impinge directly on the subject matter. The way is not easy. The bibliography is nearly exhaustive and exhausting.

Harrod, Roy F. "Domar and Dynamic Economics." ECONOMIC JOURNAL 69 (September 1959): 451-64.

A nice tidying-up article confirming that Harrod and Domar had, independently, conceived of the same general model of economic growth, with Harrod's model being more general--from Harrod's point of view.

_____. ECONOMIC DYNAMICS. New York: Macmillan, 1973. 195 p.

A pale shadow of his previous work in dynamic economics.

_____. "An Essay in Dynamic Theory." ECONOMIC JOURNAL 49 (March 1939): 14-33.

This is the classic article in growth theory. Steady state conditions are shown to be difficult to obtain and maintain. As Harrod says, "The main object of this article, however, is to present a tool of analysis, not to diagnose present conditions."

_____. TOWARDS A DYNAMIC ECONOMICS. New York: St. Martin's Press, 1948. 178 p.

A collection of Harrod's lectures on economic growth given at the University of London in February 1947. These were his first writings on economic growth since his ground-breaking 1939 article, because of World War II.

Hayek, Friedrich A. "The Mythology of Capital." QUARTERLY JOURNAL OF ECONOMICS 50 (February 1936): 199-228. Reprinted in [3].

A fine defense of the Austrian school's natural theory of capital. A list of Frank H. Knight's writings against the Austrian school is also included.

_____. THE PURE THEORY OF CAPITAL. Chicago: University of Chicago Press, 1941. 485 p.

The Austrian theory of capital is explained. Hayek thinks it might more appropriately be entitled: "Introduction to the Dynamics of Capitalistic Production."

Hicks, John R. CAPITAL AND GROWTH. New York: Oxford University Press, 1965. 351 p.

The middle work of his trilogy on capital. Hicks was slow to appreciate the importance of dynamic analysis and, consequently, time. This book is flawed on that account. However, there is still much to be learned by a critical reading.

_____. CAPITAL AND TIME: A NEO-AUSTRIAN THEORY. New York: Oxford University Press, 1973. 224 p.

This is Hicks's third and most recent book on capital. "Capital is a very large subject." He feels that Austrian analysis should be the mainstream of production-capital theory. This point of view has been taken to task in a critical review by Edwin Burmeister, "Synthesizing the Neo-Austrian and Alternative Approaches to Capital Theory: A Survey." JOURNAL OF ECONOMIC LITERATURE 12 (June 1974): 413-56.

_____. A CONTRIBUTION TO THE THEORY OF THE TRADE CYCLE. New
York: Oxford University Press, 1950. 217 p.

The first attempt to use Harrod's growth theory to build a sophisticated model of the business cycle. Hicks believes monetary reform,
to reestablish monetary security and to moderate use of fiscal controls and public investment, is an alternative that would hold out
hope for the 1950s. After twenty-five years, the cure is still being
sought.

_____. "Mr. Harrod's Dynamic Theory." ECONOMICA 16 (May 1949):
106-21. Reprinted in [5].

Hicks is critical, justifiably so, of Harrod, Roy F. TOWARDS A
DYNAMIC ECONOMICS. New York: St. Martin's Press, 1948,
because he neglects dating and slides over the question of lags.

Johnson, H[arry].G. "Money in a Neo-Classical, One-Sector Growth Model."
In his ESSAYS IN MONETARY ECONOMICS, pp. 143-78. Cambridge, Mass.:
Harvard University Press, 1967. Reprinted in [2] [16].

Outside money models are useful in demonstrating the neutrality of
money under static equilibrium conditions. Neoclassical one-sector
growth models exhibit nonneutrality of money because money is
assumed to be a non-interest-bearing asset.

_____. THE THEORY OF INCOME DISTRIBUTION. London: Gray-Mills,
1973. 292 p. Paperbound.

This book consists of Johnson's lecture notes at the London School
of Economics. Although there is a strong microfoundation, the
later chapters deal with macroeconomic subjects, especially investment and economic growth.

_____. TWO-SECTOR GROWTH MODELS. Yrjo Johnssan Lectures. Chicago:
Aldine Publishing Co., 1971. 118 p.

Johnson uses some of the standard geometrical tools from international trade theory to construct a two-sector model of production
and distribution. He examines the effects of policies and institutions on the distribution of income and, after converting his model
into a growth model, uses it to explore some of the problems of
growth theory.

Jorgenson, Dale W. "Growth and Fluctuations: A Causal Interpretation."
QUARTERLY JOURNAL OF ECONOMICS 74 (August 1960): 416-36. Reprinted
in [13].

Jorgenson tries to establish causality in dynamic input-output
analysis by means of an explicit disequilibrium theory.

Kaldor, Nicholas. "Annual Survey of Economic Theory: The Recent Controversy on the Theory of Capital." ECONOMETRICA 5 (July 1937): 201-33.

> This is a summing up of the debate between Frank Knight and the Austrian school. Also see Knight, Frank H. "On the Theory of Capital: In Reply to Mr. Kaldor." ECONOMETRICA 6 (January 1938): 63-82; and Kaldor, Nicholas. "On the Theory of Capital: A Rejoinder to Professor Knight." ECONOMETRICA 6 (April 1938): 163-76.

_____. ESSAYS ON ECONOMIC STABILITY AND GROWTH. Glencoe, Ill.: Free Press, 1960. 302 p.

> Every essay in this collection was influenced by the work of Keynes. The essays are divided into these areas: (1) "Speculation, Liquidity Preference and the Theory of Employment," (2) "The Theory of Economic Fluctuations," and (3) "The Theory of Economic Growth." The introduction gives a chronology of thought.

_____. ESSAYS ON VALUE AND DISTRIBUTION. Glencoe, Ill.: Free Press, 1960. 238 p.

> This is a collection of Kaldor's articles dealing with the problems of equilibrium, imperfect competition, welfare economics, capital and distribution. Many were published in the thirties. The introduction is most interesting reading.

Kaldor, Nicholas, and Mirrlees, J. "A New Model of Economic Growth." REVIEW OF ECONOMIC STUDIES 29 (June 1962): 174-92. Reprinted in [15] [20].

> A more sophisticated Keynesian model of economic growth, Keynesian in the sense that continued growth involves the "accelerator-multiplier" mechanism and not marginal productivities or marginal substitution ratios. Technical progress enters the system through the creation of new equipment.

Kendrick, John W. "Some Theoretical Aspects of Capital Measurement." AMERICAN ECONOMIC REVIEW 51 (May 1961): 102-11. Reprinted in [10].

> Capital, like income, may be measured in a variety of ways. Its measurement depends often on the data available.

Kennedy, Charles. "Induced Bias in Innovations and the Theory of Distribution." ECONOMIC JOURNAL 74 (September 1964): 541-47.

> To get around the problems in Sir John Hicks's theory of induced inventions (changes in relative factor prices), a model is constructed in which technical progress takes place only in the consumption sector. Kennedy shows that his innovation possibility function is really a disguised form of Nicholas Kaldor's technical progress function ("A Model of Economic Growth." ECONOMIC JOURNAL 67 [December 1957]: 591-624).

Knight, Frank H. "Profit." In ENCYCLOPEDIA OF THE SOCIAL SCIENCES, edited by E.R.A. Seligman, vol. 12, pp. 480-86. New York: Macmillan, 1934. Reprinted in [3].

What is profit? Is it a legitimate or illegitimate return on capital --human or otherwise?

Koopmans, Tjalling C. "Objectives, Constraints, and Outcomes in Optimal Growth Models." ECONOMETRICA 35 (January 1967): 1-15.

This is a survey of research on macroeconomic optimal growth models. Koopmans points out the difficulties to be encountered and the directions additional research should take.

Kregel, J.A. RATE OF PROFIT, DISTRIBUTION AND GROWTH: TWO VIEWS. Chicago: Aldine Publishing Co., 1971. 233 p.

This book is a review of the Cambridge-Cambridge debate. Each chapter focuses on a particular contribution to the debate.

Kuznets, Simon S. CAPITAL IN THE AMERICAN ECONOMY. Princeton, N.J.: Princeton University Press, 1961. 694 p.

This is a massive work. In order to examine the formation and financing of capital in the United States, it was necessary to derive a number of historical series, each with a number of variants. The time period covered is from 1869 to the 1950s.

_____. MODERN ECONOMIC GROWTH. New Haven, Conn.: Yale University Press, 1966. 547 p. Also paperbound.

This study was designed with one guiding assumption: "modern economic growth, once identified, would prove to be a significant, orderly, and distinctive body of long-term economic experience." This study is a comprehensive analysis of the quantitative characteristics of economic growth.

Lerner, Abba P. "On Some Recent Developments in Capital Theory." AMERICAN ECONOMIC REVIEW 55 (May 1965): 284-95. Reprinted in [10].

It is important to differentiate between the marginal productivity and the marginal efficiency of both capital and investment.

Levhari, David, and Patinkin, Don. "The Role of Money in a Simple Growth Model." AMERICAN ECONOMIC REVIEW 58 (September 1968): 713-53.

This paper suggests that a monetary expansion can lead to differing results depending on what use the government makes of the money it prints. The growth model is an outside money model. Also see Harkness, J. "The Role of Money in a Simple Growth Model: Comment."; Ramanathan, R. "The Role of Money in a Simple

Growth Model: Comment."; and Levhari, David, and Patinkin, Don. "Reply." AMERICAN ECONOMIC REVIEW 62 (March 1972): 177-79; 180-84; 185.

Liviatan, Nissan, and Levhari, David. "The Golden Rule in the Case of More than One Consumption Good." AMERICAN ECONOMIC REVIEW 58 (March 1968): 100-119.

The golden rule (neo-neoclassical theorem) characterizes the situation in which society maximizes the steady-state level of consumption per capita. It is possible for the golden rule to hold in the two-commodity case as well. Optimality is another question.

Lundberg, Erik. INSTABILITY AND ECONOMIC GROWTH. New Haven, Conn.: Yale University Press, 1968. 458 p.

Postwar economic instability is surveyed with regard to issues, problems, and countries.

Malinvaud, E., and Bacharach, M.O.L., eds. ACTIVITY ANALYSIS IN THE THEORY OF GROWTH AND PLANNING. New York: St. Martin's Press, 1967. 349 p.

This book is the proceedings of a 1963 conference held by the International Economic Association. The seminal article by Koopmans, Tjalling C. "Economic Growth at a Maximal Rate." QUARTERLY JOURNAL OF ECONOMICS 78 (August 1964): 355-94, also appears here (pp. 3-42).

Marchal, Jean, and Ducros, Bernard, eds. THE DISTRIBUTION OF NATIONAL INCOME. Proceedings of a conference held by the International Economic Association, 1964. New York: St. Martin's Press, 1968. 764 p.

Income distribution in capitalist, socialist, and underdeveloped countries are discussed, along with theories of distribution and income policies. It took four years from conference to publication.

Mirrlees, James A., and Stern, N.H., eds. MODELS OF ECONOMIC GROWTH. Proceedings of a conference held by the International Economic Association at Jerusalem, 1970. New York: John Wiley & Sons, 1973. 394 p.

The volume contains fifteen previously unpublished papers in the areas of: (1) growth experience, (2) growth and the short run, (3) technological growth, (4) capital growth, (5) optimal growth, and (6) growth in developing countries. An index is included. The introduction by Mirrlees, which attempts to convince the reader that growth models are useful and that their uses can be criticized, is first rate.

Nagatani, Keizo. "A Monetary Growth Model with Variable Employment." JOURNAL OF MONEY, CREDIT AND BANKING 1 (May 1969): 188-206.

This monetary growth model allows for endogenously determined employment. Both quantity and price adjustments are allowed, and stability is dependent on the relative flexibility of wages and prices.

Pasinetti, Luigi L. GROWTH AND INCOME DISTRIBUTION: ESSAYS IN ECONOMIC THEORY. New York: Cambridge University Press, 1974. 161 p.

There are six essays collected in this volume, of which three have not previously been published, five are dated 1958-62, while one of the unpublished articles was written in 1971-72. The rate of profit is exogenously determined in long-run equilibrium by the natural rate of growth divided by the capitalist's propensity to save. The theme is: In the long run, capital is independent of the rate of profit.

_____. "Rate of Profit and Income Distribution in Relation to the Rate of Economic Growth." REVIEW OF ECONOMIC STUDIES 29 (October 1962): 267-79.

If the Keynesian concepts of income determination by effective demand and of investment as a variable independent of consumption and saving are combined, there is modern content to the classical idea of a connection between the distribution of income and capital accumulation.

Phelps, Edmund S. "The Golden Rule of Accumulation: A Fable for Growthmen." AMERICAN ECONOMIC REVIEW 51 (September 1961): 638-43.

The Kingdom of Salovia searches for the golden-rule path, i.e., the optimal investment policy where consumption per capita is maximized. The brilliant peasant, Oiko Nomos, discovers the answer by setting the rate of investment equal to the competitive rate of profit, given a few assumptions here and there. A follow-up article is "Second Essay on the Golden Rule of Accumulation." AMERICAN ECONOMIC REVIEW 55 (September 1965): 793-814.

Phillips, A.W. "A Simple Model of Employment, Money and Prices in a Growing Economy." ECONOMICA 28 (November 1961): 360-70.

The model is written as a system of linear differential equations. Both the short-run problems of reducing fluctuations in the economy and the longer-run problems of employment, stable price level, and growth may be studied by it.

Ramsey, Frank. "A Mathematical Theory of Savings." ECONOMIC JOURNAL 39 (December 1928): 543-59.

Ramsey's seminal article begins with a simple sounding question: "How much of its income should a nation save?" This is the true beginning of mathematical capital theory.

Riach, P.A. "A Framework for Macro-Distribution Analysis." KYKLOS 22, fasc. 3, (1969): 542-63. Reprinted in [13].

This is a short-run theory of distribution which is heavily Kaldorian.

Robinson, Joan. THE ACCUMULATION OF CAPITAL. 3d ed. New York: St. Martin's Press, 1970. 460 p.

Basically a discussion of the theory of value. Robinson discusses the accumulation of capital assuming there is only one technique available with fixed coefficients between labor and equipment. Since there is only one technique available, new workers will require the same tools per head as existing laborers. Therefore, the new production function is dependent on accumulated capital. As long as the increase in capital follows this trend, a stable state will exist.

_____. "The Classification of Inventions." REVIEW OF ECONOMIC STUDIES 5 (February 1938): 139-42.

In this short note, Joan Robinson defines explicitly what is meant by Hicks and Harrod neutral inventions.

_____. ESSAYS IN THE THEORY OF ECONOMIC GROWTH. New York: St. Martin's Press, 1964. 148 p.

The four essays are in part reprinted and in part original. They are to be thought of as constituting an introduction to her THE ACCUMULATION OF CAPITAL. 3d ed. New York: St. Martin's Press, 1970.

_____. THE RATE OF INTEREST AND OTHER ESSAYS. New York: St. Martin's Press, 1952. 170 p.

The tone of the essays is dynamic. The following essays are included: "The Rate of Interest," "Notes on the Economics of Technical Progress," "The Generalization of the GENERAL THEORY," "Acknowledgments and Disclaimers." The penultimate essay expands the GENERAL THEORY into a dynamic model. In the last essay, she discusses the writers who have influenced her the most.

Samuelson, Paul A. "An Exact Consumption-Loan Model of Interest with or without the Social Contrivance of Money." JOURNAL OF POLITICAL ECONOMY 66 (December 1958): 467-82.

This very important article is reexamined in a paper by Cass, David, and Yaari, Menahem E. "A Reexamination of the Pure Consumption

Loan Model." JOURNAL OF POLITICAL ECONOMY 74 (August 1966): 353-67.

_____. "Parable and Realism in Capital Theory: The Surrogate Production Function." REVIEW OF ECONOMIC STUDIES 29 (June 1962): 193-206.

Another attempt to fend off the logic of Sraffa and Robinson. The factor price frontier is developed.

_____. "A Theory of Induced Innovation Along Kennedy-Weizsacker Lines." REVIEW OF ECONOMICS AND STATISTICS 47 (November 1965): 343-56.

Samuelson is willing to accept a Kennedy-Weizsacker-Samuelson hyphenation. But he will not part with the traditional production function. The Harrod-neutral labor augmentation result is possible with a variety of exogenous assumptions. See these additional notes: Kennedy, Charles. "Samuelson on Induced Innovation."; and Samuelson, Paul A. "Rejoinder: Agreements, Disagreements, Doubts, and the Case of Induced Harrod-Neutral Technological Change." Ibid., 48 (November 1966): 442-44, 444-48.

Shell, Karl, et al. "Capital Gains, Income, and Savings." REVIEW OF ECO-NOMIC STUDIES 36 (January 1969): 15-26.

They define a measure of income (Individual Purchasing Power = Disposable Income and Capital Gains) which is equal to the value of consumption that is consistent with a zero change in individuals' wealth. The implications of this new measure of consumption is considered for the traditional models of economic growth.

Sidrauski, Miguel. "Inflation and Economic Growth." JOURNAL OF POLITI-CAL ECONOMY 75 (December 1967): 796-810.

This paper is an attempt to integrate the monetary structure of the economy into the aggregative neoclassical model of economic growth. Results are consistent with the model; however, the de-mand functions for real cash balances and the saving function are not as realistic as one might hope.

_____. "Rational Choice and Patterns of Growth in a Monetary Economy." AMERICAN ECONOMIC REVIEW 57 (May 1967): 534-44.

Sidrauski uses a standard Patinkin theory of money to examine a temporal equilibrium problem from an intertemporal point of view.

Solow, Robert M. CAPITAL THEORY AND THE RATE OF RETURN. Chicago: Rand-McNally, 1963. 98 p. Paperbound.

The topics covered are: (1) "Capital and the Rate of Return," (2) "The Rate of Return and Technical Progress," and (3) "Techni-cal Progress, the Aggregate Production Function and the Rate of

Return." When these lectures were given, M.I.T. had not lost the Cambridge-Cambridge capital battle.

_____. "A Contribution to the Theory of Economic Growth." QUARTERLY JOURNAL OF ECONOMICS 70 (February 1956): 65-94. Reprinted in [20].

Solow makes the neoclassical model of economic growth more flexible (less of a knife edge) by introducing neutral technological change.

Solow, Robert M., and Stiglitz, Joseph E. "Output, Employment and Wages in the Short Run." QUARTERLY JOURNAL OF ECONOMICS 82 (November 1968): 537-60.

This is one of the many interesting shots in the Cambridge versus Cambridge capital controversy. To Solow and Stiglitz the essence of the difference is that in England the real wage clears the commodity market, while in Massachusetts it clears the labor market. Two additional notes of interest are: Weintraub, Sidney. "Solow and Stiglitz on Employment and Distribution: A New Romance with an Old Model."; and Solow, Robert M., and Stiglitz, Joseph E. "Reply." Ibid., 84 (February 1970): 144-52, 153.

Solow, Robert M., et al. "Neoclassical Growth Fixed Factor Proportions." REVIEW OF ECONOMIC STUDIES 33 (April 1966): 79-115.

This encyclopedic article examines the three special cases of technical change under many different ramifications, including the Keynesian case of output limited by effective demand.

Sraffa, Piero. PRODUCTION OF COMMODITIES BY MEANS OF COMMODITIES. New York: Cambridge University Press, 1960. 111 p. Also paperbound.

This book is a classic. Nothing since Harrod's 1939 growth article has caused such a restructuring of economic thought. The marginalists are attempting to counterattack but a widespread retreat is still going on.

Stein, Jerome L. "Monetary Growth Theory in Perspective." AMERICAN ECONOMIC REVIEW 60 (March 1970): 85-106.

In this review of monetary growth theory, Stein attempts to give answers to these central issues: (1) is money neutral, (2) do different types of money have different optimal growth, and (3) what is the most desirable stabilization policy in a growing monetary economy.

_____. MONEY AND CAPACITY GROWTH. New York: Columbia University Press, 1971. 271 p.

Mathematical monetary growth models are developed to study monetary theory, monetary policy, and economic development. A good survey of a rapidly growing area of interest.

_____. "Neoclassical and 'Keynes-Wicksell' Monetary Growth Models." JOURNAL OF MONEY, CREDIT AND BANKING 1 (May 1969): 153-71.

The basic difference between the two models is that saving always equals investment in neoclassical monetary growth models.

Stiglitz, Joseph E. "The Cambridge-Cambridge Controversy in the Theory of Capital; A View from New Haven: A Review Article." JOURNAL OF POLITICAL ECONOMY 82 (July/August 1974): 893-903.

This is a critical review of SOME CAMBRIDGE CONTROVERSIES IN THE THEORY OF CAPITAL by G.C. Harcourt. As far as Stiglitz is concerned, the controversy is basically whether the marginal productivity theory determines the interest rate or vice versa.

Swan, T.W. "Economic Growth and Capital Accumulation." ECONOMIC RECORD 32 (November 1956): 334-61. Reprinted in [20].

Swan uses two diagrams to show the connection between capital accumulation and the growth of the productive labor force.

Tobin, James. "A Dynamic Aggregative Model." JOURNAL OF POLITICAL ECONOMY 63 (April 1955): 103-15. Reprinted in [13] [19] [20].

Tobin's model allows for substitution between factors and monetary effects.

_____. "Money and Economic Growth." ECONOMETRICA 33 (October 1965): 671-84.

The first real attempt at a monetary growth model. In neoclassical monetary growth models, capital intensity will be determined by portfolio behavior and monetary factors, as well as productivity and thrift.

_____. The Neutrality of Money in Growth Models: A Comment." ECONOMICA 34 (February 1967): 69-72.

Tobin shows that with a constant saving ratio the equilibrium capital intensity is lower in a monetary model. This is in counterdistinction to Johnson, H.G. "The Neo-Classical One-Sector Growth Model: A Geometrical Exposition and Extension to a Monetary Economy." ECONOMICA 33 (August 1966): 265-87. Johnson confesses his error in "The Neutrality of Money in Growth Models: A Reply." ECONOMICA 34 (February 1967): 73-74.

Uzawa, Hirofumi. "Neutral Inventions and the Stability of Growth Equilibrium." REVIEW OF ECONOMIC STUDIES 28 (February 1961): 117-24.

> A comparison of Hicks and Harrod neutral inventions is made. A Cobb-Douglas production function with technical invention is both Harrod and Hicks neutral. Harrod neutrality is proved to exist in a stable growth equilibrium.

_____. "On the Dynamic Stability of Economic Growth: The Neoclassical versus Keynesian Approaches." In TRADE, STABILITY, AND MACROECONOMICS: ESSAYS IN HONOR OF LLOYD A. METZLER, edited by George Horwich and Paul A. Samuelson, pp. 523-53. New York: Academic Press, 1974.

> The approach used is dynamic equilibrium. The results are expected but still of interest.

_____, ed. "Symposium on the Theory of Economic Growth." JOURNAL OF POLITICAL ECONOMY 77, supplement (July/August 1969): 573-719.

> This symposium was held at the University of Chicago in November 1967. The paper by Miguel Sidrauski, "Rational Choice and Patterns of Growth," pp. 575-85, has generated the most continuing interest. This collection of papers was dedicated to his memory.

Vanek, Jaroslav. MAXIMAL ECONOMIC GROWTH. Ithaca, N.Y.: Cornell University Press, 1968. 122 p.

> This book presents a geometric approach to von Neumann's growth theory and the turnpike theorem.

Weintraub, Andrew, et al., eds. THE ECONOMIC GROWTH CONTROVERSY. New York: International Arts and Sciences Press, 1974. 248 p. Paperbound.

> A collection of conflicting answers as to the costs and benefits of growth. There are articles by E.J. Mishan, R.M. Solow, and L.C. Thurow, among others.

Weintraub, Sidney. "A Macro-Theory of Pricing, Income Distribution, and Employment." WELWIRTSCHAFTLICHES ARCHIV 102 (March 1969): 11-25. Reprinted in [13].

> This is an attempt to reconcile the theories of Joan Robinson and Nicholas Kaldor with the other theories of marginal productivity. Traditional marginal analysis must accept a subsidiary role--applicable only to factor variation and profit maximization.

Weizsacker, C.C. von. STEADY STATE CAPITAL THEORY. Springer-Verlag: New York, 1971. 102 p. Paperbound.

> This is the edited text of a series of lectures given at the University of Heidelberg the winter of 1970-71. Only the steady states of stationary and exponentially growing economies are examined. Dynamic capital theory is not touched.

Chapter 4

CENTRAL BANKING

INTRODUCTION

The lender of last resort is the central bank. To determine when there is no resort remaining is often more art than science. The art of central banking has become in part the art of international banking. This chapter tries to relate the importance of central banking without becoming entangled in international finance.

The history and theory of central banking are entwined. Two good books to read as an introduction are: Mints, Lloyd. A HISTORY OF BANKING THEORY; and Board of Governors of the Federal Reserve System. THE FEDERAL RESERVE SYSTEM: PURPOSES AND FUNCTIONS. Two additional readings which integrate history and theory quite well are by Sayers, R.S. CENTRAL BANKING AFTER BAGEHOT, pp. 1-7 and 8-19.

The practice of central banking is also covered in chapter 5, especially under the headings of "Monetary Policy," "Comparisons and Monetary Aspects of Fiscal Policy," and "Monetary Commissions."

SOURCES

History

Ashton, T.S., and Sayers, R.S., eds. PAPERS IN ENGLISH MONETARY HISTORY. New York: Oxford University Press, 1953. 167 p.

> These eleven important essays were collected and reprinted because they were written during World War II and, consequently, did not receive the readership to which they are entitled.

Bagehot, Walter. LOMBARD STREET: A DESCRIPTION OF THE MONEY MARKET. 1887. Reprint. Homewood, Ill.: Richard D. Irwin, 1962. Also paperbound.

The financial structure of the City (financial center of London) comes alive in this classic treatment. Bagehot deals with the "concrete" realities of the money market.

Board of Governors of the Federal Reserve System. THE FEDERAL RESERVE SYSTEM: PURPOSES AND FUNCTIONS. 6th ed. Washington, D.C.: 1974. 125 p. Paperbound.

This is a complete revision of the Federal Reserve's handbook of operations.

Chandler, Lester V. BENJAMIN STRONG: CENTRAL BANKER. Washington, D.C.: Brookings Institution, 1958. 495 p.

Benjamin Strong, president of the New York Federal Reserve Bank, symbolized all that was good and bad about central banking until his death in 1928.

Feavearyear, A.E. THE POUND STERLING. 2d ed. Revised by E. Victor Morgan. New York: Oxford University Press, 1963. 446 p.

This is an outstanding history of English money.

Federal Reserve Bank of Philadelphia. FIFTY YEARS OF THE FEDERAL RESERVE ACT. Philadelphia: 1964. 20 p. Paperbound.

A very good summary of how the act has been revised over time.

Fetter, Frank W. DEVELOPMENT OF BRITISH MONETARY ORTHODOXY, 1797-1875. Cambridge, Mass.: Harvard University Press, 1965. 296 p.

This book covers the period from the Bank of England's suspension of specie payments (27 February 1797) to its full emergence as a lender of last resort. The research and writing make this book a necessity for a monetary historian.

Hammond, Bray. BANKS AND POLITICS IN AMERICA: FROM THE REVOLUTION TO THE CIVIL WAR. Princeton, N.J.: Princeton University Press, 1957. 771 p.

The study of Jackson and Biddle and the Bank of the United States is especially detailed. The approach is encyclopedic. The list of the works cited is a good beginning for a reading list.

Harris, Lawrence. "Professor Hicks and the Foundations of Monetary Economics." ECONOMICA 36 (May 1969): 196-208.

This is a review article of Hicks, John R. CRITICAL ESSAYS IN MONETARY THEORY. New York: Oxford University Press, 1967. His essay advances the proposition that Hicks is a contributor to the banking school tradition--"you cannot push a string."

Hawtrey, R.G. A CENTURY OF BANK RATE. 2d ed. New York: Augustus M. Kelley, 1962. 350 p.

The importance of the Bank of England as a policy implementor is stressed. This book is based on a series of three Alfred Marshall lectures given in November 1937.

_____. CURRENCY AND CREDIT. 4th ed. New York: Longmans, Green, 1950. 475 p.

The book is divided into two parts: "Theory of Currency and Credit" and "Historical Illustrations." Keynes's TREATISE ON MONEY follows somewhat the same lines, although Keynes did not credit Hawtrey.

Hicks, John R. "Monetary Theory and History: An Attempt at Perspective." In his CRITICAL ESSAYS IN MONETARY THEORY, pp. 155-73. New York: Oxford University Press, 1967. Reprinted in [2].

Hicks looks back in history to compare Keynes and those whom he called classics. The type of monetary theory which becomes current is determined by history. The greater the challenge the better the theory.

Kock, M.H. de. CENTRAL BANKING. 3d ed. London: Staples Press, 1961. 368 p.

His thesis is that central bank control, for example over the business cycle, is drastically limited.

Krooss, Herman E., ed. DOCUMENTARY HISTORY OF BANKING IN THE UNITED STATES. 4 vols. New York: Chelsea House, 1969.

Besides the introduction by Paul Samuelson and section comments by Krooss, all the rest consists of some three hundred documents covering more than three hundred years. The first document describes the introduction of wampum into the Plymouth Colony in 1627. The last document is a June 1968 report by the Joint Economic Committee. These four volumes constitute a gold mine for the serious scholar.

Mints, Lloyd W. A HISTORY OF BANKING THEORY. Chicago: University of Chicago Press, 1945. 319 p.

The rise of central banking in Great Britain and the United States is covered from the seventeenth century until the formation of the Federal Reserve System. The "real-bills doctrine" is examined in detail and found to be unsound in all its aspects. A complete bibliography is included.

Mitchell, Wesley C. A HISTORY OF THE GREENBACKS. Chicago: University of Chicago Press, 1903. 593 p.

> This book includes not only a detailed history of the greenbacks but also their economic consequences.

Reagan, Michael D. "The Political Structure of the Federal Reserve System." AMERICAN POLITICAL SCIENCE REVIEW 55 (March 1961): 64-76. Reprinted in [14].

> A sketch of the structure of authority and historical development of the system is coupled with an analysis of the roles of each component of the system. Reagan describes how policy is made and how the system could be more effectively aligned.

Sayers, R.S. "Central Banking." In INTERNATIONAL ENCYCLOPEDIA OF THE SOCIAL SCIENCES, edited by D.L. Sills, vol. 2, pp. 1-10. New York: Macmillan-Free Press, 1968.

> Sayers provides a good historical perspective on central banking and its impact on the price system, gold reserves, and international trade.

_____. CENTRAL BANKING AFTER BAGEHOT. New York: Oxford University Press, 1957. 149 p.

> The first two (of ten) essays should be required reading of anyone majoring in monetary economics. They are entitled: "The Theoretical Basis of Central Banking" and "The Development of Central Banking after Bagehot."

Viner, Jacob. STUDIES IN THE THEORY OF INTERNATIONAL TRADE. New York: Augustus M. Kelley, 1937. 665 p.

> This is the classic work on English banking until 1865. See especially chapters 3, 4, and 5, pages 119-289. Chapters 3 and 4 deal with "The Bullionist Controversies," and chapter 5 with "English Currency Controversies, 1825-1865."

Theory

Board of Governors of the Federal Reserve System. THE FEDERAL RESERVE SYSTEM: PURPOSES AND FUNCTIONS. 6th ed. Washington, D.C.: 1974. 125 p. Paperbound.

> This is a complete revision of the Federal Reserve's handbook of operations.

Bopp, Karl R. "Central Banking Objectives, Guides, and Measures." JOURNAL OF FINANCE 9 (March 1954): 12-22. Reprinted in [14].

> The economy in which a central bank operates is dynamic; simplistic models are not of much use.

Coppock, D.J., and Gibson, N.J. "The Volume of Deposits and the Cash and Liquid Asset Ratios." MANCHESTER SCHOOL OF ECONOMICS AND SOCIAL STUDIES 31 (September 1963): 203-22.

> There seems to be no reason to reject the traditional cash ratio theory and to substitute the liquid assets theory of deposit regulation. The controversy is a continuing one.

Federal Reserve Bank of Richmond. INSTRUMENTS OF THE MONEY MARKET. Edited by J.R. Monhollon and G. Picou. Richmond, Va.: 1974. 96 p.

> This is a collection of articles from the bank's MONTHLY REVIEW.

Hawtrey, R.G. THE ART OF CENTRAL BANKING. 2d ed. New York: Augustus M. Kelley, 1962. 350 p.

> This volume of essays has a single theme, but each essay is self-contained. The most noted essay is chapter 4--the title essay. The art is surveyed from before Peal's Act to the Great Depression.

_____. A CENTURY OF BANK RATE. 2d ed. New York: Augustus M. Kelley, 1962. 350 p.

> The importance of the Bank of England as a policy implementor is stressed. This book is based on a series of three Alfred Marshall lectures given in November 1937.

_____. CURRENCY AND CREDIT. 4th ed. New York: Longmans, Green, 1950. 475 p.

> The book is divided into two parts: "Theory of Currency and Credit" and "Historical Illustrations." Keynes's TREATISE ON MONEY follows somewhat the same lines, although Keynes does not credit Hawtrey.

Meek, Paul, and Thunberg, Rudolf. "Monetary Aggregates and Federal Reserve Open Market Operations." FEDERAL RESERVE BULLETIN 57 (April 1971): 80-89. Reprinted in [17].

> Open market operations are now to be conducted with longer term objectives in mind.

Modigliani, Franco, et al. "Central Bank Policy, Money Supply, and the Short-term Rate of Interest." JOURNAL OF MONEY, CREDIT AND BANKING 2 (May 1970): 166-218.

> The FRB-MIT econometric model is used to explore and explain the way by which central bank actions are transmitted through financial markets.

Ritter, Lawrence S. "Official Central Banking Theory in the United States,

1939-61." JOURNAL OF POLITICAL ECONOMY 70 (February 1962): 14-29.

Ritter concludes that the Federal Reserve has been eclectic, pragmatic, and responsive to both experience and discussion, not dogmatic or parochial.

Roosa, Robert V. "Interest Rates and the Central Bank." In MONEY, TRADE, AND ECONOMIC GROWTH, edited by D. McCord Wright et al., pp. 270-95. New York: Macmillan, 1951. Reprinted in [19].

A good survey of the influence of the interest rate on other economic variables. The influence of the central bank on interest rates is stripped of its mystique.

Sayers, R.S. "Central Banking." In INTERNATIONAL ENCYCLOPEDIA OF THE SOCIAL SCIENCES, edited by D.L. Sills, vol. 2, pp. 1-10. New York: Macmillan-Free Press, 1968.

Sayers provides a good historical perspective on central banking and its impact on the price system, gold reserves, and international trade.

_____. CENTRAL BANKING AFTER BAGEHOT. New York: Oxford University Press, 1957. 149 p.

The first two (of ten) essays should be required reading of anyone majoring in monetary economics. They are entitled: "The Theoretical Basis of Central Banking" and "The Development of Central Banking after Bagehot."

Scott, Ira O., Jr. "The Availability Doctrine: Theoretical Underpinnings." REVIEW OF ECONOMIC STUDIES 25 (October 1957): 41-48. Reprinted in [19].

A model is set up to show the influence of a restrictive monetary policy on the availability of credit.

Thanos, C.A. "The Definition of a Central Bank and Its Practical Implications." ECONOMICA INTERNATIONALE 11 (February 1958): 113-15. Reprinted in [14].

The title of the article says it all.

Thornton, Henry. AN ENQUIRY INTO THE NATURE AND EFFECTS OF THE PAPER CREDIT OF GREAT BRITAIN. Edited by F.A. Hayek. New York: Augustus M. Kelley, 1939. 368 p.

The 1939 publication of this 1802 classic includes, in addition, Thornton's evidence given before Parliament on the Bank of England, March and April 1797; some manuscript notes; and his speeches on the Bullion Report, May 1811, with an introduction by Hayek.

Practice

Aschheim, Joseph. "Restrictive Open Market Operations Versus Reserve Require-
ment Increases." ECONOMIC JOURNAL 73 (June 1963): 254-66.

> This is a summation and reformulation of the author's initial anal-
> ysis. A large number of comments were evoked. They are cited
> in the footnotes. Also see Bain, A.D. "Monetary Control through
> Open-Market Operations and Reserve-Requirement Variations."
> ECONOMIC JOURNAL 74 (March 1964): 137-46. Aschheim's
> original article was "Open-Market Operations versus Reserve-
> Requirement Variation." ECONOMIC JOURNAL 69 (December
> 1959): 697-704.

_____. TECHNIQUES OF MONETARY CONTROL. Baltimore: Johns Hopkins
University Press, 1961. 164 p.

> This book is concerned with the operations of central banks.
> Aschheim rejects the Gurley-Shaw thesis.

Bach, G.L. FEDERAL RESERVE POLICY MAKING. New York: Alfred A.
Knopf, 1950. 282 p.

> This book is based on a report to the Hoover Commission. What
> importance does the central bank have in an era dominated by
> fiscalists?

Board of Governors of the Federal Reserve System. "Monetary Aggregates and
Money Market Conditions in Open Market Policy." FEDERAL RESERVE BULLE-
TIN 57 (February 1971): 79-104.

> A discussion of how the Federal Open Market Committee makes its
> decisions. The title of the full report is OPEN MARKET POLICIES
> AND OPERATING PROCEDURES: STAFF STUDIES. Washington,
> D.C.: 1971. 218 p. Paperbound.

_____. "Reappraisal of the Federal Reserve Discount Mechanism." FEDERAL
RESERVE BULLETIN 54 (July 1968): 545-51. Reprinted in [1].

> This was an attempt made to make the discount mechanism more
> useful to commercial banks. It has not had a great effect.

_____. REAPPRAISAL OF THE FEDERAL RESERVE DISCOUNT MECHANISM.
3 vols. Washington, D.C.: 1971-72. 276 p., 173 p., and 214 p. Paperbound.

> These three volumes contain the conclusions, recommendations, and
> research papers of a three-year, system-wide study. "The Legiti-
> macy of Central Banks" by Kenneth Boulding (vol. 2, pp. 1-14)
> is the essay with which to begin.

Brunner, Karl, ed. "The Federal Reserve Discount Policy: A Symposium." JOURNAL OF MONEY, CREDIT AND BANKING 2 (May 1970): 135-65.

Papers by Robert C. Holland, Thomas R. Atkinson, Donald D. Hester, and Deane Carson discuss the problems inherent in an independent central bank. The issues remain unsettled.

Cagan, Phillip. "Why Do We Use Money in Open Market Operations?" JOURNAL OF POLITICAL ECONOMY 66 (February 1958): 34-46.

Nonmonetary assets and commodities are less satisfactory than money, because money is a unique medium of exchange.

Canterbery, E.R. "A New Look at Federal Open Market Voting." WESTERN ECONOMIC JOURNAL 6 (December 1967): 25-38.

This article is a comment on Yohe, W.P. "A Study of Federal Open Market Voting, 1955-64." SOUTHERN ECONOMIC JOURNAL 32 (April 1966): 396-405. The question is posed: Why was there a preponderance of unanimous decisions? Also see Canterbery's "A Note on Recent Money Supply Behavior." WESTERN ECONOMIC JOURNAL 4 (Fall 1965): 91-98. Reprinted in [10].

Carson, Deane. "Is the Federal Reserve System Really Necessary?" JOURNAL OF FINANCE 19 (December 1964): 652-61. Reprinted in [14].

Carson's main proposal is to do away with reserve requirements.

Federal Reserve Bank of Richmond. INSTRUMENTS OF THE MONEY MARKET. Edited by J.R. Monhollon and G. Picou. Richmond, Va.: 1974. 96 p.

This is a collection of articles from the bank's MONTHLY REVIEW.

Guttentag, Jack M. "The Strategy of Open Market Operations." QUARTERLY JOURNAL OF ECONOMICS 80 (February 1966): 1-30. Reprinted in [4].

An exhaustive review of open market operations is made. Guttentag advances his own proposal for a complete open market strategy.

Hicks, John R. "Automatists, Hawtreyans, and Keynesians." JOURNAL OF MONEY, CREDIT AND BANKING 1 (August 1969): 307-17.

There is a need to separate the financing from policy functions of the central bank.

Jacoby, Neil [H.]. "The Structure and Use of Variable Reserve Requirements." In BANKING AND MONETARY STUDIES, edited by Deane Carson, pp. 213-33. Homewood, Ill.: Richard D. Irwin, 1963. Reprinted in [14].

Jacoby believes that reserve requirements can make a unique contribution to good monetary policy; a position in contrast to that of Friedman.

Kane, Edward J. "All for the Best: The Federal Reserve Board's 60th Annual Report." AMERICAN ECONOMIC REVIEW 64 (December 1974): 835-50.

> You need to be an expert to read between the lines. Also see, Brimmer, Andrew F. "The Political Economy of Money: Evolution and Impact of Monetarism in the Federal Reserve System." AMERICAN ECONOMIC REVIEW 62 (May 1972): 344-52.

Meltzer, Allan H. "Major Issues in the Regulation of Commercial Banks." JOURNAL OF POLITICAL ECONOMY 75 (August 1967): 482-500. Reprinted in [1].

> Many of the controls imposed on banks and nonbanks alike, fail to achieve their purpose. The benefit-cost ratio is less than one.

Roosa, Robert V. FEDERAL RESERVE OPERATIONS IN THE MONEY AND GOVERNMENT SECURITIES MARKETS. New York: Federal Reserve Bank of New York, 1956. 108 p.

> Discusses the functions of Federal Reserve as defensive (policy to guard against the consequences of accidents, e.g., seasonal shortage of reserves), or dynamic (positive policy to aid in expansion).

Ross, Myron H., and Zelder, Raymond E. "The Discount Rate: A Phantom Policy Tool?" WESTERN ECONOMIC JOURNAL 7 (December 1969): 341-48.

> Ross and Zelder express concern that an easing of discount rate rules may cause banks to explicitly maximize profits in the discount market.

Ruebling, Charlotte E. "The Administration of Regulation Q." Federal Reserve Bank of St. Louis REVIEW 2 (February 1970): 29-40. Reprinted in [1].

> Changes in the maximum interest rates payable on commercial bank time and savings deposits are discussed.

Chapter 5

STABILIZATION POLICY

INTRODUCTION

Economic stabilization policy is the proof of the theoretic pudding. Policy prescriptions are value judgments derived, at least in part, from positive theoretical input. The controversies that have arisen and the commissions appointed to deal with them give graphic testimony to the strength of opposing opinions.

SOURCES

Problems

UNEMPLOYMENT AND GROWTH

Council of Economic Advisers. "The Employment Act: Twenty Years of Policy Experience." In ANNUAL REPORT OF THE COUNCIL OF ECONOMIC ADVISERS, pp. 170-86. Washington, D.C.: Government Printing Office, 1966. Reprinted in [10] [16].

> A review of economic policy since the act was signed into law on February 20, 1946. This act gave birth to the Council of Economic Advisers.

Denison, Edward F. "How to Raise the High-Employment Growth Rate by One Percentage Point." AMERICAN ECONOMIC REVIEW 52 (May 1962): 67-75. Reprinted in [10] [16].

> The title explains perfectly what the article is about.

Domar, Evsey D. "Expansion and Employment." AMERICAN ECONOMIC REVIEW 37 (March 1947): 34-55. Reprinted in [10] [15] [16] [20].

> This paper forms a sequel to his earlier article on "The 'Burden' of the Debt and the National Income." AMERICAN ECONOMIC REVIEW 34 (December 1944): 798-827. Reprinted in [18]. Both

papers explore the economic role of growth.

Feldstein, Martin S. "Policies to Lower the Permanent Rate of Unemployment." In REDUCING UNEMPLOYMENT TO TWO PERCENT. Hearings before the Joint Economic Committee, 92d Cong., 2d sess., pp. 24-28. Washington, D.C.: Government Printing Office, 1972. Reprinted in [17].

It is necessary to use manpower programs to lower the rate of un-employment without creating inflationary pressures. Also see his "Lowering the Permanent Rate of Unemployment." Joint Economic Committee, U.S. Congress, 1973. Reprinted in [12].

Fellner, William J. "Rapid Growth as an Objective of Economic Policy." AMERICAN ECONOMIC REVIEW 50 (May 1969): 93-105. Reprinted in [10].

Capital formation which incorporates technological change is likely to be a successful way to increase economic growth. There are problems, however.

Gordon, Robert A[aron]. THE GOAL OF FULL EMPLOYMENT. New York: John Wiley & Sons, 1967. 204 p.

The question is posed: Why has the United States done so poorly, both relatively and absolutely, in reaching the goal of full employ-ment? The answers are imaginative, especially considering what has happened subsequently.

Heller, Walter W., ed. PERSPECTIVES ON ECONOMIC GROWTH. New York: Random House, 1968. 251 p.

This volume assembles the thinking of nine economists, most of whom had served as members of the President's Council of Economic Ad-visers or on the council's staff. Most of the essays have a tone of expansionary policy, reflecting the continual concern with the economy's performance.

Stein, Herbert, et al. POLICIES TO COMBAT DEPRESSION. National Bureau of Economic Research. Princeton, N.J.: Princeton University Press, 1956. 427 p.

This is the proceedings of two conferences held in Princeton, N.J., the first on October 30-31, 1953 and the second on May 14-15, 1954. There was a feeling at that time that the United States was increasingly vulnerable to an economic decline.

Worswick, G.D.N., ed. THE CONCEPT AND MEASUREMENT OF INVOL-UNTARY UNEMPLOYMENT. London: Allen and Unwin, 1976. 327 p.

Unemployment has to be defined before it can be measured.

INFLATION AND DEFLATION

Bailey, M[artin].J. "The Welfare Cost of Inflationary Finance." JOURNAL OF POLITICAL ECONOMY 64 (April 1956): 93-110.

The reason why governments seem to be willing to use inflation finance is that they do not understand all the hidden costs involved.

Ball, R.J. INFLATION AND THE THEORY OF MONEY. Chicago: Aldine Publishing Co., 1964. 313 p. Also paperbound.

One of the earlier books to emphasize the importance of money in policy matters. The intellectual forefather of a host of minibooks on inflation.

Ball, R.J., and Doyle, Peter, eds. INFLATION. Baltimore: Penguin Books, 1969. 392 p. Paperbound.

This collection of readings contains most of the pre-seventies worthwhile literature on inflation. The bibliography cites the rest of the literature. The readings cover the Keynesian revolution, the monetary revival, demand and cost inflation, and the Phillips curve.

Board of Governors of the Federal Reserve System and Social Science Research Council. THE ECONOMETRICS OF PRICE DETERMINATION. Edited by Otto Eckstein. Washington, D.C.: 1972. 397 p. Also paperbound.

The purpose of this conference was to study four equations (price adjustment, wage adjustment, price expectations, and normal utilization) which form a subsystem of a complete model. The introductory comments by James Tobin, pp. 5-15, are the place to begin.

Bronfenbrenner, Martin. "Inflation and Deflation." In INTERNATIONAL ENCYCLOPEDIA OF THE SOCIAL SCIENCES, edited by D.L. Sills, vol. 7, pp. 289-300. New York: Macmillan-Free Press, 1968.

The emphasis is on inflation. Classifications are developed and the equity aspect of inflation is explored.

_____. "Some Neglected Implications of Secular Inflation." In POST KEYNESIAN ECONOMICS, edited by Kenneth K. Kurihara, pp. 31-58. New Brunswick, N.J.: Rutgers University Press, 1955.

What are the implications of persistent inflation for the future of our economic society? Perhaps some blend of capitalism and socialism would be best for both equalitarian distribution and individual liberties. "Surely no cosmic palmist has yet read in the indifference surface of the lines of the invisible hand a zero marginal rate of substitution between equality and progress."

Bronfenbrenner, Martin, and Holtzman, F.D. "A Survey of Inflation Theory."
AMERICAN ECONOMIC REVIEW 53 (September 1963): 593-661. Reprinted
in [16].

> This is one in a series of economic survey articles supported by
> the Rockefeller Foundation. The survey is divided into these
> categories: (1) "Sources and Definitions of Inflation," (2) "De-
> mand Inflation," (3) "Supply or Cost Inflation," (4) "Quantitative
> Testing," (5) "Speed, Duration, and Extent of Inflation," (6) "Re-
> distributive Effects of Inflation," and (7) "Final Remarks." Also
> included is an extensive bibliography.

Brown, Arthur J. THE GREAT INFLATION, 1939-1951. New York: Oxford
University Press, 1955. 321 p.

> Brown's study is a work in applied econometrics. As a reviewer
> has said, ". . . by which term [applied econometrics] is meant
> the measurement of interesting things by ingeniously simple if some-
> times dubious method." This is both the strength and weakness of
> applied econometrics.

Cagan, Phillip. "Monetary Dynamics of Hyper-Inflation." In STUDIES IN THE
QUANTITY THEORY OF MONEY, edited by Milton Friedman, pp. 25-117.
Chicago: Chicago University Press, 1958.

> Hyperinflation allows one to study relations between monetary
> factors in almost complete isolation from the real sector of the
> economy. The hyperinflations of six countries are studied: Austria,
> Germany, Greece, Hungary, Poland, and Russia.

Conlisk, John. "Cross Country Inflation Evidence on the Moneyness of Time
Deposits." ECONOMIC RECORD 46 (June 1970): 222-29.

> The title tells the whole story. Given an economy with full em-
> ployment, if time deposits are money, an increase in them will
> cause inflation.

Enthoven, Alain C. "Monetary Disequilibrium and the Dynamics of Inflation."
ECONOMIC JOURNAL 66 (June 1956): 256-70.

> Because of the variety of market structures in the economy, a
> weighted sum of excess demand may provide an improved guide
> to monetary policy.

Fand, David I. "Keynesian Monetary Theories, Stabilization Policy, and the
Recent Inflation." JOURNAL OF MONEY, CREDIT AND BANKING 1 (August
1969): 556-87.

> Looking at Keynesian monetary theory through the eyes of a mone-
> tarist is disheartening. Fand feels Keynesian policies may be all
> right for developing countries, but they impart an inflationary bias

in developed countries. A good bibliography is provided. Also, look at the comments by Kenneth Boulding and Henry C. Wallich, pp. 588-99, in the same issue.

Friedman, Milton. "Government Revenue from Inflation." JOURNAL OF PO-LITICAL ECONOMY 79 (July/August 1971): 846-56.

If a government has a monopoly on the issue of fiat money, the greatest steady state command over real resources can be realized with a rate of inflation at which the income elasticity of demand for real balances is unity and real income is constant. With rising real income the growth rate must also be taken into account.

Gordon, Robert J. "Inflation in Recession and Recovery." BROOKINGS PAPERS ON ECONOMIC ACTIVITY 1, no. 1 (1971): 105-58.

His econometric wage-price model attributes the absence of a re-duction in inflation in 1970 to expectations and no increase in "disguised" unemployment. A number of simulations are carried out. Also see his article "The Welfare Costs of Higher Unemploy-ment." Ibid., 3, no. 1 (1973): 133-95.

Hansen, Bent. A STUDY IN THE THEORY OF INFLATION. New York: Augustus M. Kelley, 1951. 283 p.

This is a Swedish school interpretation of inflation. Of fundamental importance to Hansen's theory are the concepts of ex ante and ex post, with regard to investment and saving.

Johnson, Harry G. "A Survey of Theories of Inflation." INDIAN ECONOMIC REVIEW 6 (August 1963): 29-66.

Inflation is not as easy to define as one might suppose. Johnson discusses six topics: (1) a brief history of inflation problems and theory, (2) Keynesian analysis of inflation, (3) quantity theory approach to inflation, (4) cost-push versus demand-pull inflation, (5) empirical findings, and (6) policy issues.

Kessel, Reuben A., and Alchian, Armen A. "Effects of Inflation." JOURNAL OF POLITICAL ECONOMY 70 (December 1962): 521-37.

Only the implications, not the causes, are examined. Inflations are classified as being anticipated or unanticipated.

Lekachman, Robert. INFLATION. New York: Random House, 1973. 121 p. Paperbound.

Booms and busts benefit the rich and impose additional hardships on the poor.

Machlup, Fritz. "Another View of Cost-Push and Demand-Pull Inflation."
REVIEW OF ECONOMICS AND STATISTICS 42 (May 1960): 125-39. Reprinted in [10] [16].

> Machlup has defined the problem. To facilitate the analysis,
> three kinds of demand expansion are listed (autonomous, induced,
> and supportive) as well as three kinds of cost increases (responsive,
> defensive, and aggressive).

Means, Gardiner C., et al. THE ROOTS OF INFLATION. New York: Burt
Franklin, 1975. 315 p.

> Eight original essays attempt to identify the prime factors which
> cause inflation.

Mundell, R[obert].A. "Growth, Stability and Inflationary Finance." JOURNAL
OF POLITICAL ECONOMY 73 (April 1965): 97-109.

> The proper focus for authorities is the rate of monetary expansion,
> not the rate of inflation.

_____. "Inflation and the Real Rate of Interest." JOURNAL OF POLITICAL
ECONOMY 71 (June 1963): 280-83. Reprinted in [13].

> Mundell assumes that people will save more during inflation, be-
> cause their real balances have depreciated.

Niehans, Jurg, ed. "The Universities--National Bureau Conference on Secular Inflation." JOURNAL OF MONEY, CREDIT AND BANKING 5, supplement (February 1973): 237-593.

> Jurg Niehans's introduction, pp. 237-41, gives a good summary of
> the articles and comments. Niehans makes an interesting point:
> because an instable unit of account may impose costs, the unit of
> account may join the medium of exchange in the center of future
> monetary theorizing.

Phelps, Edmund S. "Anticipated Inflation and Economic Welfare." JOURNAL
OF POLITICAL ECONOMY 73 (February 1965): 1-17.

> This article provides a good survey of the "burden" of inflation.
> His conclusion is that there are times when inflation may be a
> benefit rather than a cost.

Robertson, Dennis H. GROWTH, WAGES, MONEY: THE MARSHALL LECTURES
FOR 1960. Cambridge: At the University Press, 1961. 64 p.

> "The economic stalactite of inflated demand has met a sociological
> stalagmite of upthrusting claims; and when stalactite and stalagmite
> meet and fuse in an icy kiss--I hope there is no geologist present
> to tell me I am talking through my hat--nobody on earth can be
> quite sure where the one ends and the other begins."

Rousseas, Stephen W., ed. INFLATION: ITS CAUSES, CONSEQUENCES AND CONTROL. Wilton, Conn.: Calvin K. Kazanyian Economics Foundation, 1968. 59 p. Paperbound.

The two main papers given at this symposium were: Robert M. Solow, "Recent Controversy on the Theory of Inflation: An Eclectic View," and Phillip Cagan, "Theories of Mild, Continuing Inflation: A Critique and Extension." The discussants were Albert C. Hart and James Tobin.

Rutledge, John. A MONETARIST MODEL OF INFLATIONARY EXPECTATIONS. Lexington, Mass.: Lexington Books, 1974. 144 p.

Inflation grows from expectations of investors and consumers.

Schultze, Charles L. "Recent Inflation in the United States." In EMPLOY-MENT, GROWTH, AND PRICE LEVELS. Joint Economic Committee, Study Paper no. 1, pp 4-16. Washington, D.C.: Government Printing Office, 1959. Reprinted in [10] [16].

Is inflation cause or synonym for a general price rise? It is necessary to know the type of inflation and the time span you are talking about.

Solow, R[obert].M. PRICE EXPECTATIONS AND THE BEHAVIOR OF THE PRICE LEVEL. Manchester, Engl.: Manchester University Press, 1969. 50 p. Paperbound.

Data from the United States and the United Kingdom are used to test econometrically the trade-off between inflation and unemployment. Policy recommendations are analyzed on the basis of his results.

Tarshis, Lorie. "Changes in Real and Money Wages." ECONOMIC JOURNAL 49 (March 1939): 150-54. Reprinted in [3].

Tarshis disputes Keynes's claim that real and money wages will usually move in opposite directions. Also see, Dunlup, John T. "The Movement of Real and Money Wages." ECONOMIC JOUR-NAL 48 (September 1938): 413-34.

Tulloch, J. "Effects of Stabilization." JOURNAL OF POLITICAL ECONOMY 71 (August 1963): 413-15.

When authorities attempt to steer an economy past a depression through stabilization of the money supply, there is the additional danger of sudden collapse of the currency. This note is an extension of Kessel, R.A., and Alchian, A.A. "Effects of Inflation." JOURNAL OF POLITICAL ECONOMY 70 (December 1962): 521-37.

RELATION BETWEEN EMPLOYMENT AND PRICES

Akerlof, George. "Relative Wages and the Rate of Inflation." QUARTERLY
JOURNAL OF ECONOMICS 83 (August 1969): 353-74.

There is some hope that the Phillips curve can be structurally
altered.

Bodkin, R[onald].G. THE WAGE-PRICE-PRODUCTIVITY NEXUS. Philadelphia:
University of Pennsylvania Press, 1966. 302 p.

U.S. data from 1899 to 1957 are examined using single-equation,
least-squares techniques. The trade-off necessary for price stability
is thirteen million unemployed or 18.8 percent of the labor force.

Brownlee, O.H. "The Theory of Employment and Stabilization Policy." JOUR-
NAL OF POLITICAL ECONOMY 58 (October 1950): 412-24.

Some early support for the Friedman position that automatic policies
with built-in flexibility are better than discretionary action.

Eckstein, Otto, and Fromm, Gary. "The Price Equation." AMERICAN ECO-
NOMIC REVIEW 58 (December 1968): 1159-83.

This article is part of a study to build a complete model of the
price-wage-productivity-cost structure of U.S. industries. Competitive and oligopolistic pricing structures are tested.

Holt, Charles [C.]. "Improving the Labor Market Tradeoff between Inflation and
Unemployment." AMERICAN ECONOMIC REVIEW 59 (May 1969): 135-46.

Holts's policy recommendations are aimed at reducing turnover rates
and raising the probability of placement.

Hymans, Saul H. "The Inflation-Unemployment Trade-Off: Theory and Experience." In READINGS IN MONEY, NATIONAL INCOME, AND STABILI-
ZATION POLICY, edited by W.L. Smith and R.L. Teigen, 3d ed., pp. 160-
74. Homewood, Ill.: Richard D. Irwin, 1974.

A good survey of the Phillips curve controversy.

Johnson, H[arvey].G., and Nobay, A.R., eds. THE CURRENT INFLATION.
New York: St. Martin's Press, 1971. 204 p.

The British Money Study Group's views on the Phillips curve, and so forth.

Kaldor, Nicholas, ed. CONFLICTS IN POLICY OBJECTIVES. New York:
Augustus M. Kelley, 1971. 189 p.

The lead essay is Kaldor's presidential address for Section F of the
British Association for the Advancement of Science (Economics).

He says that more wealth and a more even distribution of income are, without question, the main objectives of economic policy-- almost forever.

Lipsey, Richard [G.]. "The Relation Between Unemployment and the Rate of Change in Money Wage Rates in the United Kingdom, 1862-1957: A Further Analysis." ECONOMICA 27 (February 1960): 1-31. Reprinted in [5].

This is an exhaustive reconsideration of the hypothesis advanced by A.W. Phillips that the percentage rate of change of money wage rates in the United Kingdom can be explained to a large extent by the percentage of the labor force unemployed and the rate of change of unemployment.

Lucas, Robert E., and Rapping, Leonard A. "Real Wages, Employment and Inflation." JOURNAL OF POLITICAL ECONOMY 77 (September/October 1969): 721-54.

The parameters of the aggregate labor-supply function are estimated. The differences between labor supply in growth theory and compara- tive static theory are reconciled.

Miller, Roger L., and Williams, Raburn M. UNEMPLOYMENT AND INFLA- TION: THE NEW ECONOMICS OF THE WAGE-PRICE SPIRAL. St. Paul, Minn.: West Publishing, 1974. 118 p.

A short but careful discussion of the interdependencies between unemployment and inflation.

Palmer, John L. INFLATION, UNEMPLOYMENT, AND POVERTY. Lexington, Mass.: Lexington Books, 1973. 183 p.

A partial equilibrium analysis which treats inflation and unemploy- ment as being jointly determined. The costs and benefits of infla- tion and unemployment with regard to the poor is the focal point.

Perry, George L. UNEMPLOYMENT, MONEY WAGE RATES AND INFLATION. Cambridge, Mass.: M.I.T. Press, 1966. 158 p.

Mainly topical in nature. The wage rate is canonized.

Phelps, Edmund S. INFLATION POLICY AND UNEMPLOYMENT THEORY. New York: W.W. Norton, 1972. 350 p.

Phelps fashions a rational approach--cost-benefit or econometric-- to choosing an optimal monetary policy. Inflation and unemploy- ment are treated as being interdependent. Optimality theory is his emphasis. The introduction is especially well done.

Phelps, Edmund S., et al. MICROECONOMIC FOUNDATIONS OF EMPLOY- MENT AND INFLATION THEORY. New York: W.W. Norton, 1970. 434 p.

The best recent collection of articles about Keynes's influence on the microeconomic aspects of employment and inflation theory. The introduction by Phelps is an almost perfect precis. The two areas covered by the essays are: (1) "Employment and Wage Dynamics," and (2) "Output and Price Dynamics."

Phillips, A.W. "Employment, Inflation and Growth." ECONOMICA 29 (February 1962): 1-16. Reprinted in [15].

There is no way economic policies can be implemented to meet the problems our economy faces, if we do not understand how the economic system works.

_____. "The Relation Between Unemployment and the Rate of Change of Money Wage Rates in the United Kingdom, 1861-1957." ECONOMICA 25 (November 1958): 283-99. Reprinted in [10] [15].

This is the article in which the Phillips curve was formulated--an inverse relation between the percent unemployed and the percent change in wages or prices.

Rees, Albert. "Wage Determination and Involuntary Unemployment." JOURNAL OF POLITICAL ECONOMY 59 (April 1951): 143-53.

Rees gives a theory of wage determination in which the employees set wages which lie above the intersection of the demand and supply curves.

Samuelson, Paul A., and Solow, Robert M. "Problem of Achieving and Maintaining a Stable Price Level: Analytical Aspects of Anti-Inflation Policy." AMERICAN ECONOMIC REVIEW 50 (May 1960): 177-94. Reprinted in [8] [10] [15].

A general article on the causes of inflation. A modified Phillips curve for the United States is discussed.

Schultze, George P., and Aliber, Robert Z., eds. GUIDELINES, INFORMAL CONTROLS, AND THE MARKET PLACE. Chicago: University of Chicago Press, 1966. 357 p. Also paperbound.

Sixteen economists express their opinions with regard to guidelines in the context of the Phillips relation. Agreement is a scarce commodity.

Solow, R[obert].M. PRICE EXPECTATIONS AND THE BEHAVIOR OF THE PRICE LEVEL. Manchester, Engl.: Manchester University Press, 1969. 50 p. Paperbound.

Data from the United States and the United Kingdom are used to test econometrically the trade-off between inflation and unemployment. Policy recommendations are analyzed on the basis of his results.

Spencer, Roger W. "The Relation between Prices and Employment: Two Views." Federal Reserve Bank of St. Louis REVIEW 51 (March 1969): 15-21. Reprinted in [8] [12] [13].

> In the short run there is a trade-off; in the long run there is not. Policies should be implemented to reduce costs of obtaining employment information, improve mobility of the labor force, etc. In essence the goal is to come as close to a perfectly competitive economy as possible.

Tinbergen, Jan. ON THE THEORY OF ECONOMIC POLICY. New York: North-Holland, 1952. 78 p.

> This short booklet explores the problems inherent in converting theory to policy.

Tobin, James. "Inflation and Unemployment." AMERICAN ECONOMIC REVIEW 62 (March 1972): 1-18. Reprinted in [12] [17].

> Tobin's presidential address to the American Economic Association. There is work to be done on the welfare aspects of macroeconomics.

Tools

FISCAL POLICY

Blinder, Alan S., et al., eds. THE ECONOMICS OF PUBLIC FINANCE. Washington, D.C.: Brookings Institution, 1974. 435 p. Also paperbound.

> There are four essays on balanced budgets, taxes, public expenditures, and revenue sharing by Alan S. Blinder and Robert M. Solow, George F. Break, Peter O. Steiner, and Dick Netzer, respectively. The Blinder and Solow article relies on a budget constraint for its strange results.

Burkhead, Jesse. "The Balanced Budget." QUARTERLY JOURNAL OF ECONOMICS 68 (May 1954): 191-216. Reprinted in [18].

> The history of budget balancing is surveyed. Keynesians stress the effect of the budget but pay too little attention to its control.

Christ, Carl [F.]. "A Simple Macroeconomic Model with a Government Budget Restraint." JOURNAL OF POLITICAL ECONOMY 76 (January/February 1968): 53-67.

> When governments choose a mix of monetary and fiscal policies, they must take into account the government budget restraint. A restraint which is somewhat flexible because the government can issue fiat money.

Clark, John Maurice. "An Appraisal of the Workability of Compensatory Devices." AMERICAN ECONOMIC REVIEW 29 (March 1939): 194-208. Reprinted in [6].

> To use fiscal policy rashly is dangerous but not to use it may also be dangerous. Use fiscal policy to preserve and improve our economic and political systems.

Commission on Money and Credit, ed. FISCAL AND DEBT MANAGEMENT POLICIES. Englewood Cliffs, N.J.: Prentice-Hall, 1963. 539 p. Also paperbound.

> Eight studies were done on this topic for the commission. The authors are: W. Fellner, R.A. Musgrave, J. Tobin, J.R. Schlesinger, P.H. Coatner, I. Auerbach, R.K. Huitt, and J. Lendeman.

Eisner, Robert. "What Went Wrong?" JOURNAL OF POLITICAL ECONOMY 79 (May/June 1971): 629-41. Reprinted in [12].

> Why are not Keynesian fiscal policies working? Foreign wars are to be avoided.

Haley, Bernard F. "The Federal Budget: Economic Consequences of Deficit Financing." AMERICAN ECONOMIC REVIEW 30 (February 1941): 67-87.

> There are great inflationary worries. This is before any real government deficits had appeared.

Heller, Walter W. "CED's Stabilizing Budget Policy after Ten Years." AMERICAN ECONOMIC REVIEW 47 (September 1957): 634-51. Reprinted in [5].

> Heller is still a Keynesian. He disapproves of the assumptions made by the Committee for Economic Development that lead them to advocate a passive fiscal policy but an active monetary policy.

Lerner, Abba P. THE ECONOMICS OF CONTROL. New York: Augustus M. Kelley, 1944. 452 p.

> This book describes the essentials of government fiscal instruments: Lerner's "functional finance."

Lewis, Wilfred, Jr. FEDERAL FISCAL POLICY IN THE POSTWAR RECESSIONS. Washington, D.C.: Brookings Institution, 1962. 326 p.

> A study of federal fiscal policy during the four recessions since World War II.

McCabe, James R. "The Full-Employment Budget: A Guide for Fiscal Policy." Federal Reserve Bank of Richmond MONTHLY REVIEW 58 (May 1972): 2-8. Reprinted in [12].

> The full-employment budget is not a perfect guide, but it is the best that is available.

Ott, David J., and Ott, Attiat F. FEDERAL BUDGET POLICY. Rev. ed. Washington, D.C.: Brookings Institution, 1969. 164 p.

A book which explains the effects the federal budget has on the state of the economy; designed for the layreader.

Samuelson, Paul A. "Principles and Rules in Modern Fiscal Policy: A Neo-Classical Reformulation." In MONEY, TRADE, AND ECONOMIC GROWTH, edited by D. McCord Wright et al., pp. 157-76. New York: Macmillan, 1951.

It is impossible to come up with convenient rules-of-thumb for fiscal policy. The rules proposed are either empty or arbitrary.

Silber, William L. "Fiscal Policy, Tax Structure, and the Permanent-Income Hypothesis." KYKLOS 24, fasc. 1 (1971): 90-96. Reprinted in [12].

It is proposed that the income-based tax rates be different for saving and expenditures.

Slichter, Sumner H. "The Economics of Public Works." AMERICAN ECONOMIC REVIEW 24 (March 1934): 174-85. Reprinted in [18].

He despairs that profit maximization behavior will not maintain full employment.

Spencer, Roger W., and Yohe, William P. "The 'Crowding Out' of Private Expenditures by Fiscal Policy Actions." Federal Reserve Bank of St. Louis REVIEW 52 (October 1970): 12-24. Reprinted in [12].

When government investment takes place, private investment will be reduced.

Stein, Herbert. "Fiscal Policy--Overview." In INTERNATIONAL ENCYCLO-PEDIA OF THE SOCIAL SCIENCES, edited by D.L. Sills, vol. 5, pp. 460-71. New York: Macmillan-Free Press, 1968.

Stein summarizes the Keynesian era and the development of fiscal policy with particular attention to various multiplier effects. Policy approaches are categorized either as activist (fine-tune) or passivist (predetermined objective rule). The budget is also analyzed.

_____. THE FISCAL REVOLUTION IN AMERICA. Chicago: University of Chicago Press, 1969. 540 p. Also paperbound.

The story is told in terms of the thinking and action of leading participants at critical points in the previous forty years. Fiscal policy in the United States was not determined by one economist, one school of economic thought, one president, or one political party.

_____. "Where Stands the New Fiscal Policy?" JOURNAL OF MONEY,

CREDIT AND BANKING   1 (August 1969):   463-73.

> This is a distillation of his significant major study THE FISCAL REVOLUTION IN AMERICA. Chicago: University of Chicago Press, 1969.

Williams, John H[enry].   "Deficit Spending."   AMERICAN ECONOMIC REVIEW 30 (February 1941):   52-66.   Reprinted in [6].

> He has a low opinion of deficit spending.

MONETARY POLICY

Black, Fischer.   "Active and Passive Monetary Policy in a Neoclassical Model." JOURNAL OF FINANCE   27 (September 1972):   801-14.

> In his model, active monetary policy is never consistent with continual equilibrium in the money and bond markets.

Brunner, Karl.   "Institutions, Policies, and Monetary Analysis."   JOURNAL OF POLITICAL ECONOMY   73 (April 1965):   197-218.

> This article is, in essence, a review article of A MONETARY HISTORY OF THE UNITED STATES, 1867-1960 by Milton Friedman and Anna J. Schwartz. In order to require the Federal Reserve authorities to someday accept responsibility for the money supply, both critical assessment of their policy procedures from the outside and continual efforts of the intellectual community to contribute to the accumulation of knowledge of rational policies are needed.

_____.   "The Role of Money and Monetary Policy."   Federal Reserve Bank of St. Louis REVIEW 50 (July 1968):   9-24.   Reprinted in [4] [8] [13] [14].

> A well-constructed support of the monetarist thesis. Those critical of the monetarists are shown to be lacking in evidence and analysis.

_____, ed.   TARGETS AND INDICATORS OF MONETARY POLICY.   San Francisco: Chandler, 1969.   348 p.

> These are papers read at a 1966 conference by the same name. Additional chapters, to obtain a more representative view, were contributed by James Tobin, Lyle Gramley and Samuel Chase, Patric Hendershott, Robert Weintraub, Allan Meltzer and Karl Brunner. The conclusion is that interpretation and determination of monetary policy is a difficult problem to resolve.

Brunner, Karl, and Meltzer, Allan [H.].   "The Meaning of Monetary Indicators." In MONETARY PROCESS AND POLICY: A SYMPOSIUM, edited by George Horwich, pp. 187-217.   Homewood, Ill.: Richard D. Irwin, 1967.   Reprinted in [4].

The naive use of money supply, free reserves, or interest rates as indicators of policy is dangerous. However, the authors do attempt to reach some policy recommendations on the basis of their model.

_____. "Some Further Investigations of Demand and Supply Functions for Money." JOURNAL OF FINANCE 19 (May 1964): 240-83.

It is suggested that monetary theory, using the work of Brunner and Meltzer, may be useful in furnishing a framework for monetary policy.

Chandler, Lester V. AMERICAN MONETARY POLICY: 1928-1941. New York: Harper & Row Publishers, 1971. 371 p.

The policies of the Federal Reserve are examined in detail. He has hopes that a great depression will never happen again.

_____. "Monetary Policy." In INTERNATIONAL ENCYCLOPEDIA OF THE SOCIAL SCIENCES, edited by D.L. Sills, vol. 10, pp. 416-26. New York: Macmillan-Free Press, 1968.

The objectives, rationale, and strategies of monetary policy are discussed. The lags (recognition, administrative, and operational) inherent in any government policy make an optimum mix a fantasy.

Clower, Robert W. "Theoretical Foundations of Monetary Policy." In MONE-TARY THEORY AND MONETARY POLICY IN THE 1970's, edited by G. Clayton et al., pp. 15-28. New York: Oxford University Press, 1971.

It is important that his aphorism be kept in mind: "Goods buy money, and money buys goods--but goods do not buy goods in any organized market." The exchanges over Clower's article by Harry G. Johnson, G.L.S. Shackle, and Milton Friedman (also reprinted in this book) became quite heated.

Commission on Money and Credit, ed. IMPACTS ON MONETARY POLICY. Englewood Cliffs, N.J.: Prentice-Hall, 1963. 688 p. Also paperbound.

The importance of monetary policy over the past decade and in the future is highlighted in a number of essays by different authors. The essays on consumption by D.B. Suits, business investment by R. Eisner and R.H. Strotz, and investment and liquidity by E. Kuh and J.R. Meyer are most often cited.

_____. MONETARY MANAGEMENT. Englewood Cliffs, N.J.: Prentice-Hall, 1963. 472 p. Also paperbound.

The authors were F.M. Tamagna, W.L. Smith, C. Warburton, M.D. Rengen, C.P. Kindleberger, and R.Z. Aliber. These essays present one of the earliest confrontations of monetarists and Keynesians.

_____. MONEY AND CREDIT: THEIR INFLUENCE ON JOBS, PRICES, AND GROWTH. Englewood Cliffs, N.J.: Prentice-Hall, 1961. 300 p. Also paperbound.

> This volume is not a series of papers by economists but rather is an integrated whole. It is the commission's report on what changes were needed in the structure and performance of public and private financial institutions in the United States. The three goals of price stability, low levels of unemployment, and economic growth are assessed and policy instruments are explored.

Crawford, Arthur W. MONETARY MANAGEMENT UNDER THE NEW DEAL. Washington, D.C.: American Council on Public Affairs, 1940. 390 p.

> Every policy--nonsensible and sensible--is described.

Crouch, R[obert].L. "The Inadequacy of "New-Orthodox' Methods of Monetary Control." ECONOMIC JOURNAL 74 (December 1964): 916-34.

> If the authorities wish to control the money supply they would do better to control the cash base than the Treasury bill stock.

Culbertson, John M. "Friedman on the Lag in Effect of Monetary Policy." JOURNAL OF POLITICAL ECONOMY 68 (December 1960): 617-21.

> Culbertson feels that Friedman's long and rather variable lag does not have support. Also see Friedman, Milton. "The Lag in Effect of Monetary Policy"; and Culbertson, John M. "The Lag in Effect of Monetary Policy: Reply." JOURNAL OF POLITICAL ECONOMY 69 (October 1961): 447-66, 467-77.

Davis, Richard G. "The Role of Money Supply in Business Cycles." Federal Reserve Bank of New York MONTHLY REVIEW 50 (April 1968): 63-73. Reprinted in [4] [14].

> An attempt to clarify the relationship between money supply and peaks and troughs of cycles. He is not a monetarist. Also see his more recent article "How Much Does Money Matter? A Look at Some Recent Evidence." Federal Reserve Bank of New York MONTHLY REVIEW 51 (June 1969): 119-31. Reprinted in [4].

Dewald, William G. "Free Reserves, Total Reserves and Monetary Control." JOURNAL OF POLITICAL ECONOMY 71 (April 1963): 141-53.

> Reserve position is determined by the Federal Reserve. Open-market operations are carried on to maintain the target level of reserves.

Ellis, Howard S. "Monetary Policy and Investment." AMERICAN ECONOMIC REVIEW 30 (March 1940): 27-38. Reprinted in [6].

He believes that the market is neither a failure nor a savior, but something between.

Friedman, Milton. "Controls on Interest Rates Paid by Banks." JOURNAL OF MONEY, CREDIT AND BANKING 2 (February 1970): 15-32.

Regulation is not only not necessary, but harmful; the free market will solve the problem more efficiently. In a comparison article James Tobin argues that the aggregative effect of changes in the ceiling rate is small: "Deposit Interest Ceilings as a Monetary Control." Ibid., pp. 4-14.

_____. A PROGRAM FOR MONETARY STABILITY. New York: Fordham University Press, 1959. 120 p.

Friedman presents three basic arguments for abolishing monetary controls by the Federal Reserve: (1) instability in the stock of money has aggravated cyclical fluctuations, (2) the failure of government to provide a stable monetary framework has been the major cause of all really severe inflations and depressions, (3) counter-cyclical monetary policies should be abandoned since they do more harm than good.

_____. "The Role of Monetary Policy." AMERICAN ECONOMIC REVIEW 58 (March 1968): 1-17. Reprinted in [4] [8] [16] [17].

Friedman's position is that monetary authorities should publicly adopt the policy of achieving a steady rate of growth of the money supply. The leading spokesman of the monetarists uses price flexibility as his can opener. See Lerner, Abba P. "The Economists' Can Opener." WESTERN ECONOMIC JOURNAL 6 (March 1968): 94-96.

Galbraith, J.A. "Monetary Policy and Nonbank Financial Intermediaries." NATIONAL BANKING REVIEW 4 (September 1966): 53-60. Reprinted in [10] [14].

The destabilizing effect of shifts of funds from banks to near banks and vice versa are discussed.

Gibson, William E. "Interest Rates and Monetary Policy." JOURNAL OF POLITICAL ECONOMY 78 (May/June 1970): 431-55. Reprinted in [4].

Gibson finds that the inverse influence of money on rates of interest is rather quickly reversed at all interest rate levels by offsetting influences originating from changes in income brought about by the initial changes in money supply. An article of his in the same vein is "The Lag in Effect of Monetary Policy on Income and Interest Rates." QUARTERLY JOURNAL OF ECONOMICS 84 (May 1970): 288-300.

Goldenweiser, E.A. AMERICAN MONETARY POLICY. New York: McGraw-Hill Book Co., 1951. 391 p.

> This review of the Federal Reserve System is part of a research study undertaken for the Committee for Economic Development. He is an opponent of automatic rules, substituting "the glorious process of muddling through."

Hamburger, Michael J. "The Impact of Monetary Variables: A Survey of Recent Econometric Literature." In ESSAYS IN DOMESTIC AND INTERNATIONAL FINANCE, edited by Federal Reserve Bank of New York, pp. 37-49. New York: 1969. Reprinted in [17].

> The most often used monetary variable has been the rate of interest; interest rates have been found to be statistically significant more often in recent years; and the estimated lags appear to be quite long. There are ninety-one citations in the bibliography.

_____. "The Lag in the Effect of Monetary Policy: A Survey of Recent Literature." Federal Reserve Bank of New York MONTHLY REVIEW 53 (December 1971): 289-98.

> There is a lag in the effect of monetary policy; however, the estimates vary greatly. The most important factor to account for the differences was the specifications of the appropriate monetary policy variables.

Harris, Seymour [E.], ed. "The Controversy over Monetary Policy." REVIEW OF ECONOMICS AND STATISTICS 33 (August 1951): 179-200.

> The monetarists are Lester V. Chandler and Milton Friedman. The fiscalists are Alvin H. Hansen, Abba P. Lerner, and James Tobin. Time changes but opinions don't--often.

_____. "Controversial Issues in Recent Monetary Policy: A Symposium." REVIEW OF ECONOMICS AND STATISTICS 42 (August 1960): 245-82.

> The debt management and monetary policies of the Eisenhower administration were carefully analyzed by S.E. Harris, J.W. Angell, W. Fellner, A.H. Hansen, A.G. Hart, H. Neisser, R.V. Roosa, P.A. Samuelson, W.L. Smith, W. Thomas, J. Tobin and S. Weintraub.

Hart, Albert G[ailord]. "The 'Chicago Plan' of Banking Reform." REVIEW OF ECONOMIC STUDIES 2, no. 2 (1934-35): 104-16. Reprinted in [11].

> A proposal to do away with inside money by requiring 100 percent reserves against deposits.

Horwich, George. "Tight Money, Monetary Restraint, and the Price Level." JOURNAL OF FINANCE 21 (March 1966): 15-33. Reprinted in [13].

He finds little support for the claim that higher interest rates raise prices by raising costs.

_____, ed. MONETARY PROCESS AND POLICY: A SYMPOSIUM. Homewood, Ill.: Richard D. Irwin, 1967. 400 p.

The symposium was held during the "happy times" immediately after the 1964 tax cut--happy times for the fiscalists. The papers are gathered under four headings: (1) "High Employment and Price Stability," (2) "Possible Instability of the Financial Structure," (3) "Effects of Monetary Policy" (split into three subheadings), and (4) "International Constraints."

Jacoby, Neil H., ed. UNITED STATES MONETARY POLICY. Rev. ed. New York: Frederick A. Praeger, for the American Assembly, 1964. 243 p. Also paperbound.

The chapters contained herein were written originally as background reading for a series of American Assemblies on monetary policy.

Johnson, Harry G. "Problems of Efficiency in Monetary Management." JOURNAL OF POLITICAL ECONOMY 76 (September/October 1968): 971-90. Reprinted in [13].

Three aspects of the problem of efficiency are distinguished: (1) structural efficiency of the banking system, (2) efficiency in stabilization policy, and (3) efficiency in secular economic policy.

Leijonhufvud, Axel. "Keynes and the Effectiveness of Monetary Policy." WESTERN ECONOMIC JOURNAL 6 (March 1968): 97-111. Reprinted in [13].

Monetary policy will be futile and costly if entrepreneurial expectations are attuned to a continuous slump. If, however, expectations are sanguine, monetary policy will work.

Lerner, Abba P. "Review of Milton Friedman, 'A Program for Monetary Stability.'" AMERICAN STATISTICAL ASSOCIATION JOURNAL 57 (March 1962): 211-20. Reprinted in [8] [14].

A very readable review of Friedman's case for getting rid of authorities and having rules only.

Maisel, Sherman J. MANAGING THE DOLLAR. New York: W.W. Norton, 1973. 333 p.

A study of the use and formulation of monetary policy by a University of California professor who spent some time on the Board of Governors of the Federal Reserve System. Policy decisions are not made in a vacuum.

Mayer, Thomas. "The Inflexibility of Monetary Policy." REVIEW OF ECO-
NOMICS AND STATISTICS 40 (November 1958): 358-74. Reprinted in [19].

Mayer provides a set of empirically-determined reaction lags and
multiplier lags with regard to anticyclical monetary policy. He
determines that monetary policy produces feeble results. William
H. White has written an article in response. "The Flexibility of
Anticyclical Monetary Policy." REVIEW OF ECONOMICS AND
STATISTICS 54 (May 1961): 142-47. Reprinted in [19]. He
finds no reason to hesitate about or abandon use of cycle stabilizing measures.

———. "The Lag in the Effect of Monetary Policy: Some Criticisms."
WESTERN ECONOMIC JOURNAL 5 (September 1967): 324-42. Reprinted in
[14].

There is a lag and it appears to be long, but there is still a question about the size of the variance.

———. MONETARY POLICY IN THE UNITED STATES. New York: Random
House, 1968. 250 p. Also paperbound.

The goal, tools, and strengths of monetary policy are assessed.
Written for a layperson.

Mitchell, George W. "A New Look at Monetary Policy Instruments." JOUR-
NAL OF MONEY, CREDIT AND BANKING 3, supplement (May 1971): 381-
90.

Two questions are discussed: (1) should commercial banks and other
financial intermediaries be restricted to domestic credit and money
markets? and (2) should the Fed place greater reliance on monetary and credit aggregates? The answers are predictable if one
knows that Mitchell was a governor of the Federal Reserve when
he gave this paper.

Patinkin, Don. "On the Nature of the Monetary Mechanism." In his STUDIES
IN MONETARY ECONOMICS, pp. 143-67. New York: Harper & Row
Publishers, 1972. Reprinted in [12].

This is a reprint of part 2 of his 1967 Wicksell Lectures. He has
little faith in traditional monetary policy.

Polakoff, Murray E. "Federal Reserve Discount Policy and Its Critics." In
BANKING AND MONETARY STUDIES, edited by Deane Carson, pp. 204-12.
Homewood, Ill.: Richard D. Irwin, 1963. Reprinted in [14].

A firm supporter of the Federal Reserve's discount policy.

Poole, William. "Optimal Choice of Monetary Policy Instruments in a Simple
Stochastic Macro Model." QUARTERLY JOURNAL OF ECONOMICS 84 (May

1970): 197-216.

> A stochastic IS-LM model is used because the choice of instruments
> problem is a consequence of uncertainty. A similar problem arises
> in fiscal policy but it was not analyzed.

Rowan, D.C. "Radcliffe Monetary Theory." ECONOMIC RECORD 37 (December 1961): 420-41.

> His article was written after the release of the Radcliffe Committee's
> Report. An important distinction is made between Radcliffe mone-
> tary policy and Radcliffe monetary theory. Also see his article
> that was written before the release of the report. In it Rowan was
> quite sure a Keynes-type theory would be forthcoming. "The Rad-
> cliffe Report: A Distant View." ECONOMIC RECORD 37 (March
> 1961): 53-72.

Saving, Thomas R. "Monetary Policy Targets and Indicators." JOURNAL OF
POLITICAL ECONOMY 75 (August 1967): 446-56. Reprinted in [1] [4].

> There seems to have been a failure to distinguish clearly between
> a target and an indicator.

Sayers, R.S. "Monetary Thought and Monetary Policy in England." ECONOMIC
JOURNAL 70 (December 1960): 711-24.

> Little faith is expressed in the self-starting ability of monetary
> policy. However, in monetary policy the emphasis is on interest
> rate policy; action on the supply of bank money is purely inciden-
> tal.

Schlesinger, James R. "Monetary Policy and Its Critics." JOURNAL OF PO-
LITICAL ECONOMY 68 (December 1960): 601-16. Reprinted in [5] [10] [14].

> Some people just do not like monetary policy, especially because
> it relies on the price mechanism. Also see Schlesinger, James R.
> "Monetary-Fiscal Policy and the Growth Objective." SOUTHERN
> ECONOMIC JOURNAL 26 (April 1960): 276-80.

Simons, Henry C. "Rule Versus Authorities in Monetary Policy." JOURNAL
OF POLITICAL ECONOMY 44 (February 1936): 1-30. Reprinted in [11].

> The Chicago school's first spokesman on monetary rules. "The
> Liberal creed demands the organization of our economic life largely
> through individual participation in a game with definite rules":
> division of labor between the government and the market.

Smith, Warren L. "The Discount Rate as a Credit Control Weapon." JOUR-
NAL OF POLITICAL ECONOMY 66 (April 1958): 171-77.

> Smith feels that the discount rate has been more of a hinderance
> than a help in implementing monetary policy.

_____. "The Instruments of General Monetary Control." NATIONAL BANK-ING REVIEW 1 (September 1963): 47-76. Reprinted in [10] [17].

The three major monetary policy instruments are discussed in depth.

_____. "Time Deposits, Free Reserves and Monetary Policy." In ISSUES IN BANKING AND MONETARY ANALYSIS, edited by G. Pontecorvo et al., pp. 79-113. New York: Holt, Rinehart and Winston, 1967.

To avoid undue fluctuations in financial markets, the reserve requirements of close substitutes should be similar.

Smithies, Arthur. "Federal Budgeting and Fiscal Policy." In A SURVEY OF CONTEMPORARY ECONOMICS, vol. 1, edited by Howard S. Ellis, pp. 174-209. Homewood, Ill.: Richard D. Irwin, 1948.

The Great Depression followed by the Second World War gave government intervention in the private economy a big boost. Fiscal policy became a necessity backed up by Keynesian dogma.

Tobin, James. "Liquidity Preference and Monetary Policy." REVIEW OF ECONOMICS AND STATISTICS 29 (May 1947): 124-31; Warburton, Clark. "Comment." Ibid., 30 (November 1948): 304-14; and Tobin, James. "Rejoinder." Ibid., 30 (November 1948): 314-17. Reprinted in [18].

Demand for cash balances is shown to be interest-elastic.

Tobin, James, and Brainard, William [C.]. "Financial Intermediaries and the Effectiveness of Monetary Controls." AMERICAN ECONOMIC REVIEW 53 (May 1963): 383-400.

This is one of the early articles that formulated the Yale school view of monetary economics. See its fruitation in Tobin, James. "A General Equilibrium Approach to Monetary Theory." JOURNAL OF MONEY, CREDIT AND BANKING 1 (February 1969): 15-29.

Young, Ralph A. "Tools and Processes of Monetary Policy." In UNITED STATES MONETARY POLICY, edited by Neil H. Jacoby (for the American Assembly) Rev. ed., pp. 13-48. New York: Frederick A. Praeger, 1964.

Monetary policy is pictured as being rapid to respond and flexible, whether in expansionary or contractionary periods. Its invariant purpose is to sustain economic growth and stability of the dollar.

COMPARISONS AND MONETARY ASPECTS OF FISCAL POLICY

Andersen, Leonall C., and Jordan, Jerry L. "Monetary and Fiscal Actions: A Test of Their Relative Importance in Economic Stabilization." Federal Reserve Bank of St. Louis REVIEW 50 (November 1968): 11-24. Reprinted in [4] [13].

The results for the period tested (1952-68) suggest that monetary actions are more important, more predictable, and faster than fiscal actions. See the comment by de Leeuw, Frank, and Kalchbrenner, John. "Monetary Versus Fiscal Actions: Comments." Federal Reserve Bank of St. Louis REVIEW 51 (April 1969): 6-11. Reprinted in [13].

Ando, Albert, et al. "Lags in Fiscal and Monetary Policy." In STABILIZATION POLICIES, edited by Commission on Money and Credit, pp. 1-163. Englewood Cliffs, N.J.: Prentice-Hall, 1963.

These are two separate studies: one by John H. Karekan and Robert M. Solow and the second by Albert Ando and E.C. Brown. There is a joint introduction. Their main conclusion is that Friedman's proposition, that monetary policy has a very long and highly variable lag, does not hold water.

Bach, G.L. MAKING MONETARY AND FISCAL POLICY. Washington, D.C.: Brookings Institution, 1971. 281 p. Also paperbound.

Professor Bach has the experience to make a book of this nature readable.

Baumol, William J. "Pitfalls in Contracyclical Policies: Some Tools and Results." REVIEW OF ECONOMICS AND STATISTICS 43 (February 1961): 21-26.

Baumol joins with Friedman and Phillips to deplore and point out the dangers inherent in automatic stabilization devices.

Boughton, James M. MONETARY POLICY AND THE FEDERAL FUNDS MARKET. Durham, N.C.: Duke University Press, 1972. 192 p.

This is the first treatment of the Federal Funds market by an economist. The institutional and theoretical framework is discussed and an econometric model is constructed and tested.

Brainard, William C. "Uncertainty and the Effectiveness of Policy." AMERICAN ECONOMIC REVIEW 57 (May 1967): 411-25.

Effectiveness should be more than "bang per buck." Consequently, if a structural change is made, an empirical judgment needs to be made regarding the relative importance of different kinds of disturbances.

Chandler, Lester V. "Federal Reserve Policy and the Federal Debt." AMERICAN ECONOMIC REVIEW 39 (March 1949): 405-29. Reprinted in [11].

He objects to the Treasury's use of the Fed to maintain "an orderly market in government securities." In 1951 the Treasury and Fed reached agreement (Accord of 1951) over this issue.

Clement, M.D. "The Concept of Automatic Stabilizers." SOUTHERN ECO-
NOMIC JOURNAL 25 (January 1959): 303-14. Reprinted in [16].

> Automatic stabilizers will not prevent a major cyclical movement,
> once under way, from causing severe hardships. The built-in sta-
> bilizer arsenal is not as effective as it should be.

Commission on Money and Credit, ed. FISCAL AND DEBT MANAGEMENT POLI-
CIES. Englewood Cliffs, N.J.: Prentice-Hall, 1963. 539 p. Also paperbound.

> Eight studies were done on this topic for the commission. The
> authors are W. Fellner, R.A. Musgrave, J. Tobin, J.R. Schlesinger,
> P.H. Coatner, I. Auerbach, R.K. Huitt, and J. Lendeman.

Committee on Public Debt Policy. OUR NATIONAL DEBT. New York: Harcourt, Brace, 1949. 200 p.

> Seven pamphlets dealing with various aspects of this problem are
> published together. Their five-point program for action is as fol-
> lows: (1) control the budget, (2) reduce the debt, (3) distribute
> the debt more widely, (4) restore flexible interest rates, and (5)
> nourish a dynamic economy.

Ferguson, James M., ed. PUBLIC DEBT AND FUTURE GENERATIONS. Durham, N.C.: University of North Carolina Press, 1964. 234 p.

> This volume is a collection of twenty-three of the most important
> and representative contributions to the debate. James Buchanan
> thinks the burden does exist and Franco Modigliani, especially,
> thinks that the burden must be given a benefit-cost analysis.

Fox, Karl A., et al. THE THEORY OF QUANTITATIVE ECONOMIC POLICY.
2d ed. New York: American Elsevier Publishing Co., 1973. 638 p.

> This book extends the work done by Tinbergen and Theil on the
> theory of quantitative economic policy. Applications are made to
> economic growth, stabilization, and planning.

Friedman, Milton, and Heller, Walter W. MONETARY VS. FISCAL POLICY.
New York: W.W. Norton, 1969. 95 p. Paperbound.

> This dialogue did not solve any policy problems but it clarified
> the points of opposition between monetarists and fiscalists.

Hardy, Charles O. "Fiscal Operations as Instruments of Economic Stabilization."
AMERICAN ECONOMIC REVIEW 38 (May 1948): 395-403. Reprinted in [11].

> The monetary aspects of fiscal policy are reviewed.

Hickman, Bert G., ed. QUANTITATIVE PLANNING OF ECONOMIC POLICY.

Washington, D.C.: Brookings Institution, 1965. 292 p.

The logic of quantitative planning, specification of structures, data requirements, objectives and instruments of economic policy, and effectiveness of planning techniques are all covered. Hickman has added an informative introduction.

Holbrook, Robert S. "Optimal Economic Policy and the Problem of Instrument Instability." AMERICAN ECONOMIC REVIEW 62 (March 1972): 57-65.

Policy instruments, whether they be monetary or fiscal, are often unstable. This makes the realization of goal stability highly unlikely. "Fine tuning" of the economy might just be impossible.

Holt, Charles C. "Linear Decision Rules for Economic Stabilization and Growth." QUARTERLY JOURNAL OF ECONOMICS 76 (February 1962): 20-45.

A quadratic criterion function is used, because of its nice mathematical properties, with linear decision rules to examine growth and stability problems of the economy. The decision analysis is shown to incorporate both feedback and feed forward.

Johnson, Harry G. "Major Issues in Monetary and Fiscal Policies." FEDERAL RESERVE BULLETIN 50 (November 1964): 1400-1413. Reprinted in [8] [10].

No longer is it possible to speak only about domestic monetary and fiscal policy.

Katona, George. "Attitudes towards Fiscal and Monetary Policy." PUBLIC POLICY 18 (Winter 1970): 281-88. Reprinted in [12].

Expectations breed and multiply. Causal links are not mechanical.

Keran, Michael W. "Monetary and Fiscal Influences on Economic Activity-- The Historical Evidence." Federal Reserve Bank of St. Louis REVIEW 51 (November 1969): 5-23. Reprinted in [1].

The impact of monetary and fiscal influences on U.S. economic activity was measured from 1919 to 1969 and for selected subperiods. Money does matter.

Kuhleman, John M. "The Burden of the Debt: A Mathematical Proof." AMERICAN ECONOMIC REVIEW 56 (March 1966): 188.

"The proposition that the national debt as a liability must just equal the total of the associated assets can be stated as follows:
(1) Σ IOU's = Σ UOMe's.
If we divide both sides of the equation by OU, we have:
(2) Σ I's = Σ Me's
Q.E.D."

Laird, William E. "The Changing Views on Debt Management." QUARTERLY REVIEW OF ECONOMICS AND BUSINESS 3 (Autumn 1963): 7-17. Reprinted in [17].

> There are at least three views of debt management: countercyclical, procyclical, and neutral. Controversy has followed.

Lerner, Abba P. "The Burden of Public Debt." In INCOME, EMPLOYMENT AND PUBLIC POLICY, edited by Lloyd A. Metzler, pp. 255-75. New York: W.W. Norton, 1948.

> Most of the evils attributed to the burden of the debt are imaginary. Functional finance is the correct guide to the use of fiscal policy.

_____. "Functional Finance and the Federal Debt." SOCIAL RESEARCH 10 (February 1943): 38-51. Reprinted in [15] [18].

> In concluding this article, Lerner confesses that he has at times wrapped Functional finance (deficit financing) in the "flag" so that it will be more acceptable.

Mints, Lloyd W., et al. "A Symposium on Fiscal and Monetary Policy." REVIEW OF ECONOMICS AND STATISTICS 28 (May 1946): 60-84.

> Lloyd Mints's contribution, "Monetary Policy," pp. 60-69, is reprinted in [18]. Mints, a member of the Chicago school, emphasizes the importance of free markets, price flexibility, and monetary (versus fiscal) policy in maintaining general economic equilibrium with a high level of employment. A.H. Hansen, H.S. Ellis, A. Lerner, and M. Kalecki were part of the symposium.

Modigliani, Franco. "Long-Run Implications of Alternative Fiscal Policies and the Burden of the National Debt." ECONOMIC JOURNAL 71 (December 1961): 730-55.

> The burden of the debt is a stock-flow problem. If treated in that manner, Modigliani finds a strong case in favor of a cyclically balanced budget.

Okun, Arthur M. "Have Fiscal and/or Monetary Policies Failed?" AMERICAN ECONOMIC REVIEW 62 (May 1972): 24-30. Reprinted in [12].

> Okun feels that there has to be more effective regulation of aggregate demand.

Phillips, A.W. "Stabilization Policy and the Time-Form of Lagged Responses." ECONOMIC JOURNAL 67 (June 1957): 265-77. Reprinted in [5].

> Electronic simulators were used to solve high-order differential equations, which Phillips feels are a better representation of responses in an economic system.

_____. "Stabilization Policy in a Closed Economy." ECONOMIC JOURNAL 64 (June 1954): 290-323.

Because the simple comparative static model with a multiplier does not take time into account, Phillips develops a feedback control system. The simple multiplier model with fixed prices and interest rates is treated as the most naive model.

Theil, Henri. "Linear Decision Rules for Macrodynamic Policy Problems." In QUANTITATIVE PLANNING OF ECONOMIC POLICY, edited by B.G. Hickman, pp. 18-42. Washington, D.C.: Brookings Institution, 1965.

Quadratic preference functions with linear constraints are demonstrated. This approach combined with a Bayesian point of view allows the uncertainty problem to be handled for a wide range of circumstances.

Tinbergen, Jan. ECONOMIC POLICY PRINCIPLES AND DESIGN. New York: American Elsevier Publishing Co., 1956. 304 p.

This is a handbook on how to make economic policy. The consistency of aims and means are judged and an optimum policy is designed.

Tobin, James. "The Burden of the Public Debt: A Review Article." JOURNAL OF FINANCE 20 (December 1965): 679-82.

This is a review of Ferguson, James M., ed. PUBLIC DEBT AND FUTURE GENERATIONS. Durham, N.C.: University of North Carolina Press, 1964.

_____. "An Essay on the Principles of Public Debt Management." In FISCAL AND DEBT MANAGEMENT POLICIES, edited by Commission on Money and Credit, pp. 143-218. Englewood Cliffs, N.J.: Prentice-Hall, 1963.

The monetary and fiscal effects of the federal debt must be distinguished. Optimal debt management will never come about unless the Federal Reserve and the Treasury learn to cooperate.

INCOMES AND HUMAN RESOURCES POLICIES

Ackley, Gardner. "Incomes Policy for the 1970's." REVIEW OF ECONOMICS AND STATISTICS 54 (August 1972): 218-23. Reprinted in [17].

Sooner or later an explicit policy on income shares must be promulgated.

Feldstein, Martin S. "Policies to Lower the Permanent Rate of Unemployment." In REDUCING UNEMPLOYMENT TO TWO PERCENT. Hearings before the Joint Economic Committee, 92d Cong., 2d sess., pp. 24-28. Washington, D.C.: Government Printing Office, 1972. Reprinted in [17].

It is necessary to use manpower programs to lower the rate of un-
employment without creating inflationary pressures. Also see his
"Lowering the Permanent Rate of Unemployment." Joint Economic
Committee, U.S. Congress, 1973. Reprinted in [12].

Hansen, W. Lee, ed. INCOME, EDUCATION AND HUMAN CAPITAL. New
York: Columbia University Press, 1970. 330 p.

A collection of conference papers on education as human capital.

Harbison, F.H., and Myers, C.A., eds. MANPOWER AND EDUCATION.
New York: McGraw-Hill Book Co., 1969. 356 p.

This is a series of studies of various countries which relate manpower objectives to education.

Humphrey, Thomas M. "The Economics of Incomes Policies." Federal Reserve
Bank of Richmond MONTHLY REVIEW 10 (October 1972): 3-11. Reprinted
in [12].

As long as there are market imperfections, it may be necessary to
use incomes policies (a second-best alternative) from time to time.

Lerner, Abba P. "The Relation of Wage Policies and Price Policies." AMERI-
CAN ECONOMIC REVIEW 29 (May 1939): 158-69. Reprinted in [3].

There is a great difference between how micro and macro problems
should be handled.

Levitan, Sar A., et al. HUMAN RESOURCES AND LABOR MARKETS. New
York: Harper & Row Publishers, 1972. 637 p.

This book provides an overview of the entire human resources area.
A selected annotated bibliography is included.

Parkin, Michael, and Sumner, Michael T., eds. INCOMES POLICY AND
INFLATION. Toronto: University of Toronto Press, 1972. 295 p.

This book is the first product of a three-year research program on
the problem of inflation at the University of Manchester. Future
volumes, under the editorship of D. Laidler and M. Parkin, will
deal with inflation and the labor market and inflation and expectations.

Parkin, Michael, et al. "A Survey of the Econometric Evidence of the Effects
of Income Policy on the Rate of Inflation." In INCOMES POLICIES AND IN-
FLATION, edited by Michael Parkin and Michael T. Sumner, pp. 1-29.
Toronto: University of Toronto Press, 1972.

The econometric evidence is not clear-cut at best and confusing
at worst. Over forty references are cited.

Poole, William. "Wage-Price Controls: Where Do We Go From Here?"
BROOKINGS PAPERS ON ECONOMIC ACTIVITY 3, no. 1 (1973): 285-99.

> Poole believes the distortions caused by wage-price controls invalidate their use--ever.

Thurow, Lester C. POVERTY AND DISCRIMINATION. Washington, D.C.:
Brookings Institution, 1969. 214 p.

> Econometric methods are applied to these twin problems.

Policy Controversies

Andersen, Leonall C., and Jordan, Jerry L. "Monetary and Fiscal Actions:
A Test of Their Relative Importance in Economic Stabilization." Federal Reserve
Bank of St. Louis REVIEW 50 (November 1968): 11-24. Reprinted in [4] [13].

> The results for the period tested (1952-68) suggest that monetary
> actions are more important, more predictable, and faster than fiscal
> actions. See the comment by de Leeuw, Frank, and Kalchbrenner,
> John. "Monetary Versus Fiscal Actions: Comments." Federal
> Reserve Bank of St. Louis REVIEW 51 (April 1969): 6-11. Re-
> printed in [13].

Brunner, Karl. "The Monetarist Revolution in Monetary Theory." WELTWIRT-
SCHAFTLICHES ARCHIV 105, no. 1 (1970): 1-30.

> The building blocks of monetarist analysis are: (1) the price theo-
> retical approach to the transmission mechanism, (2) the stability of
> the private sector's internal dynamics, (3) the dominance of mone-
> tary impulses, and (4) the approximate separation of allocative and
> aggregative forces. All four will influence the choice of policy.

_____ , ed. PROCEEDINGS OF THE FIRST KONSTANZER SEMINAR ON
MONETARY THEORY AND MONETARY POLICY. Berlin: Duncker and Humbolt,
1972. 410 p.

> The conference was designed to encourage empirical and analytic
> work in Europe in the field of monetary policy and monetary anal-
> ysis. Of most interest were the articles by K. Brunner and A.H.
> Meltzer, L.C. Andersen and R.S. Masera relating to a monetarist
> framework for aggregative analysis and economic stabilization.

Davis, J. Ronnie. "Chicago Economists and the Early 1930's." AMERICAN
ECONOMIC REVIEW 58 (June 1968): 476-82.

> This is the guts of his book THE NEW ECONOMICS AND THE
> OLD ECONOMICS. Chicago economists were stressing fiscal
> policy, to stem the depression, even before the GENERAL THEORY.

_____. THE NEW ECONOMICS AND THE OLD ECONOMICS. Ames: Iowa State University Press, 1971. 186 p.

The view is presented and substantiated that Keynes was not alone in his advocacy of fiscal policy. The views of the Chicago school are given most prominence.

Diamond, James J., ed. ISSUES IN FISCAL AND MONETARY POLICY: THE ECLECTIC ECONOMIST VIEWS THE CONTROVERSY. Chicago: De Paul University, 1971. 91 p. Paperbound.

Five leading economists rehash the monetarist-fiscalist controversy. Okun, Arthur M. "Rules and Roles for Fiscal and Monetary Policy" is reprinted in [17].

Fand, David I. "A Monetarist Model of the Monetary Process." JOURNAL OF FINANCE 25 (May 1970): 272-89. Reprinted in [1] [4].

The monetarists' and fiscalists' monetary models are compared and contrasted. Monetarists believe in a monetary theory of the price level, a real theory of the interest rate, and a theory relating rising (or high) nominal market interest rates to rising prices. The fiscalists believe the contrary.

Friedman, Milton. THE COUNTER-REVOLUTION IN MONETARY THEORY. Institute of Economic Affairs, Occasional Paper 33. New York: Transatlantic Arts, 1970. 28 p.

The rate of growth of the quantity of money influences the rate of growth of nominal income, with an average delay of six to nine months. This, together with the proposition that a change in monetary growth affects interest rates in one direction at first but in the opposite direction later on, emphasizes the importance of money. The question that arises is: Can monetary policy handle this important role? Of course there is another side to the question.

Friedman, Milton, and Heller, Walter W. MONETARY VS. FISCAL POLICY. New York: W.W. Norton, 1969. 95 p. Paperbound.

This dialogue did not solve any policy problems but it clarifies the points of opposition between monetarists and fiscalists.

Johnson, Harry G. INFLATION AND THE MONETARIST CONTROVERSY. New York: North-Holland, 1972. 116 p.

Inflation is discussed as a problem in international monetary dynamics. The conflicts and comparisons between three theoretical approaches--the Dutch, the Keynesian, and the monetarist are analyzed.

_____. "The Keynesian Revolution and the Monetarist Counter-Revolution."

AMERICAN ECONOMIC REVIEW 61 (May 1971): 1-14.

The virtues and strengths of the two revolutions are examined. The monetarist counterrevolution is useful because it challenged a great deal of Keynesian intellectual nonsense. Its own success, however, is thought to be transitory because its policy issue--inflation--is less important than unemployment. Only time will tell.

Kaldor, Nicholas. "The New Monetarism." LLOYDS BANK REVIEW, no. 97 (July 1970): 1-18. Friedman, Milton. "The New Monetarism: Comment."; and Kaldor, Nicholas. "The New Monetarism: Reply." LLOYDS BANK REVIEW, no. 98 (October 1970): 52-55.

Kaldor, a British Keynesian, attacks and is counterattacked. A good survey of the debate is provided by Brunner, Karl. "The Monetarist View of Keynesian Ideas." LLOYDS BANK REVIEW, no. 102 (October 1971): 35-49.

Rasche, Robert H. "Comments on a Monetarist Approach to Demand." Federal Reserve Bank of St. Louis REVIEW 54 (January 1972): 26-32. Reprinted in [12].

The monetarist models have a creditable forecasting record. However, more work is necessary, especially in the area of price-adjustment, if realistic comparisons between Keynesian and monetarist models are to be made. Also see his article "A Comparative Static Analysis of Some Monetarist Propositions." Ibid., 53 (December 1973): 15-23.

Stein, Jerome L. "Unemployment, Inflation, and Monetarism." AMERICAN ECONOMIC REVIEW 64 (December 1974): 867-87.

If specifications of the IS-LM model are done carefully, they will imply either fiscalist or monetarist conclusions. With the right input the computer can solve the controversy.

Teigen, Ronald L. "A Critical Look at Monetarist Economics." Federal Reserve Bank of St. Louis REVIEW 54 (January 1972): 10-25. Reprinted in [12] [17].

Both Keynesians and monetarists have oversimplified their opponents' views. So let us remember that "to belittle is to be little." Support for the monetarist position is given in Andersen, Leonall C. "A Monetarist View of Demand Management: The United States Experience." Federal Reserve Bank of St. Louis REVIEW 53 (September 1971): 3-11. Reprinted in [12] [17].

Weintraub, Sidney, et al. KEYNES AND THE MONETARISTS AND OTHER ESSAYS. New Brunswick, N.J.: Rutgers University Press, 1973. 239 p.

A critical examination of the monetarists' position vis-a-vis his own

Keynesian one. Weintraub's position is Keynesian in the sense
that its microfoundations are Marshallian. There are nine essays
(most published previously). The issues discussed are inflation,
full employment, income distribution, and monetary policy.

Monetary Commissions

Aliber, Robert Z. "The Commission on Money and Credit: Ten Years Later."
JOURNAL OF MONEY, CREDIT AND BANKING 4 (November 1972): 915-
29.

> The background, economics, and impact of the commission are
> described, discussed, and appraised.

Brunner, Karl. "The Report of the Commission on Money and Credit." JOUR-
NAL OF POLITICAL ECONOMY 69 (December 1961): 605-20. Reprinted in
[19].

> Brunner's review has more good to say than bad. Over eighty
> recommendations were advanced and some of the underlying analysis
> was well done.

_____, ed. "A Symposium: The President's Commission on Financial Structure
and Regulation." JOURNAL OF MONEY, CREDIT AND BANKING 3 (February 1971): 1-34.

> Five economists were asked to discuss the role and function of the
> president's commission. What are the social costs and benefits of
> the existing regulations and constraints?

Commission on Money and Credit. MONEY AND CREDIT: THEIR INFLUENCE
ON JOBS, PRICES, AND GROWTH. Englewood Cliffs, N.J.: Prentice-Hall,
1963.

> This volume contains the conclusions reached by the commission.
> For the supporting papers, see Fox, Bertrand, and Shapiro, Eli, eds.
> THE LIBRARY ON MONEY AND CREDIT. 9 vols. Englewood
> Cliffs, N.J.: 1961-63. The nine volumes are entitled: (1) IM-
> PACTS OF MONETARY POLICY, (2) STABILIZATION POLICIES,
> (3) MONETARY MANAGEMENT, (4) FISCAL AND DEBT MANAGE-
> MENT POLICIES, (5) FEDERAL CREDIT AGENCIES, (6) FEDERAL
> CREDIT PROGRAM, (7) PRIVATE CAPITAL MARKETS, (8) PRIVATE
> FINANCIAL INSTITUTIONS, and (9) INFLATION, GROWTH, AND
> EMPLOYMENT. The nine volumes contain fifty-eight individual
> essays. A list of the authors that participated and other publica-
> tions relating to the commission may be found in Schriftgiesser,
> Karl. THE COMMISSION ON MONEY AND CREDIT: AN AD-
> VENTURE IN POLICY-MAKING. Englewood Cliffs, N.J.:
> Prentice-Hall, 1974. Pp. 163-65.

Dewald, William G. "The National Monetary Commission: A Look Back."
JOURNAL OF MONEY, CREDIT AND BANKING 4 (November 1972): 930-
56.

>The record is reviewed. Both the quantity and the quality of
>money should be taken into account. The basic sources are in-
>cluded in the literature cited.

Fox, Bertrand, and Shapiro, Eli, eds. THE LIBRARY ON MONEY AND CREDIT.
9 vols. Englewood Cliffs, N.J.: Prentice-Hall, 1961-63.

>See above, under Commission on Money and Credit. These are
>papers written for the commission.

Gordon, Scott. "Two Monetary Inquiries in Great Britain: The Macmillan
Report of 1931 and the Radcliffe Report of 1959." JOURNAL OF MONEY,
CREDIT AND BANKING 4 (November 1972): 957-77.

>Gordon's opinion is that these two reports came to very different
>conclusions. See Griffiths, Brian. "Two Monetary Inquiries in
>Great Britain. A Comment." Ibid., 6 (February 1974): 101-14,
>for the other side of the coin.

Gurley, John G. "The Radcliffe Report and Evidence." AMERICAN ECONOMIC
REVIEW 50 (September 1960): 672-700. Reprinted in [19].

>This is a lukewarm review of the committee's analysis of Britain's
>financial system. Bank rate was deemed the only worthwhile in-
>strument of monetary policy because of the extreme variability of
>velocity.

Kaufman, Herbert M., and Marcis, Richard G. "The Hunt Commission Recommendations and the Determination and Control of the Money Supply." JOUR-
NAL OF MONEY, CREDIT AND BANKING 7 (August 1975): 343-58.

>In no sense should the recommendations be accepted as an improve-
>ment of monetary control. A piecemeal adoption may bring chaos.
>Much of the relevant literature is cited. But also see the com-
>ments by G.J. Benston, D.M. Jaffee, S. Peltzman, and A.H.
>Meltzer in JOURNAL OF MONEY, CREDIT AND BANKING 4
>(November 1972): 985-89, 990-1000, 1001-4, 1005-9.

Schriftgiesser, Karl. THE COMMISSION ON MONEY AND CREDIT: AN
ADVENTURE IN POLICY-MAKING. Englewood Cliffs, N.J.: Prentice-Hall,
1974. 165 p.

>The commission was created in 1958 by the Committee for Economic
>Development and supported by grants from the Ford Foundation.
>The book concentrates on a number of the commission's eighty-odd
>recommendations. A bibliography of the commission's publications
>and other relevant writings is included.

Wallich, Henry C.   "One Chance in a Generation: Guideposts for the Commission on Financial Structure and Regulation."   JOURNAL OF MONEY, CREDIT AND BANKING   3 (February 1971):   21-30.

> The successor to the Commission on Money and Credit is given some advice as to the trouble spots in the U.S. financial community.

AUTHOR INDEX

This index includes authors, editors, compilers, and others who have contributed to works mentioned either in text or in notes. Numbers refer to page numbers. Alphabetization is letter by letter.

A

Abramovitz, Moses 102, 124, 191, 195
Ackley, Gardner 38, 156, 243
Adams, F. Gerard 102
Adelman, Frank L. 102
Adelman, Irma 102
Akerlof, George 224
Akerman, Johan 24
Alchian, Armen A. 133, 182, 221, 223
Alessio, Frank J. 39
Alexander, Sidney S. 102
Alhadeff, Charlotte P. 77
Alhadeff, David A. 77, 86
Aliber, Robert Z. 226, 231, 248
Allais, Maurice 95
Allen, R.G.D. 38
Almon, Shirley 147
American Bankers Association 86
American Bibliographic Service 48
American Economic Association 46-47
Ames, Edward 38, 165
Andersen, Leonall C. 77, 86, 103, 238, 245, 247
Anderson, W.H. Locke 147
Ando, Albert 103, 140, 156, 157, 239
Andreano, Ralph L. 45

Angell, J.W. 16, 106, 234
Apilado, Vincent P. 27
Archibald, G.C. 123, 124, 164
Arrow, Kenneth J. 17, 69, 77, 79, 124, 133, 162, 163, 191
Aschheim, Joseph 38, 87, 213
Ashton, T.S. 207
Atkinson, Thomas R. 13, 214
Auerbach, I. 228, 240
Augustine, Saint 2

B

Bach, G.L. 13, 213, 239
Bacharach, M.O.L. 17, 200
Bagehot, Walter 207
Bailey, Martin J. 39, 140, 147, 219
Bain, A.D. 178, 213
Baird, Charles W. 39, 124
Baird, Robert N. 39
Balbach, Anatal 179
Ball, R.J. 124, 164, 219
Ballabon, Maurice B. 48
Baran, Paul A. 24
Barger, Harold 34
Barrett, C.R. 156
Barrett, Nancy S. 39
Barro, Robert J. 34, 124, 133
Barthelme, Donald 1n
Baumol, William J. 39, 78, 87,

251

Author Index

124, 147, 148, 156, 164, 165, 177, 239
Becker, Gary S. 165
Beckmann, Martin 125
Benassy, Jean-Pascal 133
Benavie, Arthur 133
Benston, George J. 87, 249
Bentzel, Ragnar 24
Besen, Stanley M. 35
Bicksler, James L. 78
Bierwag, G.O. 78, 165
Bilas, Richard A. 39
Bilkes, Gerrit 165
Bischoff, C.W. 148
Black, Fischer 230
Black, J. 17, 162
Blake, Robert 24
Blaug, Mark 39
Blinder, Alan S. 107, 227
Bliss, C.J. 191
Board of Governors of the Federal Reserve System 207, 208, 210, 213, 219
Bodkin, Ronald G. 124, 164, 224
Boorman, John T. 26
Bopp, Karl R. 210
Boughton, James M. 35, 239
Boulding, Kenneth E. 2n, 16, 134, 184, 191, 213, 221
Bowers, David A. 39
Brady, Dorothy S. 140
Brainard, William C. 87, 92, 111, 238, 239
Branson, William H. 39
Break, George F. 227
Brechling, F.P.R. 15, 81, 82, 126, 133, 134
Brems, Hans 148
Brill, Daniel H. 87
Brimmer, Andrew F. 215
Britto, Ronald 59n, 192
Bronfenbrenner, Martin 25, 103, 119, 165, 192, 219, 220
Brooman, Frederick 39
Brown, Arthur J. 220
Brown, E. Cary 239
Brown, J.A.C. 17, 162
Brown, M. 161
Brownlee, O.H. 224
Brubaker, Earl R. 161
Brumberg, Richard 145

Brunhild, Gordon 39
Brunner, Karl 10n, 13-14, 64n, 78, 96, 156, 165-66, 178, 179, 183, 214, 230, 231, 245, 247, 248
Bruno 15
Bryan, William R. 87
Buchanan, James M. 82
Burger, Albert E. 35, 77, 86, 179
Burkhead, Jesse 227
Burmeister, Edwin 15, 40, 59n, 103, 192, 195, 196
Burns, Arthur F. 103, 104, 109
Burrows, Paul 40
Burstein, M.L. 35, 124, 125, 164, 167
Burton, Robert H. 39
Buse, A. 187
Butters, J. Keith xiv, 33

C

Caff, J.T. 156
Cagan, Phillip 18, 79, 179-80, 181, 214, 220, 223
Campagna, Anthony S. 40
Campbell, Colin D. 35
Campbell, Rosemary G. 35
Cannan, Edwin 166
Canterbery, E.R. 214
Cantillon, R. 95
Carleton, Willard T. 87
Carlson, Keith M. 103
Carson, Deane xiii, 13, 26, 64n, 84, 132, 214, 236
Cass, David 26, 192, 202
Cassel, Gustav 183
Castaneda, Carlos 1n, 3n
Catt, A.J.L. 78, 166
Chambers, Edward J. 40
Champernowne, D.G. 17, 30, 116, 128, 162
Chandler, Lester V. 16, 35, 208, 231, 234, 239
Chang, J. 166
Chase, Samuel B., Jr. 14, 88, 89, 230
Chenery, Hollis 148
Chetty, V. Karuppan 166
Chow, Gregory C. 112, 167
Christ, Carl F. 78, 104, 125, 227
Clark, John J. 26

Clark, John Maurice 104, 157, 228
Clayton, George 14, 88, 231
Clemence, Richard V. 28, 108
Clement, M.D. 240
Clower, Robert W. xii, xiii, 27, 52n, 63, 65n, 69, 75, 84, 96, 124, 125, 129, 133, 134, 164, 167, 170, 176, 183, 231
Coatner, P.H. 228, 240
Cobb, Charles W. 161
Cochran, John A. 35
Cochrane, James L. 40
Coddingham, Alan 135
Cohen, J. 49
Cohen, Jacob 112
Cohen, Kalman J. 88
Cohen, Morris 26
Commission on Money and Credit 146, 149, 157, 228, 231-32, 239, 240, 243
Committee on Public Debt Policy 240
Comptroller of the Currency, U.S. Treasury Department 88
Conard, Joseph W. 183
Conference on Research in Income and Wealth 14
Conlisk, John 220
Conover, Helen F. 47
Cooper, J. Phillip 104
Copeland, Morris A. 112
Coppock, D.J. 211
Cornford, John 40
Council of Economic Advisers 217
Crawford, Arthur W. 232
Crick, W.F. 82
Croome, David R. 12, 14, 20, 55
Crouch, Robert L. 40, 232
Culbertson, John M. 35, 40, 82, 187, 232

D

Dacey, W.M. 180
Darby, Michael R. 40
Dasgupto, Ajit K. 148
Dauten, Carl A. 40
David, Paul A. 24, 193
Davidson, Paul 67, 69, 96, 99, 135, 167, 168
Davis, J. Ronnie 245-46

Davis, Joseph S. 144
Davis, Richard G. 232
Davis, T.E. 141
Dean, Edwin 95
de Leeuw, Frank 90, 105, 147, 168, 239, 245
Demsetz, Harold 79, 168
Denison, Edward F. 162, 193, 217
Department of Economics, University of Pittsburgh 49
DePrano, Michael 156, 157
Dernberg, Thomas F. 11, 41
Dewald, William G. 232, 249
Diamond, James J. 246
Diamond, Peter A. 193
Dillard, Dudley 116
Dobb, Maurice 3n, 29
Dobell, Rodney A. 40
Dodds, J.C. 187
Doenges, R. Conrad 34
Dolan, Edwin G. 42
Domar, Evsey D. 19, 193, 217
Douglas, Paul H. 161
Doyle, Peter 219
Ducros, Bernard 200
Duesenberry, James S. 60, 69, 79, 105, 141, 169
Dunkman, William E. 35
Dunlup, John T. 223

E

Easterlin, R.A. 194
Eccles, Marriner S. 24
Eckaus, Richard S. 157
Eckstein, Otto 15, 188, 219, 224
Edwards, Edgar O. 160
Eishner, A.S. 137
Eisner, Robert 60n, 148-49, 150, 152, 194, 228
Eliot, T.S. 2n
Elliott, J. Walter 41, 60n, 149, 152
Ellis, Howard S. 11, 13, 113, 159, 168, 232, 238, 242
Eltis, W.A. 24
Encarnacion, Jose 96
Enthoven, Alain C. 194, 220
Entine, Alan D. 27
Evans, Michael K. 41, 106, 157
Ezekiel, Mordecai 106

Author Index

F

Fabriant, S. 112
Fair, Ray C. 41
Fama, Eugene F. 187
Fand, David I. 180, 220, 246
Farrell, M.J. 141
Feaveryear, A.E. 208
Federal Reserve Bank of New York 234
Federal Reserve Bank of Philadelphia 208
Federal Reserve Bank of Richmond 211, 214
Feeney, George J. 80
Feige, Edgar I. 85, 168
Feiwel, G.R. 99
Feldstein, Martin S. 188, 218, 243
Fellner, William J. xiii, 11, 16, 27, 59, 69, 161, 183, 194, 218, 228, 234, 240
Ferber, Robert 60, 141–42, 147, 150, 152
Ferguson, C.E. 194
Ferguson, James M. 240, 243
Fetter, Frank W. 208
Feyerabend, Paul 135
Fischer, Gerald C. 88
Fischer, Stanley 104
Fisher, Douglas 35
Fisher, F.M. 142, 194
Fisher, Gordon 106
Fisher, Irving 95, 96, 183
Fisher, Malcolm R. 160
Flannery, Mark J. 88
Fleming, Miles 35, 169
Fletcher, John 45
Foley, Duncan K. 41, 79
Ford, J.W. 187
Fortson, James 158
Fox, Bertrand 248, 249
Fox, Karl A. 240
Frazer, William J., Jr. 36, 190
Freeman, Jo Fisher 184
Friedman, Milton 4n, 11, 14, 19, 60, 64n, 69, 75, 76, 79, 85, 86, 95, 96, 97, 98, 106, 142, 156, 157, 158, 169, 180, 220, 221, 230, 231, 232, 233, 240, 246, 247

Friedman, Rose D. 140
Friend, Irwin 79
Frisch, Ragnar 106, 135
Fromm, Gary 105, 106, 168, 224
Frost, P.A. 89
Fuchs, Victor 112
Fundaburk, Emma Lila 45

G

Galbraith, J.A. 89, 233
Galloway, Lowell E. 125
Garegnani, P. 15, 29, 195
Garrett, G. 118
Garvy, George 109
Gaskin, M. 166
Gayer, A.D. 24
Geisel, Martin S. 147
Gibson, N.J. 211
Gibson, William E. xiii, 27, 184, 233
Gies, Thomas G. 27
Gilbert, J.C. 170
Glahe, Fred R. 41
Goldberger, Arthur S. 104, 107, 109
Goldenweiser, E.A. 234
Goldfeld, Stephen M. 89, 107
Goldsmith, R.W. 89
Goodhart, C.A.E. 36
Goodman, Oscar R. 89
Goodwin, R.M. 107, 157
Gordon, Robert Aaron xiii, 28, 61, 69, 107, 218
Gordon, Robert J. 69, 96, 221
Gordon, Scott 249
Gorman, W.M. 142, 194
Gramley, Lyle E. 14, 89, 230
Gramlich, Edward M. 105
Green, H.A. John 6n, 142
Greenbaum, Stuart I. 89
Griffin, Appleton P.C. 47
Griffiths, Brian 249
Griliches, Zvi 161, 163, 195
Grossman, Herschel I. 34, 125, 133
Grove, M.A. 78, 165
Guarnieri, Raymond L. 79
Gurley, John G. 63, 69, 82, 83, 175, 194, 249
Guthrie, Harold W. 80, 142, 170

Guttentag, Jack M. 90, 184, 214

H

Haavelmo, Trygve 150, 158
Haberler, Gottfried xiii, 15, 28, 30, 59, 69, 99, 101, 107-8, 117, 126, 129, 195
Hagen, Everett E. 99
Hague, D.C. 15
Hahn, Frank H. 6n, 15, 18, 28, 81, 82, 98, 124, 126, 133, 134, 170, 184, 195
Hahn, L. Albert 117
Haitovsky, Y. 112
Haley, Bernard F. xiii, 11, 27, 59, 69, 144, 195, 228
Hall, R.J. 60n
Hamberg, Daniel 41
Hamburger, Michael J. 143, 173, 188, 190, 234
Hammer, Frederick S. 88
Hammond, Bray 208
Hansen, Alvin H. 24, 28, 57, 70, 95, 101, 108, 117, 126, 234
Hansen, Bent 63, 70, 127, 221
Hansen, W. Lee 244
Harbison, F.H. 244
Harcourt, G.C. 28, 31, 64, 70, 113, 150, 195, 205
Hardy, Charles O. 240
Harkness, J. 199
Harris, Lawrence 208
Harris, Seymour E. xiii, 15, 16, 29, 59, 70, 112, 117, 120, 121, 161, 234
Harrod, Roy F. 7, 19, 24, 30, 36, 55, 57n, 58, 70, 114, 118, 128, 195-96, 197
Hart, Albert Gailord 16, 18, 36, 234
Havrilesky, Thomas M. 26
Hawkins, C.J. 150
Hawtrey, R.G. 100, 180, 209, 211
Hayek, Friedrich A. 19, 135, 150, 196, 212
Hazlitt, Henry 118
Heller, Walter W. 218, 228, 240, 246
Hendershott, Patric H. 14, 90, 108, 230

Herman, Edward S. 90
Hester, Donald D. 13, 29, 80, 83, 87, 157, 158, 214
Hickman, Bert G. 108, 240, 243
Hicks, Sir John R. 11, 19, 24, 41, 57, 58, 68, 70, 80, 103, 108, 118, 127, 160, 170, 192, 196-97, 208, 209, 214
Higgins, Benjamin 102
Hines, A.G. 136
Hirshleifer, Jack 60, 70, 136, 150-51, 170
Hitch, C.J. 60n
Hitiris, Theodore 40
Hoffmann, Banesh 3n
Hogan, Warren P. 164
Holbrook, Robert S. 241
Holland, Robert C. 13, 214
Hollis, Martin 135
Holt, Charles C. 224, 241
Holtzman, F.D. 220
Homer, Sidney 184
Horvitz, Paul M. 36
Horwich, George 16, 24, 41, 159, 165, 167, 168, 177, 206, 230, 234-35
Hosek, William R. 42
Houthakker, H.S. 143, 145
Howitt, P.W. 136
Hsieh, Ching-Yao 38
Huffnagle, John D. xiv, 34, 61, 73
Huitt, R.K. 228, 240
Humphrey, Thomas M. 244
Hunt, E.K. 29
Hutchinson, Harry D. 36
Hutt, W.H. 52n, 118, 127
Hymans, Saul H. 143, 224
Hynes, J. Allan 127

I

Institute for Scientific Information 50
International Committee for Social Science Documentation 47
Ireland, Thomas R. 42

Author Index

J

Jacoby, Henry A. 39
Jacoby, Neil H. 214, 235, 238
Jaffe, William 127
Jaffee, Dwight M. 88, 90, 249
Janankar, P. 151
Jevons, W.S. 171
Johnson, Elizabeth 18, 116
Johnson, Harry G. xii, 12, 14-15, 16, 20, 29, 42, 54n, 55, 83, 84, 85, 127-28, 168, 171, 197, 205, 221, 224, 231, 235, 241, 246
Johnson, M. Bruce 60, 70, 143
Johnson, Walter L. xiii, 29
Jordan, Jerry L. 179, 180, 238, 245
Jorgenson, Dale W. 60, 149, 150, 151, 161, 195, 197
Juster, F.T. 112

K

Kahn, Richard F. 21, 56, 99, 158
Kalchbrenner, John 239, 245
Kaldor, Nicholas 6n, 17, 21, 126, 136, 162, 198, 224, 247
Kalecki, Michal 17, 21, 56, 70, 99, 136, 242
Kamerschen, David R. xiii, 29
Kane, Edward J. 171, 188, 215
Kareken, John H. 181
Karnosky, Denis 187
Katona, George 90, 143, 241
Kaufman, George G. xiii, 27, 36
Kaufman, Herbert M. 249
Keiser, Norman F. 29, 42
Kendrick, John W. 112, 161, 198
Kennedy, Charles 161, 163, 198, 203
Kennedy, Peter E. 42
Keran, Michael W. 241
Kessel, Reuben A. 188, 189, 221, 223
Keynes, John Maynard 5, 51, 53n, 55, 71, 95, 100, 101, 114
Keynes, Milo 115
Kindleberger, C.P. 231
Klein, Benjamin 171

Klein, John J. 36
Klein, Lawrence R. xiii, 25, 28, 60n, 61, 69, 104, 106, 107, 109, 119, 152, 183
Klise, Eugene S. 36
Knight, Frank H. 184, 199
Knox, A.D. 152
Koch, R.R. 190
Kock, M.H. de 209
Kogiku, K.C. 42
Kondratieff, Nikolai D. 109
Koopmans, Tjalling C. 17, 21, 109, 111, 199, 200
Kornai, Janos 71, 136
Koyck, L.M. 152
Kregel, J.A. 42, 67, 71, 136, 137, 199
Krooss, Herman E. 76, 209
Kuenne, R.E. 128
Kuh, Edwin 42, 60, 72, 152, 154, 162, 231
Kuhleman, John M. 241
Kuhn, Thomas S. 4n, 17, 137
Kurihara, Kenneth K. 24, 61, 71, 116, 119, 122, 128, 131, 145, 146, 219
Kuznets, Simon S. 112, 113, 144, 153, 199

L

Lachmann, L.M. 137
Laidler, David 36, 171-72
Laing, N.F. 28, 64, 70
Laird, William E. 242
Lakatos, Imre 4n, 17, 137
Lange, Oscar 57, 71, 119, 128
Latane, Henry A. 80, 172
Latsis, Spiro J. 4n, 137
Latta, Cynthia M. 188, 190
Laumas, G.S. 172
Lawrence, Robert 91
Lee, Maurice W. 42
Lee, Thomas A. 144
Lee, Tong Hun 91, 166, 173
Leijonhufvud, Axel 6n, 52n, 65, 71, 115, 125, 127, 128, 134, 138, 162, 235
Lekachman, Robert xiii, 30, 63, 71, 113, 128, 221

Lendeman, J. 228, 240
Leon, Paolo 162
Leontief, Wassily 120
Lerner, Abba P. 16, 17, 22, 30, 97, 120, 128, 129, 138, 153, 173, 185, 199, 228, 233, 234, 235, 242, 244
Leser, C.E.V. 173
Levhari, David 15, 195, 199, 200
Levitan, Sar A. 244
Lewis, Wilfred, Jr. 228
Library and Documentation Center of the Economic Information Service 46
Lindauer, John xiv, 30, 42
Lindsay, Robert 90
Lindsey, David 42
Lippitt, Vernon C. 42
Lipsey, Richard G. 17, 123, 124, 162, 164, 165, 225
Liviatan, Nissan 125, 129, 167, 200
Lloyd, Cliff L. 129, 185
Long, Clarence D. 160
Lougee, Duane 91
Lovell, Michael C. 43
Lubell, Harold 144
Lucas, Robert E. 225
Luckett, D.G 91
Lund, Phillip J. 153
Lundberg, Erik 107, 200
Lutz, Friedrich A. xiv, 15, 30, 59, 71, 120, 126, 131, 153, 175, 185, 188
Lutz, Vera 153

M

McCabe, James R. 228
McCulloch, J. Juston 36
McDougall, Duncan M. 41
Machlup, Fritz 120, 222
Mack, Ruth P. 144
McKean, Roland N. 173
McKenna, Joseph P. 43
McKenzie, Lionel W. 26
Maisel, Sherman J. 235
Malinvaud, E. 17, 200
Malkiel, Burton G. 78, 147, 188, 189, 190
Mansfield, Edwin 163

Marchal, Jean 200
Marcis, Richard G. 249
Marget, Arthur W. 121
Marglin, S.A. 153
Markowitz, Harry 64n, 80
Marschak, Jacob 79, 144, 173
Marshall, Alfred 22, 53, 71, 100
Marshall, Robert H. 36
Martial, Alfred 171
Martin, George 173
Marty, Alvin L. 83, 85, 129, 162
Masera, R.S. 189, 245
Masui, Mitsuzo 48
Matthews, R.C.O. 109, 195
Maurois, Andre 2n, 3n
Mayer, Thomas 43, 60, 71, 129, 144, 156, 157, 165, 236
Meade, James E. 17, 43, 57n, 121, 162, 181
Means, Gardiner C. 222
Meek, Paul 211
Meigs, A. James 98, 181
Meinich, Per 130
Meiselman, David 156, 157, 189, 191
Melitz, Jacques 173
Melnik, Arie 81
Meltzer, Allan H. 14, 78, 96, 156, 165-66, 171, 174, 179, 181, 215, 230-31, 245, 249
Merklein, Helmut 43
Metzler, Lloyd A. 22, 25, 62n, 102, 109, 121, 122, 126, 130, 141, 153, 157, 242
Meyer, Hermann H.B. 48
Meyer, John R. 60, 72, 154, 231
Michaelsen, Jacob B. 189
Miller, Merton H. 43, 154, 174
Miller, Roger L. 225
Minsky, Hyman P. 110
Mints, Lloyd W. xiv, 17, 30, 59, 71, 126, 131, 175, 207, 209, 242
Mintz, I. 112
Mirrlees, James A. 17, 162, 198, 200
Mishan, E.J. 160, 174, 206
Mitchell, George W. 236
Mitchell, Wesley C. 104, 109, 110, 209
Mitchell, William E. xiv, 30

Author Index

Mittra, S. xiv, 31
Modigliani, Franco 13, 25, 57, 60, 90, 103, 104, 118, 119, 121, 126, 130, 140, 144-45, 154, 156, 157, 174, 184, 189-90, 211, 242
Monhollon, J.R. 214
Moore, Basil 36, 81
Moore, G.E. 112
Moore, G.H. 110
Morgan, E. Victor 174, 208
Morishima, Michio 15, 43, 195
Morrison, George R. 81, 91, 168
Morton, J.E. 51
Mueller, E. 143
Mueller, M.G. xiv, 31, 61, 72, 99
Mundell, Robert A. 22, 130, 222, 228, 240
Musgrave, Alan 17, 137
Musgrave, R.A. 228, 240
Myers, C.A. 244
Myrdal, Gunnar 56, 72, 100, 122

N

Nadiri, M.I. 149, 154
Nagatani, Keizo 201
National Bureau of Economic Research 110
Negishi, Takashi 174
Neher, Philip A. 43
Neisser, Hans 16, 102, 234
Nell, Edward 135
Nelson, Charles R. 104, 190
Nelson, Richard R. 162
Netzer, Dick 227
Newlyn, W.T. 37, 181
Niehans, Jurg 18, 175, 222
Nobay, A.R. 16, 224
Nuti, D.M. 29

O

O'Bannon, Helen B. 37
Ohlin, Bertil 100
Okun, Arthur M. 242, 246
Ornstein, Robert E. 3n
Orr, Danial 174
Ostroy, Joseph M. 138, 175
Ott, Attiat F. 229

Ott, David J. 43, 229

P

Palmer, John L. 225
Parker, R.R. 31, 113
Parkin, Michael 18, 81, 85, 244
Pasinetti, Luigi L. 15, 22, 195, 201
Patinkin, Don 22, 25, 61, 62, 63n, 72, 81, 83-84, 96, 98, 119, 123, 125, 126, 131, 133, 170, 175, 185, 199-200, 236
Peacock, Alan T. 176
Pearce, D.W. 148, 150
Peltzman, Sam 81, 249
Perry, George L. 145, 225
Pesek, Boris P. 37, 63, 72, 83, 84, 85
Peston, M.H. 156, 158
Peterson, Wallace C. 43
Phelps, Edmund S. 192, 201, 222, 225
Phillips, A.W. 201, 226, 242-43
Phillips, Chester Arthur 84, 181
Picou, G. 214
Pierce, D.G. 37
Pierson, Gail 190
Pigou, A.C. 95, 100, 121, 131, 181
Plumb, J.H. 2n
Polakoff, Murray E. 37, 236
Polanyi, Michael 121
Pontecorvo, Givcio 31, 238
Poole, William 236, 245
Popper, Karl 17
Post, George R. 149
Powelson, John P. 113
Prager, Jonas 32
Prest, A.R. 154
Pringle, Robin 76

R

Rakshit, M.K. 125, 167, 176
Ramanathan, R. 199
Ramsey, Frank 201
Rapping, Leonard A. 225
Rasche, Robert H. 104, 145, 247
Reagan, Michael D. 210

Reddaway, W.B.   30, 57n, 122, 128
Reder, Melvin W.   24
Rees, Albert   226
Reichenbach, Hans   2n
Rengen, M.D.   231
Riach, P.A.   202
Richardson, G.B.   138
Ritter, Lawrence S.   32, 37, 132, 211
Robbins, Lionel   101
Robertson, Dennis H.   22, 25, 37, 100, 101, 182, 185, 222
Robinson, E.A.G.   30, 54n, 116, 128
Robinson, Joan   6n, 17, 24, 29, 57, 72, 116, 122, 136-37, 139, 154, 162, 163, 202
Robinson, Roland I.   38, 91
Rock, James M.   128
Roll, Eric   139
Roll, Richard   190
Roosa, Robert V.   16, 212, 215, 234
Ross, Myron H.   43, 215
Rousseas, Stephen W.   18, 223
Rowan, D.C.   43, 237
Rowe, David M.   102
Rudra, Ashok   145
Ruebling, Charlotte E.   215
Ruggles, Nancy D.   1n, 13, 113
Ruggles, Richard   113
Russell, Thomas   85
Rutledge, John   223
Rutner, Jack L.   42
Ryder, Harl   125

S

Salant, William A.   158
Samuelson, Paul A.   14, 15, 16, 17, 24, 25, 30, 57, 72, 78, 96, 112, 122, 129, 159, 162, 163, 165, 176, 177, 192, 195, 202-3, 206, 226, 229, 234
Sargent, Thomas J.   186
Savage, L.J.   79
Saving, Thomas R.   37, 63, 72, 83, 84, 168, 171, 237
Sayers, R.S.   38, 76, 207, 210, 212, 237
Schilpp, Paul Arthur   2n

Schlesinger, James R.   228, 237, 240
Schmalansee, Richard L.   42
Schmookler, Jacob   163
Schriftgiesser, Karl   248, 249
Schultz, Theodore W.   112
Schultze, Charles L.   223
Schultze, George P.   226
Schumpeter, Joseph A.   110, 116, 176
Schwartz, Anna Jacobson   64, 69, 75-76, 106, 169, 180, 230
Schwartz, Jesse G.   29
Scott, Ira O., Jr.   212
Selby, Edward B., Jr.   38
Seligman, Edmund R.A.   50, 113, 184
Sen, Amartya   32, 64, 72
Sen, S.R.   99
Senior, Nassau W.   176
Shackle, G.L.S.   2n, 5n, 8n, 53n, 67, 72, 101, 122, 139, 186, 231
Shapiro, Edward   xiv, 32, 38, 44
Shapiro, Eli   38, 248, 249
Sharp, Carl S.   113
Sharpe, William F.   81
Shaw, D.M.   37
Shaw, Edward S.   63, 69, 76, 82, 83, 175, 194
Shaw, G.K.   44
Shell, Karl   33, 203
Sheppard, David   106
Sheshinski, Eytan   15, 33, 195
Shove, Gerald   160
Sidrauski, Miguel   18, 41, 79, 203, 206
Siebert, C.D.   149, 152
Siegal, Barry N.   44
Silber, William L.   37, 82, 132, 229
Sills, David L.   11, 50, 76, 97, 124, 139, 146, 148, 150, 174, 210, 212, 219, 231
Simmons, Edward C.   176
Simons, Henry C.   237
Skinner, A.S.   99
Slade, William Adams   48
Slichter, Sumner H.   229
Smith, Adam   52, 72
Smith, Paul E.   125
Smith, Vernon L.   60, 72, 91-92, 154

Author Index

Smith, Warren L. xiv, 16, 33, 44, 92, 122, 177, 182, 190, 224, 231, 234, 237-38
Smithies, Arthur 33, 110, 145, 238
Solow, Robert M. 17, 18, 44, 155, 162, 163-64, 192, 194, 203-4, 206, 223, 226, 227
Somers, Harold M. 132, 183, 186
Sowell, Thomas 52n, 132
Spencer, Roger W. 227, 229
Spiro, Alan 145
Sprinkel, Beryl Wayne 98
Sprinkel, Case M. 172
Sraffa, Piero 64, 72, 204
Starr, Ross M. 140, 176
Stein, Herbert 18, 62, 73, 218, 229
Stein, Jerome L. 86, 132, 204-5, 247
Steiner, Peter O. 227
Steinhaur, L. 166
Stekler, H.O. 110, 111
Stern, N.H. 17, 200
Stewart, Michael 140
Stigler, George J. 160
Stiglitz, Joseph E. 33, 192, 204, 205
Stigum, B.P. 142, 194
Stone, Richard 17, 162
Stone, Robert W. 92
Streeten, Paul P. 122
Strotz, Robert H. 149, 159, 231
Strumpel, Burkhard 25
Suits, Daniel B. 111, 146, 231
Sumner, Michael T. 244
Sutch, Richard 189-90
Swan, Craig 147
Swan, T.W. 205
Swanson, Rodney B. 36
Sweeney, Richard J. 44
Sweezy, Paul M. 30, 123, 129

T

Tamagna, F.M. 231
Tarshis, Lorie 146, 223
Taubman, Paul 105, 106
Taylor, Lester D. 143, 145
Teigen, Ronald L. xiv, 33, 172, 177, 182, 224, 247

Telser, Lester G. 171, 190
Terrell, William T. 190
Thanos, C.A. 212
Theil, Henri 146, 243
Thomas, W. 16, 234
Thompson, Earl A. 177
Thorn, Richard S. xiv, 33, 38, 61, 73
Thornton, Henry 20, 212
Thunberg, Rudolf 211
Thurow, Lester C. 146, 155, 206, 245
Timberlake, Richard H., Jr. 38, 158
Timlin, M.F. 123
Tinbergen, Jan 111, 227, 243
Tobin, James 1n, 13, 14, 15, 16, 18, 25, 29, 64, 73, 76, 80, 82, 83, 84, 85, 86, 87, 92, 95, 96, 98, 111, 146, 147, 160, 177-78, 194, 205, 219, 223, 227, 228, 230, 233, 234, 238, 240, 243
Tolly, G.S. 182
Treadway, Arthur B. 155
Trivedi, P.K. 155
Tsiang, S.C. 86, 159, 186
Tucker, Donald 92, 140, 182
Tulloch, J. 223
Turvey, Ralph 154, 159, 186
Tuttle, Donald L. 80

U

Ulrey, Ann P. 87
U.S. Department of Commerce 113
U.S. Government Printing Office 51
Upton, Charles W. 43
Uzawa, Hirofumi 18, 33, 164, 206

V

Valavanis, Stefan 132
Valentine, Lloyd M. 40
Van Dahm, Thomas E. 38
Vanek, Jaroslav 206
Veendorp, E.C.H. 126
Vernon, Jack 92
Villard, Henry H. 13, 55

Viner, Jacob 30, 123, 129, 210
Vining, Rutledge 109
Vonnegut, Kurt, Jr. 2n

W

Wadsworth, J.E. 77
Wallace, Neil 112, 178, 189
Wallich, Henry C. 221, 250
Walras, Leon 52, 73
Walters, Alan A. 156, 159
Wan, Henry Y., Jr. 44
Warburton, Clark 111, 231, 238
Ward, Richard C. 33
Weintraub, Andrew 206
Weintraub, Robert 14, 230
Weintraub, Sidney 13, 16, 99,
    132, 204, 206, 234, 247
Weiss, Steven J. 93
Weizsacker, C.C. von 206
Wells, Paul 155
Whitaker, J.K. 142, 195
White, William H. 155, 236
Whittlesey, C.R. 25
Wicker, Elmus R. 35
Wicksell, Knut 56n, 73, 101, 187
Williams, Harold R. xiv, 34, 61,
    73
Williams, John Henry 230

Williams, Raburn M. 225
Wilson, J.S.G 25
Witte, James G., Jr. 133, 155
Wolf, Harold A. 34
Wolfe, J.N. 25, 129
Wong, Stanley 4n
Wonnacott, Paul 44, 178
Wood, John H. 93, 191
Woodworth, G. Walter 82
Worswick, G.D.N. 218
Wright, David McCord 25, 123,
    185, 212, 229
Wrightsman, Dwayne 38

Y

Yaari, Menahem E. 192, 202
Yeager, Leland B. 178
Yohe, William P. 93, 187, 214,
    229
Young, Ralph A. 238

Z

Zahn, Frank 44
Zarnowitz, Victor 111-12
Zelder, Raymond E. 215
Zellner, Arnold 147

TITLE INDEX

This index includes only books cited in the text or in notes. In some cases titles have been shortened. Alphabetization is letter by letter.

A

Accounting for United States Economic Growth, 1929-1969 193
Accumulation of Capital, The 154, 202
Activities and Associated Writings: Rethinking Employment and Unemployment Policies, 1929-31 114
Activities and Associated Writings: Shaping the Post-War World, 1940-46 114
Activities and Associated Writings: The End of Reparations, 1922-32 114
Activities and Associated Writings: The Return to Gold and Industrial Policy, 1924-29 114
Activities and Associated Writings: Treaty Revision and Reconstruction, 1920-22 114
Activities and Associated Writings: War Finance, 1940-45 114
Activities and Associated Writings: World Crises and Politics in Britain and America, 1931-39 114
Activities 1906-1914: India and Cambridge 114
Activities 1914-1919: The Treasury and Versailles 114
Activity Analysis in the Theory of Growth and Planning 17, 200

After Keynes 116
Against Method 135
Age of Keynes, The 115, 128
Aggregate Economic Analysis 43
Aggregate Economics and Public Policy 44
Aggregation in Economic Analysis 6n, 142
Albert Einstein: Creator and Rebel 3n
Albert Einstein: Philosopher-Scientist 2n
Allocation of Economic Resources 124
American Banking Structure 88
American Monetary Policy 234
American Monetary Policy: 1928-1941 231
Annual Report of the Council of Economic Advisers 217
Annual Volumes of the Journal of Economic Literature 46
Anti-Equilibrium 71
Art of Central Banking, The 211
Aspects of the Theory of Risk-Bearing 77

B

Bank Credit 84, 181
Banking and Monetary Studies 26, 64n
Banking in Britain 76
Banking Markets and Financial Institutions 27

Title Index

Banks and Politics in America 208
Banks and the Monetary System in the U.K., 1959-71, The 77
Basic Macroeconomics: Principles and Reality 42
Behavior of Interest Rates, The 190
Benjamin Strong: Central Banker 208
Bibliography and Index 114
Bibliography of Finance, A 48
Brookings Model: Some Further Results, The 105, 106
Brookings Quarterly Econometric Model of the United States, The 105, 106
Business Cycle, The 109
Business Cycle Indicators 110
Business Cycle in the Post-War World, The 107
Business Cycles and Economic Growth 105
Business Cycles and Forecasting 40
Business Cycles and National Income 108
Business Cycles and Unemployment 110
Business Cycles: The Problem and Its Setting 110
Business Cycle Today, The 111
Business Fluctuations, Growth, and Economic Stabilization 26
Business Looks at Banks 90

C

Capital and Growth (Harcourt and Laing) 28, 70
Capital and Growth (Hicks) 196
Capital and Time: A Neo-Austrian Theory 192, 196
Capital in the American Economy 199
Capital Investment Appraisal 150
Capital Theory and the Distribution of Income 191
Capital Theory and the Rate of Return 203
Central Banking 209
Central Banking after Bagehot 207, 210, 212
Century of Bank Rate, A 211
Checklist of U.S. Public Documents, 1789-1909 51
Collected Economic Papers 23

Collected Writings of John Maynard Keynes, The 53n, 54, 114
Commercial Bank Behavior and Financial Activity 89
Commercial Banking Industry, The 86
Commission on Money and Credit: An Adventure in Policy-Making 248, 249
Competition and Controls in Banking 86
Concept and Measurement of Involuntary Unemployment, The 218
Confessions, The 3n
Conflicts in Policy Objectives 224
Consumer Demand in the United States 143, 145
Consumer Response to Income Increases 143
Contribution to the Theory of the Trade Cycle, A 58, 70, 103, 108, 197
Control of the Money Supply 178
Controversy over the Quantity Theory of Money, The 95
Cost-Benefit Analysis 148
Counter-Revolution in Monetary Theory, The 246
Credit Rationing and the Commercial Loan Market 90
Crisis in Economic Theory 36
Crisis in Keynesian Economics, The 68, 70
Critical Essays in Monetary Theory 19, 70, 118, 208
Criticism and the Growth of Knowledge 4n, 17, 137
Critics of Keynesian Economics, The 118
Critique of Economic Theory, A 29
Cumulative Bibliography of Economics Books 49
Currency and Credit 209, 211
Current Inflation, The 16, 224
Cyclical Behavior of the Term Structure of Interest Rates 188

D

Death of the Past, The 2n

Demand for Money, The 36, 172
Depression, Inflation, and Monetary Policy 23
Determinants and Effects of Changes in the Stock of Money, 1875–1960 179, 181
Determinants of Investment Behavior, The 150
Development of British Monetary Orthodoxy, 1797–1875 208
Development of the Monetary Sector, Prediction and Policy Analysis in the FRB–MIT–Penn Model 104
Dimensions of Macroeconomics xiv, 31
Distributed Lags and Investment Analysis 152
Distribution of National Income, The 200
Documentary History of Banking in the United States 76, 209
Dollars and Deficits 19

E

Econometric Model of the United States, 1929–1952, An 104, 107, 109
Econometrics of Price Determination, The 15, 219
Economic Abstracts 46
Economic Accounts and Their Uses 112
Economic Analysis of Labour 160
Economic Articles and Correspondence XI 114
Economic Articles and Correspondence XII 114
Economic Consequences of the Peace, The 114
Economic Dynamics (Baumol) 39
Economic Dynamics (Harrod) 195
Economic Essays 19
Economic Essays in Honor of Gustav Cassell 106
Economic Essays in Honour of Erik Lindahl 24
Economic Growth (NBER) 112
Economic Growth (Wan) 44
Economic Growth and Development 43
Economic Growth Controversy, The 206
Economic Heresies 72, 139

Economic Implications of an Electronic Monetary Transfer System, The 88
Economic Policy Principles and Design 243
Economic Power of Commercial Banks, The 86
Economics 1, 13
Economics of Control, The 228
Economics of Employment 129
Economics of Illusion, The 117
Economics of John Maynard Keynes, The 116
Economics of Money and Banking, The 35
Economics of Public Finance, The 227
Economics Selections: An International Bibliography 48
Economic Stability and Growth: The American Record 107
Economic Theory in Retrospect 39
Economic Titles 46
Elementary Mathematical Macroeconomics 39
Elements of Pure Economics 52, 73
Employment and Equilibrium 100
Employment, Growth, and Price Levels 223
Encyclopedia of the Social Sciences 50
Enquiry into the Nature and Effects of the Paper Credit of Great Britain 212
Epistemics and Economics 2n, 67, 72, 139
Essays in Domestic and International Finance 234
Essays in Economic Analysis 22
Essays in Economics 23, 73
Essays in Modern Economics 18
Essays in Monetary Economics 20
Essays in Money and Banking in Honor of R.S. Sayers 25
Essays in Money and Interest 22
Essays in the Theory of Economic Growth (Domar) 19, 193
Essays in the Theory of Economic Growth (Robinson) 23, 202
Essays in the Theory of Risk–Bearing 77
Essays on Biography 114

Title Index

Essays on Economic Policy 21
Essays on Economic Stability and
Growth 21, 198
Essays on Interest Rates 184
Essays on John Maynard Keynes 115
Essays on Persuasion 114
Essays on the Theory of Optimal Eco-
nomic Growth 33
Essays on Value and Distribution 21,
198
Essentials of Macroeconomic Analysis,
The 39
Expectations, Investments, and Income
122
Expectations, Uncertainty and the Term
Structure of Interest Rates 187

F

Failure of the "New Economics," The
118
Federal Budget Policy 229
Federal Credit Agencies 248
Federal Credit Program 248
Federal Fiscal Policy in the Postwar
Recessions 228
Federal Reserve Operations in the
Money and Government Securities
Markets 215
Federal Reserve Policy Making 213
Federal Reserve System: Purposes and
Functions, The 207, 208, 210
Fifty Years of the Federal Reserve
Act 208
Finance and Capital Markets 112
Financial Institutions and Markets 37
Financial Intermediaries in the Ameri-
can Economy Since 1900 89
Financial Markets: The Accumulation
and Allocation of Wealth 38
Financial Markets and Economic Activ-
ity 29, 83
Fiscal and Debt Management Policies
228, 240, 243, 248
Fiscal Revolution in America, The
62, 73, 229
Forecasts and Simulations from the
Wharton Econometric Model, 1974-
1975 Edition 102
Foundations of Economic Analysis
57, 72

Foundations of Money and Banking,
The 37
Four Quartets 2n
Free Reserves and the Money Supply
181
Full Employment and Free Trade 121
Further Essays in Monetary Economics
20

G

General Competitive Analysis 69,
124
General Theory and After, Part I,
The 114
General Theory and After, Part II,
The 115
General Theory of Employment, In-
terest and Money, The 5, 25, 51,
68, 71, 101, 114, 115, 122, 127
General Theory of the Price Level,
Output, Income Distribution and
Economic Growth 132
Gilletts: Bankers at Banbury and
Oxford 76
Gilletts in the London Money Market:
1867-1967 76
Goal of Full Employment, The 218
Great Books of the Western World 3n
Great Inflation, 1939-1951, The 220
Growth and Income Distribution:
Essays in Economic Theory 22, 201
Growth & Stability in a Mature Econ-
omy 40
Growth and Stability of the Postwar
Economy 108
Growth Economics 32, 72
Growth Theory: An Exposition 44
Growth, Wages, Money 161
Guidelines, Informal Controls, and
the Market Place 226
Guide to Keynes, A 57, 70
Guilty Pleasures 1

H

History of Banking Theory, A 207,
209
History of Interest Rates, A 184
History of the Greenbacks, A 209
Household Behavior: Consumption,
Income and Wealth 60, 70, 143

Human Behavior in Economic Affairs 25
Human Resources 112
Human Resources and Labor Markets 244

I

Illusions 2n
Image: Knowledge in Life and Society, The 2n
Impact Multipliers and Dynamic Properties of the Klein-Goldberger Model 107
Impacts of Monetary Policy 231, 248
Income: Analysis and Policy 43
Income and Value Measurement 144
Income and Wealth 38
Income Distribution Theory 192
Income, Education and Human Capital 244
Income, Employment, and Economic Growth 43
Income, Employment, and Public Policy 25, 102
Income, Saving and the Theory of Consumer Behavior 60, 69, 141
Incomes Policy and Inflation 244
Index of Economic Articles in Journals and Collective Volumes 47
Indian Currency and Finance 114
Induction: Growth and Trade 24
Inflation (Ball and Doyle) 219
Inflation (Lekachman) 221
Inflation: Its Causes, Consequences and Control 18
Inflation and the Monetarist Controversy 246
Inflation and the Theory of Money 219
Inflation, Growth, and Employment 248
Inflation Policy and Unemployment Theory 225
Inflation, Unemployment, and Poverty 225
Instability and Economic Growth 200
Instruments of the Money Market 211, 214
Intellectual Capital of Michal Kalacki 99
Interest Rates and Asset Prices 186

Intermediate Macroeconomics: Output, Inflation, and Growth 43
International Bibliography of the Social Sciences: International Bibliography of Economics 47
International Encyclopedia of the Social Sciences 50
Introduction to Applied Macroeconomics 42
Introduction to Macroeconomic Models, An 42
Introduction to Monetary Economics 35
Introduction to Monetary Theory and Policy, An 38
Introduction to Money and Banking 38
Introduction to Money and Banking, An 35
Introduction to the Theory of Employment 57, 72, 122
Introduction to the Theory of Finance, An 37, 81
Introduction to the Theory of Interest, An 183
Introduction to the Theory of Macroeconomic Policy, An 44
Invention and Economic Growth 163
Investment: Theories and Evidence 151
Investment: The Study of an Economic Aggregate 153
Investment and Production 60, 72, 154
Investment Decision, The 60, 72, 154
Investment, Interest, and Capital 60, 70, 151
Investment Portfolio Decision-Making 78
Issues in Banking and Monetary Analysis 31
Issues in Fiscal and Monetary Policy 246
Issues in Monetary Economics 16
Is the Business Cycle Obsolete? 103

J

John Maynard Keynes 115
Journal of Economic Literature, The 45
Journey to Ixtlan: The Lessons of Don Juan 1n

Title Index

K

Keynes and After 140
Keynes and the Classics 138
Keynes and the Monetarists and Other Essays 247
Keynes' General Theory: Reports of Three Decades xiii, 30, 63, 71, 128
Keynesianism: Retrospect and Prospect 118
Keynesian Kaleidics 67n, 139
Keynesian Revolution, The 119
Keynesian System, The 123
Keynes' Monetary Thought 115
Keynes's "General Theory": A Retrospective View 121

L

Lapses for Full Employment 121
Lectures on Political Economy 73, 101
Lessons of Monetary Experience, The 24
Library on Money and Credit, The 248, 249
Life of John Maynard Keynes, The 70, 114
Linear Aggregation of Economic Variables 146
Liquidity Preferences of Commercial Banks 81, 91
List of the More Important Books in Library of Congress on Banks and Banking, A 47
List of Works Relating to the First and Second Banks of the United States, A 47
Lombard Street: A Description of the Money Market 207

M

Macroeconomic Activity 41
Macroeconomic Analysis (Elliott) 41
Macroeconomic Analysis (Shapiro) 44
Macroeconomic Readings xiv, 30
Macroeconomics (Crouch) 40
Macroeconomics (Darby) 40
Macroeconomics (Keiser) 42
Macroeconomics (Kennedy) 42

Macroeconomics (Lindaur) 42
Macroeconomics (Merklein) 43
Macroeconomics (Smith) 43
Macroeconomics (Wonnacott) 43
Macroeconomics: Analysis and Policy 40
Macroeconomics: A Neoclassical Introduction 43
Macroeconomics: An Integration of Monetary, Search, and Income Theories 39
Macroeconomics: An Introduction to Theory and Policy 39
Macroeconomics: Fluctuations, Growth, and Stability 42
Macroeconomics: Income and Monetary Theory 38
Macroeconomics: Measurement, Theory, and Policy 43
Macroeconomics: Selected Readings (Johnson and Kamerschen) xiii, 29
Macroeconomics: Selected Readings (Shapiro) xiv, 32
Macroeconomics: The Measurement, Analysis, and Control of Aggregate Economic Activity 41
Macroeconomics: Theory and Policy 41
Macroeconomics: Theory and Practice 40
Macroeconomics and Monetary Theory 42
Macroeconomics Before Keynes 40
Macroeconomic Theory (Ackley) 38
Macro-Economic Theory (Allen) 38
Macroeconomic Theory (Brunhild and Burton) 39
Macroeconomic Theory (Burrows and Hitiris) 40
Macroeconomic Theory (Hosek) 42
Macroeconomic Theory (Ott, et al.) 43
Macroeconomic Theory: Selected Readings xiv, 34, 61, 73
Macroeconomic Theory and Policy (Branson) 39
Macroeconomic Theory and Policy (Zahn) 44
Macroeconomic Theory and Stabilization Policy 40
Macro-Economic Thinking and the Market Economy 137

Macro Theory with Micro Foundations, A 44

Making Monetary and Fiscal Policy 239

Management of Bank Funds 91

Management of Cyclical Liquidity of Commercial Banks, The 82

Managing the Dollar 235

Manpower and Education 244

Mathematical Methods in the Social Sciences, 1959 163

Mathematical Theories of Economic Growth 40

Maximal Economic Growth 206

Measurement in Economics 145

Measurement in Economics: Studies in Mathematical Economics and Econometrics in Memory of Yehirda Grunfeld 78

Measuring Business Cycles 104

Microeconomic Foundations of Employment and Inflation Theory 225

Milton Friedman's Monetary Framework 69, 96

Model of Macroeconomic Activity, A 41

Models of Economic Growth (Hamberg) 41

Models of Economic Growth (Mirrlees and Stern) 17, 200

Modern Banking 38

Modern Economic Growth 199

Monetarist Model of Inflationary Expectations 223

Monetary and Fiscal Policy in a Growing Economy 41

Monetary Conference Series 15

Monetary Economics 37

Monetary Economics: Controversies in Theory and Policy 32

Monetary Economics: Readings 27

Monetary Economics: Readings on Current Issues xiii, 27

Monetary Equilibrium 56, 72, 100, 122

Monetary History of the United States, A 69, 75, 76, 180

Monetary Management 231, 248

Monetary Management Under the New Deal 232

Monetary Policy and the Federal Funds Market 239

Monetary Policy and the Financial System 36

Monetary Policy in the United States 236

Monetary Process: Essentials of Money and Banking, The 36

Monetary Process and Policy: A Symposium 16

Monetary Statistics of the United States 76

Monetary Theory (Clower) xiii, 27, 63, 69

Monetary Theory (Miles) 35

Monetary Theory (Mundell) 22

Monetary Theory and Monetary Policy in the 1970's 14

Monetary Theory and Policy (Thorn) xiv, 33, 61, 73

Monetary Theory and Policy (Ward) 33

Monetary vs. Fiscal Policy 240, 246

Money (Burstein) 35

Money (Harrod) 36

Money (Ritter and Silber) 37

Money (Robertson) 37

Money and Banking (Culbertson) 35

Money and Banking (Fisher) 35

Money and Banking (Klise) 36

Money and Banking (Shapiro) 38

Money and Banking (Timerlake and Shelby) 38

Money and Banking (Van Dahm) 38

Money and Banking: A Selected List of References 34

Money and Banking: Theory, Analysis, and Policy xiv, 31

Money and Banking Theory, Policy, and Institutions 37

Money and Capacity Growth 204

Money and Capital Markets 91

Money and Credit: Their Influence on Jobs, Prices, and Growth 232, 248

Money and Economic Activity 32

Money and Finance xiii, 26

Money and Inflation 36

Money and Markets 98

Title Index

Money and the Economy 36
Money and the Mechanism of Exchange
   171
Money and the Real World 67, 69,
   135
Money, Banking and Public Policy 34
Money, Banking and the Economy 35
Money, Banking, and the U.S. Econ-
   omy 36
Money, Capital, and Prices 41
Money, Credit, and Banking 35
Money, Debt and Economic Activity
   36
Money, Employment and Inflation 34
Money in a Theory of Finance 63,
   69, 83
Money in Britain: 1959-1969 14
Money, Information and Uncertainty
   36
Money, Interest, and Prices 61, 72,
   123, 125, 131, 133
Money Matters 98
Money Supply, Money Demand, and
   Macroeconomic Models 26
Money Supply Process, The 35, 179
Money, the Financial System and
   the Economy 36
Money, Trade, and Economic Growth
   20
Money, Trade, and Economic Growth:
   In Honor of John Henry Williams
   25
Money, Wealth, and Economic Theory
   63, 72, 83, 84
Monthly Catalog of U.S. Government
   Publications 51

N

National Economic Environment, The
   42
National Income Accounts and Income
   Analysis 113
National Income Analysis and Fore-
   casting 40
National Income and Flow-of-Funds
   Analysis 113
National Income and the Price Level
   39
National Income and the Public Wel-
   fare 113

National Product since 1869 144
Nations and Households in Economic
   Growth 24, 193
Nature of Income and Capital, The
   183
Neo-Classical Theory of Economic
   Growth, A 43
New Economics: Keynes' Influence
   on Theory and Public Policy, The
   xiii, 29, 59, 70, 117
New Economics and the Old Econom-
   ics, The 245, 246

O

OECD Economic Outlook: Occasional
   Studies 106
Official Papers 22
On Keynesian Economics and the
   Economics of Keynes 65, 71, 115-
   16, 127, 138
On the Notion of Equilibrium in Eco-
   nomics 6n, 126, 136
On the Reappraisal of Keynesian Eco-
   nomics 136
On the Theory and Measurement of
   Technological Change 161
On the Theory of Economic Policy
   227
Open Market Policies and Operating
   Procedures 213
Optimum Quantity of Money, The
   19, 69, 85, 86, 98
Our National Debt 240

P

Papers in English Monetary History
   207
Permanent Income, Wealth, and Con-
   sumption 60, 71, 144
Perspectives on Economic Growth 218
Policies to Combat Depression 18,
   218
Policy Issues and Research Opportuni-
   ties in Industrial Organization 112
Policy Simulations with an Econometric
   Model 105, 106, 107
Population, Labor Force, and Long
   Swings in Economic Growth 194
Portfolio Behavior of Financial Insti-
   tutions 82

Portfolio Selection: Efficient Diversification of Investment 64n, 80

Portfolio Theory: The Selection of Assets 78

Portfolio Theory and Capital Markets 81

Post Keynesian Economics 24, 61, 71, 119

Postwar Productivity Trends in the United States 161

Pound Sterling, The 208

Poverty and Discrimination 245

Powerful Consumer, The 143

Price Expectations and the Behavior of the Price Level 227

Price Flexibility and Employment 57, 71, 119

Principles of Economics 53, 71, 100

Principles of Macroeconomics and Money 42

Principles of Monetary Economics, The 35

Principles of Money, Banking, and Financial Markets 37

Private Capital Markets 248

Private Financial Institutions 248

Problems of Economics and Planning 24

Proceedings of the First Konstanzer Seminar on Monetary Theory and Monetary Policy 245

Production of Commodities by Means of Commodities 72, 204

Profits, Interest and Investment 19, 150

Program for Monetary Stability, A 233

Prosperity and Depression 99

Psychology of Consciousness, The 3n

Public Debt and Future Generations 240, 243

Public Expenditures and Taxations 112

Purchasing Power of Money, The 96

Pure Theory of Capital, The 196

Q

Quantitative Economic Research 112

Quantitative Planning of Economic Policy 240

Quarterly Check-List of Economics and Political Science 48

R

Rate of Interest and Other Essays 23, 202

Rate of Profit, Distribution and Growth: Two Views 199

Rational Economic Man 135

Readings in British Monetary Economics 29

Readings in Business Cycles xiii, 28, 61, 69, 107

Readings in Business Cycles and National Income 28

Readings in Business Cycle Theory xiii, 28, 59, 69, 108

Readings in Fiscal Policy xiv, 33

Readings in Macroeconomics xiv, 31, 61, 72

Readings in Macroeconomics: Current Policy Issues xiv, 30

Readings in Macroeconomics: Theory, Evidence and Policy 29

Readings in Monetary Theory xiv, 30, 59, 71

Readings in Money and Banking 34

Readings in Money, National Income, and Stabilization Policy xiv, 33

Readings in the Concept and Measurement of Income 31, 113

Readings in the Modern Theory of Economic Growth 33

Readings in the Theory of Growth 28

Readings in the Theory of Income Distribution xiii, 27, 59, 69

Reappraisal of the Federal Reserve Discount Mechanism 213

Reconstruction of Political Economy, The 67, 71, 136

Reference Materials and Periodicals in Economics 45

Rehabilitation of Say's Law, A 52n, 127

Revision of the Treaty, A 114

Risk Aversion and Portfolio Choice 80

Roots of Inflation, The 222

Title Index

S

Say's Law 52n, 132
Scheme of Economic Theory, A 8n
Selected Essays in Employment and Growth 21, 56
Selected Essays on the Dynamics of the Capitalist Economy, 1933-1970 21, 56, 70, 99
Selected List of Books with References to Periodicals Relating to Currency and Banking 47
Selected List of References on the Monetary Question 48
Selected Readings in Macroeconomics and Capital Theory from Econometrica 26
Slaughterhouse-Five 2n
Social Science Citation Index 50
Some Cambridge Controversies in the Theory of Capital 195, 205
Sources of Economic Growth in the United States and the Alternatives before Us 162, 193
Special Bibliography in Monetary Economics and Finance 49
Stabilization Policies 248
Statistical Testing of Business Cycle Theories 111
Steady State Capital Theory 206
Stock Market and Economic Efficiency, The 87
Strategic Factors In Business Cycles 104
Structural Change and Growth in Capitalism 162
Structure of Scientific Revolutions, The 137
Student Economist's Handbook, The 45
Studies in Banking Competition and the Banking Structure 88
Studies in Income and Wealth 14
Studies in Mathematical Economics and Econometrics 128
Studies in Monetary Economics 22, 63n, 84
Studies in the Theory of International Trade 210
Studies of Portfolio Behavior 80

Study in the Theory of Inflation, A 221
Study in the Theory of Investment, A 150
Study of Aggregate Consumption, A 142
Study of Money-Flows in the United States, A 112
Survey of General Equilibrium, A 63, 70, 127

T

Targets and Indicators of Monetary Policy 14, 230
Techniques of Monetary Control 213
Technology, Economic Growth, and Public Policy 162
Term Structure of Interest Rates, The (Masera) 189
Term Structure of Interest Rates, The (Meiselman) 189, 191
Term Structure of Interest Rates, The (Nelson) 190
Term Structure of Interest Rates: Expectations and Behavior Patterns, The 189
Term Structure of Interest Rates: Financial Intermediaries and Debt Management 189
Term Structure of Interest Rates: Theory, Empirical Evidence and Applications, The 189
Theories of Value and Distribution Since Adam Smith 3n
Theory of Capital, The 15
Theory of Economic Growth, The (Kregel) 42
Theory of Economic Growth, The (Morishima) 43
Theory of General Economic Equilibrium, The 128
Theory of Idle Resources, The 118
Theory of Income Distribution 197
Theory of Interest, The (Fisher) 183
Theory of Interest, The (Lutz) 185
Theory of Interest Rates, The 15
Theory of Macroeconomic Policy, The 39
Theory of Money 37

Theory of Prices, The 121
Theory of Quantitative Economic
  Policy 240
Theory of the Consumption Function,
  A 60, 69, 142
Theory of Unemployment, The 100
Theory of Wages, The 160
Three Essays on the State of Economic
  Science 21
Three Lectures on the Value of Money
  176
Towards a Dynamic Economics 58,
  70, 196
Tract on Monetary Reform 114
Trade, Stability, and Macroeconomics
  24
Treatise on Money, A 5, 71, 114,
  115, 127
Treatise on Probability 114
Two-Sector Growth Models 197

U

Understanding Money 38
Unemployment and Inflation: The
  New Economics of the Wage-Price
  Spiral 225

Unemployment, Money Wage Rates
  and Inflation 225
United States Monetary Policy 235
Use of Economics Literature, The
  45

V

Value and Capital 41, 57, 70, 127
Value, Capital, and Growth 25
Veil of Money, The 101

W

Wage-Price-Productivity Nexus, The
  224
Wealth of Nations, The 52, 72
Wharton Econometric Forecasting
  Model, The 106
World After Keynes, The 139

Y

Years of High Theory, The 53n, 72,
  101

SUBJECT INDEX

Underlined numbers refer to main areas covered in the text. Alphabetization is letter by letter.

A

Abramovitz, Moses 24, 193
Acceleration principle 112, 148, 149, 156-59
Accord of 1951 239
Accumulation. See Golden rules of accumulation
Aggregate demand 10, 52, 133
Aggregate supply 10
Aggregation 5-6, 11, 140, 142, 145, 211
American Economic Association 27, 28, 30, 33
Angell, J.W. 16, 234
Antibullionists 207, 208, 209, 210, 212
Archibald, G.C. 124
Asset effect. See Real balance effect
Augustine, Saint 2
Availability doctrine 212

B

Balance budget theory. See Multipliers, balance budget
Ball, R.J. 164
Banking school 207, 208, 209
Banking theory 210-12
Bank of England 25, 77, 207, 208, 209, 210, 211
Bank of the United States (First and Second) 208

Banks, commercial 25, 86-93
    history 75, 76
    vs. nonbank intermediaries 82, 87, 90, 91, 93. See also Financial intermediaries
    See also Creation of money
Barter economy 10, 133, 140, 171, 176-77
"Bastard" Keynesians 64, 118
Bodkin, Ronald G. 124, 164
Boulding, Kenneth E. 3, 16
Brookings model 105, 106, 107
Brunner, Karl 166, 195
Budget, full employment 228
Budget constraint 227
Buffer stocks 66n, 138
Bullionists 207, 208, 209, 210, 212
Bullion report (1811) 212
Burmeister, Edwin 15, 195
Business cycles 11, 58, 102-12, 121, 232

C

Cambridge-Cambridge controversy 15, 59, 64, 137, 195, 199, 203, 204, 205
Capital markets 33, 91
Capital theory 15, 23, 28, 192, 196, 203, 206
    neoclassical capital theory 149, 151, 152
Cassel, Gustav 106

Castaneda, Carlos 4
Central banking 207-15, 230-43,
    248-50. See also Bank of
    England; Bank of the United
    States; Federal Reserve System
Chandler, Lester V. 16, 234
Chicago plan 234
Chicago school 17, 19, 245. See
    also Quantity theory of money,
    Friedmanite
Choice theory 77, 78, 79, 81, 133
Classical economics 52, 96, 165,
    167, 176
Clower, Robert W. 65, 124
Commercial banks. See Banks,
    commercial
Commission on Money and Credit
    13, 248-50
Committee for Economic Development
    228, 234
Competition, perfect and imperfect
    7, 19, 21, 53
Conferences and symposiums 13-18
    capital theory 15
    Federal Reserve Bank policy 13
    fiscal policy 17
    growth theory 17
    inflation 16, 18
    interest rates 15
    monetary economics 13, 14, 15,
        16, 17, 18
    national income accounting 15
    price determination 15
Consumption 23, 59, 140-47
    absolute income hypothesis 145
    life-cycle hypothesis 140, 144,
        145
    permanent income hypothesis 142,
        229
    psychological law 60
    relative income hypothesis 140,
        141
    second psychological law 66
Contra-quantity theory 98, 99
Cost-push inflation. See Inflation
Council of Economic Advisers 217,
    218
Creation of money 82, 83, 84, 174,
    181
Credit rationing 90, 92, 140
Currency school 207, 208, 209
Cycles. See Business cycles

D

Davidson, Paul 67
Debt. See National debt
Deficit financing. See Fiscal policy
Deflation. See Inflation
Demand for labor. See Labor market
Demand for money. See Money,
    demand
Demand-pull inflation. See Inflation
Depression, economic 18, 23, 128,
    211, 218. See also Great
    Depression
Dichotomy 61n, 132
Discount mechanism 213, 214, 215,
    236, 237. See also Monetary
    instruments
Disequilibrium economics 125, 133-40
Disinvestment. See Investment
Distribution effects and theory 11,
    21, 22, 27, 32, 58, 67n,
    132, 191, 192, 201, 202
Dual-decision hypothesis 65, 133-34
Duesenberry-Eckstein-Fromm model
    105, 106

E

Eckstein, Otto 105
Economic growth 17, 18, 19, 21,
    22, 23, 24, 25, 191-206.
    See also Growth models
Economic welfare 219, 220, 221,
    222, 225, 227, 240
Economy. See Barter economy;
    Money, economy
Effective demand 10, 52, 119, 138
Einstein, Albert 2, 3n
Ellis, Howard S. 17
Employment Act (1946) 104, 217
Employment theory 11, 21, 22, 118,
    119, 121, 122, 123, 129, 217,
    218
Equilibrium economics 123-33
Expectations, economic 19, 122,
    139, 168, 184, 187, 191, 227

F

Federal budget 227-29
    constraints 227
    effects on the economy 229

full employment 228
history of 227
stabilization of 228
Federal Funds market 239
Federal Open Market Committee.
See Federal Reserve System,
Open Market Committee
Federal Reserve Act (1913) 208
Federal Reserve-MIT-Penn model
103, 104, 105, 211
Federal Reserve System (FED) 13,
75, 208, 209, 210, 211, 231,
234, 235, 236
Board of Governors 235
financial intermediaries and 92
Open Market Committee 213
operations 210
See also Creation of money; Banks,
commercial; Central banking
Feedback control systems 128
Financial intermediaries 75-93, 173,
233, 238. See also Banks,
commercial; Stock market
Fiscal policy 17, 227-30
Fisher, Irving 24
Flow of funds analysis. See Money,
flows
Forecasting of business cycles 102-12
FRB-MIT econometric model. See
Federal Reserve-MIT-Penn model
Free reserves 232, 238. See also
Federal Reserve System
Friedman, Milton 16, 64, 96, 234
Fromm, Gary 105
Full employment. See Employment
theory
Functional finance 228, 242

G

General equilibrium analysis 92,
126, 127, 177, 184
Gibson paradox 186
Golden rule of accumulation 33,
200, 201
Government purchases of goods and
services. See Fiscal policy
Great Depression 10, 13, 51, 54
Gross national product (GNP). See

National income accounting
Growth models 191-206
consumption-loan model 192,
202
Harrod-Domar 19, 58, 193, 195,
196, 197
Hicks 58, 103, 108, 197
Kaldor 59, 198
Keynes-Wicksell 205
money 199, 203, 204
Solow 59, 204
See also Economic growth
Grunfeld, Yehirda 79
Gurley, John G. 64

H

Hansen, Alvin H. 16, 17, 25, 242
Harrod, Roy F. 24, 58
Harrod-neutral 161, 163, 164.
See also Growth models,
Harrod-Domar
Hart, Albert G.
Hayek, Friedrick A. 20
Hicks, Sir John R. 25, 134, 161
Hicks-neutral 161, 163, 164. See
also Growth models, Hicks
Hoover Commission 213
Human capital resources 199, 244
Hunt Commission 14, 248, 249
Huxley, Aldous 3n

I

Illiquidity. See Money, demand
Illusion. See Money, illusion
Imperfect competition. See Competi-
tion, perfect and imperfect
Income accounting. See National
income accounting
Income-constrained process. See
Dual-decision hypothesis
Income determination 122, 132
Income distribution. See Distribution
effects and theory
Incomes policy 243-45
Index problem of macroeconomic and
monetary theory 6, 35, 180

Subject Index

Inflation 16, 18, 219-22, 224, 246, 247
  burden of. See Economic welfare
  cost-push 219, 220, 221, 222
  demand-pull 219, 220, 221, 222
  hyper 220
  secular 219, 220
Information cost 66, 133, 135, 136, 138
Innovations and inventions 161, 163, 164, 194, 198, 206. See also Economic growth; Growth models
Inside money. See Money, inside and outside
Interest rates 19, 22, 23, 153, 233
  term structure 187-91
  theory 182-87
International Colloquium in the Philosophy of Science (1965) 17
International Economic Association 15, 17
International economics 12, 20, 22, 24, 25, 33, 207, 211
Inventory theory 147-56
Investment theory 19, 60, 120, <u>147-56</u>, 232
Invisible hand doctrine 32, 58, 62, 99, 160
IS-LM model 57, 118, 128, 132, 237

J

Jevons's Law of Indifference 7
Johnson, Harry G. 54

K

Kalecki, Michal 24
Kaleidic factor 8, 67
Katona, George 25
Keynes, John Maynard 114-40
  contributions of 54-55, 114-15
  interpretations of 18, 56-57, 115-23
  re-interpretations of 63, 64-68, 133-39
  vs. classics 11, 100
  vs. Keynesians 118, 138

Keynesian revolution 54, 101, 114-40
Keynesians, bastard. See "Bastard" Keynesians
Keynesians vs. classics 58
Keynesians vs. monetarists. See Monetarists vs. fiscalists
Keynesian-Walrasian model 57, 127, 130
Kuhnian "revolutions" 4, 137

L

Labor market 160-61. See also Employment; Phillips relation
Lakatosian "research programs" 4, 137
Leijonhufvud, Axel 66
Lender of last resort. See Central banking
Lindahl, Erik 24
Liquidity. See Money, demand
Liquidity preference 112, 121, 175, 177. See also Money, demand
Liquidity trap (Keynesian trap) 58, 61, 65, 172
LM curve. See IS-LM model
Loanable funds vs. liquidity preference. See Interest rates, theory

M

Marginal efficiency of capital 153
Marginal efficiency of investment. See Investment theory
Marginal propensities to consume. See Consumption
Margin requirements 207, 208. See also Monetary instruments
Marshallian microeconomics. See Microeconomics
Medium of exchange. See Money, functions
Meiselman, David 158
Methodologies and modeling of economic theory 4, 21
Metzler, Lloyd A. 24
Microeconomics 5, 100, 127, 132, 155, 167, 225

Monetarists vs. fiscalists 20, 230, 231, 240, 245–48
Monetary base. See Money, supply
Monetary economy 67n, 134, 140
Monetary instruments 14, 211, 213–15, 232, 236, 237, 238
Monetary policy 11, 12, 13, 14, 20, 25, 97, 230–43
Monetary theory 10, 11, 12, 13, 20, 22, 25, 164–82
Money
  biological analogies 171
  definition 8, 19, 167, 169, 171, 172, 173
  demand 19, 60–61, 66, 164–78
  economy 10, 167, 176, 207
  finance motive 167
  flows 37, 112
  functions 19
  illusion 2, 7, 58, 130, 173
  inside and outside 20, 63, 82–84, 177, 181, 234
  motives for holding money. See Money, demand
  multipliers. See Multipliers
  purchasing power of 52
  substitutes. See Near moneys
  supply 178–82, 211
Money Study Group 14, 16
Multipliers 21, 56, 99, 112, 120, 122, 156–59
  balance budget 156, 157, 227
  deviation-amplifying 66
  deviation-counteracting 66
  monetary 156, 157, 159
Mutual savings banks. See Financial intermediaries

N

National debt
  burden of 217, 241, 242, 243
  management of 239, 240, 242, 243
National income accounting 15, 54, 112–14. See also Money, flows
Near moneys 166
Neoclassical model 123, 124, 131, 193, 194

Neoclassical synthesis 56, 61, 62
Neo-Keynesians 59, 63, 64. See also Cambridge–Cambridge controversy
Neutrality of money 22, 58, 61, 174, 178, 180, 197, 205
New York Federal Reserve Bank 208

O

Open Market Committee. See Federal Reserve System
Open market operations 93, 211, 213, 214, 215. See also Monetary instruments
Operation Twist 190
Optimal propensity to consume 119
Optimal quantity of money 19, 20, 84–86, 174
Orthodox consensus 55, 61
Ostroy, Joseph M. 133
Output relations 161–64
Outside money. See Money, inside and outside

P

Palmer Rule (Rule of 1832) 207, 208, 209, 210
Paradox of saving 19
Peal's Act (Bank Act of 1844) 211
Perfect competition. See Competition, perfect and imperfect
Phillips relation 16, 219, 224, 225, 226, 227
Pigou effect. See Real balance effect
Planning 24
Policy. See Stabilization policy
Population growth 101
Portfolio analysis 77–82
  banks 77, 80, 81, 82
  consumers 80
  firms 78, 80
President's Commission on Financial Structure and Regulation. See Hunt Commission
Price flexibility 119
Price level 226, 227, 234
Price system 15, 21, 68, 219

Subject Index

Principle of Reflux. See Real-bills
  doctrine
Production functions. See Output
  relations
Profits 19
Pump-priming effect 61-62
Pyramiding of monetary reserves 209

Q

Quantity theory of money, classical
  95, 96
  Friedmanite 22, 63, 75, 76,
    96, 97, 98

R

Radcliffe Committee and Report 12,
  15, 132, 166, 180, 237, 249
"Ramsey problem" 33, 201
Real balance effect 62-63, 99, 125,
  127, 129, 131, 170, 175.
  See also Wealth effect
Real-bills doctrine 207, 208, 209,
  210
Real wage rate. See Wages
Regulation Q 215
Re-interpreters of Keynes. See
  Keynes, John Maynard
Reserve requirements 213, 214.
  See also Monetary instruments
Risk. See Choice theory
Robinson, Joan 6, 7, 64, 206
Rules vs. authorities 237, 239

S

Samuelson, Paul A. 4n, 76
Saving 19, 120, 142, 201. See
  also Paradox of saving
Savings and loan associations. See
  Financial intermediaries
Sayers, R.S. 25
Say's law (equality, identity) 52,
  96, 127, 132
Say's principle 125, 134
Shackle, G.L.S. 4, 8
Shaw, Edward S. 64
Speculative motive. See Liquidity
  preference; Money, demand

Stabilization policy 10, 217-50
Stock-flow analysis 8, 164, 183,
  185, 186
Stock market 87, 145
Strong, Benjamin 208
Surveys of macro-monetary economics
  business cycles 11
  capital theory 192
  distribution theory 11
  employment policy and theory 11
  growth theory 191, 192
  macroeconomic theory 11, 13
  monetary policy 11, 12, 13, 20
  monetary theory 10, 11, 12, 13,
    20
Swedish school (Stockholm school)
  100, 101

T

Tatonnement 127
Taxes. See Fiscal policy
Technology. See Output relations;
  Innovations and inventions
Term structure. See Interest rates,
  term structure
Trade cycles. See Business cycles
Transactions cost 164, 174
Transactions motive. See Money,
  demand
Transfer payments. See Fiscal
  policies
"Treasury view" 6

U

Uncertainty. See Kaleidic factor
Unemployment. See Employment
  theory
Utility. See Choice theory

V

Value system 3, 122
Value theory 11, 21, 121, 123,
  164
Veil of money 58, 101
Velocity. See Money, demand
Victorian economists 53

W

Wage-price controls 245
Wages 222, 224, 225, 226
Walrasian microeconomics. See
   Microeconomics
Walrasian system 52, 125
Walras law 133
Wealth effect 82-84

Welfare. See Economic welfare
Wharton econometric model 102
Wicksell, Knut 124

Y

Yale school 13, 23, 29, 37, 64,
   80, 81, 82